The Global Politics of Contemporary Travel Writing

To what extent do bestselling travel books, such as those by Paul Theroux, Bill Bryson, Bruce Chatwin and Michael Palin, tell us as much about world politics as newspaper articles, policy documents and press releases? Debbie Lisle argues that the formulations of genre, identity, geopolitics and history at work in contemporary travel writing are increasingly at odds with a cosmopolitan and multicultural world in which 'everybody travels'. Despite the forces of globalisation, common stereotypes about 'foreignness' continue to shape the experience of modern travel. *The Global Politics of Contemporary Travel Writing* is concerned with the way contemporary travelogues engage with, and try to resolve, familiar struggles in global politics such as the protection of human rights, the promotion of democracy, the management of equality within multiculturalism and the reduction of inequality. This is a thoroughly interdisciplinary book that draws from international relations, literary theory, political theory, geography, anthropology and history.

Debbie Lisle is Lecturer in Politics and Director of Cultural and Media Studies in the School of Politics, International Studies and Philosophy at Queen's University Belfast. She received the BISA Best Thesis Prize for her PhD in International Relations at Keele University.

The Global Politics of Contemporary Travel Writing

Debbie Lisle

CAMBRIDGE
UNIVERSITY PRESS

CAMBRIDGE UNIVERSITY PRESS
Cambridge, New York, Melbourne, Madrid, Cape Town, Singapore, São Paulo

Cambridge University Press
The Edinburgh Building, Cambridge CB2 2RU, UK

Published in the United States of America by Cambridge University Press,
New York

www.cambridge.org
Information on this title: www.cambridge.org/9780521867801

First published 2006

Printed in the United Kingdom at the University Press, Cambridge

A catalogue record for this publication is available from the British Library

ISBN-13 978-0-521-86780-1 hardback
ISBN-10 0-521-86780-0 hardback

For my Mom and Dad

Epigraph

Those who believe in the resistance of the real and continue to be surprised that men can live and die for words have little to teach us about the bitter knowledge of travel.

Jacques Rancière

Contents

List of illustrations   *page* ix
Preface   xi
'Travelogue'   xiii

1   Introduction: the global imaginary of contemporary
    travel writing   1

2   Between fact and fiction: the generic boundaries
    of travel writing   27

3   The cosmopolitan gaze: rearticulations of modern
    subjectivity   68

4   Civilising territory: geographies of safety and danger   134

5   Looking back: utopia, nostalgia and the myth
    of historical progress   203

6   Engaging the political: contemporary travel
    writing and the ethics of difference   260

    Bibliography   279
    Index   295

Illustrations

1. Tété-Michel Kpomassie in Greenland
   Photograph from *An African in Greenland* by Tété-Michel Kpomassie, © 1981, Flammarion, Paris, English translation by James Kirkup © 1983 by Harcourt Brace & Company and Martin Secker & Warburg Ltd., reprinted by permission of Harcourt *page* 88
2. Michael Palin performing a traditional Maori greeting in New Zealand
   Photograph: Maori Acceptance from *Full Circle* by Michael Palin (2004) © Basil Pao 103
3. Theroux's map of *The Great Railway Bazaar*
   From *The Great Railway Bazaar* by Paul Theroux (1976) 144

Text credits

Epigraph: from Jacques Rancière (trans. James B. Swenson), *Short Voyages to the Land of the People*, © 1990 Editions du Seuil, English translation © 2003 by the Board of Trustees of the Leland Stanford Jr. University. All rights reserved. Used with the permission of Stanford University Press, www.sup.org.

'Travelogue' by Linda Pastan. From *The Last Uncle*, published by W. W Norton, 2002.

Every effort has been made to trace all the copyright holders, but if any have been inadvertently overlooked, Cambridge University Press will be pleased to make the necessary acknowledgements at the first opportunity.

Preface

I remember the exact moment this book began. I was sitting in a café in Saigon (sounds glamorous – it wasn't). It was April 1993 and I was chatting with other like-minded backpackers from Canada, Australia and Germany. We were revelling in our self-importance and congratulating ourselves that we got to Vietnam before the *other* travellers spoiled it. Embarrassingly, I think we honestly felt that we were the first Westerners in Saigon since the war ended. In any case, I wanted to trade a novel I had finished – Milan Kundera's *The Joke* – and an American fellow offered me Paul Theroux's *The Happy Isles of Oceania* in return. I had never read a travelogue before, but I eagerly exchanged books. I thought Theroux would inspire me on my impending solo journey through Asia and Africa. It was, and I stick to this judgement, one of the worst books I have ever read – boring, nasty and offensive in equal measure. The problem was that I didn't have a critical language to express my distaste. Intuitively, I knew this wasn't just a bad book; there was something *wrong* with this book and something *wrong* with travel writing in general. Ultimately, I came to the conclusion that there was also something *wrong* with my own rite of passage as a smug Western backpacker. Over a decade later, this is the result. Although the arguments presented here are a little more developed (and hopefully a little more complex), I think there is a lot to be said for my initial judgement of Theroux's book specifically, and travel writing more generally. There may be good travelogues and bad travelogues, but as a whole, the genre encourages a particularly conservative political outlook that extends to its vision of global politics. This is frustrating because travel writing has the potential to re-imagine the world in ways that do not simply regurgitate the status quo or repeat a nostalgic longing for Empire. To be sure, a small part of me remains hopeful that travel writing might take hold of its transformative potential, but I have to admit that it is a very small part indeed.

Many people have provided intellectual support for this project over the years, and I would like to offer them my heartfelt thanks. Initially, it was Rob Walker's encouragement that led me to pursue the idea that travelogues are political texts that are significant for the study and practice of International Relations. I hope I have managed to balance the interdisciplinary framework he introduced me to with a simultaneous foregrounding of the political. More significantly, I want to thank him for offering words of encouragement while I got more and more tangled in the knot of travel, power, difference, culture and representation. As a PhD student pursuing these questions, I benefited greatly from the support of two people in particular: firstly, my supervisor Andrew Linklater, who was both intellectually challenging and fantastically patient; and secondly, my colleague and friend Martin Coward, who was theoretically inspiring, critically generous and unfailingly loyal. For their helpful suggestions on transforming a halting PhD thesis into a less halting manuscript, I would like to thank Alex Danchev and Cindy Weber. For their excellent critical insights and positive suggestions for the manuscript, I would like to thank John Haslam at Cambridge and three anonymous readers. For granting a sabbatical in 2003 to complete the manuscript, I would like to thank the School of Politics and International Studies at Queen's University. Along the way, I have presented my work at numerous conferences, workshops and seminars, and I have had informal discussions about my work with several peers and colleagues. For their comments, suggestions and support on these occasions, I would like to thank Simon Bainbridge, Tarak Barkawi, David Campbell, James Der Derian, Mick Dillon, David Dwan, Jenny Edkins, Vince Geoghegan, Larry George, Eamonn Hughes, Richard Kirkland, Warren Magnusson, Peter Mandaville, Kate Manzo, John McMillan, Claire Moon, David Mutimer, Peter Nyers, Louisa Odysseos, Jan Jindy Pettman, Michael Shapiro, Kara Shaw, Steve Smith, Adrian Streete, Hidemi Suganami, Caroline Sumpter and Maja Zehfuss.

Among the wider community of people who have supported me while writing this book, I would like to thank a variety of football players at the universities of Keele and Queen's who have allowed me the privilege of kicking them in the shins twice a week without fail. I can't begin to express how therapeutic it has been. To friends who have put up with my ambivalent passion for travel writing over the years, and to my family who are too far away, I would like to say thank you for unconditionally supporting my intellectual adventures. Without a doubt, this book is dedicated to them. Finally, I would like to thank Andrew — passionate sceptic, creative interlocutor, hopeful Luton supporter and ardent mischief-maker — who helped this book on its way by nurturing my intellectual curiosity and making me laugh every day.

Travelogue

I always take a book along,
raising it between my eyes and
whatever landscape I've come
so far to see — blue mountains,
or vineyards with their musky
purpling grapes; often a bay
or ocean unfolding just as far
as the horizon of the book
whose pages turn like surf
beneath my fingertips.

Perhaps I could simply stay at home
and have some cardboard scenery
shuffled at intervals. The story
I inhabit would be the same: a mystery
or poem, the memoir of some other
traveller in some other
more indelible century.
But sometimes in early morning,
or at scented dusk, what I see
and read converge

into a kind of symmetry,
a blending of sight and syllable,
a language as new to me
as the most tropical landscape.
So that when night finally falls
and I lie in the strange dark,
the rustling I think I hear could be
leaves, or wings, or pages turning,
and on the winding road to sleep
I could be anywhere.

Linda Pastan

1 Introduction: the global imaginary of contemporary travel writing

As literary representations of journeys across the globe, travelogues express political commitments that are barely visible beyond their received status as a minor literary genre. This book politicises travelogues by revealing their connection to the 'serious' business of world affairs, and their significance to the study and practice of global politics. It argues that the quasi-fictional genre of travel writing is at least as useful for understanding issues of international importance as the policy documents, government press releases, parliamentary debates and media stories that are usually privileged in this context. In fact, travelogues have a distinct advantage because they are read widely by a number of people, and thus provide valuable information about how artefacts of popular culture produce common assumptions about power relations at the international level. Historically, travel writing participated in the international realm by disseminating the goals of Empire: stories of 'faraway lands' were crucial in establishing the unequal, unjust and exploitative relations of colonial rule. While many post-colonial scholars have examined the role of travel writing during Empire, I am particularly interested in how contemporary travel writing is addressing its colonial legacy by engaging – or not engaging – with wider intellectual and cultural debates about global politics.[1]

---

[1] In *Orientalism* (New York: Vintage, 1978), Edward Said argued that the travel writing of famous authors such as Richard Burton and Gustave Flaubert was central to the apparatus of Orientalism. Many post-colonial scholars have pursued Said's initial argument by illustrating the extent to which travel writing reinforced or transgressed colonial rule; see especially Ali Behdad, *Belated Travelers: Orientalism in the Age of Colonial Dissolution* (Durham: Duke University Press, 1994); Steve Clark, ed., *Travel Writing and Empire: Postcolonial Theory in Transit* (London and New York: Zed Books, 1999); Sara Mills, *Discourses of Difference: An Analysis of Women's Travel Writing and Colonialism* (London and New York: Routledge, 1991); Mary Louise Pratt, *Imperial Eyes: Travel Writing and Transculturation* (London and New York: Routledge, 1992); David Spurr, *The Rhetoric of Empire: Colonial Discourse in Journalism, Travel Writing, and Imperial Administration* (Durham: Duke University Press, 1993); and Nicholas Thomas, *Colonialism's Culture: Anthropology, Travel and Government* (Cambridge: Quality Press, 1994).

The contemporary travel writer's efforts to abandon his/her colonial heritage is understandable: it mimics the efforts of statesmen, diplomats, civil servants, journalists, researchers and scholars who are currently searching for more equal and just ways of arranging our post-colonial world. In other words, we are all dealing with the legacy of Empire, whether in popular stories of travel or in policy documents on Third World debt. For this reason, many critics have argued that it is 'virtually impossible to consider travel writing outside the frame of postcolonialism'.[2]

Why, then, are travelogues still being written in our supposedly 'enlightened' age? And why are they still so popular? If the Empire that sustained travel writing was dismantled with the various decolonisation movements of the twentieth century, why hasn't travel writing itself disappeared? To address those questions, this book examines popular travelogues written in English since 1975. This time period is significant not only because it encompasses the modern 'renaissance' of travel writing inaugurated by Paul Theroux's *The Great Railway Bazaar: By Train through Asia*, but also because it reveals how travelogues are currently addressing their colonial past in a context of rapid globalisation.[3] However one wants to interpret the vast debates over globalisation (e.g. as new or old, as good or bad, as killing the state or saving it), there is no doubt that the enormous changes in technology, economics, politics and culture in the last thirty years have been reflected in, and produced by, travel writing.[4] This is not to say that the historical forces of globalisation have never made themselves felt in travel writing.

---

[2] Brian Musgrove, 'Travel and Unsettlement: Freud on Vacation', in Clark, *Travel Writing and Empire*, p. 32. Musgrove goes on to say that 'the revival of critical interest in travel writing was co-incident with the rise of postcolonial theory'.

[3] Paul Theroux, *The Great Railway Bazaar: By Train through Asia* (New York: Ballantine Books, 1976). Critic Paul Fussell argues that *The Great Railway Bazaar* is one of the few good travelogues to emerge from our age of mass tourism: see *Abroad: British Literary Travelling between the Wars* (Oxford: Oxford University Press, 1980), pp. 39–40. Introducing Fussell at the 1999 'Writing the Journey' conference at the University of Pennsylvania, David Epsey echoed these comments and signified *The Great Railway Bazaar* as the origin point for the renaissance of modern travel writing: for a transcript of his comments, see http://www.english.upenn/edu/Ytravel99/Fussell.html.

[4] This literature is vast, but the best introduction to the debates on globalisation is David Held and Anthony McGrew, eds., *The Global Transformations Reader: An Introduction to the Globalization Debate* (Cambridge: Polity Press, 2000); see also Zygmunt Bauman, *Globalization: The Human Consequences* (Oxford: Blackwell, 1998); John Beynon and David Dunkerley, eds., *Globalization: The Reader* (London: Athlone Press, 2000); Eleanore Kofman and Gillian Youngs, eds., *Globalization: Theory and Practice* (London: Pinter, 2001); Debbie Lisle, 'Globalization', in Iain McKenzie, ed., *Political Concepts: A Reader and a Guide* (Edinburgh: Edinburgh University Press, 2005); Jan Aarte Scholte, *Globalization: A Critical Introduction* (London: Palgrave, 2000).

Indeed, as Ali Behdad argues in his excellent book *Belated Travelers*, travel writing was crucial to the late nineteenth-century dissolution of Empire and Orientalism. Rather, this book is concerned with how contemporary travel writing participates in, and responds to, the anxieties created by late twentieth-century globalisation. For example, how is travel writing coping with the embarrassment of its colonial past while also recognising that there are no undiscovered places left to explore? Given this precarious position, can travelogues tell us anything relevant, let alone provocative, about contemporary global life?

This book examines how travel writing is currently resuscitating itself in the face of globalisation by pursuing two simultaneous strategies. Firstly, travel writers alleviate the anxieties created by globalisation by recalling the assurances of Empire. As travel writer Robyn Davidson explains:

It's as if the genre has not caught up with the post-colonial reality from which it springs. One would think it should collapse under the weight of its paradoxes, but quite the opposite is happening. There is a passion for travel books harking back to a previous sensibility when home and abroad, occident and orient, centre and periphery were unproblematically defined. Perhaps they are popular for the very reason that they are so deceptive. They create the illusion that there is still an uncontaminated Elsewhere to discover, a place that no longer exists, located, indeed, somewhere between 'fiction and fact'.[5]

As Davidson suggests, it is easy to see how contemporary travel writing continues in the colonial tradition: it reproduces a dominant Western civilisation from which travel writers emerge to document other states, cultures and peoples. In this sense, travel writers continue to secure their privileged position by categorising, critiquing and passing judgement on less-civilised areas of the world. As Joanne P. Sharp argues, 'Western travellers have tended to adopt a colonialist style of writing which assumes the superiority of the traveller's cultural and moral values and which leads to this figure taking possession of what he [sic] sees in a voyeuristic gaze.'[6] In short, travel writers maintain their relevance in a globalised world by mimicking their colonial forebears. This book argues that contemporary travel writing reproduces the logic of Empire through a *colonial vision*. This is not, however, an unreconstructed version of Orientalism. Rather, the post-colonial framework

---

[5] Robyn Davidson, 'The Trip Trap', edited extract of her introduction to *The Picador Book of Journeys*, in the *Guardian*, 4 August, 2001, p. 2; reprinted as the introduction to Robyn Davidson, ed., *Journeys: An Anthology* (London: Picador, 2002), p. 6.

[6] Joanne P. Sharp, 'Writing over the Map of Provence: The Touristic Therapy of *A Year in Provence*', in James Duncan and Derek Gregory, eds., *Writes of Passage: Reading Travel Writing* (London and New York: Routledge, 1999), p. 203.

at work in this book does not condense cross-cultural encounters to 'simple relations of domination and subordination.'[7] When I argue that a particular travel writer employs a colonial vision, I certainly mean to foreground the tropes of power, control and exclusion at work in the text. But I also mean to reveal the anxieties, insecurities and difficulties that arise when simple logics of dominance/subordination are reproduced in a context of late twentieth-century globalisation. In other words, 'colonial vision' is a contested term in this book: it reveals anachronistic forms of authority but also questions, disrupts and interrogates the foundations upon which that authority is grounded.

This brings us to the second strategy by which travel writing is currently resuscitating itself in the face of globalisation. Many travel writers make deliberate efforts to distance themselves from the genre's implication in Empire by embracing the emancipatory possibilities created by an interconnected 'global village.' Rather than 'harking back to a previous sensibility', these authors celebrate the interdependence and common aims of all cultures. In this sense, they 'lead from the front' by teaching us how to appreciate cultural difference and recognise the values common to all of humanity. Unlike their colonial predecessors, these writers frame encounters with others in positive ways – they reveal moments of empathy, recognitions of difference, realisations of equality and insights into shared values. To the extent that travel writers seek to jettison their colonial heritage by focusing on the harmonising effects of globalisation, they employ what I call a *cosmopolitan vision*. I think contemporary travel writing is at its most interesting when it confronts readers and writers with the problem of global community – of what values might cut through cultural difference and make it possible to develop a global order based on shared understandings, norms and sensibilities. Indeed, as Jim Philip argues, 'it may be possible, after all, to read these texts as a site of the emergence, however tentatively, of a new kind of international *society*'.[8] This optimistic understanding of travel writing has its corollary in the arguments for cosmopolitan democracy articulated by, amongst others, David Held.[9] This approach is very clear

---

[7] Steve Clark, 'Introduction', in *Travel Writing and Empire*, p. 3. Indeed, the post-colonial approach at work here draws explicitly from the Clark text, as well as from the work of Behdad, Mills and Pratt.

[8] Jim Philip, 'Reading Travel Writing', in Jonathan White, ed., *Recasting the World: Writing after Colonialism* (Baltimore and London: Johns Hopkins University Press, 1993), p. 251 (italics his).

[9] The cosmopolitan ideal informs all of Held's work, but the most succinct formations of it can be found in 'Democracy and the New International Order', in Daniele Archibugi and David Held, eds., *Cosmopolitan Democracy: An Agenda for a New World Order* (Cambridge: Polity Press, 1995), pp. 96–120 and 'Cosmopolitan Democracy and the

about the kinds of values, norms and understandings upon which a global cosmopolitan democracy should be based. My point is that the cosmopolitan vision embedded in contemporary travel writing and espoused by many liberal thinkers is not as emancipatory as it claims to be; rather, it is underscored by the remnants of Orientalism, colonialism and Empire. In effect, travel writers currently articulating cosmopolitan visions of the world do not avoid the 'embarrassing' attitudes of their colonial predecessors – they actually produce new forms of power that mimic the 'previous sensibility' of Empire. I want to subject the certainty of this cosmopolitan vision to Jacques Derrida's questions: 'Where have we received the image of cosmopolitanism from? *And what is happening to it?*'[10] By drawing on more critical understandings of cosmopolitanism, this book reveals how contemporary travel writing operates in a contested, antagonistic and uncertain political terrain that is haunted by the logic of Empire.[11]

This book argues that contemporary travel writing engages most profoundly in the wider debates of global politics through its structuring tension between *colonial* and *cosmopolitan* visions. These two visions cannot be understood separately; it is not enough simply to chart how travel writing reproduces the categories of Empire in an effort to ward off the homogenising forces of globalisation, nor is it enough to argue that travel writing has successfully resolved its irrelevancy by championing the principles of global civil society and cosmopolitanism. Rather, these two visions exist in a complex relationship with one another – sometimes antagonistic, sometimes symbiotic, sometimes ambiguous. In examining this relationship, this book asks whether the cosmopolitan vision is merely a blander mutation of the colonial vision, or if it really

New International Order', in David Held, ed., *Democracy and the Global Order: From the Modern State to Cosmopolitan Governance* (Cambridge: Polity Press, 1995), pp. 267–86. For a more nuanced and recent engagement with these questions, see Steven Vertovec and Robin Cohen, eds., *Conceiving Cosmopolitanism: Theory, Context, Practice* (Oxford: Oxford University Press, 2002), in which Held has an essay entitled 'Culture and Political Community: National Global, and Cosmopolitan', pp. 48–58.

[10] Jacques Derrida, *On Cosmopolitanism and Forgiveness*, trans. Mark Dooley and Michael Hughes (London and New York: Routledge, 2001), p. 3.

[11] Along with Derrida's work, critical approaches to cosmopolitanism are best articulated in Pheng Cheah and Bruce Robbins, eds., *Cosmopolis: Thinking and Feeling beyond the Nation* (Minneapolis: University of Minnesota Press, 1998), especially Bruce Robbins, 'Introduction, Part I: Actually Existing Cosmopolitanisms', pp. 1–19; as well as in Vertovec and Cohen, *Conceiving Cosmopolitanism*, especially Craig Calhoun, 'The Class Consciousness of Frequent Travellers: Towards a Critique of Actually Existing Cosmopolitanism', pp. 86–109. From a more literary perspective, Timothy Brennan pursues these questions in *At Home in the World: Cosmopolitanism Now* (Cambridge and London: Harvard University Press, 1997).

does allow for difference, heterogeneity and contingency in the global realm. To what extent do the Western values of recognition, equality and tolerance embedded in the cosmopolitan vision carry traces of their colonial heritage? Is contemporary travel writing able to encourage a radically diverse global community unconstrained by Enlightenment notions of civilisation and progress? At the heart of these questions is the production of difference in the global realm. It is not that difficult to see how superior Western subjects employing a colonial vision construct inferior 'others' in order to justify the continuation of hierarchical global relations. Likewise, it is not that difficult to see how a self-proclaimed international community employing a cosmopolitan vision articulate universal standards of civilisation by which they judge all cultures. But what *is* difficult to see – and what this book seeks to illustrate – is the extent to which these competing productions of difference both fuse together and fall apart in contemporary travel writing.

Double vision: the production of difference in Paul Theroux and Bill Bryson

In order to illustrate how colonial and cosmopolitan visions operate, it is useful to see how two masters of contemporary travel writing – Paul Theroux and Bill Bryson – utilise conventional geopolitical categories to produce difference in the global realm. In *The Old Patagonian Express: By Train through the Americas* (the follow-up to *The Great Railway Bazaar*), Theroux makes an epic train journey from Boston to Patagonia and back again. Early on in the book, he crosses the border from Laredo, Texas into Nuevo Laredo, Mexico, and makes the following observation:

the garlic seller was the personification of Latin America. He was weedy and wore a torn shirt and greasy hat; he was very dirty; he screamed the same words over and over. These attributes alone were unremarkable – he too had a counterpart in Cleveland. What distinguished him was the way he carried his merchandise. He had a garland of garlic cloves around his neck and another around his waist and ropes of them on his arms, and he shook them in his fists. He fought his way in and out of the crowd, the clusters of garlic bouncing on his body. Was there any better example of cultural difference than this man? At the Texas end of the bridge he would have been arrested for contravening some law of sanitation; here he was ignored. What was so strange about wearing bunches of garlic around your neck? Perhaps nothing, except that he would not have done it if he were not a Mexican, and I would not have noticed it if I hadn't been an American.[12]

---

[12] Paul Theroux, *The Old Patagonian Express: By Train through the Americas* (New York: Washington Square Press, 1979), p. 51.

What is remarkable about this passage is the way Theroux uses the category of modern statehood to produce, interpret and judge the difference he encounters. In other words, his observations about the garlic seller are made meaningful to the extent that they draw upon already established oppositions between Mexico and America. Theroux and the garlic seller are different because they come from different countries (e.g. 'he would not have done it if he were not a Mexican, and I would not have noticed it if I hadn't been an American'). Theroux's colonial vision is quite explicit here: he uses the border between Mexico and America to invoke a series of cultural, political, economic and structural differences whereby Mexico is always inferior to America. As geographer Doreen Massey explains, Theroux 'does not seem to doubt for a minute his right to pass the sweeping judgements he records', and those judgements always reinforce a hierarchical relationship between Mexico and America.[13] Theroux's marking of difference through a colonial vision not only provides moral justification for the geopolitical border between Mexico and America, it also legitimates the wider cultural, political, economic and structural inequalities that exist between these two states. Theroux's loaded description of the garlic seller is exemplary in this regard: the weedy, dirty, screaming Mexican could not be more opposed to the rational, observant American travel writer. Theroux's judgement of the garlic seller resonates with readers because it calls upon many other shared interpretations of the unequal relationships between Mexico and America (e.g. developed and under-developed, civilised and primitive, First World and Third World). Suddenly, the heavy security presence at the US border begins to make sense to Theroux's readers – America *needs* to be protected from those hordes of filthy characters symbolised by the garlic seller. By augmenting the Mexican-American border with descriptions of cultural difference inherited from a colonial past, Theroux invites his readers to sanction the structures of power that justify America's most militarised and violent national border.

Conversely, Bill Bryson's travelogue *Neither Here Nor There: Travels in Europe* is an effort to celebrate diversity rather than judge it according to a colonial vision. Just after the fall of the Berlin Wall, Bryson sets forth from his home in England to see the major European cities between

---

[13] Doreen Massey, 'Imagining the World', in John Allen and Doreen Massey, eds., *Geographical Worlds* (Oxford: Oxford University Press in association with the Open University, 1995), p. 40. Massey's critical reading of Theroux is more compelling than the formal critique offered by Fussell in *Abroad*, p. 159, where he argues that *The Old Patagonian Express* is a 'failure' because of an 'absence of sufficient resonance, and allusion and nuance'. In other words, it is *badly written*.

Stockholm and Istanbul. What follows is an affectionate reaffirmation of the minute foibles and national stereotypes of Europe. But Bryson is keen to distance himself from the negative judgements that colonial travel writing encouraged, and therefore represents European stereotypes in positive and humorous ways. This allows him to celebrate the differences that make Europe unique, and counter the 'American habit of thinking of Europe as one place and Europeans as essentially one people'.[14] Thus, the rudeness of French waiters is reassuring (and waning under pressure from the French Tourist Board), the crazy Italians are chaotic and wonderful (especially when they park their cars on top of each other) and German cities are admirable for their order and efficiency. Unlike Theroux, Bryson rejoices in the differences he encounters:

One of the small marvels of my first trip to Europe was the discovery that the world could be so full of variety, that there were so many different ways of doing essentially identical things, like eating and drinking and buying cinema tickets. It fascinated me that Europeans could at once be so alike – that they could be so universally bookish and cerebral, and drive small cars, and live in little houses in ancient towns, and love soccer, and be relatively unmaterialistic and law-abiding, and have chilly hotel rooms and cosy and inviting places to eat and drink – and yet be so endlessly, unpredictably different from each other as well. I loved the idea that you could never be sure of anything in Europe.[15]

The differences that Bryson documents in Europe are not threatening or damaging; rather, they are precisely what make the place worth visiting. What is interesting in this passage is how Bryson translates particular characteristics through a cosmopolitan vision; he assumes that everybody the world over eats, drinks and buys cinema tickets because these are universal habits. The challenge for him as a travel writer is to show how these universal activities are performed differently (and thus humorously) in each particular nation of Europe. Like Theroux, Bryson is keen to mark out difference – it's just that Bryson's cosmopolitan approach seems much more benign. While Theroux despises the 'poverty and degradation' of Mexico, Bryson thinks the states of Europe are 'nifty' discoveries. They are not better or worse than his English home – they are simply different. By focusing on the diversity of Europe – from their 'little houses' to their 'love of soccer' – Bryson articulates resistance to the visible signs of cultural homogenisation (e.g. the ubiquity of McDonalds, Starbucks and Gap).

[14] Bill Bryson, *Neither Here Nor There: Travels in Europe* (London: Black Swan, 1998), p. 86.
[15] Bryson, *Neither Here Nor There*, p. 40.

Bryson's cosmopolitan vision of the world does *not* mean homogenisation; rather, it means encouraging, celebrating and securing cultural differences. This makes the travelogue the perfect vehicle for Bryson's message, and *Neither Here Nor There* inaugurates his bumbling efforts to learn about, appreciate and celebrate difference rather than judge it negatively.

What is significant in these passages is that while Theroux and Bryson articulate competing global visions – one colonial and the other cosmopolitan – both rely on stable geopolitical boundaries to locate difference and secure identity. Both narratives assume that there are 'natural' boundaries separating different cultures – it's just that in Theroux's narrative those boundaries are necessary to protect privileged identities from uncivilised others, and in Bryson's narrative those boundaries simply indicate diverse cultural traditions. Neither author thinks about, let alone interrogates, the givenness of these categories, and both assume that boundaries operate as simple markers of difference rather than complex and contingent formations of power. While Bryson's cosmopolitan vision may offer a more palatable approach for these 'enlightened' times, he relies on the same logics of differentiation and demarcation embedded in Theroux's colonial vision. The problem here is that while travel writers spend much of their time crossing cultural and national borders, they fail to address the intricate and ambiguous power relations at work in these sites. In Theroux's narrative, his judgemental production of difference ignores the everyday transgressions that occur along the Mexican-American border – the physical struggles between illegal Mexican immigrants and American law enforcers, the transfer of capital between international banks and multinational corporations, the interactions between female workers, union activists and wealthy entrepreneurs in Maquilladora factories, and the constant installation and maintenance of American surveillance technology. Similarly, Bryson's more optimistic production of difference ignores the contingency of Europe as a political entity – the mobility of Europe's eastern border during the different phases of enlargement, the continuing antagonisms in Northern Ireland, Cyprus and Bosnia, and EU decisions that consolidate elite power and exclude disempowered groups across the continent (e.g. migrant workers, asylum seekers, refugees). So while Theroux's colonial vision depicts the Mexican-American border as an effective mechanism for protecting the 'civilised' Americans from the 'uncivilised' Mexicans, and Bryson's cosmopolitan vision depicts the borders of Europe as essentially benign containers of quirky cultural differences, neither writer questions how his simple depiction of crossing a border hides a number of problematic assumptions about power, culture and difference. To enter into this kind of epistemological interrogation would place the position of the travel writer in doubt: how could Theroux produce and judge difference if the boundary securing his home and his identity were to be questioned? How could Bryson celebrate the differences of Europe if he began to doubt the very boundaries he cherishes?

If the colonial and cosmopolitan visions of Theroux and Bryson are similar in their uncritical reproduction of geopolitical boundaries, they differ in their political urgency. Because Theroux's colonial vision allows him to make negative judgements about the places he visits, it is easy to see how his texts reproduce the prevailing ideologies of his time. Indeed, many of my engagements with Theroux's texts are efforts to reveal his conservative outlook and privileged position within the status quo. But it is the travel writers who enact a cosmopolitan vision who are most alarming, for they smuggle in equally judgemental accounts of otherness *under the guise* of equality, tolerance and respect for difference. While cosmopolitan travel writers might be part of a larger cultural effort to critique colonial power relations, I want to argue that they simultaneously rearticulate the logic of Empire through new networks, structures and boundaries. Travel writers like Bryson might refrain from making the negative judgements that characterise Theroux's writing, but his playful celebration of difference can be picked up and mobilised in the construction of new global hegemonies. For example, cosmopolitan travel writers fail to recognise the privileged conception of global mobility embedded in the genre. Much of this writing would have us believe that the increase in mobility brought about by globalisation results in the equal movement of people, goods and ideas around the world. But there is an enormous difference between a wealthy Western travel writer like Bryson bumbling his way across Europe funded by a healthy advance from his publisher and, say, a teenager from Macedonia forced through the organised prostitution networks of Rome, Paris and London in order to 'work off' her debt and buy back her freedom. The idea that 'everybody moves freely' in a globalised world is a fallacy: only those who can afford to move, or those who are willing to take the risks associated with migration, are able to cross established geopolitical borders with ease. While travel writers might be aware of these global inequalities, they are often unaware of how the act of writing about travel *itself* engenders contemporary power formations that are as unequal, unjust and exploitative as those forged during Empire. While Bryson's efforts to reveal the funny side of difference might seem like a step in the right direction, I want to argue that even those 'benign' efforts can be used to justify and legitimate new forms of global exclusion, domination and violence.

In the departure lounge: discourse, power and materiality

Travel writing shapes and influences the way we understand the world. Historically, our knowledge of the world has come to us, in part, through the famous travel stories of figures like Marco Polo, Magellan and Lawrence of Arabia. In short, we *know* there are faraway lands on the other side of the world because certain travellers have made journeys there and recorded them in travelogues. But travel writing has not remained static over the years – it is also shaped by the very world it seeks to document. Think of how the genre has changed in line with significant global shifts: while eighteenth-century travelogues happily categorised foreign plants, animals and peoples into ordered taxonomies, that Enlightenment confidence had dissipated by the late nineteenth century, and many travel writers expressed fear and anxiety as the structures of Empire began to collapse.[16] The difficulty with this formulation – texts shaping reality and reality shaping texts – is that it reproduces a 'correspondence' understanding of representation. In other words, it assumes there is a single, incontrovertible reality awaiting documentation by travel writers, and each travelogue can be judged for how accurately it represents this reality. For example, Theroux's *The Old Patagonian Express* could be considered a vehicle for the seamless transmission of 'real' cultural difference and inequality from the world, to the author, to the text, and finally to the reader. The book's subsequent success with the public could then be understood as testament to the truth and accuracy of Theroux's interpretation of Latin America. But representation is never a simple literary event: reading, writing and interpretation are political acts that involve complex power relations between readers, writers and the social worlds they inhabit. To argue that travel writing is connected to the world it documents in a more complex way than simple correspondence, it is necessary to examine the forces and structures that shape the text/reality relationship. This book argues that stories of travel are connected to the social worlds inhabited by readers and writers by a number of competing *discourses*.

[16] See Pratt, *Imperial Eyes*, 'Part I. Science and Sentiment, 1750–1800', pp. 15–107, for an excellent account of the relationship between taxonomies of knowledge and eighteenth-century travel writing; see Behdad, *Belated Travelers*, for a detailed account of the travelogue's participation in the nineteenth-century dissolution of Empire.

Although discourse is a difficult and contested term, it is most easily understood as a set of images, vocabularies and material conditions that expresses prevailing truth claims about the world and positions subjects and objects accordingly. As the work of Michel Foucault makes clear, discourses attach all texts, utterances and representations to the social, political, cultural and economic forces that give rise to their production, circulation and value. His method of discourse analysis examines how power arranges certain subjects, objects and meanings into an incontrovertible reality and excludes other possible ways of being and knowing.[17] This is not a 'correspondence' understanding of representation at all; indeed, discourse analysis resists the idea that we are handcuffed to a stable and single reality that we can somehow 'get wrong' by not being accurate enough in our representations and interpretations. This is precisely why Foucault explains that the world does not 'turn a legible face towards us' that we can decipher according to a transcendental framework. Acts of writing and speaking are given meaning through prevailing discourses and actually *do violence* to the world because they are an imposition of ordered meaning on an otherwise ambiguous reality. Travel writing is no exception: it organises the world through a number of prevailing discourses, and sediments that world into a seemingly incontrovertible reality. Travelogues are politically interesting texts because they mask that process of discursive ordering and offer their observations as neutral documentations of a stable, single and ordered reality. In order to identify and reveal the prevailing discourses at work in contemporary travel writing, it is necessary to track the *continuity* of statements and meanings that come to be understood as true and real. Indeed, Foucault argues that discourses become *hegemonic* when the gathering of statements and

---

[17] Michel Foucault's detailed empirical and historical studies on insanity, criminality and sexuality exemplify the methodology of discourse analysis at work in this book: see *Madness and Civilization: A History of Insanity in the Age of Reason*, trans. Richard Howard (New York: Random House, 1973); *Discipline and Punish: The Birth of the Prison*, trans. Alan Sheridan (New York: Pantheon Books, 1977); and *The History of Sexuality*, Vol. I: *An Introduction*, trans. Robert Hurley (New York: Vintage Books, 1980). In addition, I am also drawing from Foucault's three key 'method' texts: *The Order of Things: An Archaeology of the Human Sciences* (New York: Vintage Books, 1973), which provides a discursive reading of the human sciences; *The Archaeology of Knowledge and the Discourse on Human Language* (New York: Pantheon Books, 1972), which explores the relationship between discourse and language; and 'The Order of Discourse', in Michael Shapiro, ed., *Language and Politics* (Oxford: Basil Blackwell, 1984), pp. 108–37, which outlines a discursive genealogy. This famous lecture by Foucault was originally given at the College de France on 2 December 1970 and is also reproduced as 'A Discourse on Language' in the back of the American publication of *The Archaeology of Knowledge*.

meanings around various truth claims continues uninterrupted until it sediments into a 'clear' picture of reality.[18]

With this in mind, *The Global Politics of Contemporary Travel Writing* uses Foucauldian discourse analysis to identify the prevailing discourses shaping contemporary travelogues and illustrate how the same discourses are at work in the study and practice of global politics. With this discursive approach, power is never situated wholly within the travelogue text, the travel writer, the reading audience or the 'reality' that is being documented. Rather, power is always located in the discourses that *connect* texts, subjects and realities. Foucault's point is that this connection is never neutral – which is why we need discourse analysis to trace hegemonic discursive formations and reveal their political effects. With respect to *The Old Patagonian Express* and *Neither Here Nor There*, we can see that discourses locate subjects, objects and meanings in differential positions. The discourses at work in *The Old Patagonian Express* ensure that the myriad of possible relationships between Mexico and America are jettisoned in favour of a superior/inferior relationship that is rendered 'natural' and therefore placed beyond question. This hierarchy is secured every time Theroux reinforces his superiority as a rational and objective American travel writer against objectified others such as the dirty, weedy, Mexican garlic seller. Conversely, the discourses at work in *Neither Here Nor There* insist that every country in Europe is different, and that happy coexistence is Europe's 'natural' mode of being. Unlike Theroux's strategy, Bryson's 'quirky' and unthreatening observations are less about judging difference, and more about contrasting the marvellous Europeans with his own infantile, shambolic and ungainly self. But this humour does not neutralise Bryson's travelogue; rather, it helps to place his production of difference beyond question, for how can the playful celebration of difference be a *bad* thing?

What differentiates Foucauldian discourse analysis from the more over-determined ideological examinations of culture offered by the Frankfurt School (amongst others) is its claim that resistance is embedded in all discourses. While a Foucauldian approach locates the truth claims reinforced by discourses, it also reveals the *discontinuity* of all discourses and their failure to completely exclude other subjects, objects and meanings. In this way, discourse analysis uncovers and gives voice to that which is made silent within the discursive imposition

---

[18] In *The Archaeology of Knowledge*, Foucault explains that discursive continuity occurs through the following practices: a continuing reference to the same object, a common style in the production of statements (e.g. the vernacular of science), a constant usage of the same concept and a repeated referral to common themes (pp. 31–9).

of order: it reveals the ambiguities, ruptures and repetitions that are covered over every time we agree to interpret the world according to a single and incontrovertible reality. For example, what possibilities are precluded and silenced by the confident authorial voice of the travel writer? What would the Mexican garlic seller make of Theroux's observations? How do the Spanish and Portuguese feel at being excised from Bryson's European odyssey? Ernesto Laclau and Chantal Mouffe build on Foucault's arguments about the discontinuity of discourse by explaining that resistance is located precisely in the *failure* of discourses to achieve hegemony and totality. We understand the failure of hegemony primarily because history is full of powerful struggles against various discursive totalities. If discourses were completely successful at organising meaning into a hegemonic bloc, there would be no struggle, no antagonism and no debate. In short, there would be no politics. If we accepted all truth claims as the foundation for an incontrovertible reality, there would be nothing to hegemonise and no continual need for discourses to repeat themselves. So while the superior/inferior relationship between America and Mexico structures the narrative of *The Old Patagonian Express*, it never completely silences the history of political and cultural antagonism between these two states − a history that includes the nineteenth-century Mexican-American War, Cesar Chavez's creation of the United Farm Workers Union in the 1960s, various anti-NAFTA movements all across North America in the early 1990s, and the Zapatista resistance movement led by Subcomandante Marcos. Likewise, while Bryson depicts Europe as a diverse and happy family of nations, his humour never completely silences the horrors of European history. In other words, Bryson's shambling tour of 'little houses in ancient towns' and 'cosy and inviting places to drink' is haunted by the battlefields of the Somme, the Allied cemeteries in Normandy and the memorials at Auschwitz and Birkenau.

Laclau and Mouffe make a further political intervention in Foucault's work by explaining how discourses achieve continuity and permanence by continually changing their boundaries over time. When discursive limits are questioned and transgressed by counter-hegemonic forces (i.e. when moments of resistance are revealed), new limits and new mechanisms of regulation must be formed and repeated to hold truth claims in place.[19] Laclau and Mouffe explain this malleability of discursive limits

---

[19] As Laclau and Mouffe argue, 'the two conditions of a hegemonic articulation are the presence of antagonistic forces and the instability of the frontiers which separate them... [W]ithout equivalence and without frontiers, it is impossible to speak of hegemony'; see Ernesto Laclau and Chantal Mouffe, *Hegemony and Socialist Strategy: Towards a Radical Democratic Politics* (London: Verso, 1985), p. 136.

through the Gramscian idea of assimilation: discursive hegemony continues because it is able to assimilate and neutralise the forces of resistance it encounters. This is precisely what is occurring in contemporary travel writing as authors make efforts to distance themselves from the genre's complicity in Empire. It might seem that Bryson's harmless and unthreatening depictions of cultural difference are *better* than Theroux's explicit neocolonial judgements. But as this book argues, the shift from a colonial to a cosmopolitan vision is profoundly depoliticising because it smuggles in the logic of Empire under the banner of universalism. In other words, messages of global harmony and international unity are being trumpeted by a genre that *claims* to have jettisoned its colonial past, but all the while is casually producing new forms of colonial power. Because many contemporary travel writers fail to address the powerful influence of the genre's colonial history, they end up imposing values they believe to be universal (e.g. equality, tolerance, cultural diversity) without realising the particular Western heritage of those values. My point is that by assimilating certain messages of 'political correctness', travel writing actually perpetuates an unreconstructed colonial vision while claiming to celebrate equality, tolerance and cultural diversity.

If we assume that discourses are only about textual and linguistic matters, then this analysis of travel writing would be limited to the formal, aesthetic and stylistic questions of whether or not a particular travelogue is well written. To maintain the political edge of discourse analysis, it is necessary to pursue one of Foucault's most troubling and enduring insights, that discourses are actually *material* things. While discourses are certainly a function of language and its orders, they also have very real effects – on our bodies, in our homes, in our institutions, in our minds. One of the most serious misunderstandings of Foucault is that his work is purely theoretical, linguistic and historical, and that his concern with discourse is simply an obsession with language and thought. But the strength of Foucault's work – especially his early research on prisons and clinics – is its empirical richness and historical detail. For Foucault, discourses are never just about language and texts – they make the crucial political link between representations and their material effects. And this is precisely the argument that causes the most anxiety, for while we are able to accept the discursive construction of meaning according to a grid of power and knowledge, we are much less willing to accept that discourses shape our material world. As Foucault argues, the inclusion of materiality is exactly what the struggles for discursive hegemony are designed to do away with: 'in every society the production of discourse is at once controlled, selected, organized and redistributed by a certain number of procedures whose role it is to ward off its powers and dangers, to gain mastery over its chance events, to evade its ponderous, formidable materiality'.[20] Laclau and Mouffe are even more explicit than Foucault in arguing for the materiality of discourse. For them, there is nothing at all outside of discourse – not even material objects – because the discursive field is infinite. In other words, discourses cover both linguistic and non-linguistic spheres.[21] Suggesting that 'nothing is outside of discourse' is, by logical extension, a suggestion that material artefacts such as tables, mountains and guns do not actually *exist* without discourses to articulate them. These artefacts are somehow animated by our language and meaning, but prior to that encounter they are not entities at all. While Laclau and Mouffe accept that objects do, in fact, exist externally to our thinking about them, they also deny that objects 'could constitute themselves as objects outside any discursive condition of emergence'.[22] As they explain, 'as a member of a certain community, I will never encounter an object in its naked existence – such a notion is a mere abstraction; rather, that existence will always be given as articulated within discursive totalities'.[23]

If material objects are as discursively constructed as language, then the discourse analysis at work in this book necessarily invokes the 'real' world of global travel just as it invokes the 'literary' world of travel writing. To claim that travelogues are 'just books' is to ignore their participation in wider discursive structures, and the material effects that are produced within those structures. For example, the discourses invoked by Theroux in his judgement of the Mexican garlic seller are the same discourses used by American law enforcers when they apprehend illegal immigrants at the Mexican-American border. Likewise, the discourses embedded in Bill Bryson's text are the same discourses used by EU bureaucrats as they redefine the role of NATO in a globalised world. Insisting on a discursive field that is infinite – that is material as well as linguistic – is the best way to foreground the possibility of

---

[20] Foucault, 'The Order of Discourse', p. 109.
[21] Laclau and Mouffe claim: 'This totality which includes within itself the linguistic and the non-linguistic, is what we call *discourse*.' They provide a very clear explanation of this relationship through the example of building a brick wall: see Ernesto Laclau and Chantal Mouffe, 'Post-Marxism without Apologies', *New Left Review*, No. 166, Nov./Dec. 1987, p. 82. A helpful translation of Foucault, Laclau and Mouffe's work in politics is David Howarth, Aletta J. Norval and Yannis Stavrakakis, eds., *Discourse Theory and Political Analysis: Identities, Hegemonies and Social Change* (Manchester: Manchester University Press, 2000).
[22] Laclau and Mouffe, *Hegemony and Socialist Strategy*, p. 108.
[23] Laclau and Mouffe, 'Post-Marxism without Apologies', p. 85.

resistance within even the most oppressive discourses. For example, lurking within the discourses that frame Theroux's judgement of Mexico are alternative formations of power that require more just and equitable relationships between people located on either side of the border. Likewise, embedded within the discourses that Bryson draws upon to frame Europe as a 'friendly' collection of cultural differences are alternative formations of power that reveal longstanding political antagonisms and public memories of violence and bloodshed. By foregrounding an infinite discursive field characterised as much by resistance as it is by oppression, it is possible to show how travel writing enables the reproduction of global hegemonies, but also has the potential to disrupt and transform these logics of rule.

The road not taken: disciplinary starting points

There has been considerable debate in a number of areas over how best to apply discourse analysis to cultural products.[24] All discursive approaches start from the premise that cultural products both reflect and produce their social contexts; that is, a cultural product cannot be understood in isolation from its social and political environment. This means that any formal appreciation of, say, a painting (e.g. the perspective, the brushstrokes) must be supplemented by an account of how that painting reflects, comments on and contributes to its social and political environment (e.g. what does the painting mean? What is its message?). Beyond this starting point, however, scholars diverge on the locus of analysis. One direction, inspired explicitly by the work of Foucault, pursues a 'content analysis' of particular cultural texts (e.g. advertisements, novels, photographs, magazines, films, paintings, fashion, architecture) and reveals how hegemonic constellations of power/knowledge are both articulated and challenged. This is very much the spirit of discourse analysis that guides this book. However, these arguments are not divorced from 'institutional' approaches that widen the focus from the text itself and examine the producers (e.g. artists, writers, directors, curators), institutions (e.g. galleries, museums, the film industry, the publishing industry) and audiences (e.g. readers, listeners, viewers) that interact with specific cultural products. While this book is certainly attuned to the producers of travel writing (e.g. travel writers) as well as its consumers (e.g. readers), its primary focus is

---

[24] Although focusing on visual culture, Gillan Rose provides the most compelling account of these debates; see *Visual Methodologies: An Introduction to the Interpretation of Visual Materials* (London: Sage, 2001), pp. 135–203.

to examine the variety of discourses *embedded within travelogues themselves* and ask what those discourses tell us about competing colonial and cosmopolitan visions. This is not to ignore the claims of travel writers and readers; indeed, I am very concerned with how prevailing discourses constitute the subject positions of 'the reader' and 'the writer'. But the focus of this book does not extend to a detailed taxonomy of reading groups, or an ethnography of popular travel writers. While there is much work to be done on the cultures of production and consumption surrounding contemporary travel writing, I am concerned here primarily with the colonial and cosmopolitan visions that are currently shaping the genre itself.[25]

The Global Politics of Contemporary Travel Writing is not a detailed examination of global politics, nor is it an exhaustive study of contemporary travelogues. Rather, it contributes to the academic debates about travel writing by situating the genre in the interdisciplinary space between International Relations and Cultural Studies. It is perhaps unorthodox to ask what contemporary travel writing can tell us about the *serious* business of global politics – about borders and states, about cultures and conflicts, and about security and order. After all, these are books written to amuse, entertain and possibly to educate. It is not surprising, then, that travel writing, or 'Trip Lit', has become one of the new and fashionable areas for literary criticism. As one commentator suggested, travel writing is 'the most recent darling of the trendy humanities and lit-crit set, who scour travel books, both well known and hopelessly obscure, for evidence of postcolonialism, postimperialism, patriarchy and other evils'.[26] However, this 'new' area of criticism has, for the most part, been content to focus on travel writing from the colonial era, which has left contemporary travel writing relatively free of

---

[25] Two potential areas of research emerge here: firstly, a 'political economy' of travel writing that would examine the publishing industry, book sales, marketing strategies and the publicity of certain travel writers. Indeed, as Patrick Holland and Graham Huggan argue, 'A comprehensive industry analysis of the travel writing business would also be useful' (*Tourists with Typewriters: Critical Reflections on Contemporary Travel Writing* (Ann Arbor: University of Michigan Press, 1998)), p. ix. Secondly, an examination of the specific reading cultures of travel writing (e.g. book groups dedicated to the genre) which would draw from the 'sociology of texts' literature; see Tony Bennett, 'Texts, Readers, Reading Formations', *Literature and History*, Vol. 9, No. 2, 1983, pp. 214–27; Jenny Hartley and Sarah Turvey, *Reading Groups* (Oxford: Oxford University Press, 2001); Jerome J. McGann, *The Textual Condition* (Princeton: Princeton University Press, 1991); and D. F. McKenzie, *Bibliography and the Sociology of Texts* (Cambridge: Cambridge University Press, 1999).

[26] Jason Wilson, 'The Travails of Travel Writing', 'On Media' section, *Philadelphia City Paper*, 17–24 June 1999; see http://www.citypaper.net/articles/061799/news.onmedia1.shtml.

critical analysis. Patrick Holland and Graham Huggan's 1998 book *Tourists with Typewriters* corrects this oversight – and sets the stage for my own analysis – by examining how colonial power relations continue to inform contemporary travel writing. Their work is framed around the various historical claims that travel writing, as a separate literary genre, is over. As they argue, '[travelogues] have a habit of justifying their own limitations by anticipating their own decline'.[27] Literary and social critic Paul Fussell has made the most powerful case for the demise of the genre, arguing that with the emergence of post-1945 mass tourism, the age of 'real' travel – and thus 'real' travel writing – had ended.[28] What Holland and Huggan provide is a powerful refutation of Fussell's claim, and a broad study of why the opposite has occurred – why travel writing has actually flourished with the onslaught of mass tourism. When six major publishing houses established new lines dedicated specifically to travel writing at the end of the 1980s, one publisher commented: 'We are in the midst of a great and somewhat unexpected boom in travel writing. Authors borne by air are exploring distant corners of the globe with an ease unimaginable 25 years ago . . . And publishers are rushing to jump on the bandwagon . . . The whole subject has exploded.'[29]

In examining the increasing popularity of travelogues in the context of mass tourism, Holland and Huggan argue that these texts remain 'a refuge for complacent, even nostalgically retrograde, middle-class values'.[30] In other words, travel writing remains popular because it feeds on images of otherness utilised by colonial writers and, as such, provides a sanctuary from contemporary 'politically correct' attitudes about race, gender, sexuality and class. Holland and Huggan trace how contemporary travel writers recapture the sense of discovery that was central to colonial travel writing by creating new and original ways to make the familiar world seem strange. This is what accounts for the powerful sense of nostalgia that pervades contemporary texts: 'travel writers . . . hearken back to their precursors, seeking solace for a troubled

---

[27] Holland and Huggan, *Tourists with Typewriters*, p. 1.

[28] Fussell, *Abroad*, p. vii. Gary Krist argues that 'much of [Fussell's] hatred for the age of tourism results from the fact that even his mail carrier can now afford to take the seat next to him on the plane to Zanzibar' ('Ironic Journeys: Travel Writing in the Age of Tourism', *Hudson Review*, Vol. 45, No. 4, Winter 1993, p. 594).

[29] Jim Miller, 'Literature's New Nomads', *Publisher's Weekly*, Vol. 114, No. 7, 14 August 1989, pp. 50–1; for more specific information on the new lines established by publishers, see Carolyn Anthony, 'Travel Reading for Pleasure', *Publisher's Weekly*, Vol. 237, No. 3, 19 January 1990, pp. 32–4; see also Michael Kowalewski, 'Introduction: The Modern Literature of Travel', in Michael Kowalewski, ed., *Temperamental Journeys: Essays on the Modern Literature of Travel* (Athens, GA, and London: University of Georgia Press, 1992), pp. 5–6.

[30] Holland and Huggan, *Tourists with Typewriters*, p. viii.

present in nostalgic cultural myths'.[31] With this in mind, we might say that Holland and Huggan are also concerned with the articulation of a colonial vision in contemporary texts. However, while *Tourists with Typewriters* is critical of the colonial ethos that continues to contaminate contemporary travelogues, it is equally concerned with re-imagining travel writing in a more ethical and non-reductive manner. Thus, Holland and Huggan explain that travel writing endures because otherness can be transformed and enveloped within larger ideas about global unity. Instead of signalling the demise of travel writing, globalisation and mass tourism have led to its 'democratisation'. Not only are different kinds of people now writing travelogues (including those who were previously colonised), but the readership is also becoming more global and democratic. Thus, we might also say that Holland and Huggan examine how a more cosmopolitan vision is developing in contemporary travel writing.

Tourists with Typewriters is an important text because it uses literary and post-colonial criticism to reveal both the exclusionary and the emancipatory possibilities of travel writing. Holland and Huggan argue that travelogues can be a positive influence when writers and readers use images of otherness to reflect on their privileged cultural assumptions:

[this study] deviates, for example, from the commonly held view that travel writing upholds freedom, arguing instead that it can be seen — though not exclusively — as an imperialist discourse through which dominant cultures (white, male, Euro-American, middle-class) seek to ingratiate themselves, often at others' expense. Travel writing, though, has another side... [it] can be seen as a useful vehicle of cultural self-perception; as a barometer for changing views on other ('foreign', 'non-Western') cultures; and as a trigger for the informational circuits that tap us into the wider world. Travel writing ... may yet show its readers the limits of their ambition and remind them of their responsibilities.[32]

By revealing the possibilities of critique and reflection, Holland and Huggan make a compelling case for the endurance of travel writing in a globalised world. While they are keen to illustrate the continuing colonial legacy of travelogues, they are not wholly preoccupied with the 'evils' of the genre. Given the arguments made by Holland and Huggan, it should be clear that I am sympathetic to *Tourists with Typewriters*, not least because it is the most comprehensive and critical academic engagement with contemporary travel writing produced so far. However, because it is the first sustained critique of these texts, I see

---

[31] Holland and Huggan, *Tourists with Typewriters*, p. xi.
[32] Holland and Huggan, *Tourists with Typewriters*, p. xiii.

it as a starting point for the questions, issues and difficulties under scrutiny in my own analyses. While I share the ethical imperative of *Tourists with Typewriters* – to politicise contemporary travel writing and reveal its continuing colonial ethos – I am specifically interested in how travel writing aligns with the changing debates and practices of global politics. Let me be clear: I agree with Holland and Huggan that these texts are powerful statements on the legacy of colonialism, but I want to extend their analysis outside of literary criticism and connect it to the interdisciplinary concerns currently being articulated by International Relations and Cultural Studies.

Although scholars working in International Relations – from realists to post-structuralists – have not dealt with travelogues explicitly, the latter have certainly engaged with the underlying theoretical concepts that make it possible to understand travelogues as significant to the study and practice of global politics. By focusing on power relations across global space rather than sovereign arrangements of authority, post-structural scholars have made powerful critiques of the statist ontology of the discipline.[33] More importantly, these scholars have established a much wider interdisciplinary context for research by insisting that culture is a crucial site of global power relations.[34]

[33] Significant post-structural texts in International Relations include Richard Ashley and R. B. J. Walker, eds., *International Studies Quarterly* (Special Edition), Vol. 34, No. 3, 1990; David Campbell, *Writing Security: United States Foreign Policy and the Politics of Identity* (Manchester: Manchester University Press, 1992) and *National Deconstruction: Violence, Identity and Justice in Bosnia* (Minneapolis: University of Minnesota Press, 1998); James Der Derian and Michael J. Shapiro, *International/Intertextual Relations: Postmodern Readings of World Politics* (Lexington: Lexington Books, 1989); Jim George, *Discourses of Global Politics: A Critical (Re)introduction to International Relations* (Boulder: Lynne Rienner Publishers, 1994); Michael J. Shapiro, *Reading the Postmodern Polity: Political Theory as Textual Practice* (Minneapolis: Minnesota University Press, 1992); and R. B. J. Walker, *Inside/Outside: Political Theory as International Relations* (Cambridge: Cambridge University Press, 1993).

[34] I am not referring here to the argument made by Yosef Lapid and Friedrich Kratochwil in *The Return of Culture and Identity in IR Theory* (Boulder: Lynne Rienner Publishers, 1997). Their framework is unhelpful in politicising travel writing because it fails to make a sufficient critique of the prevailing statist ontology. For Lapid and Kratochwil, the sphere of culture is understood as *secondary* to International Relations – it is something that reflects the more fundamental and natural limits of sovereignty. David Campbell's essay 'Violent Performances: Identity, Sovereignty, Responsibility' stands out as a critical voice in this collection because it deconstructs the foundations of culture and identity that the book fails to problematise adequately. Campbell's work is part of a more critical approach to culture first articulated in International Relations by Michael Shapiro's *The Politics of Representation: Writing Practices in Biography, Photography and Policy Analysis* (Madison: University of Wisconsin Press, 1988). More recent examples of this body of research include a special issue of *Millennium: Journal of International Studies* entitled 'Images and Narratives in World Politics', Vol. 30, No 3, 2001; David Campbell, 'Salgado and the Sahel: Documentary Photography and the

Not surprisingly, this has led to productive interdisciplinary connections with Cultural Studies, which has always foregrounded how power shapes our cultures, identities and communities in both local and global sites.[35] While scholars in Cultural Studies accept that power may be wielded most effectively by the state and its institutions, they are keen to show how issues such as identity (e.g. race, class, gender and sexuality) participate in that process and in some cases challenge the state's legitimacy.

With this interdisciplinary departure in mind, Holland and Huggan's claim that contemporary travel writing involves the continuation of colonialism alongside more positive and democratic possibilities is worth pursuing. If the genre is indeed being democratised, at what point does the expansion of democratic ideas become an imperial project? In other words, will travel writers – no matter where they are from or what experiences of oppression they have – always interpret their encounters with difference through some kind of colonial vision? If travelogues written during globalisation focus on cosmopolitan messages of equality, toleration and dialogue, how do those ideals play out in areas radically different from the West? And if travel writers employ a cosmopolitan framework of dialogue, inclusion and tolerance, what happens when

Imaging of Famine', in Cindy Weber and François Debrix, eds., *Rituals of Mediation: International Politics and Social Meaning* (Minneapolis: University of Minnesota Press, 2003), pp. 69–96; James Der Derian, *Virtuous War: Mapping the Military-Industrial-Media-Entertainment Network* (Boulder: Westview Press, 2001); Mark Lacey, 'War, Cinema and International Relations', *Alternatives*, Vol. 28, No. 5, Nov./Dec. 2003, pp. 611–36; Patricia Molloy, 'Theatrical Release: Catharsis and Spectacle in *Welcome to Sarajevo*', *Alternatives*, Vol. 25, No. 1, Jan./Mar. 2000, pp. 75–90; Cindy Weber, 'IR: The Resurrection OR New Frontiers of Incorporation', *European Journal of International Relations*, Vol. 5, No. 4, 1999, pp. 435–50 as well as her introductory textbook that uses popular film to explain the different theoretical approaches to the discipline, *International Relations Theory: A Critical Introduction* (London and New York: Routledge, 2001); and Jutta Weldes, *Science Fiction and World Politics* (London: Palgrave Macmillan, 2003).

[35] Since the institutionalisation of Cultural Studies at the Centre for Contemporary Cultural Studies in Birmingham in the 1970s, the forces of globalisation have been central to the discipline's research agenda; see, for example, Arjun Appadurai, *Modernity at Large: Cultural Dimensions of Globalization* (Minneapolis: University of Minnesota Press, 1996); Paul Du Gay, *Production of Culture/Cultures of Production* (London: Sage and Open University, 1997); Simon During, 'Popular Culture on a Global Scale: A Problem for Cultural Studies?' *Critical Inquiry*, Vol. 23, No. 4, 1997, pp. 808–34; Mike Featherstone, *Undoing Culture: Globalization, Postmodernism and Identity* (London: Sage, 1995); and John Tomlinson, *Cultural Imperialism* (London: Pinter Press, 1991). For a good intellectual history of the discipline of Cultural Studies in a UK context, see Graeme Turner, *British Cultural Studies* (London: Routledge, 1996); for an analysis of how British Cultural Studies has been exported to other countries, see Valda Blundell, John Shepherd and Ian Taylor, eds., *Relocating Cultural Studies: Developments in Theory and Research* (London: Routledge, 1993).

they confront subjects who are intolerable – who do not accept the basic values of liberal democracy? These questions are foregrounded in many other cultural products – in Hollywood films like *Black Hawk Down*, in periodicals like *Time* and *Newsweek*, in newspapers like the *Washington Post* and in television shows like *The West Wing*. It is easy to see how these products of popular culture exert a powerful influence on the way global politics is understood and practised. This book argues that contemporary travel writing is an equally important cultural voice in these debates because it reveals how previously colonised, marginalised and silenced groups are engaging and struggling with the hegemonic power relations currently shaping the global sphere. While Holland and Huggan certainly introduce the tension between colonial and cosmopolitan visions in contemporary travel writing, their disciplinary framework does not include an examination of how those visions align with and draw from current debates in global politics. Therefore, *The Global Politics of Contemporary Travel Writing* should be seen as an effort to extend the arguments made by Holland and Huggan in such a way that travel writing is positioned at the heart of debates between globalising forces and various forms of cultural resistance.

The proposed route: mapping the discourses of contemporary travel writing

Given the methodological and interdisciplinary concerns of this book, my focus on the discursive construction of contemporary travel writing develops simultaneously in two directions. Firstly, it argues that the discourses through which colonial and cosmopolitan visions are articulated become politically interesting when they achieve hegemony, that is to say, when they are repeated in such a way over time that they acquire the authority of truth. The second direction of my study is more complex: it is an attempt to show how these discourses – even the most powerful ones – are *incomplete* articulations of power that offer compelling moments of resistance. This 'double narrative' strategy unfolds through a detailed examination of the four main discourses that shape contemporary travel writing. Chapter 2 uses the *discourse of literary genre* to open up the object of study under scrutiny. It examines the literary regulations of travel writing by asking 'what is and what is not a travelogue'. Because travelogues must negotiate the contradictory authorities of fact and fiction, they are best understood as a strange collection of other genres (fiction, autobiography, memoir and history). By exploring the indistinct generic boundaries of travel writing through the work of Tzvetan Todorov and Jacques Derrida, it is possible to reflect upon the larger question of how objects of knowledge are disciplined – in both senses of the word – in the humanities and social sciences.

Chapter 3 outlines the most explicit political question of travel writing by examining how the colonial vision is being transformed through a *discourse of liberal subjectivity*. While travel writers like Theroux continue to repeat colonial tropes, a new hegemonic position has emerged with writers like Bill Bryson and Michael Palin who pursue a cosmopolitan vision through bemusement, tolerance and understanding. This position has been fortified by a democratisation of the genre; indeed, travelogues are now written by previously excluded subjects (e.g. women, Asians, gays and lesbians, African-Americans, people with disabilities). What is interesting about the discourse of liberal subjectivity is the extent to which it is able to cover over its own complex and difficult exclusions. In other words, by making it possible for anyone to write a travelogue, the discourse of liberal subjectivity effaces the powerful discriminations enacted by *all* travel writers – no matter what age, race, gender or sexual orientation. Travel writers still need *other* places and people to visit and write about – which means that travel writers must always engage in the production of difference. The political issue at stake here is how travel writers produce, project and pass judgement on this difference. This chapter works against the liberal travel writer's insistence that the cosmopolitan ethos of inclusion and acceptance resolves the logic and legacy of Empire. Instead, it argues that the subject position of the travel writer is a contested site that encourages competing visions of both the genre's colonial heritage and the travel writer's cosmopolitan desires.

The following chapter examines how the forces of globalisation are not only democratising the subject position of the travel writer, they are also transforming his/her chosen destinations. It argues that all travel writing requires an important distinction between home and elsewhere, and thus draws upon a *discourse of modern cartography*. The travelogue's geographical distinction of home/elsewhere relies on underlying assumptions about civilisation and security: there are civilised places on the globe that are safe, and there are uncivilised places that are dangerous. Contemporary travelogues are full of the desire to escape the clutches of the 'safe' tourist circuit and rediscover the authenticity of elsewhere. In order to get away from the ever-encroaching tourist gaze, travel writers like Robert Kaplan are being forced into inhospitable places where tourism is not allowed – war-zones, ghettoes, deserts, glaciers and shantytowns. As the all-consuming tourist gaze swallows up exotic destinations, travel writing has become polarised in its search for difference. Travel writers are either searching out sites of global atrocity and danger (e.g. new 'hearts of darkness' like West African slums), or sites where nothing 'political' ever happens (e.g. suburbia, Antarctica, the desert). By drawing on critical scholars in International Relations and Geography, this chapter re-imagines the discourse of modern cartography that underscores the polarisation of travel writing and asks whether the genre can address the logic of Empire embedded in its cartographic history.

Chapter 5 argues that the spatial assumptions encouraged by liberal travel writers are secured by a linear understanding of history. Travel writing locates the objects of its gaze (i.e. foreign places and people) farther back in the queue of history, whereas those who are actively writing are placed at the apex of the present. As Heather Henderson argues, 'the pervasive desire to reimagine the past leads to one of the central preoccupations of travel literature, the search for the lost innocence of a Golden Age'.[36] My point is that travel writers long to 'reimagine the past' because their linear understanding of temporality is constantly being threatened by the forces of globalisation. If the rest of the world is 'catching up' with the West, then the world is becoming a single homogeneous place with no obvious hierarchies of difference, and no guaranteed cultural superiority for Western writers. To re-establish the teleological historical queue, travel writers produce a powerful *discourse of nostalgia* in order to cultivate a longing for the past. At least during colonialism people knew their place – 'they' were elsewhere, and 'they' were behind 'us', dutifully marching along the road to civility, progress and emancipation. The difficulty, of course, is that these 'backward' places now reveal signs of modernity and Westernisation – they are just as globalised, cosmopolitan and sophisticated as home. The discourse of nostalgia is crucial in travel writing because it provides a retreat into an air-brushed past which allows both readers and writers to avoid the anxieties and difficulties of a post-colonial and globalised present.

Given these insights on knowledge, identity, space and time, *The Global Politics of Contemporary Travel Writing* ends with the problem of how to judge contemporary travel writing in a context of globalisation. How can we adjudicate between travelogues on *political* grounds rather than simply on formal, aesthetic and stylistic grounds? To what extent can those judgements be informed by critical interdisciplinary research that takes questions of power, difference and mobility seriously? In a genre so predicated on setting down limits – between self and other,

---

[36] Heather Henderson, 'The Travel Writer and the Text: "My Giant Goes With Me Wherever I Go"', in Kowalewski, *Temperamental Journeys*, p. 233.

here and there, now and then — this task is immensely difficult. Despite the growing literature available on travel writing, it is easy to end up with apolitical conclusions suggesting that *sometimes* travelogues are hegemonic, and *sometimes* they are transgressive. The challenge, then, is to establish political criteria from which to evaluate travel writing and to acknowledge simultaneously that the establishment of *any* criteria is itself a political act. And it is here that the ethical commitment of this book's post-structural and post-colonial approach is revealed most clearly. Discourse analysis does not just critique metanarratives and truth claims, it also makes robust arguments for establishing an ethical framework within which global political life can flourish. With that in mind, the book ends by asking whether travelogues are *better* when they reflect upon their indeterminate generic position, critique the relationship between colonial and cosmopolitan visions, and challenge the spatiotemporal assumptions that make these narratives complicit in the reproduction of Empire.

2   Between fact and fiction: the generic boundaries of travel writing

I don't believe in coming clean.

Bruce Chatwin to Paul Theroux

How had he travelled from here to there? How had he met this or that person? Life was never so neat as Bruce made out.

Paul Theroux on Bruce Chatwin

Before Bruce Chatwin died in 1989, he and Paul Theroux discussed whether travel writing was legitimised primarily by fact or fiction.[1] Although both authors routinely drew from the intellectual fields of literature, science, anthropology, poetry, politics and history, Theroux believed that travel writers 'record what the eye sees', whereas Chatwin – who hated the term travel writer – preferred to 'embroider' his adventures with fictional embellishments. Chatwin was much happier concealing the mundane aspects of his own journey in favour of more fantastic literary descriptions, whereas Theroux believed the challenge of travel writing was including the 'how' of travel – the minutiae about how you get from one place to another – alongside personal observations and descriptions of foreign cultures. Chatwin and Theroux never doubt these twinned authorities, they simply disagree

---

[1] This discussion was made public at the Royal Geographic Society in London when the two authors gave a combined lecture about their respective books on Patagonia – Chatwin's *In Patagonia* (1977) and Theroux's *The Old Patagonian Express* (1979). Chatwin argued that the talk 'completely bewildered types like Lord Hunt, as we took the audience breathlessly through a literary excursion to the Antipodes', whereas Theroux argued that Chatwin was 'something of a mythomaniac and had a screaming laugh and bizarre conceits that provoked him to such behaviour as monologuing to the mountaineers Lord Hunt and Chris Bonington about great climbs he had made'; see Nicholas Shakespeare, *Bruce Chatwin* (London: Harvill Press, 1999), p. 534. Theroux gives a more detailed account of the evening in 'Chatwin Revisited', *Granta*, Vol. 44, 1993 (*The Last Place on Earth*), pp. 213–21, as well as in an interview with George Plimpton at The Poetry Centre in New York in 1989; see Casey Blanton, '"Lying Travelers": Bruce Chatwin', in *Travel Writing: The Self and the World* (London and New York: Routledge, 1995), pp. 102–3.

27

over which should be emphasised, and which is more persuasive for the reader. The different positions advocated by Chatwin and Theroux reveal the tension at the heart of all travel writing: it must authorise itself through both fact *and* fiction. This chapter examines the different ways in which facts and fictions are arranged in travel writing and argues that these competing authorities cannot be divorced from the legacy of colonialism.

The conjunction between fact, fiction, travel and Empire was first explored by Edward Said in *Orientalism*. Said argued that the vacillation between fact and fiction in travel writing was part of the colonial division of knowledge between academic and popular information.[2] Although colonial travel writers were uncomfortable with the term 'popular', they cited a wide range of authorities and knowledges in order to differentiate their work from narrow and obscure academic pursuits.[3] This meant that travelogues not only disseminated particular 'facts' about the Orient (e.g. economic, political, religious, cultural and scientific knowledge), but also offered a much more encompassing 'way of knowing' the Orient delivered by more popular 'fictional' strategies. For Said, the combination of factual statements and fictional descriptions meant that colonial travel writing was best placed to 'flesh out' the bare bones of the Orient/Occident dichotomy:

The increasing influence of travel literature, imaginary utopias, moral voyages, and scientific reporting brought the Orient into sharper and more extended focus... But all such widening horizons had Europe firmly in the privileged center, as main observer... even as Europe moved itself outwards, its sense of cultural strength was fortified. From travelers' tales, and not only from great institutions like various India companies, colonies were created and ethnocentric perspectives secured.[4]

Colonial travel writing was very effective at widening and popularising the scope of Orientalism: unlike academic texts, travelogues were able to disseminate the power relations of Empire to a much wider audience.

---

[2] Said argues that 'even the most innocuous travel book – and there were literally hundreds written after mid-century – contributed to the density of public awareness of the Orient', (*Orientalism*, p. 192). See also Richard Bevis, *Bibliotheca Cisorientalia: An Annotated Checklist of Early English Travel Books on the Near and Middle East* (Boston: G. K. Hall and Co., 1973).

[3] Said explains how this justification was exemplified by Richard Burton: '[he] seems to have taken a special sort of infantile pleasure in demonstrating that he knew more than any professional scholar, that he had acquired many more details than they had, that he could handle the material with more wit and tact and freshness than they' (*Orientalism*, p. 194).

[4] Said, *Orientalism*, p. 117.

The combination of factual statements and fictional descriptions made colonial travelogues popular with readers of history, science and current affairs *as well as* with readers of fiction. Their factual citations made them accurate and authoritative representations of life in the colonies, and their fictional references made them descriptive, enlightening and entertaining. While the democratisation of contemporary travel writing has forced the genre to at least recognise its colonial heritage, it has not significantly altered the basic structure of these texts. As the debate between Chatwin and Theroux reveals, contemporary travel writers still rely on a peculiar combination of fact and fiction to authorise and legitimate their narratives. How, then, might we update Said's argument? Can the formal, aesthetic and stylistic elements of these texts be politicised? Are there *structural* similarities between colonial and contemporary travel writing? This chapter examines how the twinned authorities of fact and fiction construct the generic boundaries of travel writing and shape colonial and cosmopolitan visions. Moreover, it argues that purely 'literary' discussions about the formal, aesthetic and stylistic elements of travel writing are depoliticising because they fail to take account of how *both* form and content are complicit in wider discourses of power.

Formal examinations of the genre are difficult because there is no consensus over how to define travel writing or its structural elements. As Paul Fussell explains, 'Criticism has never quite known what to call books like these.'[5] Despite efforts to set down generic boundaries, travel writing has always been saturated with the formal elements of other literary genres. As Terry Caesar explains: 'it seems more important, finally, to locate travel writing ... as a practice that writes across generic boundaries, whether those of memoir or essay, journalism or pastoral, fiction or ethnography'.[6] While the practice of 'writing across' literary genres sounds emancipating, it is not without its own

---

[5] Fussell, *Abroad*, p. 202. For Fussell's comments on travel writing as a literary genre, see his chapter 'Travel Books as Literary Phenomena', pp. 202–15.

[6] Terry Caesar, *Forgiving the Boundaries: Home as Abroad in American Travel Writing* (Athens, GA: University of Georgia Press, 1995), pp. 80, 115. Caesar's comments are echoed by Holland and Huggan: 'Travel writing, it need hardly be said, is hard to define, not least because it is a hybrid genre that straddles categories and disciplines. Travel narratives run from picaresque adventure to philosophical treatise, political commentary, ecological parable, and spiritual quest. They borrow freely from history, geography, anthropology, and social science, often demonstrating great erudition, but without seeing fit to respect the rules that govern conventional scholarship'. (*Tourists with Typewriters*, pp. 8–9).

limitations. This chapter argues that a powerful *discourse of literary genre* arrests the travelogue's potentially transgressive vacillation between fact and fiction by positioning it within a hierarchy of literature. While travelogues draw on many different types of writing, they are most closely associated with the novel and the guidebook: they are understood as *inferior* to the novel, but more *sophisticated* than the travel guidebook. Travelogues will never achieve the status of the novel because the travel writer's imagination is always handcuffed to the narration of brute facts. This 'non-fiction' classification makes Fussell wonder how worthy travelogues are in terms of literary merit: 'how serious artistically and intellectually can a travel book be? Is there not perhaps something in the genre that attracts second-rate talents?'[7] The spectre of fiction looms large here — it is positioned as an ideal that the travelogue can never quite achieve.[8] However, it is precisely the freedom to translate 'brute facts' through the strategies of fiction that makes travelogues *better* than guidebooks. As Caesar explains, 'the strategies of fiction are necessary to romance fact into existence as a condition of certifying the real.'[9] Guidebooks must list the mundane facts of negotiating foreign places (e.g. history, how to get there, accommodation, eating and drinking, sightseeing, practical matters), whereas travelogues have more freedom to interpret and embellish these facts. Therefore, a travelogue that is *too* real and descriptive is boring (too much like a guidebook), but a travelogue that is *too* imaginative and metaphoric is a lie (too much like a novel). Travelogues are thus governed by a hierarchical discourse of literary genre: fiction, as symbolised by the more popular and widely influential novel, reigns supreme over the travelogue, but the travelogue outranks the factual descriptions exemplified by the pedantic guidebook.

---

[7] Fussell, *Abroad*, p. 212.

[8] As Holland and Huggan suggest, 'their "factual" disclosures are screens for cannily structured fictions'; see *Tourists with Typewriters*, p. xi. Terry Caesar has also remarked on the generic blurring between travel writing and fiction: 'These decades only reveal two things: how permeable the boundaries between travel writing and fiction are, and how most of the movement across has led to the absorption of travel writing by fiction... And yet travel books still appear, either more careless of the guidebook model... or more accommodating of fiction. How to classify them? How to understand them?' (*Forgiving the Boundaries*, pp. 137–41).

[9] Caesar, *Forgiving the Boundaries*, p. 125. Caesar goes on to suggest that as a literary form, travelogues were closer to the guidebook between 1945 and 1975 but have since moved closer to fiction. For a more specific historical discussion of the relationship between the guidebook and the travelogue, see Behdad, *Belated Travelers*, pp. 35–52.

From formal to political: fact, fiction, history and genre

Despite its indeterminate literary status, the travelogue's ability to 'write across' literary genres is potentially transgressive. Fussell's claim that nobody quite knows what to call travelogues should not be cause for alarm; rather, it should foreground the possibility that the genre's 'in-between' position might be the key to its political transformation. Indeed, Fussell himself goes on to say that the boundaries up for discussion in travel writing include metaphysical, psychological, artistic, religious, political and ethical.[10] I want to argue that the generic uncertainty of travel writing emerges, in part, from the impossibility of defining and categorising the topic at hand. 'Travel' is never simply about physically crossing boundaries and encountering different people: the act of border crossing potentially opens up wider epistemological questions about how truth claims are represented in language. In this sense, the discourse of literary genre regulates travel writing on two levels: firstly, by trying to categorise a practice as diverse and ambiguous as travel; and secondly, by trying to order the complex manner in which travel writing uses both fact and fiction to authorise itself. For me, the awkward generic position of travel writing – stuck between the imagination of the novel and the realism of the guidebook – illustrates how the discourse of literary genre ultimately fails to discipline even 'second-rate' books like travelogues.

In *Tourists with Typewriters*, Holland and Huggan claim that travelogues are 'fictions of factual representation' that can be used to 'chart the limits of knowledge and to test the claims of information'.[11] While they refer to historiographer Hayden White's studies of fiction and history in this passage, they fail to elaborate on how travel writing employs the twinned authorities of fact and fiction to 'chart' and 'test' our accepted limits of knowledge. They do suggest that bad travel writing is 'profit-driven or entertainment-oriented' and good travel writing is able to ask wider questions about the limits of knowledge, but they do not explain how those judgements are derived from the genre's formal arrangement of fact and fiction. It seems to me that in an otherwise politically engaged analysis, Holland and Huggan fail to pursue a crucial point here. For me, White's arguments about history and fiction are necessary in any analysis that claims to politicise literary texts. White argues that *all* forms of historical writing use narrative strategies to interpret and deliver facts, and if historians

---

[10] Fussell, *Abroad*, p. 214.
[11] Holland and Huggan, *Tourists with Typewriters*, p. 10 and p. 221, note 10.

didn't use these 'storytelling' techniques, they would be stuck listing a sequential order of facts in a chronology.[12] In *Metahistory*, White argues that historical narratives are shaped by four basic literary tropes: metaphor, metonymy, synecdoche and irony.[13] While this might seem like a purely formal literary argument, it marks the beginning of White's more radical political approach. The contentious arguments in his first two books rest upon the claim that there is nothing in the historical record itself, nothing inherent in the chronological arrangement of events, that makes historians choose one narrative style over another. Each of the four tropes is equally capable of arranging time/space-specific events into a structure that can translate the 'chaotic' nature of the past as we find it.[14] For White then, a history book uses the same narrative devices as a novel in order to legitimate a particular ordering of historical events:

> Although historians and writers of fiction may be interested in different kinds of events, both the forms of their respective discourses and their aims in writing are often the same. In addition, in my view, the techniques or strategies that they use in the composition of their discourses can be shown to be substantially the same ... the aim of the writer of a novel must be the same as that of the writer of a history. Both wish to provide a verbal image of 'reality'.[15]

Although White stresses the similarities of these two forms of writing, he is clear that historical events are different from fictional events. He is not saying that the historical record is 'made up' just like fiction. Rather, he distinguishes between history and fiction by arguing that historical events are observable and located in a specific time and place, whereas fictional events are products of the imagination. He is not claiming that a time/space-specific event did not happen, or cannot be said to have happened, until its arrangement into a historical narrative. Rather, White is concerned with how the narrative structures of history disprove any claim historians might make about providing objective representations of reality.

Although the problem of narration is historiography's 'thorniest issue', it is not limited to representations of history. The use of narrative

---

[12] Hayden White, 'The Value of Narrativity in the Representation of Reality', in *The Content of the Form: Narrative Discourse and Historical Representation* (Baltimore: Johns Hopkins University Press, 1987), pp. 1–25.

[13] Hayden White, *Metahistory: The Historical Imagination in Nineteenth-Century Europe*, (Baltimore: Johns Hopkins University Press, 1973).

[14] Hayden White, *The Tropics of Discourse: Essays in Cultural Criticism* (Baltimore: Johns Hopkins University Press, 1978), p. 84; see also Wulf Kansteiner, 'Hayden White's Critique of the Writing of History', *History and Theory*, Vol. 32, No. 3, 1993, p. 279.

[15] White, *Tropics of Discourse*, pp. 121–2.

strategies to interpret facts happens in a variety of genres – including contemporary travel writing. Like policy documents, eye-witness accounts, newspaper stories and documentaries, travel writing is part of the discursive terrain that shapes the 'real world' of global politics. To put it another way, travel writing is an important part of the *narration* of global politics – it is one of many types of representation that shape time/space-specific events according to wider structures of global power. Instructive here is David Campbell's explanation of how travel writing shaped global policy towards Bosnia:

Rebecca West's pre-World War II *Black Lamb and Grey Falcon* influenced in both style and substance Robert Kaplan's *Balkan Ghosts*, which in turn was read by President Clinton and others at a critical juncture in 1993 and helped make possible – because of the story of ancient and violent animosities it told – the American reluctance to take action. The more important issue, of which this example is but one illustration, is that conceptions of history and identity are not descriptive but constitutive of a terrain of possibility through which events are framed and responses debated.[16]

Campbell's explanation of why a travelogue, rather than a history book, influenced the most powerful political actors in the world during the Bosnian conflict indicates something compelling in the genre's ability to narrate the 'facts' of global politics. Like other 'non-fiction' books on history and politics, travelogues are engaged in delivering time/space-specific facts and events to audiences in intelligible ways. But as White reminds us, *all* these forms of writing use similar narrative strategies to translate facts and events and make the historical record meaningful. What makes travel writing particularly interesting in this respect is its vacillation between the authorities of fact and fiction: it is well positioned to contest the hierarchy of literature that prevents us from identifying important discursive connections between different types of writing.

The discourse of literary genre stabilises the travelogue's precarious position by categorising these narratives and distinguishing them

---

[16] David Campbell, 'Contra Wight: The Errors of Premature Writing', *Review of International Studies*, Vol. 25, No. 2, April 1999, p. 321. Campbell is one of the few scholars to apply Hayden White's work to global politics; see especially 'MetaBosnia: Narratives of the Bosnian War', *Review of International Studies*, Vol. 24, No. 2, April 1998, pp. 261–81, which is then expanded in greater detail in 'Ontopology: Representing the Violence in Bosnia', in Campbell, *National Deconstruction*, pp. 33–81. From a more analytical framework, White's arguments are also addressed by Hidemi Suganami in *On the Causes of War* (Oxford: Oxford University Press, 1996), and 'Stories of War Origins: A Narrativist Perspective on the Causes of War', *Review of International Studies*, Vol. 23, No. 4, 1997, pp. 401–18.

from the other texts they steal from. Literary theorist Tzvetan Todorov outlines the continuity of this discourse in an essay entitled 'The Origins of Genre' (1976). Todorov argues that it was only when the novel emerged in the early eighteenth century that the separation of modern literary genres was established.[17] And it is here that we get the first 'border anxieties' caused by the simultaneous birth of the novel and the modern travelogue. As Von Martels explains, 'often it is subject to discussion whether we may still speak of travel writing, for instance, where the distinction between travel writing and fiction becomes small, and the novel comes into being'.[18] Todorov argues that despite the clear birth of modern literary genres in the eighteenth century, it is no longer possible to organise texts into distinct generic categories. He is particularly concerned with Maurice Blanchot's suggestion that modern literature *as a whole* has become a singular and self-reflexive genre: today there is no intermediary between the particular, individual work and literature as a whole, the ultimate genre; there is not, because the evolution of modern literature consists precisely in making of each work a questioning of the very being of literature.[19] Blanchot's point is that if every piece of literature contests generic categories, then the concept of genre has lost its currency. What Todorov explains here is an important debate between structural accounts of genre and post-structural claims that the limits of genre must be 'shattered'. But Todorov's position is clear: he wants to resuscitate the category of genre at precisely the moment when genre has become irrelevant. Unlike Blanchot, Todorov refuses to abandon generic distinctions, for he believes they reveal something important about the state of modern literature as a whole, and about specific 'types' of literature as well. This does not, however, continue an Enlightenment project of establishing universal and transcendental categories by which all literary

---

[17] Tzvetan Todorov, 'The Origin of Genres', *New Literary History: A Journal of Theory and Interpretation*, Vol. 8, No. 1, Autumn 1976, pp. 159 –70; for a commentary on Todorov's position, see Christine Brooke-Rose, 'Historical Genres/Theoretical Genres: A Discussion of Todorov on the Fantastic' in the same issue, pp. 145–58. For a discussion of the emergence of the novel and its relation to the bourgeois class, see Ian Watt, *The Rise of the Novel: Studies in Defoe, Richardson and Fielding* (Harmondsworth: Penguin, 1963).

[18] Zweder Von Martels, *Travel Fact and Travel Fiction: Studies on Fiction, Literary Tradition, Scholarly Discovery and Observation in Travel Writing* (Leiden: E. J. Brill, 1994), p. xi. For a more specific explanation of the generic distinction between novels and travelogues, see Percy G. Adams, *Travel Literature and the Evolution of the Novel* (Lexington: University Press of Kentucky, 1983).

[19] Todorov, 'The Origin of Genres', p. 159; he is referring here to Maurice Blanchot's work, *Le Livre à Venir* (Paris, 1959).

efforts must be judged. Rather, Todorov's structuralist approach contextualises all generic boundaries within the social and political worlds they arise from by combining 'general poetics' with 'literary history'. Todorov identifies those widely recognised rules and norms that we understand to be generic (general poetics) alongside more historically embedded questions about where, when and how those rules emerged (literary history). In this way, he explains how genres are defined as 'classes of texts' and charts how they have come to be recognised as such over time. Todorov's synthesis of structural and historical questions identifies how the constituent limits of a genre get established and taken to be natural and universal: 'It is because genres exist as an institution that they function as "horizons of expectation" for readers, and as "models of writing" for authors.'[20] This structural and historical codification of language into genres amounts to a *discourse of literary genre*: a coherent set of rules and disciplining mechanisms that divide literature into discrete categories such as 'travel writing' and 'novel' and subsequently constrain and enable what kind of literature can be produced at any given time. With Todorov's arguments in mind, what are the generic boundaries of travel writing, and how have they been established as such over time?

Generic criteria: a 'general poetics' of travel writing

A journey can include a mixture of leaving home, finding oneself, going through a rite of passage, seeking one's fortune, experiencing a dangerous adventure or simply getting away from it all. Whatever the scope of that movement, from climbing Mount Everest to visiting a shopping mall, the *telling* of the journey has several distinct features.[21] As Caesar explains, the generic stasis of the travelogue can be located in practices of observation and evaluation: 'the genre's mode of knowing does not change. Knowledge in each text remains saturated by

---

[20] Todorov, 'The Origin of Genres', p. 163.
[21] Although there has been no in-depth study of the generic criteria of travel writing, all critical studies have an implicit sense of what these texts consist of. The following studies offer accounts of the generic boundaries of travel writing, and have been useful in developing a 'general poetics' of the genre: Blanton, *Travel Writing: The Self and the World*, pp. 1–29; Caesar, *Forgiving the Boundaries*, pp. 81–92, 137–43; Paul Fussell (ed.), *The Norton Book of Travel* (New York: W. W. Norton and Co., 1987), pp. 13–17; Holland and Huggan, *Tourists with Typewriters*, pp. 8–13; Mills, *Discourses of Difference*, pp. 73–94; Anna Stella Karlsdottir Stubseid, 'Travelogues as Indices of the Past', *Journal of Popular Culture*, Vol. 26, No. 4, 1993, pp. 89–100; and Reul K. Wilson, *The Literary Travelogue: A Comparative Study with Special Relevance to Russian Literature from Fonvizin to Pushkin* (The Hague: Martinus Nijhoff, 1973), pp. 1–27.

the experience of observation. Furthermore, the observation is always evaluative (this man good, that experience bad, etc.)'.[22] Likewise, Casey Blanton sees travel writing as a 'family' of collected literatures: 'the more narrow group of narratives that we have come to call "the modern travel book" has inherited elements of all its predecessors as well as its close cousins. This complex family, then, includes memoirs, journals, and ships' logs, as well as narratives of adventure, exploration, journey, and escape.'[23] Despite the fact that travelogues borrow heavily from other forms of writing, Caesar's formulation of generic stasis provides a useful starting point to outline the basic shape of these texts. A purely structuralist analysis would suggest that the journey provides the foundation (content) and the story provides the framework (form). But Todorov's idea of 'general poetics' makes it possible to identify coherent generic criteria of travel writing, and illustrate how those rules and regulations operate in a particular text. For this task, let us go back to one of the travelogues that opened this book: Paul Theroux's *The Old Patagonian Express.*

Travelogues are about journeys

All travelogues are based on a journey metaphor that expresses the common affliction of wanderlust – the need to go elsewhere. Indeed, our physical movements across space are etymologically and linguistically encoded: a metaphor means 'a change of place', and the verb 'to go' is paramount in linguistic teachings (subservient only to the verbs 'to be', 'to have' and possibly 'to give').[24] Since the beginning of written and recorded history, the journey metaphor has been central to the way peoples and cultures locate themselves and tell stories about the world they are living in. Theroux's *The Old Patagonian*

---

[22] Caesar, *Forgiving the Boundaries*, p. 143. Caesar's formulation of generic stasis is echoed by Von Martels: 'Travel writing seems unlimited in its forms of expression, but though we may therefore find it hard to define the exact boundaries of the genre it is generally understood what it contains' (*Travel Fact and Travel Fiction*, p. xi).

[23] Blanton, *Travel Writing: The Self and the World*, p. 2. Blanton goes on to list her own succinct 'general poetics' of contemporary travel writing: 'Among the chief characteristics are a narrator/traveller who travels for the sake of travel itself; a narrative style that borrows from fiction in its use of rising and falling action, character, and setting; a conscious commitment to represent the strange and exotic in ways that both familiarize and distance the foreign; a writerly concern with both language and literature; and finally, thematic concerns that go beyond descriptions of people and places visited' (p. 5).

[24] Mary B. Campbell, *The Witness and the Other World: Exotic European Travel Writing, 400–1600* (Ithaca: Cornell University Press, 1988), pp. 1–2.

Express exemplifies this common desire to go elsewhere, to leave home and venture into foreign places. His journey begins as he sets out from his home on the outskirts of Boston: he travels south on his own, has a series of adventures and returns home again to write up his narrative. In this particular case, it is boredom that spurs Theroux on to South America – he is bored with his middle-class life teaching creative writing at a small college, he cannot seem to find inspiration for a new novel, and, above all, he desires solitude. Armed with a rucksack and a railway timetable, Theroux embarks on a physical journey by train from Boston to the tip of Patagonia and back to Boston.

Travelogues are stories

Travelogues have a narrative framework that follows the linear passage of beginning, middle and end. However, travelogues assume that 'living happily ever after' means reaching a destination, or more commonly, returning home after a successful journey. Therefore, the narrative structure of travel writing is contained in the journey and vice versa: beginning–middle–end is inseparable from home–away–home. For Fussell, this combined structure reveals the travelogue's debt to the romance:

A travel book, at its purest, is addressed to those who do not plan to follow the traveller at all, but who require the exotic or comic anomalies, wonders, and scandals of the literary form *romance*, which their own place or time cannot entirely supply ... aren't all travel books really romances in the old sense, with the difference that the adventures are located within an actual, often famous, topography?[25]

In *The Old Patagonian Express*, we are introduced to Theroux as he boards the train in Boston (home/beginning), accompany him on his long journey to Patagonia (away/middle) and return with him to Boston as the story concludes (home/end). That narrative closure is accompanied by a powerful sense of resolution and catharsis: Theroux returns home invigorated, he is now ready to begin his new novel and reinstate himself into the familiarity of his American life.

---

[25] Fussell, *Abroad*, pp. 203, 207. Fussell argues that travel writing reproduces specific versions of quest, picaresque and pastoral romances, pp. 207–12. Caesar, Holland and Huggan also cite Romantic literature as having a profound influence on the genre of travel writing because it is posed as the ultimate in subjective fiction in opposition to the tedious guidebook; see Caesar, *Forgiving the Boundaries*, pp. 2–3, 88–92, and Holland and Huggan, *Tourists with Typewriters*, pp. 8–11.

Travelogues are classified as non-fiction

Although disdainful of guidebooks, travelogues authorise their claims about foreign places and people through recourse to 'facts'. The non-fiction status of travelogues allows them to employ strategies and methodologies similar to those used in the natural and social sciences. In this sense, travelogues assume a 'real' world that can be known and accessed via proper methods of investigation (e.g. identifying, categorising, analysing, proving and testing empirical facts about the world). For Fussell, this factual reliance arises because the audience wants to have it both ways – it wants to have adventures in faraway lands, but 'at the same time wants to feel itself within a world declared real by such up-to-date studies as political science, sociology, anthropology, economics and contemporary history'.[26] In *The Old Patagonian Express*, Theroux is explicit about the factual authorities he cites in order to legitimate his personal observations. For example, when he is at the border between Texas and Mexico, his understanding of inequality is authorised by neoclassical economics: 'Laredo had the airport and the churches; Nuevo Laredo, the brothels and basket factories. Each nationality had seemed to gravitate to its own special area of competence. This was economically sound thinking: it followed to the letter the theory of comparative advantage outlined by the distinguished economist David Ricardo.'[27] In passages such as this one, Theroux's personal observations are given weight by the authority of economic indicators. When Theroux suggests that it is somehow 'natural' for Mexicans to be competent at basket weaving and prostitution while their American counterparts are more 'naturally' predisposed to run airports and have organised religions, he reproduces some of the most problematic assumptions of neoclassical economics. The very categories by which neoclassical economics operate (e.g. rational actors, optimal outcomes, profit motives) require scholars to ignore the social and political contexts within which these economic 'facts' exist.[28] For example, Ricardo's theory of comparative advantage cited by Theroux is built upon a number of problematic assumptions about autonomous agents

---

[26] Fussell, *Abroad*, p. 207.

[27] Theroux, *The Old Patagonian Express*, p. 49.

[28] The critiques of neoclassical economics are vast but usually begin with Karl Polanyi, *The Great Transformation: The Political and Economic Origins of Our Time* (Boston: Beacon Press, 1947) and continue with Martin Hollis and Edward Nell, *Rational Economic Man: A Philosophical Critique of Neo-Classical Economics* (Cambridge: Cambridge University Press, 1975). A more recent critique is Jon Mulberg, *Social Limits to Economic Theory* (London: Routledge, 1995).

behaving rationally within immutable systems of capitalist exchange. No attention is paid to the particular structural, historical, material – and in this case colonial – inequalities that determine, shape and influence economic behaviour. Theroux's reliance on factual authorities that lie elsewhere – in this case in neoclassical economics – leads us back into the problem posed by Hayden White: if facts are shaped and given meaning by the same narrative techniques used in fiction, how is it possible to represent 'reality' in accurate and truthful ways?

Travelogues use fictional means to interpret facts

While a textbook on economics might be discouraged from including fictional devices such as metaphor, symbolism and personification, travelogues *welcome* these efforts at elaboration. Indeed, it is these fictional devices that distinguish Theroux's *The Old Patagonian Express* from, for example, the Lonely Planet guidebook *Latin America on a Shoestring*.[29] To convince his readers of the factual authority of comparative advantage, Theroux fills out a purely economic reading of the Mexico/America relationship through symbolism and synecdoche:

> At first glance, this looked like the typical sort of mushroom-and-dunghill relationship that exists at the frontiers of many unequal countries. But the longer I thought about it, the more Laredo seemed like all of the United States, and Nuevo Laredo like all of Latin America. This frontier was more than an example of cozy hypocrisy; it demonstrated all one needed to know about the morality of the Americas, the relationship between the puritanical efficiency north of the border and the bumbling and passionate disorder – the anarchy of sex and hunger – south of it ... Crossing the national boundary and seeing such a difference on the other side had something to do with it: truly, every human feature there had the resonance of metaphor.[30]

In this passage, Theroux's use of descriptive adjectives and metaphors gives the reader a much more elaborate picture of what is entailed in the unequal relationship between Mexico and America. Even if the reader has never heard of economist David Ricardo, they can guess at the kind of asymmetrical relationships that are explained and justified by comparative advantage. However, in suggesting that this unequal relation is 'all one needed to know about the morality of the Americas', Theroux discourages readers from questioning the factual authorities

---

[29] This is not to say that guidebooks are innocent in their descriptions of foreign places. As Rudi Koshar argues, the history of the Baedeker is underscored by a powerful colonial sensibility; see Koshar, *German Travel Cultures* (London: Berg, 2000).
[30] Theroux, *The Old Patagonian Express*, p. 49.

he cites. In effect, all we need to do is listen to Theroux's statements on such matters – statements that are both well informed (i.e. he understands neoclassical economics) and eloquently rendered (i.e. he is a beautiful and evocative writer).

Travelogues are primarily about difference

All travelogues pursue an engagement with difference, with something *other* than the usual, everyday experiences of home, and organise that engagement through the categories of subjectivity, space and time. Travelogues are written by an observing subject about observed objects – they are written in the first person from the point of view of the individual making the journey. This results in a firmly established narrator/subject, an active 'I' that uses all of his or her senses to absorb and assimilate the surrounding data and makes sense of it during the act of writing. In this way, we can see how the 'eye' and the 'I' become mutually dependent in travel writing.[31] Todorov's ideas about a 'general poetics' of travel writing are developed in an argument about difference and cultural encounter in an essay called 'The Journey and Its Narratives' (1995).[32] Todorov argues that travel writing is important primarily because it facilitates encounters with people different from ourselves and displays 'a certain tension (or a certain balance) between the observing subject and observed object. This is what, in its way, the term *travel narrative* designates: narrative, that is, personal narration and not objective description; but also travel, and therefore a framework of circumstances exterior to the subject'.[33] It is through the subject position of the travel writer that a clear distinction is forged between an observing subject and observed objects. As Caesar explains, 'authors choose to write travel rather than fiction (especially the many, like Theroux, who write both) because they want to try to *embed* a "self" in a certain way'.[34] *The Old Patagonian Express* is written confidently in the first person: Theroux is the autonomous 'I' on the train making observations about his surroundings, categorising them, dividing them and comparing them to what is already known and understood – which means that during his travels, his solitude keeps him detached from all he encounters. Theroux's self-representation in *The Old Patagonian*

---

[31] Von Martels, *Travel Fact and Travel Fiction*, pp. xi–xviii.
[32] Tzvetan Todorov, 'The Journey and Its Narratives', in *The Morals of History*, trans. Alyson Waters (Minneapolis: University of Minnesota Press, 1995), pp. 60–70.
[33] Todorov, 'The Journey and Its Narratives', p. 67.
[34] Caesar, *Forgiving the Boundaries*, p. 144.

Express is primarily figured by autonomy. His observations do not
alter the self he wants to project, nor do they affect his already honed
skills of judgement. As critic Lynn Barber argues, 'he is somehow self
enclosed. He lacks empathy, he doesn't seem to "read" other people
very well; if the people he encounters in his travels seem to behave rather
weirdly, it could be because Theroux has behaved weirdly towards
them. You feel he has observed the human race intensely but at
a distance, through literature, or through train windows.'[35] In order
to secure this autonomy, Theroux's observations about the difference
of Latin America must reinforce opposing truth claims about his
individuality and his home. As we saw with his judgements of the garlic
seller in Mexico, Theroux calls upon a prevailing colonial vision to
secure his own identity at the expense of objectified others. As Sally
Tisdale argues, 'his travels are filled with the "fat lady" and "the cripple"
and "the zombie", with drunks and bigots, stupid people, boring
people. He's only gotten more sour the farther he's gone. (He's a
walking example of how travel doesn't necessarily broaden you) ...
Theroux's rudeness seems constitutional, a part of his personality.'[36]
While Theroux's misanthropy is extreme, it is indicative of how the
genre requires a particular kind of subject who can fulfil the role of
the travel writer – one that continually secures a self in contrast to the
difference of others.

   However, the distinction between self/other in travel writing is not
just about subjectivity – others are made foreign to the extent that they
are physically located elsewhere. Travelogues *require* spatial movement:
the surest way to guarantee an encounter with difference is to physically
go elsewhere. According to Todorov, it is spatial movement that links
the journey itself (its ontological status) and the resulting narratives
about those journeys (their epistemological status): 'Movement in
space is the first sign, the easiest sign, of change; life and change
are synonymous. Narrative is also nourished by change; in this sense
journey and narrative imply one another.'[37] Todorov is particularly
concerned to illustrate the necessary spatial distance between observer

---

[35] Lynn Barber, 'Making Waves', *Observer*, 20 February 2000, p. 41.
[36] Sally Tisdale, 'Never Let the Locals See Your Map: Why Most Travel Writers
   Should Stay at Home', *Harper's Magazine*, Vol. 291, No. 1744, September 1995,
   p. 67. More revealing here are musician Randy Newman's comments on Paul
   Theroux: 'I'm not like a giant grim walking around. Basically, I'm extroverted and
   sorta happy. I... I'm not like Paul Theroux. I mean he's *unreadable*. He hates people
   so much. He travels, and everybody he meets he *hates!* So what the fuck do I want
   to read him for? I can't stand him anymore' (*Guardian*, 'Weekend', 31 July 1999).
[37] Todorov, 'The Journey and Its Narratives', p. 60.

and observed by insisting that a 'true' travel narrative 'recounts the discovery of *others*, either savages of faraway lands or the representatives of non-European civilizations — Arab, Hindu, Chinese and so on'.[38] In other words, national, cultural and civilisational differences are guaranteed by spatial distance, and the farther one travels away from home, the more significant these differences become. But Todorov's argument is not oblivious to the logic of Empire underscoring the spatial boundaries crossed by travel writers; indeed, these national, cultural and civilisational differences were initially used by Europeans to describe the new worlds they encountered during colonial exploration.[39] For Todorov, then, the spatial coding of home/away in travel writing always entrenches a Western and European point of view: 'A journey in France would not result in a "travel narrative". It is not so much that such narratives do not exist, but they clearly lack the feeling of alterity in relation to the people (and the lands) described.'[40] In *The Old Patagonian Express*, the spatial border between Mexico and America appears almost immediately and functions as a model through which Theroux can make comparisons between home (where he belongs) and away (where he is travelling). Home is what he knows and understands, and away is what he is making sense of in relation to home — it must therefore be strange, different, and other: 'Looking out across the river, I realized that I was looking toward another continent, another country, another world. There were sounds there — music, and not only music but the pip and honk of voices and cars. The frontier was actual: people did things differently there.'[41] Theroux's marking of difference resonates because difference is located *there* as opposed to *here*. The point is not that 'people did things differently there', but that Theroux judges that difference as inferior to the way *he* does things at home in America.

The self/other and home/away structure of travel writing is further secured by the inscription of temporal difference. As Todorov explains, this arrangement is guaranteed primarily by the distance between readers and narrators: 'the narrator must be different from us, but not too different, not, in any case, as different as the people who are the subject of his narrative. The typical narrator would therefore be a European, belonging to the long period that extends from the

---

[38]   Todorov, 'The Journey and Its Narratives', p. 68.
[39]   Sayed Manzuril Islam provides a helpful explanation of how the categories of modern cartography and Euclidian space become complicit in Empire; see *The Ethics of Travel: From Marco Polo to Kafka* (Manchester: Manchester University Press, 1996), p. 61.
[40]   Todorov, 'The Journey and Its Narratives', p. 68.
[41]   Theroux, *The Old Patagonian Express*, p. 47.

Renaissance to about 1950...at least one generation separating reader and writer is necessary.'[42] If we expand and update Todorov's criteria to suggest that travel writers are primarily Western and within the Anglo-American literary establishment, contemporary travel writers like Paul Theroux are easily accommodated. He is 'different from us' (Todorov's assumed Western audience) because he is brave enough to make a solo journey to Patagonia and back, 'but not too different' because we can identify with his Western point of view. Quite apart from Todorov's distinction between the travel writer and the reader, the temporal distance in travel writing is sharpened in relation to the *others* being written about. Not only are they located elsewhere, they are also located 'back' in time. By journeying elsewhere, the travel writer is able to 'go back in time' and experience more primitive historical eras that were once populated by colonial explorers. The others encountered in Latin America are different not just because they exist elsewhere, but also because they are not quite evolved, not yet civilised and not ready to experience the level of modernisation enjoyed by Theroux. In *The Old Patagonian Express*, the negative coding of others (e.g. Mexicans as weedy and unclean, Mexico full of 'bumbling passionate disorder') is accompanied by a powerful sense of paternalism. Theroux has the advantage of looking back upon the linear grand narrative of Western history and showing how others are always scrambling up the ladder of modernisation. In this way, the narrative closure of the story is also a confirmation of the present: others elsewhere have been observed and plotted in terms of their progress, and all are still 'catching up' with Theroux's position as civilised observer.

These five reference points constitute the basic generic criteria for travel writing – in structuralist terms, a 'general poetics'. While these categories are certainly not absolute, they reflect, more or less, the shape of travel writing over the last three centuries. As Caesar explains, 'the core elements of a travel book remain unchanged, no matter now that the course of travel writing enables us to understand these elements as if distilled with a kind of precious clarity'.[43] Caesar is right to argue that it is still possible to identify some similarities between contemporary texts and their post-Renaissance counterparts. Indeed, the resilience of this genre exemplifies how the discourse of literary genre is able to establish and reproduce seemingly 'transcendental' rules and regulations for specific groups of texts. But to what extent have travelogues always adhered to this set of criteria? Is the epic of Gilgamesh similar to

---

[42] Todorov, 'The Journey and Its Narratives', p. 69.
[43] Caesar, *Forgiving the Boundaries*, p. 142.

Theroux's journey? To follow through on a structuralist approach, it is not enough to explain exactly *what* travelogues are, it is also necessary to explain *how* they have come to be this way.

Generic development: a 'literary history' of travel writing

In 'The Journey and Its Narratives', Todorov argues that the evolution of travel writing is best understood through the dialectic relationship between internal and external journeys. At different times in history, travel writing has either focused on the emotional and personal transformations experienced by the author, or on the author's physical movement across space. But Todorov insists that both are always present in the journey narrative and reformulates the internal/external dialectic onto a continuum: 'Particular narratives can thus occupy every imaginable point along an axis that leads from the purely exterior to the purely interior.'[44] The best journey narratives refrain from both the excessive solipsism of internal quests (navel gazing) and the corporeal delights of external journeys (hedonism). For Todorov then, the subjectivity and behaviour of the author are central to the historical development of the genre: it is the travel writer's negotiation of interiority and exteriority, rather than the travelogue's depiction of foreign lands, that has changed over time. Keeping in mind Todorov's concerns with difference, he does not suggest that the internal/external continuum is universal. Rather, he examines how internal journeys are privileged over external journeys in Western societies and shows how this hierarchy originated in the search for the Holy Grail. He describes how the Knights of the Round Table realised how their material (external) search for a sacred object was, in fact, a spiritual (internal) journey that only the purest were able to complete (i.e. Galahad and Percival). Thus, material journeys like the search for the Holy Grail are legitimised and given credibility only to the extent that they manifest a more important spiritual quest. For Todorov, the privileging of internal journeys frames Western travel writing from early Christianity until the present: these texts will only countenance material movements across territory if they are accompanied by the necessary spiritual component.[45]

---

[44] Todorov, 'The Journey and Its Narratives', p. 63.

[45] Texts that privilege spiritual discovery over material exploration are also categorised as literature of 'the quest'. For a collection of quest narratives (especially in relation to mythologist Joseph Campbell's work), see Harold Schechter and Jonna Gormely Semeiks, eds., *Discoveries: Fifty Stories of the Quest*, 2nd edition

Todorov's focus on the subjectivity of the travel writer is made explicit in his claim that all travelogues are founded upon a commitment to self-discovery: 'it is the education of the soul that is the goal of these movements of the body... Although the goal is self-knowledge, the journey is no less indispensable: it is by exploring the world that one begins to discover oneself.'[46] In this way, internal and external journeys fuse in the subject of the travel writer: physical journeys to faraway places provoke us into self-discovery, just as spiritual questioning is provoked by an encounter with other places and people. With this in mind, Todorov further re-imagines the internal/external continuum by arguing that more recent travel writing is based on allegory and impression. Earlier spiritual quests (e.g. for the Holy Grail) have been rearticulated in accordance with the secular nature of modern life – which means that, more than ever, travelogues focus on the thoughts, observations and memories of the travel writer. On the one hand, the material elements of the journey are only relevant to the extent that they are framed allegorically through issues of wider significance – when travel writers use their physical journeys to make sense of larger and more symbolic worlds. For example, *The Old Patagonian Express* can be read as an allegory about relations between North and South America – Theroux uses his physical journey through Latin America to comment on the wider economic, social, political and cultural differences between what he has left behind and what he confronts. On the other hand, the drastically reduced currency of spiritual ideas in the modern world has resulted in a different order of internal revelation. Gone are the days when travel writers used their journeys to provide 'transcendental' meditations on human nature – these have been replaced by the solipsistic and 'personal' impressions of the author. Todorov argues that travelogues detailing the self-discovery and personal reflections of authors are not only replacing earlier 'spiritual' narratives, they

---

(Oxford: Oxford University Press, 1992). These spiritual narratives display two interesting generic elements: firstly, they further complicate the relationship between travel writing, fiction and autobiography because the physical component of travel is not necessary; secondly, the spiritual narratives foreshadow the current subgenre of self-help travel narratives that introduce a 'new age' element to the literature. In these cases, the journey is a metaphorical one that is not necessarily tied to physical movement; see, for example, Ambika Wauters, *Journey of Self-Discovery* (London: Piatkus Books, 1995), and Beth Hevda, *Journey from Betrayal to Trust: A Universal Rite of Passage* (Long Island, NY: Celestial Arts, 1992).

[46] Todorov, 'The Journey and Its Narratives', p. 65.

are also replacing travelogues based around an allegorical structure.[47] Casey Blanton goes even further in this claim; she argues that in the more autobiographical narratives of today, 'social and psychological issues are more important than facts about places and events'.[48] It is as if travel writers have recognised that what readers *really* want is a gripping tale full of instinctive and often 'taboo' judgements about other places and people — which is precisely what we get in *The Old Patagonian Express* every time Theroux delivers his masterly judgements about the 'featureless, night-haunted republics of Latin America'.[49]

Todorov's developmental history of travel writing culminates with an argument that contemporary texts have three distinct features. The first, and most important, is the idea that the self only becomes salient through encounters with difference. Because one does not travel in a vacuum, the most challenging feature of the journey is that one must encounter the other — other people, other places, other ways of thinking, living, expressing oneself. For Todorov, this mutually consti-tutive encounter carries significant political weight in terms of relations between peoples and cultures:

the *I* does not exist without a *you*. One cannot reach the bottom of oneself if one excludes others. The same holds true for knowledge of foreign countries and different cultures: the person who knows only his own home always runs the risk of confusing culture with nature, of making custom the norm, and of forming generalizations based on a single example: oneself.[50]

For Todorov, travelogues are politically important because they provoke self-reflexivity: they force us to ask questions about difference, questions about our own encounters with otherness and, ultimately, questions about ourselves and our identities in relation to difference. His hope is that travel writers can 'discover other men and women whose vision of the world is different, even if only slightly, from theirs. This, in turn, could change them and lead them to be a little more just.'[51] The encounter with difference also shapes the second and third characteristics of contemporary travel writing: spatial distance between

---

[47] Todorov argues that the texts inaugurating this modern split of allegory/impression are Chateaubriand's: his voyage to America is allegorical in that it 'submits the traveller's observations to a preconceived design that they are used to illustrate'; and his voyage to the Orient is impressionistic because it 'neglects the world and concentrates on the self, recounting the successive impressions of that self' ('The Journey and Its Narratives', p. 67).

[48] Blanton, *Travel Writing: The Self and the World*, p. 4.

[49] Theroux, *The Old Patagonian Express*, p. 47.

[50] Todorov, 'The Journey and Its Narratives', p. 65.

[51] Todorov, 'The Journey and Its Narratives', p. 66.

the narrator and the object (e.g. Western authors documenting others 'Arab, Hindu, Chinese, and so on'), and temporal distance between the reader and the author (e.g. 'at least one generation separating the reader and writer is necessary'). In this sense, the earlier 'general poetics' of travel writing are not that different to where Todorov ends up in his developmental history. The key point to take from Todorov's argument is that travel writing is based on an encounter with difference, and the travel writer's internal/external continuum must be understood as part of a wider network of self–other relations and cross-cultural encounters. In this sense, Todorov rightly suggests that the history of journey narratives is related to a colonial history where European powers dominated much of the world: 'in order to ensure the tension necessary to the travel narrative, the specific position of the colonizer is required: curious about the other, and secure in his own superiority'.[52] But how does this encounter with difference play out in recent travel writing? Is it constrained or enabled by a hierarchy of literature? And is it managed more competently by those who write *both* novels and travelogues?

Reading generic boundaries: Rushdie outside in and Theroux inside out

Salman Rushdie's *The Jaguar Smile: A Nicaraguan Journey* exemplifies the constraints and regulations placed on travelogues by the discourse of literary genre. In this case, the generic limits of travel writing are so powerful that Rushdie's usually complex and subtle treatment of difference is disregarded when he comes to write a travelogue. It is as if the provocative questions about identity, mobility, hybridity and exile that emerge in Rushdie's fiction are aborted when he switches genres. In this narrative about the aftermath of Nicaragua's populist left-wing revolution, Rushdie takes the opportunity to reveal his own political sympathies. But his idealised vision of Ortega's regime – bolstered by his left-leaning political agenda – prevents Rushdie from recognising the complexity of the political shifts occurring in Nicaragua in the late 1980s. Unlike the multi-layered portrayal of characters and communities in his fiction, *The Jaguar Smile* celebrates the singularity, strength and resilience of the Nicaraguan people – characteristics that are expressed in the popular Sandanista revolution: 'Nicaragua was an imperfect state. But it was also engaged in a true revolution: in an

---

[52] Todorov, 'The Journey and Its Narratives', p. 69.

attempt, that is, to change the structures of society in order to improve the lives of its citizens. And imperfection, even the deep flaw of censorship, did not constitute a justification for being crushed by a superpower's military and economic force.'[53] Tolerating 'imperfection' in the name of a higher goal means covering over the moments of injustice, exclusion and violence committed by the 'true revolutionaries' of Nicaragua. It may be imperfect, but this is *morally superior* imperfection. Rushdie's unwavering support for the revolution makes for a particularly unreflexive narrative – not the characteristics usually attributed to his works of fiction. Rushdie presents Nicaragua under the leadership of Daniel Ortega as noble and exemplary, especially in comparison to the atrocities committed by the previous Somoza regime. This devotion prevents Rushdie from exploring difficult questions: how is the newly governed state of Nicaragua imagining and creating a collective identity for its citizens? How is it establishing a legitimate political authority? Most importantly, how is it producing a coherent national memory by vilifying the time before the revolution in order to legitimate the present regime? My point is that the lack of reflexivity in *The Jaguar Smile* is constituted by the generic boundaries of travel writing. In the end, it is disappointing that Rushdie's travelogue fails to pursue the linkages between narration, belonging, identity and community that make his fiction and criticism so important for those of us trying to re-imagine the prevailing discourses of global politics.[54]

Part of Rushdie's blindness here derives from his sense of solidarity with Nicaragua's experience under colonialism. This shared background of 'subcontinentalism' is explained at the beginning of the book when Rushdie describes what drew him to Nicaragua in the first place:

It was perhaps also true that those of us who did not have our origins in the countries of the mighty West or North had something in common – not, certainly, anything as simplistic as a unified 'third world' outlook, but at least some knowledge of what weakness was like, some awareness of the view from underneath, and of how it felt to be there, on the bottom, looking up at the descending heel.[55]

[53] Salman Rushdie, *The Jaguar Smile: A Nicaraguan Journey* (London: Picador, 1987), p. 49.
[54] These themes are present in all of Rushdie's fiction, but his political approach is best expressed in *Imaginary Homelands: Essays and Criticism 1981–1991* (London: Picador, 1991).
[55] Rushdie, *The Jaguar Smile*, p. 12. He goes on to make more specific comparisons between India and Nicaragua in the following passage: 'In my first hours in the city streets, I saw a number of sights that were familiar to eyes trained in India and

This image of subservience to larger global forces is never questioned in *The Jaguar Smile* as it is in *Midnight's Children* (where the multifaceted post-colonial histories of India are told as a series of disruptions to Indira Ghandi's post-independence policies), or *The Satanic Verses* (where an undercurrent of resistance to all kinds of Western, British, Indian, masculine and Islamic dogmatism is carefully and humorously constructed). Rushdie has written about several places in his fiction – India, Pakistan and the UK in his earlier works, but also Spain, New York City and Mexico in his more recent works – all of which are depicted as complex, multicultural and hybrid sites. What is remarkable about the depiction of Nicaragua in *The Jaguar Smile* is its lack of multiplicity: these are a united people, pursuing a noble revolution under a righteous leader. It is almost as if by winning the revolution, the Sandanistas are credited with establishing a kind of left-wing Third World utopia.[56]

Rushdie's acquiescence to the generic limitations of travel writing illustrates the power of factual and empirical authorities that govern travelogues from below. While a travelogue can translate empirical facts by fictional devices, the travel writer cannot ignore the empirical world altogether – that would lift the travelogue out of its precarious in-between position and shove it head first into fiction. All of which begs the question: why write a travelogue when you could write a novel? The hierarchy of literature – especially the idealisation of fiction – is reinforced by the assumption that Rushdie is 'slumming it' in the genre of travel writing. To write fiction is to finally disown the ball and chain of fact and luxuriate in a superior genre where facts and truths can be rendered according to the writer's imagination. *The Jaguar Smile* is revealing because it illustrates how the generic boundaries of travel writing are capable of constraining a writer as gifted as Rushdie.

Pakistan: the capital's few buses, many of them donated by Alfonsin's new Argentina, were crammed to bursting point with people, who hung off them in a very subcontinental way. And the roadside shanties put up by the *campesinos* (peasants) who had come to Managua with hope and not much else, echoed the *bustees* of Calcutta and Bombay' (p. 17).

[56] Holland and Huggan give another reason for Rushdie's refusal to see the complexity of the Nicaraguan revolution. As a 'literary guest' of the country, Rushdie is escorted through Nicaragua in the company of the cosmopolitan literary and cultural elite. This has the effect of producing a superficial and almost cartoon-like caricature of Nicaragua in *The Jaguar Smile*. But this attention to surfaces offers Rushdie moral protection as well: 'his utopian rhetoric of displacement... allows him to resist the state that continues to give him service, and to move about the world in search of a solidarity of the oppressed'; see Holland and Huggan, *Tourists with Typewriters*, pp. 53–5.

While his fiction portrays the complexity, diversity and mobility of post-colonial life, his travelogue offers unreflexive, uncontested and uninteresting platitudes about the revolution in Nicaragua.

Paul Theroux's work takes us in the opposite direction. As Rushdie's text cannot escape its factual foundations, Theroux's work cannot escape its fictional ambitions. *The Great Railway Bazaar: By Train through Asia*, published in 1975, was an instant bestseller that prompted Theroux to divide his subsequent writing career between novels and travelogues. The journey itself begins and ends in London but moves in a circuitous route through Europe, Turkey, Iran, Afghanistan, India, Sri Lanka, Thailand, Malaysia, Singapore, Vietnam, Japan, the USSR and then back to London. His principal mode of travel is the train, including the Orient Express, the bullet train to Kyoto, and the Trans-Siberian Railway (although poor rail connections sometimes force him to take buses and aeroplanes).[57] Although *The Great Railway Bazaar* is not Theroux's first book, it is his first travelogue. As such, there is a sustained effort throughout the text to relate it to the literary form he is most familiar with: the novel. In order to switch genres effectively, Theroux possesses a relatively clear understanding of the rules and norms of travel writing and how they differ from those of the novel: 'the difference between travel writing and fiction is the difference between recording what the eye sees and discovering what the imagination knows'.[58] Theroux's notion that novels offer more depth than travelogues is shared by Caesar: 'the joy of travel writing is not "pure", and it is not pure because it has already been contaminated by fiction.

---

[57] The journey takes him approximately four months to complete, from September 1973 to early January 1974, and four months to write, which meant that the book was published early in 1976. These dates can be discerned from the text itself: he quotes a November 1973 newspaper when in Singapore; he positions himself chronologically in relation to the previous cease-fire in Vietnam (December 1973, p. 244); the last leg of his trip through Siberia is in December as he races to get home for Christmas; and his only footnote in the entire book explains the situation in Vietnam at the time the book goes to the publisher (April 1975). These dates are confirmed in Theroux's account of writing *The Great Railway Bazaar*, 'First Train Journey', *Granta*, Vol. 29, Winter 1989 (*New World*), pp. 167–72.

[58] Theroux, *The Great Railway Bazaar*, p. 341; for a description of Theroux's relationship between actual travel and the writing process, see Elton Glaser, 'The Self-Reflexive Traveller: Paul Theroux on the Art of Travel and Travel Writing', *Centennial Review*, Vol. 3, No. 3, Summer 1989, pp. 193–206. While this essay is useful in thinking about the literary authorities embedded in *The Great Railway Bazaar*, Glaser's rendering of Theroux as 'self-reflexive' can be somewhat misleading; see also Edward T. Wheeler, 'What the Imagination Knows: Paul Theroux's Search for the Second Self', *Commonweal*, Vol. 121, 20 May 1994, pp. 18–22.

Fiction has been, all along, the name of the boundary between recording and discovering, seeing and knowing.'[59] Theroux's reproduction of the hierarchy of literature is borne out in *The Great Railway Bazaar* through a continual idealisation of fiction. While he makes great efforts to explain why it is he travels alone, Theroux is always accompanied by other texts – literary, local and instructive – that consolidate *The Great Railway Bazaar*'s position somewhere beneath the much-venerated novel.[60]

The first fictional authorities in *The Great Railway Bazaar* are the great works of literature Theroux is either reading or quoting from. Whatever Theroux sees, experiences and records is conveyed to the reader by cross-referencing great writers such as Browning, Byron, Dickens, Eliot, Joyce, Kipling and Maugham. For example, a simple crossing of the Bosphorus is infused with much more historical and cultural meaning when accompanied by a few lines of Byron.[61] Theroux's continual literary references and quotations position his 'observing eye' firmly within the Anglo-American literary canon and legitimate Theroux as a *literary* traveller rather than a common tourist or an illiterate local.[62] Theroux's reliance on the Anglo-American literary canon reveals his assumption about the universality of 'great literature': it doesn't matter where Theroux is on his Grand Tour, the literature he calls upon resonates at the universal level of humanity. In other words, literary greatness transcends geographical and historical context. But this assumption about universality is also revealed in Theroux's practical and professional relationship with the canon. He funds his train journey through Asia by giving lectures on American

---

[59] Caesar, *Forgiving the Boundaries*, p. 125.
[60] This framework is loosely based on Glaser's structure of intertextuality; see 'The Self-Reflexive Traveller', pp. 198–201.
[61] Theroux, *The Great Railway Bazaar*, p. 36.
[62] Literary references in *The Great Railway Bazaar* include the following: James Joyce (prologue, p. 133), T. S. Eliot (p. 23), William Burroughs (p. 24), Graham Greene (p. 41), Rudyard Kipling (pp. 85, 187), V. S. Naipaul (pp. 96, 121), Mark Twain (pp. 107, 123), E. M. Forster (p. 129), Somerset Maugham (p. 133), Robert Browning (pp. 133, 197), Charles Dickens (p. 178), André Gide (p. 229), Joseph Conrad (pp. 253, 262, 307), William Blake (p. 255), Anton Chekhov (p. 283) and Saul Bellow (p. 291). Indeed, it reads like a syllabus for an American college class on 'Great Modern Writers'. Theroux also has respect for others (travellers or locals) who display knowledge of the Western literary canon. The most sympathetically portrayed characters all show some respect for great works of literature: Yashar in Turkey, Mr Barnard in Burma and Mr Thanoo in Thailand. To those who share his passions for a solitary engagement with literature, Theroux offers respect: 'Mr. Thanoo, the aged traveller in my compartment sat reading *Colonel Sun* by Kingsley Amis. He said he had been saving it for the trip, and I didn't want to interrupt him in his reading. I went into the corridor' (*The Great Railway Bazaar*, p. 214).

Literature along the way: the first is in Turkey, followed by India, Sri Lanka, Vietnam and Japan. He markets himself as an authority not only because he is an established writer himself, but also because he lectures and teaches on American Literature.[63] Although Theroux makes frequent comments about the practicalities and social opportunities that arise in these intellectual gatherings, the only hint at the *content* of these lectures comes at the end of his trip in Japan: 'Over three months earlier, in Istanbul, I had spoken on the tradition of the American novel, implying that it was special and local. In India I contradicted most of this, and by the time I got to Japan I had come full circle, claiming that there was no real tradition in American writing that was not also European.'[64]

In effect, the content of these lectures is secondary to Theroux's position as a literary expert. Moreover, his choice of reading material, coupled with his lectures, implies a specific readership that, like Theroux, is conversant with the Anglo-American literary canon. If the reader has no familiarity with the works of Eliot, Kipling, Dickens or Byron, Theroux's citations and references are lost. But if the reader is conversant with the canon, they enjoy the pleasure of sharing 'expert' literary knowledge with a master like Theroux. That implied readership, coupled with Theroux's literary authority, sets up the principal intertextual relationship in *The Great Railway Bazaar* between travelogues and 'great' works of Anglo-American fiction.

The second element of intertextuality appears in *The Great Railway Bazaar* through 'local' novels, or works of fiction written by people who live in the places he is travelling through. Not many of these texts are included in *The Great Railway Bazaar*, presumably because Theroux cannot identify a consistent 'literary tradition' in the vast area of Asia that he covers. Therefore, his brief encounters with local texts are restricted to the discussions he has with authors and scholars who attend his lectures. Because these interactions link Theroux with a local literary elite which is already trained in the Anglo-American canon (and the English language), he is never forced to encounter literary traditions wholly 'other' to his own. His reading and interactions are framed in advance by already circumscribed boundaries and orthodox interpretations of the Anglo-American literary canon. His encounters with 'local novels' begin at his first lecture in Turkey where he admits

---

[63] Theroux has held teaching posts and 'writer-in-residence' positions at Urbino, Kampala, Malawi, Singapore and Virginia.
[64] Theroux, *The Great Railway Bazaar*, p. 285.

that he has only ever read one Turkish novel, Yashar Kamal's *Mehmet My Hawk*. He spends the rest of his time in Turkey with Yashar and his wife, discussing great works of Anglo-American literature, and concludes, 'Yashar's complexity is the Turkish character on a large scale.'[65] Western works of 'great literature' rule the rest of Theroux's journey through India, Burma, Thailand and Vietnam until he decides to read novels by Japanese authors in order to prepare himself for his visit. Along with Shushako Endo's *Silence* (which he enjoys), Theroux reads Edogawa Rampo's collection of stories, of which he says the following: 'His fictional inventions were ungainly, and his shin-barking prose style was an irritation; and yet I was held, fascinated by the very ineptitude of the stories... Here was another glimpse of the agonized Japanese spirit.'[66] Perhaps Rampo was not clear on the 'universal' qualities that make a novel great. Even so, Theroux shows no sympathy for the cross-cultural misreadings and misinterpretations of literature: Rampo's novel is inept according to a universal standard of literature that Theroux – as expert – has mastered. More revealing is how Theroux relegates these local texts to a subordinate literary status through the use of synecdoche: Yashar's complexity comes to stand in for the whole of Turkey, and Rampo's text shows us the entire agonised Japanese spirit. While authors like Eliot and Dickens show us the *universal* conditions of humanity, local writers give us insight into the *particular* characteristics of each country (e.g. Turkey's complexity and Japan's agony). Because Theroux accesses local fiction through an already stipulated hierarchy of literature, these texts can only ever work as secondary confirmations of the standards that Theroux takes to be universal. It is only when he cannot find a universally recognised modern author to inscribe a country for him (as Kipling, Twain and Naipaul do for him in India) that he is forced to look to indigenous writers to verify what he is witnessing.

The third literary authority in *The Great Railway Bazaar* belongs neither to fiction nor to travel writing; rather, it is the much-maligned guidebook. Because *The Great Railway Bazaar* is so over-coded with canonical fictional authority, there is little room for the banalities of the guidebook. And this is precisely the point: Theroux's general disdain for these texts is another way of reinforcing the hierarchy of literature. Sourcing one's knowledge and inspiration in famous literature

[65] Theroux, *The Great Railway Bazaar*, p. 44.
[66] Theroux, *The Great Railway Bazaar*, p. 276.

is so much better than sourcing it in factual guidebooks that even *tourists* read:

I slowed down and, with Nagel's *Turkey* in my hand, began sightseeing, an activity that delights the truly idle because it seems so much like scholarship, gawping and eavesdropping on antiquity, flattering oneself with the notion that one is discovering the past when really one is inventing it, using a guidebook as a scenario of swift notations.[67]

Although one assumes Theroux had maps and guidebooks with him at all times, he mentions them only rarely – he prefers to give the impression that the route he travels is a meandering, unplanned and spontaneous one.[68] Guidebooks are only mentioned as a last resort: if literary references inspire his imagination and creativity, and local texts add a more 'indigenous' flavour to his universal understandings, then guidebooks – however infrequently – show the reader that Theroux's observations are rooted in established knowledge. Moreover, Caesar suggests that references to guidebooks in contemporary travel writing symbolise the growing presence of tourism in the genre: 'The profound influence of the guidebook on the travel text is explained by the need to pay tribute to the sheer power of tourism, and not merely disdain it.'[69] But disdain is Theroux's hallmark, and his unwillingness to acknowledge the guidebooks that frame his journey is simply another strategy to create distance between himself and the tourists who use guidebooks as bibles. Not only is Theroux a *literary* expert (i.e. he constantly references great works of fiction), he is also a *travel* expert (i.e. he doesn't rely on guidebooks to navigate foreign cultures).

The limits of structuralism: ontological, contextual and post-colonial horizons

To read Rushdie and Theroux through a structuralist framework is to reveal how the generic boundaries of travel writing shape and influence the content of these narratives. While Rushdie's *The Jaguar Smile* illustrates how generic regulations can constrain even the most creative writers, Theroux's *The Great Railway Bazaar* illustrates how generic regulations are enforced by a continual subordination to

---

[67] Theroux, *The Great Railway Bazaar*, p. 34.
[68] The relatively few references to guidebooks are the following: *Murray's Handbook* appears in Simla (p. 109); a forty page handbook called *Visit Vietnam* is all he has to guide him in that country (p. 244); and there is mention of the *Sapporo Handbook* when he is in Japan.
[69] Caesar, *Forgiving the Boundaries*, p. 92.

'great literature'. In this way, Rushdie's text shows the continuity of a discourse of literary genre in travel writing, while Theroux's text shows how that discourse is constantly shifting between the much-valued novel and the much-maligned guidebook. Within a structuralist framework, then, these texts engage with cultural difference within the limits of prevailing generic regulations. While I am sympathetic to Todorov's structuralist framework and his account of the journey narrative, I want to argue that his approach is politically limited. Todorov not only fails to engage with the ontological significance of the journey metaphor, he also fails to adequately politicise the concept of genre. Consequently, his arguments about the travelogue's engagements with difference lack the critical edge of post-colonial and post-structural analysis and cannot account for how and why the legacy of Empire continues to shape the genre.

Todorov begins his analysis of travel writing with a provocative statement, 'What is *not* a journey?', and goes on to explain the impossibility of categorising these texts because 'the journey coincides with life, no more, no less ... everything is a journey ... one cannot isolate the journey from what it is not'.[70] This is an acute observation, not least because it interrupts any clear structuralist definition that 'travelogues are about journeys'. What is curious about Todorov's following analysis is the refusal to see how this question destabilises any simple 'general poetics' or 'historical development' of travel writing. This takes us back to Todorov's larger concerns about resuscitating literary genre as a viable analytical tool in the face of post-structural efforts – led by Blanchot – to 'shatter the limits of genre'. Todorov wants to hold on to genre as a significant (if compromised) organising category even when the topic at hand – travel – cannot be easily defined. In the case of travelogues, he argues, 'If one cannot isolate the journey from what it is not, one can, somewhat more successfully, attempt to distinguish within this vast confused medley several kinds of journeys, several categories that allow us to clarify particular types of journeys.'[71] In effect, Todorov wants to provide a taxonomy of journey narratives as they have developed over time in order to establish the generic criteria for this type of literature. But failing to define

---

[70] Todorov, 'The Journey and Its Narratives', pp. 60, 62. This question is explored in greater depth in Michel de Certeau, *The Practice of Everyday Life*, trans. Steven Rendall (Berkeley and Los Angeles: University of California Press, 1984), and Georges Van Den Abeele in *Travel as Metaphor: From Montaigne to Rousseau* (Minneapolis: University of Minnesota Press, 1992).

[71] Todorov, 'The Journey and Its Narratives', p. 62.

the limits of a journey makes it equally impossible to define the limits of the genre through which those journey narratives are told. How can you have distinct generic boundaries when the subject matter of the genre is itself infinite? I want to argue that Todorov's initial question – 'what is *not* a journey?' – is more important than his general poetics and literary history because it prompts us to question the ontological security of all generic boundaries. Moreover, this question places the travelogue with its indeterminate status and complex citation of fact and fiction in the ideal position to pursue Blanchot's desire and shatter the limits of genre.

Todorov is aware that his resuscitation of genre as an analytical tool must take account of how the rules and regulations of literature are shaped by their social context. Indeed, his structuralist approach stipulates that a 'general poetics' must be historicised in order to show how generic boundaries are both reflections and productions of their social environments.[72] The problem is that Todorov's efforts at context-ualisation do not go far enough – an inadequacy that is made pain-fully obvious when he comes to analyse travel writing. Since his structural arguments on genre emerged in the 1970s, genre theory has developed much more critical frameworks that foreground issues of social context, rhetorical conditions and power relations. Following Bakhtin's arguments in *The Dialogic Imagination* (1981), scholars began to focus on the social aspects of genre in terms of how they reflected and shaped their users. As Catherine Schryer explains: 'All genres have a complex set of relations with past texts and with other present texts: genres come from somewhere and are transforming into some-thing else. Because they exist before their users, genres shape their users, yet users and their discourse communities constantly remake and reshape them.'[73] Carolyn Miller's seminal piece 'Genre as Social Action' (1984) and John Swayles' *Genre Analysis* (1990) made the break from a transcendental 'recipe theory' of genre by focusing on *how* language is used in specific social contexts, and how generic rules and

---

[72] Todorov expresses his discontent with a purely linguistic analysis of genre when he concludes that a discourse is not divorced from the subject that produces it. The 'series of sentences' that makes up a discourse suddenly becomes politicised when the producer is located and attached to his or her enunciations. For Todorov, then, sentences are always uttered in a context and always enunciated by a subject, which means that 'a discourse is always and necessarily a speech act', ('The Origin of Genres', p. 162).

[73] Catherine F. Schryer, 'The Lab vs. the Clinic: Sites of Competing Genres', pp. 105–24, in Aviva Freedman and Peter Medway, eds., *Genre and the New Rhetoric* (London: Taylor and Francis, 1994), p. 108.

regulations condition that use in specific times and places.[74] But scholars also began to focus on the 'plasticity and freedom' of generic boundaries by insisting that all genres are radically contingent categories that evolve, develop and decay. What we are left with now is an understanding of genres as thoroughly context-bound and unstable. As Schryer argues, a genre should be properly understood as 'a stabilized-for-now or stabilized-enough site of social and ideological interaction'.[75]

Todorov's failure to pursue the ontological and contextual elements of genre analysis compromises his arguments about the colonial legacy of travel writing. Although his understanding of the colonial encounter was made clear in a much more popular and well-received study, *The Conquest of America: The Question of the Other*, Todorov's argument that travel writing is founded on an encounter between self and other seems woefully apolitical.[76] To be sure, Todorov ends his study by arguing that travel writing requires the 'specific position of the colonizer', but does not explain how that subject position continues to mobilise powerful discursive hegemonies. For Todorov, it is more important to examine why readers keep going back to colonial travel narratives for respite and comfort, rather than ask why and how the logic of Empire continues to shape these narratives:

> as today's readers, we retain the advantage of colonialist ideology; but at the same time we derive the benefit brought about by the period of decolonisation since we can still say to ourselves: but we are *not* those authors. The alienation so dear to Brecht, occurring here in relation to the narrators of these tales, allows us to retain our pleasure without having to face the criticism that could be levelled at our elders.[77]

Todorov goes on to explain his own preference for an old colonial travel narrative as opposed to new ones: 'it offers me the prism I need in

---

[74] See Carolyn R. Miller, 'Genre as Social Action', *Quarterly Journal of Speech*, Vol. 70, 1984, pp. 151–67, and her follow-up piece 'Rhetorical Community: The Cultural Basis of Genre', pp. 67–78, in Freedman and Medway's *Genre and the New Rhetoric*; see also John Swayles, *Genre Analysis* (Cambridge: Cambridge University Press, 1990). More recently, Wanda Orlikowski and JoAnne Yates have developed the context-bound nature of genres in more specific directions: see 'Genres of Organizational Communication: A Structurational Approach to Studying Communication and Media', *Academy of Management Science Review*, Vol. 17, No. 2, 1992, pp. 299–326, and *Genre Systems: Structuring Interaction through Communicative Norms* (Cambridge, MA: MIT Press, 1998).

[75] Schryer, 'The Lab vs. the Clinic', p. 107.

[76] Tzvetan Todorov, *The Conquest of America: The Question of the Other*, trans. Richard Howard (Ithaca: Cornell University Press, 1982).

[77] Todorov, 'The Journey and Its Narratives', p. 70.

order to really take advantage of my trip... an image of the traveller with which I identify while at the same time distancing myself from it, and which thus absolves me of all guilt'.[78] While I accept the slightly facetious tone of Todorov's conclusion, it exemplifies the depoliticised nature of his entire argument about travel writing because it reveals his inability to see how power relations are embedded in formal generic boundaries *as well as* in the content of particular narratives. Todorov certainly suggests that travel writing has been shaped by colonialism, but he fails to illustrate how colonial relations are constitutive of both the historical development of the genre *and* its general poetics. In short, Todorov's account does not explain how the production of difference is not just restricted to *what* is written in travelogues (i.e. the content), it is also embedded in the rules and regulations that determine *how* things are written (i.e. the form). Given the limitations of Todorov's analysis, I want to re-visit the initial problem of genre through a post-structural position. What would it look like if we politicised travel writing through Blanchot's desire to 'shatter the limits of genre'?

Contaminating genres: re-imagining the boundaries of travel writing

One of the significant problems with a structuralist approach to travel writing is that it cannot conceive of generic indeterminacy as transgressive. As *Gulliver's Travels* proves, there have always been travelogues that escape the bounding practices of literary genre.[79] If we apply a rigid 'general poetics' of travel writing, then anomalous texts actually reinforce the boundary by either proving the genre's existence (the anomaly remains excluded) or by reincorporating itself inside the generic boundaries (the anomaly becomes assimilated). To foreground the perpetual instability that results from the travelogue's vacillation between fact and fiction, a different reading of literary genre is required. To this end, we follow Blanchot's desire and approach Jacques Derrida's essay 'The Law of Genre' (1980).[80] For Derrida, the value of genre is in its ability to place laws on language: genres give us specific codes of the 'do' and 'do not' variety. In this way, genre instigates a number of norms and limits that are either respected or transgressed — so far not

---

[78] Todorov, 'The Journey and Its Narratives', p. 70.
[79] Frederik N. Smith, ed, *The Genres of Gulliver's Travels* (Newark: University of Delaware Press, 1990).
[80] Jacques Derrida, 'The Law of Genre', trans. Avital Ronell, *Critical Inquiry*, Vol. 7, No. 1, 1980, pp. 55–81.

too different from Todorov's formulation. Derrida's first departure comes in his distinction between epistemological genres and literary genres. The term *Physis* refers to a more general determination of boundaries that are related to nature, and are most easily understood as taxonomic classifications. This general use of genre relates to Foucault's idea of discursive continuity – how a specific 'order of things' is organised into differences and hierarchies and made to seem natural over time. But Derrida also argues that genres are about a specific *typology* that governs questions of style, technique and grammar. And it is within this specific understanding of genre that we can pursue an alternative to Todorov's structuralist formulation.

Derrida starts with the promise that he will be responsible and not mix literary genres – but in typical fashion, he spends the rest of the argument exploring what is at stake in the mixing of genres. Any desire to avoid this mixing requires a previous understanding of genres as pure and bounded entities in the first place. For Derrida, pure genres do not and cannot exist. The original law of generic purity is disrupted by an *a priori* law of contamination, a 'counter-law' that is the very condition of possibility for generic purity to exist in the first place.[81] Thus, the counter-law is a perpetual disruption of the sense, order and reason of genre: the law of generic purity is continually transgressed by its own counter-law. Derrida argues that this generic disruption happens in the following manner: each law or limit is threatened *in advance* by a counter-law that works as an outside against which the original law is constituted and given identity. That 'always already' relationship threatens the 'original' identity of generic purity: it cannot be said to exist without its other, its outside, its counter-law. As Derrida explains, 'The law and the counter-law serve each other citations summoning each other to appear, and each recites the other in this proceeding'.[82] It is this dialectic of original and counter-law that makes it difficult to separate genres from one another, and to accept their boundaries as historically and structurally stable. Despite starting with the proposition of mixing genres, Derrida accepts that literary genres are identified by shared common traits that we rely on in order

---

[81] Derrida's use of law here can also be understood as limit: it is the stipulation of some kind of boundary upon which infinite possibilities of inclusion and exclusion rest. For an explanation of Derrida's deconstructive understanding of laws and limits, see Jacques Derrida, 'Force of Law: The "Mystical Foundation of Authority"', in David Gray Carlson, Drucilla Cornell and Michael Rosenfeld, eds., *Deconstruction and the Possibility of Justice* (London: Routledge, 1992) pp. 3–67.

[82] Derrida, 'The Law of Genre', p. 58.

to decide whether a given work corresponds to a given set of criteria. These traits help us decide if texts will acquire membership in a specified genre, where membership is attained by the successful display and repetition of these common traits over time. But Derrida takes this dialectic understanding apart in two ways. Firstly, the very trait that guarantees belonging to a genre also *doesn't belong*, that is to say, it is haunted and punctured by all those other traits that it has excluded in its search for membership. Like the logic of law and its built-in counter-law, any trait that appears to be stable and 'criteria forming' is actually made possible through the exclusion of an infinite number of other counter-traits. Derrida's crucial point here is that those 'other' traits are never quite expelled. In effect, the stability of a set of generic traits is a continually performed illusion designed to stabilise a definitive set of generic boundaries against an already established outside. Very simply, generic membership of any trait or text is illusory. Derrida's second disruption of a dialectical understanding of genre has to do with repetition: the common trait that establishes membership in a genre is *not* identical each time it is repeated. As he explains, 'perhaps someone has noticed that, from one repetition to the next, a change had insinuated itself into the relationship between the two initial utterances'.[83]

These two shifts – failed exclusions and always-changing repetitions – constitute Derrida's most explicit departure from a structuralist formulation of literary genre. But Derrida also questions Todorov's entire project of examining the 'origin' of genres. There can be no such thing as an origin point of a genre, because each moment of origin is always already contaminated with past and future moments that it has tried unsuccessfully to expel. In other words, all origin points are constituted in advance by the 'teleological ordering of history'. Deconstructing the temporality assumed in the grand narrative of Western history is Derrida's way of problematising our assumed end points of enlightenment – transparent knowledge, metaphysical presence and ontological security. More specifically, re-imagining Todorov's teleological formulation of genre takes away the necessary end point of all travelogues being impressionistic, superficial renditions of otherness. Derrida's formulation of genre reverses Todorov's linear process of discursive codification by proposing that the law of genre is essentially a principle of contamination. Genres work in a 'parasitical economy' so that a pure or original genre never exists: it is always already

---

[83] Derrida, 'The Law of Genre', p. 58.

contaminated by other (not-quite-expelled) counter-laws, other rules, other traits and other genres. And that contamination is what frames generic instability: 'a text cannot belong to no genre, it cannot be without or less a genre. Every text participates in one or several genres, there is no genreless text; there is always a genre and genres, yet such participation never amounts to belonging.'[84] For Derrida, the principle of contamination requires participation in a discursive economy *without* membership. Although genres work to organise texts, they also resist their own self-identification as a genre during the process of organisation. For Derrida, a genre should not be understood as a law or a limit, but rather as a 'floodgate'. So while Todorov explores how the limits and laws of a genre are historically established, Derrida refuses that containment and resists generic closure: 'at the very moment that a genre or a literature is broached, at that very moment, degenerescence has begun, the end begins'.[85]

Disrupting content and form: the travels of Bruce Chatwin

If we pose Derrida's deconstruction of genre against Todorov's structural account, we can begin to see how the precarious location of travelogues between fact and fiction works constantly to disrupt and contaminate stable generic boundaries. But what kind of travelogue would express this contamination? And even if it could do this, would it still be a travelogue? Bruce Chatwin's *The Songlines* is a text that defies simple categorisation. Some argue that this provocative mixture of memoir, fiction, philosophy and anthropology constitutes a travelogue, while others − including Chatwin himself − claim it is 'more obviously a work of fiction'.[86] More than any of his texts, *The Songlines* illustrates how Chatwin's own migrations and thoughts on travel push against our usually static relationships to land, home, history and self. The structure of the book, a combination of traditional journey narrative plus a collection of notes, is borrowed from two obscure

---

[84] Derrida, 'The Law of Genre', p. 65.
[85] Derrida, 'The Law of Genre', p. 66.
[86] Disregarding his publisher's advice, Chatwin 'insisted' on calling *The Songlines* a novel. As Nicholas Shakespeare explains, 'Within Jonathan Cape [Chatwin's publishers] there had been confusion over how to market the book. Bruce was adamant: he did not wish to be regarded as a travel writer'; see Shakespeare, *Bruce Chatwin*, p. 486; see also Blanton, '"Lying Travellers": Bruce Chatwin', in *Travel Writing: The Self and the World*, pp. 95−105.

Modernist texts: Edith Sitwell's *Planet and Glow-Worm* and Cyril Connolly's *Palinarus: The Unquiet Grave*.[87] The first two-thirds of the book can be considered more or less a straightforward travelogue. Chatwin is drawn to the 'parched hide' of Australia because he is curious about the Aboriginal Dreaming Tracks, an ancient way of mapping the land through song. In *The Songlines*, Chatwin uses that image to make sense of his own thoughts on movement; that is, the Dreaming Tracks allow him to discuss how the figure of the nomad disrupts our modern understandings of identity and location. In the first two-thirds of the book, these questions arise in a series of dialogues between Chatwin and a Russian émigré called Arkady who was living and working with Aboriginal communities. Arkady explains the essence of the Dreaming Tracks to Chatwin in the following way: 'each totemic ancestor, while travelling through the country, was thought to have scattered a trail of words and musical notes along the lines of his footprints ... these Dreaming-tracks lay over the land as "ways" of communication between the most far-flung tribes'.[88] In order to deepen his understanding, Chatwin accompanies Arkady on his travels with Aboriginal communities in order to discover what the Dreaming Tracks can tell him about nomads. However, the conventional travel narrative that makes up the first two-thirds of the text is soon abandoned. The last third of *The Songlines* is a collection of aphorisms, tales, thoughts and stories from Chatwin's own moleskin notebooks:

I had a presentiment that the 'travelling' phase of my life might be passing. I felt, before the malaise of settlement crept over me, that I should reopen those notebooks. I should set down on paper a résumé of the ideas, quotations and encounters which had amused and obsessed me; and which I hoped would shed light on what is, for me, the question of questions: the nature of human restlessness.[89]

At the same point that the text shifts from travelogue to notebook, Chatwin's own journey through Australia gives way to his countless other journeys around the world in search of an answer to the question that haunts him. And this is where Chatwin's text differs so markedly from standard travelogues: his narrative is not built upon a home-away-home/beginning-middle-end structure. One does not get any sense of

[87] While Chatwin read Sitwell's book at school, he only arrived at the solution of this 'cut-up' method after seventeen years of struggling with his text on nomads; see Shakespeare, *Bruce Chatwin*, pp. 69, 458.

[88] Bruce Chatwin, *The Songlines* (London: Penguin, 1987), p. 13.

[89] Chatwin, *The Songlines*, p. 161.

where either home or away are for Chatwin – it is as if he simply appears in places and then disappears again.

The Songlines is particularly interesting with respect to issues of genre because it disrupts the formal boundaries of travel writing. As Graham Huggan explains, the most interesting journey in The Songlines is actually the narrative journey from travelogue to notebook: 'Chatwin's thesis that migratory instincts are not particular to nomadic societies, but are common to the human species, gains support from the "migratory instincts" of his own narrative. Chatwin's notes thus effectively sketch a songline of his own, a concatenation of semi-connected voices charting the uneven territory of the text.'[90] By taking 'travel' as its subject matter, The Songlines inserts a meta-discussion about nomadology, movement and restlessness into the conventional structure of the travelogue. Very simply, a change in form (from travelogue to notebook) effects a change in content (from exploring Australia to exploring 'the nature of human restlessness'). But The Songlines also departs from other travelogues because it reveals its fictional and factual citations. The notebook section of the text is a pseudo-academic document in which Chatwin calls explicitly upon the natural and social sciences to legitimate his broader argument that the natural state for humans is movement rather than stasis. In this mobilisation of sources, he cites Darwin, child psychologists, philologists, Max Weber, genetic determinists, economists, archaeologists and especially anthropologist Theodor Strehlow. But the notebooks also rely on another form of authorisation – Chatwin augments his academic claims with numerous literary quotations (e.g. Pascal, Wordsworth, Blake, Heidegger, Vico and Kinglake) and metaphors (e.g. the biblical story of Cain and Abel). When science and social science don't resonate, Chatwin is quite happy to insert historical and philosophical musings on travel – and vice versa. These explicit authoritative citations work to displace the subject position of the travel writer: Chatwin does not play the role of author in the notebook section, rather, he steps back and lets these other voices – from anthropologists to poets – speak for themselves.

Many critics have argued that the unorthodox structure of The Songlines amounts to a 'tremendous misuse of poetic license' that

---

[90] Graham Huggan, 'Maps, Dreams, and the Presentation of Ethnographic Narrative: Hugh Brody's "Maps and Dreams" and Bruce Chatwin's "The Songlines"', Ariel: A Review of International English Literature, Vol. 22, No. 1, January 1991, p. 65.

perpetuates lies about Australian Aborigines.[91] As one New Zealand anthropologist argued:

The book itself is ... a mixture of half-truths and fabrications. Such warped images are typical of the book as a whole ... Where does fiction begin, or end, and how is the mixture to be interpreted? ... Chatwin's *Songlines* won't help readers who don't know much about the Aboriginal ... situation, and it is likely to infuriate those who do.[92]

I am not bothered by Chatwin's rather shambolic and unorthodox mobilisation of literary and scientific sources to examine the question of nomadology. But what I *am* bothered about is how the venerated position of *The Songlines* as a 'radical' travelogue obscures Chatwin's reproduction of a colonial vision in *both* form and content. To this extent, I disagree profoundly with Blanton's claim that Chatwin's observations 'neither romanticise nor glorify the nomad and the exile'.[93] Many anthropologists who study Aboriginal communities – including those who appear in *The Songlines* itself – suggest that Chatwin is not a cosmopolitan aesthete or modern-day Renaissance man, but rather, the latest in a long line of colonial explorers. As Geoff Bagshaw, who works with Aboriginal groups in Australia, argued: 'It's a Dances-With-Wolves syndrome, that you need a white guy to mediate and render Aborigines intelligible. Bruce is part of a uniquely English tradition of men in rumpled white shirts at the far-flung corners of the world.'[94] Even more revealing are the words of Toly Sawenko, the man upon whom Chatwin based his character Arkady:

Bruce hadn't sorted the protocols through. He hadn't sat down with any Aborigine. He gets his information second-hand and repeats it ... Aboriginal people are capable of dealing with the world in a philosophical way. The problem is, he just wasn't there long enough, he didn't get involved at any depth. That was anathema to Bruce ... He would have had to get to know some aboriginal people, which he just didn't do. He uses me as a convenient artifice, but it's still a white man speculating over how interesting Aboriginal culture is.[95]

There are two parts to this charge against Chatwin: firstly, that in a 'non-fiction' genre like travel writing, Chatwin misrepresents the

---

[91] Critic Christopher Pearson, quoted in Shakespeare, *Bruce Chatwin*, p. 489.
[92] Catherine H. Berndt, 'Review of *The Songlines*', *Parabola*, Vol. 13, No. 1, Spring 1988, pp. 130–2.
[93] Blanton, *Travel Writing: The Self and the World*, p. 105.
[94] Geoff Bagshaw, as quoted in Shakespeare, *Bruce Chatwin*, p. 412.
[95] Toly Sawenko, as quoted in Shakespeare, *Bruce Chatwin*, p. 490. Petronella, the woman upon whom Chatwin bases the character Marion, echoes Sawenko's claim: 'he [Chatwin] doesn't grant the Aborigines any voice at all. He reproduces the white-fella-as-boss colonial relation' (p. 490).

Dreaming Tracks of Australia, and secondly, that these failures are the result of Chatwin's colonial vision of Aborigines as 'romantic' nomads. Charges of 'false' or 'mis' representations come from (in this case) social scientists and locals claiming to *know* Aboriginal culture better than Chatwin, either because they rely on academically rigorous research or because they have lived and worked with Aboriginal communities for a long time. In effect, *The Songlines* reveals that Chatwin is a poor anthropologist (his visit too brief, his ethnography too superficial) whose travel writing is limited by his Western, neocolonial privilege.

Interesting, then, that literary circles offer an altogether different interpretation – especially writers who accept Chatwin's claim that *The Songlines* was a novel and not a travelogue. Anthropologists and locals claim that the lack of intellectual rigour in *The Songlines* fails to satisfy the non-fiction criteria of travel writing, and consequently does a disservice to Aboriginal groups. But novelists like Thomas Keneally, the Australian author of *Schindler's Ark*, have quite the opposite view: 'It's a dangerous thing to say, but I think he did Aboriginal Australia a service ... I don't know how scientifically reliable it was, but I was willing to take it as a hopeful fable for human kind, a fortifying myth.'[96] Likewise, Salman Rushdie – an author who knows all about the trouble that fiction can cause – travelled with Chatwin in Australia when *The Songlines* was being written. When critics made accusations that Chatwin's book 'misused' the truth, and that Rushdie himself was the basis for the character Arkady, Rushdie responded thus:

Later, after the book is published, Bruce tells someone that 'of course' I am Arkady. This isn't true. I know one person in Alice Springs, like Arkady an Australian of Russian descent, also highly knowledgeable about aboriginal religion, who is a much more obvious model. Nor do I recognize a single line of our conversation in *The Songlines*. The truth is, 'of course', that Bruce is Arkady as well as the character he calls Bruce. He is both sides of the dialogue.[97]

Similarly, writer and politician Mario Vargas Llosa had no problem with Chatwin's mixing of fact and fiction, a skill that he claims is the 'most demanding and imperishable of human enterprises'.[98] Novelists and writers, it seems, had no problem with Chatwin's romantic image of the nomad, or his depictions of Australian Aborigines. By accepting the book as a novel rather than a travelogue, Chatwin and his colleagues are released from the burden of factual representation. In effect, fictional status is the ultimate 'get-out' clause when criticism comes from more

---

[96] Thomas Keneally, as quoted in Shakespeare, *Bruce Chatwin*, p. 488.
[97] Rushdie, 'Travels with Chatwin', in *Imaginary Homelands*, p. 233.
[98] Mario Vargas Llosa, as quoted in Nicholas Shakespeare, *Bruce Chatwin*, p. 491.

'factual' sources – in this case anthropologists. It is no surprise, then, that Rushdie was so quick to defend Chatwin's 'imaginary' narrative. Although *The Songlines* was published a year before *The Satanic Verses*, it mobilised a much less violent version of the debate that culminated in Rushdie's Fatwa in February 1989. Not only were these authors *irresponsible* in their representations of otherness, their rejoinder of fictionality – 'I made it all up!' – rang even more hollow in the ears of those being written about (i.e. Muslims, Australian Aboriginals).

While I agree with the anthropologist's claim that Chatwin's popular and supposedly 'progressive' text smuggles in well-known colonial prejudices, I don't think anthropology's rendering of 'facts' about foreign cultures is any less problematic. Indeed, as James Clifford and others have argued, the ethnographic function of anthropology cannot be divorced from its own colonial history.[99] And while I support the novelist's requirement of freedom of speech, that does not mean writers like Chatwin (and Rushdie for that matter) are somehow placed outside of everyday operations of power and cultural difference. Indeed, it is precisely the privileges enjoyed by writers like Chatwin and Rushdie – including the freedom of mobility – that blinds them to the prejudices and exclusions enacted in the name of cosmopolitanism. So while *The Songlines* might tweak the prevailing narrative strategies of travel writing, Chatwin still reproduces nomads – including Tuareg, Sufi and Bedouin as well as Australian Aborigines – according to romanticised projections of the colonial other. Moreover, as post-colonial critic David Taylor argues, Chatwin's colonial vision is not just limited to the content of his narrative:

[his writing's] distinctiveness lies not in merging fact and fiction, but in the striking combination of the persona of aesthete-traveller with an ostentatious fastidiousness of style... Its formal ingenuity allows it to sidestep its intellectual failings and faults in characterisation... [Chatwin] is clearly vulnerable to the charge of avoidance of the more immediate dynamics of cultural encounter, explanation and opinion, his stylistic virtuosity a refusal to engage with the actualities of human and political contact.[100]

Taylor's point is significant: the colonial vision so prevalent in travel writing is embedded in the stylistic, formal and aesthetic features of these texts. Moreover, to politicise *both* form and content is to work

---

[99] See James Clifford, *The Predicament of Culture: Twentieth Century Ethnography, Literature and Art* (Cambridge, MA: Harvard University Press, 1988), and James Clifford and George Marcus, eds., *Writing Culture: The Poetics and Politics of Ethnography* (Berkeley: University of California Press, 1986).

[100] David Taylor, 'Bruce Chatwin: Connoisseur of Exile, Exile as Connoisseur', in Clark, *Travel Writing and Empire*, pp. 199, 207, 210.

against the prevailing consensus that it is OK to ignore Chatwin's reproduction of colonial relations because he is such a good writer. Taylor's position is clear: Chatwin's 'finely wrought language' must be condemned, for his stylistic devices are 'mere ciphers for an ultimately reactionary nostalgia'.[101]

Should we then dismiss *The Songlines* because its innovative style and unorthodox structure are mapped onto a problematic colonial vision? Todorov doesn't think so: he argues that we can enjoy travel writing as long as we *know* we are different from writers in the colonial tradition. Within Todorov's framework then, it is possible to enjoy *The Songlines* if we, as readers, do not romanticise nomads in the same way that Chatwin does. But Taylor does not accept that our aesthetic appreciations of travel writing are innocent; indeed, he argues that readers cannot help but buy into the 'taxonomies of the colonialist' that Chatwin perpetuates. In other words, our appreciation of Chatwin's generic disruptions and his writing style cannot be divorced from what Taylor calls an 'ethnographic neo-colonialism for a post-colonial world'.[102] All of this makes the popularity of Chatwin worth thinking further about. Many critics have argued that since his death in 1989, it is Bruce Chatwin *the figure*, rather than his texts, that attracts the most attention. As Nicholas Shakespeare suggests, Chatwin's carefully constructed self is central to the appeal of *The Songlines*: '*The Songlines* is as much about nomads as it is about Bruce inventing himself as his best, most achieved character: intrepid and practical traveller, humble sage, sharp-witted inquisitor. This was Chatwin as he liked to see himself, a Hemingway hero full of deep feeling yet economical with words.'[103] Chatwin has become the modern iconic hero for global travellers – the epitome of the sophisticated, cosmopolitan nomad – and *The Songlines* has become a 'must read' for anyone with similar pretensions.[104] More than any other figure, the mercurial, clever and charming Chatwin is central to understanding the current formation of the genre: his subjectivity functions as the cosmopolitan ideal which other travel writers aspire to.

---

[101] Taylor, 'Bruce Chatwin: Connoisseur of Exile', p. 208.
[102] Taylor, 'Bruce Chatwin: Connoisseur of Exile', p. 195.
[103] Shakespeare, *Bruce Chatwin*, p. 420.
[104] For a sense of Chatwin's current heroic status, see the spate of biographies, anthologies and reviews that have recently been published about Chatwin: his editor Susannah Clapp's *With Chatwin: Portrait of a Writer* (London: Jonathan Cape, 1997); Shakespeare's *Bruce Chatwin*, and the two collections of his writing published posthumously, *Anatomy of Restlessness* with Jan Borm and Matthew Graves (London: Picador, 1997) and *What Am I Doing Here?* (London: Vintage, 1998). Chatwin's texts have been resuscitated in popular spheres as well as academic ones – anthropologists have used Chatwin's work to 'correct the paternalism of previously undisputed Western methodologies' (Shakespeare, *Bruce Chatwin*, p. 541).

3   The cosmopolitan gaze: rearticulations of modern subjectivity

I was reminded of the damage that liberals can do

Graham Greene[1]

Graham Greene is a symbolic figure for contemporary travel writers. As one of the first modern writers to publish both novels and travelogues, he serves as a model for 'cross-over' authors like Paul Theroux, Jonathan Raban and Pico Iyer. Many of Greene's novels are infused with exotic myths: for example, *The Quiet American* is a story about love, loss and moral action which is brought into relief by its setting in pre-war Vietnam. Greene also translates larger moral questions through an exotic lens in his travelogues – in Liberia he thinks of lost innocence (*Journey without Maps*, 1936) and in Mexico he thinks of faith and violence (*The Lawless Roads*, 1939).[2] Greene's travelogues are certainly significant for their exotic registers, but they also inaugurate a new era of introspection for the travel writer. Countering Todorov's claim that modern travelogues record the 'fleeting' impressions of authors, Greene's writing suggests that travel

---

[1] This quotation appears in the recent screen adaptation of Greene's 1955 story *The Quiet American* (Miramax Films, 2002: Dir. Phillip Noyce). It synthesises several conversations between Fowler (Michael Caine) and Pyle (Brendan Fraser) over the proper course of action in Vietnam and captures Fowler's doubts about Pyle who was 'impregnably armoured by his good intentions and his ignorance' (Graham Greene, *The Quiet American* (London: Vintage, 2002)). Lest we think that Greene's moral concerns about democracy and imperialism are outdated, we should remind ourselves that it is *precisely* these questions that so upset American audiences about the recent film adaptation. Indeed, the film-makers delayed the release of the film until well after the American administration had translated the events of 11 September into policy action against the 'War on Terror'. As support for these actions began to wane – no Bin Laden, no Saddam Hussein, no weapons of mass destruction – American audiences did not want to be reminded of how their liberal intentions in Vietnam caused the nation's greatest and most humiliating defeat; see David Thompson, 'Their Man in Saigon', *Guardian*, 2 November 2002, 'Review', p. 18.

[2] Graham Greene, *Journey without Maps* (London: Heineman, 1978) and *The Lawless Roads* (London: Penguin, 1982). The latter emerged from Greene's research for his novel *The Power and the Glory*.

writers are profoundly self-reflexive. As Blanton suggests, Greene's travelogues are 'the real beginning of heightened subjectivity in the genre' – a subjectivity which resonates deeply when posed against exotic, foreign and often hostile locations.[3] This chapter examines the condition of self-reflexivity in contemporary travel writing and asks how it shapes the cross-cultural encounters between travel writers and those they write about.

While Todorov's desire to resuscitate the category of genre might be problematic, his specific claims about the central role of the travel writer are insightful: one cannot study an object of knowledge (the travelogue) without also examining the subjects who produce that knowledge (travel writers). We know that the generic design of travel writing involves a constant negotiation between the competing authorities of fact and fiction. Because travel writers are never sure whether to call upon fact or fiction to authorise their narratives, they must be simultaneously objective observers (fact) and creative writers (fiction). But the competition between factual and fictional sources is hidden beneath the travel writer's unquestioned power to faithfully represent foreign places and people. To secure this agency, the travel writer must be clearly distinguished from everything else – he/she must be fashioned over and against a series of others who are denied the power of representing themselves. This hierarchy of authors and others opens up the second powerful discourse at work in travel writing: the *discourse of modern subjectivity*. Of particular interest here is how the contemporary travel writer becomes a site of struggle between a masculine, imperial subjectivity (what Mary Louise Pratt calls the 'monarch-of-all-I-survey') and a liberal, cosmopolitan subjectivity that actively resists the colonising and patronising aspects of cultural encounter.[4]

By requiring an analysis of subjectivity alongside questions of genre, it becomes possible to ask *who* is doing the representing, *who* is being represented, and how those subject positions are aligned with wider structures of power. In this sense, post-colonial scholars are right to argue that contemporary travel writers carry on the imperial project by assuming a moral universe of Western superiority. In addition, feminist scholars are right to argue that the superiority of the imperial gaze in travel writing is secured by the attending structures of patriarchy. All this is to say that, despite significant social and political changes (e.g. decolonisation, women's liberation, civil rights, feminism), many travel writers continue to secure their own identities by producing difference

---

[3] Blanton, *Travel Writing: The Self and the World*, p. 60.
[4] Pratt, *Imperial Eyes*, pp. 201–27.

on racial and gendered grounds. Certainly, Paul Theroux's negative judgements about others make it easy to see how contemporary travel writers continue to resuscitate an imperial, masculine subjectivity: he constructs a confident, self-assured narrative voice that makes well-informed judgements about what he finds at the edges of the civilised world.[5] However, many contemporary travel writers go to great lengths to *avoid* the imperial and patriarchal attitudes of their predecessors, opting instead for self-reflexive narratives that either foreground connections between global cultures, or use humour and self-deprecation to send up the notion of 'adventure'. That both modes of travel writing continue to be produced attests to what Holland, Huggan and others have called the 'democratisation' of travel writing – the fact that anyone can become a travel writer regardless of race, gender, sexual orientation, age and so on. In this way, travel writing has become another cultural site for the expression of identity politics – these texts create a valuable space for previously marginalised groups to articulate their claims for recognition within wider cultural and political communities. Within this cultural landscape, travel writers resuscitating colonial and patriarchal attitudes are finding it difficult to reproduce narratives in which other people are racially inferior and feminised. As Holland and Huggan argue, the moral universe of the 'Englishman Abroad' has 'outlived its usefulness'.[6] In short, the moral superiority and easy judgements of colonial travel writers are no longer acceptable in a world where states, cultures and people are – at least theoretically – afforded equal status within an international community.

I am interested in how contemporary travel writers are responding to the pressures of identity politics by negotiating the colonial and patriarchal heritage of the genre. This response is contradictory: travel writers either secure their subject positions by clinging onto an outdated paradigm of superior, masculine selves and inferior, feminised others, or find security through a more cosmopolitan approach where difference and otherness are reproduced on equal footing. While the latter response might seem more attractive, I want to argue that embedded in the cosmopolitan vision of many travel writers is a reconstructed framework of colonialism and patriarchy. As Todorov argues, this is why 'openly racist' colonial travel narratives continue to be popular with Western readers: 'We are all in favour of people's right to

---

[5]   Pratt, *Imperial Eyes*, pp. 217–21.

[6]   Holland and Huggan, *Tourists with Typewriters*, pp. 28, 39. They go on to say, 'The role of the "gentleman abroad" here, however ridiculous, is enabling: it springs from the ironic awareness that the Empire has collapsed, but that the traveller is free – or, better, can *pretend* to be free – to act as if it never had' (p. 46).

self-determination, and we all profess faith in the natural equality of races. Yet for all that we have not stopped believing in the superiority of our civilization over "theirs"; and why would we, since they all seem to want to imitate us and dream of coming to work in our countries?'[7] My point is that the cosmopolitan vision in travel writing does not necessarily contradict or escape its colonial and patriarchal heritage. All travel writing requires the production of difference – it requires the author to discriminate between what is familiar and what is exotic so that readers are satisfied that they are encountering people and places that are sufficiently *foreign*. Those practices of discrimination do not simply disappear when travel writers realise it is unacceptable – even taboo – to make negative judgements about cultural difference in an era of global diversity and multiculturalism. Rather, by claiming to celebrate difference under the auspices of cosmopolitanism, travel writers rely on the same mechanisms of discrimination they always have – only these mechanisms emerge in more subtle and imaginative ways. While it may be unfashionable for travel writers to make explicit judgements about other people (e.g. these locals good, those locals bad), it *is* acceptable if those judgements are made in the right spirit – in an effort to reveal the commonalities that exist between cultures. This chapter argues that colonial and cosmopolitan visions in contemporary travel writing are united most explicitly by their reproduction of modern subjectivity.

Matrices of race and gender: Orientalism, patriarchy and colonial travel writing

In asking how we 'do violence' to the world and to others in our acts of representation, Foucault provides a compelling critique of liberal-humanist conceptions of individuality. He exposes the discourse of modern subjectivity by taking away the 'substance' or 'essence' of the human subject and placing all identity formations in their social, political and discursive contexts.[8] For Foucault, the discursive construction of modern subjects is based on a logic of identity/difference that confers power on a set of 'selves' and denies it to a set of 'others'. In other words, the logic of identity/difference enables the modern subject to know itself and acquire a stable identity by locating others through visible signs of difference. Thus, we can say that modern

---

[7] Todorov, 'The Journey and Its Narratives', p. 70.
[8] Foucault states that the subject 'is not a substance; it is a form and this form is not above all or always identical to itself'; see Michel Foucault, 'The Ethic of Care for the Self as a Practice of Freedom', in J. Bernauer and David Rasmussen, eds., *The Final Foucault* (Cambridge, MA: MIT Press, 1988), p. 10.

identity and selfhood develop according to the logic of the 'I' and the 'not-I'. The political consequences of this logic emerge each time the 'difference' side of the equation is negatively judged and positioned according to the 'identity' norm. An example might be the following: the rational/unified/conscious 'I' of the travel writer transforms all those who fall outside of that description into irrational/chaotic/ignorant 'others'. As William E. Connolly argues, it is impossible to break out of the continual formulation of the identity/difference logic:

> when you remain within the established field of identity and difference, you become a bearer of strategies to protect identity through devaluation of the other; but if you transcend the field of identities through which the other is constituted, you lose the identity and standing needed to communicate with those you sought to inform. Identity and difference are bound together, it is impossible to reconstitute the relation to the second without confounding the experience of the first.[9]

Recognising the inescapability of the logic that shapes 'I', 'me', 'you', 'us' and 'them' does not liquidate the power relations manifest in each formulation of the identity/difference logic. As Foucault's work suggests, what needs to be worked out are the specific practices by which a particular subject position comes to be thought of as fixed and natural within the prevailing order of things.[10]

Many post-colonial and feminist scholars have used Foucault's methods to politicise the formulations of identity/difference at work in colonial travel writing. For Said, colonial travel writers were crucial in reproducing Orientalism: they opened up exotic places as laboratories for the operation of Western knowledge, and they packaged the Orient

---

[9] William E. Connolly, 'Identity and Difference in World Politics', in Der Derian and Shapiro, *International/Intertextual Relations*, p. 329.

[10] By thinking of all identity formations as *subject positions* within the discursive field, the 'fixed' and 'natural' characteristics of individuals are revealed as effects of the continual installation of the identity/difference logic. The easiest way to understand 'subject positions' is to say that discourses set up locations within which subjects form and identities are conferred. Foucault explains the concept of the subject position in *The Archaeology of Knowledge*: 'It is a particular, vacant place that may in fact be filled by different individuals; but, instead of being defined once and for all, and maintaining itself as such throughout a text, a book, or an *oeuvre*, this place varies — or rather it is variable enough to be able either to persevere, unchanging, through several sentences, or to alter with each one' (p. 95). Thinking about how subjects are *constructed* at the same time as they are *located* in the discursive field suggests that we do not simply drift along as pre-formed bodies and slot into discursive positions as they become available. Rather, we, as subjects, only come into presence to the extent that we are attached to, and formed by, circulating discourses. By calling it a 'vacant place', Foucault suggests that the fitting together of bodies, subjects, discourses and positions is a highly co-dependent process.

in modern terminology to be received by literate Western audiences.[11] In Said's formulation, travel writers produced and reflected Orientalism in three ways: epistemologically (how we know the Orient), materially (how we encounter the 'actual' space of the Orient) and textually (how the Orient is represented). Because travel writers always inscribed the East through Western codes of knowledge, travelogues were understood as authoritative and truthful representations of life in the colonies. Because the logic of identity/difference operated through the more general coding of East and West, the travel writer was constructed as the typical Western scholar, adventurer and explorer, and all others were constructed as variously uncivilised, dangerous, mysterious, untrustworthy and so on. The authority of the travel writer was enabled principally by their exteriority: the morality of the author was placed outside the Orient in order for him (and less often her) to speak for it, represent it and make it visible to the West. As Said explains, this moral disengagement allowed travel writers to categorise and know the people and places of their journey through an already accepted understanding of Oriental inferiority.[12] Likewise, this disengagement allowed authors to write over the material and everyday aspects of the Orient according to their own mythology of superiority and enlightenment. Said explains how travel writer Alexander Kinglake 'wrote over' the Orient:

it is interesting how little the experience of actually seeing the Orient affected his opinions. Like many other travellers he is more interested in remaking himself and the Orient (dead and dry – a mental mummy) than he is in seeing what there is to be seen. Every being he encounters merely corroborates his belief that Easterners are best dealt with when intimidated, and what better instrument of intimidation than a sovereign Western ego?[13]

For Said, that moral superiority was further sanctioned by the authors' ability to move *physically* inside and outside of the Orient. Travel writers were not constrained by the material and geographical distinctions between East and West because their movements within the Orient were always accompanied by the opportunity to stand outside it and represent it 'objectively'.

---

[11] Said, *Orientalism*, pp. 424–44. As Said argues, imaginative and travel literature 'strengthened the divisions established by Orientalists between the various geographical, temporal, and racial departments of the Orient ... this literature is especially rich and makes a significant contribution to building the Orientalist discourse' (p. 99). He goes on to say 'even the most innocuous travel book – and there were literally hundreds written after mid-century – contributed to the density of public awareness of the Orient' (p. 192).

[12] Said, *Orientalism*, p. 42.

[13] Said, *Orientalism*, p. 193.

While it is possible to understand the processes by which Western travel writers inscribed an inferior Orient, many feminist critics have argued that the identity/difference logic operates on a more complex register when questions of gender are introduced.[14] Sara Mills's *Discourses of Difference* analyses how patriarchal values shaped women's travel writing during colonialism.[15] Initially, audiences and literary circles in the eighteenth and nineteenth centuries had great difficulty situating colonial travel writing by women. Because it was thought that women could not possibly engage in the kind of adventures that men could (after all, they were only *women*), women's travel writing was considered to be either impossible or untruthful. Mills explains how the literary establishment positioned colonial women's travel writing as either extraordinary ('true' accounts of how 'even *women* can travel'), or mundane (individual diaries detailing domestic life in colonial territories). With these two characterisations, travel narratives by colonial women failed to live up to the rigorous literary standards required by the newly established genre of travel writing. But Mills explains that colonial women travel writers inhabited a much more conflicted subject position than simple subordination: they were both feminist and imperial. By escaping the constraints of sanctioned gender roles in their homes and seeking an alternative life in colonial outposts, many 'adventuresses' actively resisted the discourse of patriarchy. Having said that, these same powerful women who contravened the status quo at home often reproduced colonial power structures while abroad. These women travel writers were not purely colonisers without sympathy (for their femininity made them empathise with natives), nor were they purely sentimental missionaries fighting against the injustices of colonialism (for their privilege allowed them to judge natives according to Western standards of civilisation). By adding women to the framework of Orientalism, Mills shows how these 'adventuresses' present an anomaly in the operation identity/difference: women travel writers do not fit within a strictly coloniser/colonised or Orient/Occident framework. Because women travel writers adhere to both sides of the coloniser/colonised framework (i.e. women colonise and patronise

---

[14] For gendered critiques of *Orientalism*, see Reina Lewis, *Gendering Orientalism: Race, Femininity and Representation* (London: Routledge, 1996), and Mayda Yegenoglu, *Colonial Fantasies: Towards a Feminist Reading of Orientalism* (Cambridge: Cambridge University Press, 1998).

[15] In addition to Mills's analysis, see Karen R. Lawrence, *Penelope Voyages: Women and Travel in the British Literary Tradition* (Ithaca: Cornell University Press, 1994), and Cheryl McEwan, *Gender, Geography and Empire: Victorian Women Travellers in West Africa* (Aldershot: Ashgate, 2000).

natives overseas but are colonised and patronised by men at home), they cannot be easily recovered in the binary framework of Orientalism. And because they inhabit *both* sides of the coloniser/colonised framework, women travel writers often get marginalised within post-colonial analyses that *supposedly* uncover previously silenced voices.

Mills's analysis is an important adjunct to *Orientalism* because it suggests that colonial encounters were more complex than a simple equation of domination/subordination. Including gender in an analysis of travel writing starts the process of deconstructing its Orientalist foundations – first by locating the discourses of patriarchy as well as Orientalism, but also by revealing that 'coloniser' and 'colonised' are not the only subject positions at stake in the experience of Empire. But how have these complex understandings of race and gender affected contemporary travel writing? We know that contemporary travel writers are unable to locate, translate and expose 'undiscovered' cultures in the same fashion as their colonial predecessors. Simultaneously, travel writers – like all producers of Western cultural products – have had to respond to the profound social and political critiques launched by subjects who have been excluded from Western narratives. Indeed, as 'new identities' become travel writers and re-imagine the genre, we see the publication of books such as *An Anthology of Women's Travel Writing*, and *Stranger in the Village: Two Centuries of African-American Travel Writing*.[16] However, alignments between coloniser/colonised and masculine/feminine continue to shape how travel writers produce difference – even when they want to avoid the colonial and patriarchal legacy of the genre.

Taxonomies of difference: globalisation, subjectivity and power

Contemporary travel writers certainly recognise how the forces of globalisation have changed cultural encounters for ever. Some respond by reviving matrices of colonialism and patriarchy and foregrounding cultural difference (i.e. 'they' are still different from 'us'). Unhappy with the colonial and patriarchal tone of that project, other travel writers seek to *manage* cultural difference – to locate, place and administer it within a framework of universal norms. Cosmopolitan travel writers seek out

---

[16] Sara Mills and Shirley Foster, eds., *An Anthology of Women's Travel Writing* (Manchester: Manchester University Press, 2002); Farah J. Griffin and Cheryl J. Fish, eds., *Stranger in the Village: Two Centuries of African-American Travel Writing* (Boston: Beacon Press, 1999).

difference in order to welcome it, include it and celebrate it: it doesn't matter if 'they' are different from 'us', as long as 'we' – and that means everyone – can join together and celebrate those differences. Although these two responses to globalisation contradict one another, they indicate the primary ways in which the identity/difference logic is currently operating in contemporary travel writing – either reviving cultural difference through colonial and patriarchal binaries, or synthesising and celebrating it through a cosmopolitan vision. My point is that *both* of these responses are enabled by an identity/difference logic that positions the travel writer as the principal and unquestioned subject in the text. Difference in any form is domesticated by the travel writer's power to arrange events, others and objects into a coherent narrative. In this way, 'writing the self' in contemporary travelogues is also a sustained writing of difference – identifying, locating and categorising difference is the most effective way to bolster the subject position of the travel writer.

The particular manifestation of identity/difference in travel writing is explained by Foucault's argument about the internal and external forces of that logic: 'This form of power applies itself to immediate everyday life which categorises the individual, marks him by his own individuality, attaches him to his own identity, imposes a law of truth on him which he must recognise and which others must recognise in him. It is a form of power which makes individuals subjects.'[17] When external discursive pressures are used to shape individuals, we are witnessing a process of *subjectification*. In this case, individuals are literally *made* into subjects: they achieve presence and acquire identities through the external discourses that shape them. Primarily, these external forces construct hegemonic subject positions (e.g. the travel writer) by locating and marginalising other subject positions that display characteristics of difference (e.g. the 'others' who are written about). In this sense, the process of subjectification requires a world external to the subject: securing identity is about projecting difference outward. But practices of power do not only shape subjects from the outside in. Subjects are not Pavlovian dogs: we do not simply respond to regulations from 'out there' and act accordingly (just as power does not simply move 'top down' from structure to subject). The discursive rules and regulations that discipline us as subjects are also created by us; in other words, the boundaries installed between identity and difference do not exist without attending selves and others to perpetuate these limits.

---

[17] Michel Foucault, 'The Subject of Power', in H. L. Dreyfus and Paul Rabinow, eds., *Michel Foucault: Beyond Structuralism and Hermeneutics* (Brighton: Harvester Press, 1982), p. 212.

The external forces that position subjects are also mirrored by powerful internalising practices. We, as subjects, keep ourselves intact by internalising practices of power that tell us who we are and how to behave. This insertion of self-consciousness, or 'turning inward', is what Foucault calls *subjection*. Rather than repeat the legacy of humanism that insists subjects achieve full consciousness by possessing individual agency and free will, Foucault argues that the subject literally *produces itself* as an autonomous entity by internalising the mechanisms of repression and control meant to keep them docile and 'in place'.

What Foucault's work teaches us is that the discourse of modern subjectivity consists of simultaneous processes of *subjectification* (directed at external others) and *subjection* (directed inward on the self).[18] What I am particularly interested in is how these practices shape the contemporary travel writer's contradictory responses to globalisation. Whether reviving colonial and patriarchal binaries, or overcoming them through a cosmopolitan vision, the travel writer secures his/her position through various manifestations of the identity/difference logic. Whether cultural difference is foregrounded, managed or ignored, it is always present and always shaping the travel writer as a confident subject capable of negotiating, organising and translating unfamiliar territory. I want to argue that contemporary travel writers secure their subjectivity by projecting difference primarily onto two external others: the tourist and the local. Simultaneously, travel writers turn inward and fashion a self characterised by solitude, masculinity and irony.

Producing others

Travellers and tourists

Part of the attraction of reviving colonialism and patriarchy in travel writing is that they enable travel writers to mimic the adventures of great colonial explorers – being the first to discover a place, and the first to translate and represent it in a travelogue. While the forces of globalisation have certainly ruined this opportunity for travel writers, it is more specifically modern tourism that has made these discoveries impossible. Because the tourist can go anywhere the travel writer can, the travel writer now secures his/her subject position by producing an other that is easy to hate: the tourist. The traveller/tourist binary is an explicit formation of the identity/difference logic – the former installed as the hero of the text, and the latter disdained as an unfortunate

---

[18] Foucault, 'The Subject of Power', p. 208.

by-product of globalisation. The tourist represents a particularly useful combination of similarity and difference for the travel writer to work against: similar in that the tourist is also pursuing adventure in faraway lands (and is most likely from the same Western culture as the travel writer), but different in that the tourist's manner of travel is wholly abhorrent to the travel writer. As Sally Tisdale explains, the traveller/tourist dichotomy is a central feature of contemporary travel writing:

A particular distinction between travel and tourism marks modern travel writing, which sometimes goes to acrobatic lengths to frame it. The self-anointed traveller despairs at the nearness of other visitors, the tiniest evidence of travellers having passed this way before, and is touchy indeed at being mistaken for one of the crowd. What he hates most about tourism is tourists... [travelogues] serve as flattery for all who wish to separate from the rabble — those other people, those *tourists*.[19]

By disparaging the behaviour of tourists, travel writers assume that there is a more authentic way to engage with cultural difference. Moreover, they can maintain the fantasy that it is still possible to locate and experience places in the world that are as yet untouched by mass tourism. By claiming to be 'intrepid travellers', travel writers are able to affirm their subject positions by denouncing the mechanical and routine movements of tourists. Travel writers often represent tourists as pathetic creatures, unable to manage foreign countries on their own — they must be led, pandered to and taken care of like spoiled children.[20] But the characteristic that marks tourists off most explicitly from travel writers is their herd-like mentality — their constant need for affiliation with other tourists. In *The Wind in My Wheels* (1992), travel writer Josie Dew interrupts her cycling voyage through North Africa to observe a group of

---

[19]   Sally Tisdale, 'Never Let the Locals', p. 67. In 'Mindless in Gaza', travel writer Jack Shamash argues that this distinction is not particular to modern travel writing but also characterised earlier texts: 'Since then [Victorian times] travellers have thought of themselves as faintly noble and they look down on mere tourists who stay in comfortable hotels and ride in air-conditioned buses. To travellers it is a mark of pride to suffer as much as possible. They get a perverse joy from spending all day squatting over a sordid cesspit'. See Geoff Barton, ed., *Travel Writing: Oxford Literary Resources* (Oxford: Oxford University Press, 1993), p. 1. For a discussion of the history of the traveller/tourist distinction, see James Buzard, *European Tourism, Literature and the Ways to Culture, 1800–1918* (Oxford: Clarendon Press, 1993). For a critical and theoretical discussion of the traveller/tourist distinction, see Dean MacCannell, *The Tourist: A New Theory of the Leisure Class* (New York: Schocken, 1976) and *Empty Meeting Grounds: The Tourist Papers* (London and New York: Routledge, 1992).

[20]   As John Urry explains, this 'childlike' characteristic is especially prominent in tour groups: 'One is told where to go, how long to go for, when one can eat, how long one has to visit the toilet, and so on' (*The Tourist Gaze: Leisure and Travel in Contemporary Societies* (London: Sage, 1990), p. 101).

British tourists: 'As we skidded to a stop in the gravelled tourist park, monstrous coaches with gaping exhaust pipes, like colossal colons, were spewing forth their noxious waste. Phalanxes of lard-white sightseers spilled out of their air-conditioned capsules through tinted double doors, all of them skimplily clad even though it was not yet hot.'[21] Likewise, during Bill Bryson's hiking trip along the Appalachian Trail in *A Walk in the Woods* (1998), he describes a group of greedy American tourists invading the Smokey Mountain National Park: 'crowds of overweight tourists in boisterous clothes, with cameras bouncing on their bellies, consuming ice-creams, cotton candy and corn dogs, sometimes simultaneously ... throngs of pear-shaped people in Reeboks wandered between food smells, clutching grotesque comestibles and bucket-sized soft-drinks.'[22] Because Dew and Bryson are embarrassed that these creatures are from their own countries (Britain and America respectively), they make great efforts to differentiate themselves from the awkward behaviour of their fellow citizens.

Instead of the contrived situations experienced by tourists, travel writers insist that they are involved in journeys of their own making – their itineraries are prepared so as *not* to participate in common tourist practices. As much as possible, travel writers move 'off the beaten track' and thus outside the convenience, familiarity and mechanics of the constructed tourist gaze. It is not that travel writers do not experience the Eiffel Tower or the Pyramids, but the act of 'travelling' requires a certain independence and autonomy that mass tourism does not allow. By marking themselves off as travellers and not tourists, travel writers maintain the belief that they are escaping the already-scripted nature of tourism and engaging with a much more *genuine* reality than the one constructed through the tourist gaze. It is only the subject position of the travel writer that has access to 'real' difference, whereas tourists are not willing to be deprived of comfort and leisure in their collective encounters with difference. As journalist and travel writer Robert Kaplan states, 'I wanted to map the future, perhaps the "deep future", by ignoring what was legally and officially there and, instead, touching, feeling, and smelling what was really *there*.'[23] And this is the key: to claim the identity of a travel writer is to separate yourself from the

---

[21] Josie Dew, *The Wind in my Wheels: Travel Tales from the Saddle* (London: Little Brown and Co. Ltd., 1992), p. 30.

[22] Bill Bryson, *A Walk in the Woods* (London: Doubleday, 1997; reprint, London: Black Swan Books, 1998), p. 139.

[23] Robert Kaplan, *The Ends of the Earth: As a Journey at the Dawn of the Twenty-First Century* (London: Macmillan Papermac, 1997), p. 6 (italics his).

'hordes' of tourists — it is to be a modern-day pioneer, adventurer, explorer, moving ever closer to the *real* world. As Tisdale explains:

This isn't something most travellers will admit, but they know that if you really want to stand out in a strange place, show up late and on foot. Act according to the belief that the locals will want to get to know you as much as you hope to get to know them. The single traveller, the one with the small backpack and the notebook, the one looking for the 'real' Java, the 'real' Sudan, wants something the tour group does not. He wants to be the centre of attention; he yearns to be taken behind the scenes. Knowing he can't 'pass' as a local, the traveller (credit card and all) tries to pass as something else — a pilgrim, a nomad, ever on the move, belonging to no one.[24]

This quest for 'the real' is echoed by travel writer Robert Stone: 'I felt that wherever authenticity resided, it must be elsewhere. And needless to say, I was in search of authenticity. What else is there?'[25] Travel writers disdain tourists because they cannot tell the difference between 'authentic' cultural difference (e.g. a 'real' voodoo ritual in rural Haiti) and 'staged' cultural difference put on for their benefit (e.g. an evening of 'voodoo culture' at the Hilton Hotel in Port-au-Prince). Illustrating how tourists allow themselves to be fooled by 'fake' displays of cultural difference is crucial in the identity formation of travel writers: it allows them to take comfort in their moral superiority, and continue to believe that they, alone, are intrepid explorers experiencing authentic encounters with other cultures.[26]

Travel writers are able to pursue authenticity while distinguishing themselves from tourists because they have a certain freedom in solitude: travel writers deliberately move alone, and through alternative and lesser-known circuits. For example, when travel writer Monica Furlong plans her journey through the Australian outback in *Flight of the Kingfisher* (1996), she believes that her independent route will get her closer to Aboriginal culture: 'There were, of course, "tours" which would take me to Kakadu, say, and give me a "taste" of Aboriginal life while smoothing out the awkwardness for me. Maybe it was snobbery,

---

[24] Tisdale, 'Never Let the Locals', p. 72.
[25] Robert Stone, as quoted in Russell Banks, Jan Morris, Robert Stone and William Styron, 'Itchy Feet and Pencils: A Symposium', *New York Times Book Review*, Vol. 96, 18 August 1991, p. 24.
[26] The relationship between cultural difference, authenticity and tourism is discussed in Dean MacCannell, 'Staged Authenticity', in *The Tourist*, pp. 91–107. In *Empty Meeting Grounds*, MacCannell develops this idea and sees the pilgrimage of the modern tourist in the following terms: 'A secondary effect of the alleged globalization of relations is the production of an enormous desire for, and corresponding commodification of, *authenticity*' (pp. 169–70).

but the idea made me uneasy.'[27] Travel writers like Furlong are made anxious by the thought of not being able to gain independent access to authenticity and translate it on their own terms – to give up on the quest for authenticity makes travel writers exactly like tourists. But as travel writer Katherine Govier explains during her journey in Morocco, the circuitry of mass tourism is almost impossible to escape:

Sometimes the apparatus of travel overwhelms the event. There are trips when I feel that everything set in place to facilitate tourists is in fact preventing me from seeing the place the way I want to see it. The journey becomes a game of fox and hounds as I try to escape the tour operators, translators, souvenir sellers, crowds, staged events, and advice givers of all kinds to discover the 'real' Japan, Hong Kong, or, in this case, Morocco.[28]

What is particularly significant about Govier's desire to escape the tourist circuit is her sense that it is always encroaching on her 'real' experience. The touch of paranoia here is telling, because it reveals that travel writers are losing the 'game of fox and hounds' with tourists. While many travel writers lament the growth of the tourist industry – for it takes them further away from their colonial predecessors – others see it as an inevitable consequence of globalisation and no longer bother to maintain their distance from tourism. This decision is born out of necessity rather than desire, as many travel writers realise that globalisation has made the intrepid traveller all but obsolete. In effect, it is a futile exercise to get 'off' the beaten track because the world has already been discovered.

In *Neither Here Nor There: Travels in Europe*, Bill Bryson is happy to place himself alongside other tourists – in trains, at tourist offices, in hotels, at restaurants and at various tourist sites. Indeed, Bryson spends much of his time in Europe augmenting his collection of kitsch tourist souvenirs: 'I have a certain weakness for tacky memorabilia...One of the worst parts about living in the 1990s is that crappy souvenirs are *so* hard to find these days.'[29] But even as Bryson jokes his way through the European tourist circuit, he is also worried about what the onslaught of tourism is doing to the places he wants to visit:

It is of course hypocritical to rail against tourists when you are one yourself, but none the less you can't escape the fact that mass tourism is ruining the very things it wants to celebrate. And it can only get worse as the Japanese and other

---

[27] Monica Furlong, *Flight of the Kingfisher: A Journey among the Kukatja Aborigines* (London: HarperCollins Publishers, 1996), p. 20.
[28] Katherine Govier, 'In Fez without a Guide', in Katherine Govier, ed., *Without a Guide: Contemporary Women's Travel Adventures* (Toronto: Macfarlane, Walter and Ross, 1994), p. 89.
[29] Bryson, *Neither Here Nor There*, pp. 172–3.

rich Asians become bolder travellers. When you add in the tens of millions of eastern Europeans who are free at last to go where they want, we could be looking back on the last thirty years as a golden age of travel. God help us all.[30]

Bryson accepts that he is a tourist, but simultaneously laments the growth of the tourist industry. He is happy to enjoy the benefits that tourism brings but is worried that some tourists – Japanese, rich Asians, Eastern Europeans – will not respect other cultures in the same way that he does. Rather than portray himself as an intrepid traveller who disdains other tourists, Bryson recognises his own participation in the tourist industry and engages in a more subtle form of projection. He can no longer negatively position the tourist without coming off as a hypocrite, but he can certainly secure his own position as a 'good' tourist by making judgements about the 'bad' tourist behaviour of others. When wandering through the streets in Paris, Bryson is sympathetic to locals who have to deal with the 'bad' tourists who infiltrate the city in the summer months. Speaking of the apartments overlooking Notre Dame, Bryson states: 'I cannot imagine tiring of that view, though I suppose in August when the streets are clogged with tour buses and a million tourists in Bermuda shorts that SHOUT, the sense of favoured ecstasy may flag.'[31] Despite his recognition that the traveller/tourist distinction is problematic, Bryson continues to employ the identity/difference logic by positioning himself as a 'good' tourist, and others as 'bad' tourists. What this suggests is that cosmopolitan travel writers no longer claim the privileged position of traveller, but they do claim to be *ethical* tourists: they want to learn about difference, protect the environment and respect the cultural heritage of the local communities they visit. To the extent that others are doing the same, they can be part of the same community as the travel writer; to the extent that others contravene those ethical principles and behave badly, they can be derided, mocked and insulted. Bryson is often magnanimous in his descriptions of others who share his passion for the 'right' way to travel, that is, those that share his values. To be sure, there will always be fat, unprepared, culturally ignorant tourists to poke fun at (the 'bad' tourists), but Bryson holds open the possibility that other travellers might share his approach to travel – they might be 'good' tourists. What is interesting about Bryson's distinction between good and bad tourism is that it reveals the same process of subjectification that has always secured the travel writer: it projects difference onto others. But somehow, the 'bad' tourist-as-other does not quite satisfy the travel writer's desire for authenticity – in order to secure

---

[30] Bryson, *Neither Here Nor There*, p. 199.
[31] Bryson, *Neither Here Nor There*, p. 50.

his/her subject position properly, the travel writer requires a more *concrete* example of otherness. Enter the 'real' other.

The exotic and the celebrated

Tourists are different, but not different enough: they don't exhibit the obvious traces of the exotic and the primitive that travel writers require as markers of difference. The subject position of the travel writer is secured to an even greater extent when it can project excessive difference onto the foreign subjects who live elsewhere.[32] In effect, the more difference displayed by locals, the more authentic the encounter is. Once Josie Dew arrives in North Africa, she finally confronts the 'real' otherness she came looking for:

Within moments we were engulfed by a crowd of boisterous, bare-footed youngsters dressed in clothes that people back home would use only for wiping oily hands. Many had open sores (a magnet for flies) and filthy faces, with noses that had never been wiped.... we found a small hotel but it provided no respite from the clamouring crowds. It was full of noisy and continuously hawking locals who banged relentlessly on our door and shouted and shrieked through the broken window.[33]

It is not difficult to see how the identity/difference logic works here: Dew secures her position as the morally enlightened and superior traveller by depicting the locals as cartoonish, primitive beasts. But Dew is an amateur of negative projection when compared with a master like Theroux. His depiction of the 'weedy' Mexican garlic seller is only the beginning: throughout his train journey in Asia, the Iranians are 'stupid starved creatures', Afghans are 'lazy, idle, and violent', the Singhalese are 'idle, stumbling and negligent', and Bengalis are 'irritable, talkative, dogmatic, arrogant, and humourless'.[34] For Theroux, others are at their

---

[32] Holland and Huggan argue that judgements of others work to remind readers of the superiority of the travel writer's own culture: the 'English Gentleman Abroad' is 'an avid student and consumer of other, mostly non-European cultures whose impressive erudition affords another reminder of the imagined superiority of his own imperial national culture' (*Tourists with Typewriters*, p. 28). Sally Tisdale agrees when she argues that contemporary travel writers express 'a collision of British gentility with the primitive world' ('Never Let the Locals', p. 70).

[33] Dew, *Wind in My Wheels*, pp. 38, 49.

[34] Theroux, *The Great Railway Bazaar*, pp. 63, 72, 155, 176. Theroux's interactions with others occur most often in the form of a rude interrogation that displays little sensitivity for others. For example, he repeatedly questions the mysterious and elusive Duffill in their dark compartment on the way to Turkey (p. 16), he pesters Indian writer V. G. Deshmukh on his views about poverty (p. 122), he badgers and patronises the family planning officers from Bangladesh and suggests that they are elitist hypocrites (pp. 226–9) and he mocks Mr Watanabe's 'Engrish' in Sapporo (pp. 282–3).

most primitive and ignorant when they fail to achieve the self-consciousness and individuality so central to modern subjectivity. The Japanese are the worst offenders in this sense, as their inability to think for themselves makes them almost inhuman: 'The strong impression I had was of a people who acted together because of a preconceived plan: a people programmed. You see them queuing automatically in the subway, naturally forming lines at ticket counters and machines, and it is difficult to avoid the conclusion that the people all have printed circuits.'[35] Theroux's self-consciousness and independent mind allow him to locate, translate and interpret foreign cultures through the universal logic of identity/difference: others are always different, and always inferior.

Theroux's skill at rendering the foreign in familiar terms takes precedence over any other interpretation – especially those expressed by locals. This effort of 'writing over' the other is exemplified when Theroux travels to Jaipur, India, and enlists the help of Mr Gopal, an incompetent and ignorant local guide:

He had ridiculed the handbook I had been carrying around: 'You have this big book, but I tell you to close it and leave it at hotel because Jaipur is like open book to me.' Unwisely, I had taken his advice . . .

'Whose is it [the fortress]?'

'The Maharajah's.'

'No, who built it?'

'You would not know his name.'

'Do *you?*'

Mr Gopal walked on . . .

'What's this?' I asked. I hated him for making me leave my handbook behind . . .

Mr Gopal was doing his best, but he was a hard man to escape from. So far I had been travelling alone with my handbook and my Western Railway timetable; I was happiest finding my own way and did not require a liaison man . . .

Outside the museum I said, 'When was this built?'

'About fifteen fifty.'

He hadn't hesitated. But today I had my handbook. The building he had placed in the mid-sixteenth century was the Albert Hall, started in 1878 and finished in 1887. In 1550 Jaipur did not exist, though I didn't have the heart to tell that to Mr Gopal, who had sulked when I contradicted him the previous day. Anyway, a weakness for exaggeration seemed a chronic affliction of some Indians.[36]

[35] Theroux, *The Great Railway Bazaar*, p. 270.
[36] Theroux, *The Great Railway Bazaar*, pp. 124–7.

As a modern subject who possesses the self-consciousness and individuality needed to translate Jaipur through more universal categories,
Theroux's 'foreign' interpretation transcends Mr Gopal's 'local' knowledge. Although Theroux is a foreigner, he is an enlightened traveller
whose self-possession allows him to place the sites of Jaipur – its
fortresses, its museums – on a *universal* scale of world history. Theroux's
subject position as an omniscient travel writer explaining cultural
artefacts of universal interest is guaranteed by his denigration of Mr
Gopal's local knowledge and behaviour. Subjects like Mr Gopal lack the
ability to locate and understand their own existence within the universal
categories of 'history', 'politics' and 'culture'. Indeed, ignorance about
one's position in the wider world expresses a lack of understanding of
what it means to be civilised. For Theroux, the primitive attachment to
locality is evidence of a superstitious mind that is not fully conscious of
what 'the world' consists of. In other words, subjects who do not
appreciate their own heritage, people who cannot attach their own
history, politics and culture to the wider world, are people of an inferior
civilisation.

Given the general ignorance of Mr Gopal, Theroux's refusal to
admonish him reveals another facet of the coloniser/colonised binary.
Because the other is primitive and ignorant, he/she must be taken care of
and guided in a paternal manner towards the enlightenment possessed
by the civilised travel writer. In this way, the supposed 'ignorance' of
primitive others can be understood through a more romantic vision:
locals are not superstitious, but are 'noble savages' that remind the
Western world of what it has lost in its pursuit of modernity. Although
describing the travelogues of George Woodcock, the following description applies equally to writers like Theroux:

he is, in the main, travelling to the least, not the best developed parts of the
earth. He always seems to be searching for evidence that other supposedly
primitive people have clung to some organic wisdom we lost long ago, about how
to live together without creating institutions which harm us. It's also no
coincidence that he writes mostly...about places once colonized by the
European powers, for it's the survival of the genuine against all odds that
intrigues him most.[37]

Romanticising the other is the flip side to colonial judgements: instead of
reading the ignorance of others negatively, better to read it as an
expression of ancient wisdom that has been lost in the modern world.
In this case, others should be valued because they are closer to the

---

[37] Douglas Fetherling, 'George Woodcock: A Graceful Voyager on a Road Well-
Travelled', *Globe and Mail*, 1 May 1993, p. C9.

mysteries of nature, spirituality and the universe. This romantic paradigm characterised many colonial travelogues: others were figures to be subjugated and governed by a 'sovereign Western ego', but they were also figures of great mystery, to be discovered, honoured, gazed upon and wondered at. What makes travelogues – both colonial and contemporary – provocative translations of difference is that others are rendered in contradictory ways. This juxtaposition of difference as both inferior and romantic is evident in Dew's text when she cycles further into the 'heart' of Africa. While the North Africans contravened her European notions of civility, Dew changes her tune when she encounters the 'wondrous land of the Tuaregs – the Blue Men of the desert'. Much like the nomads in Bruce Chatwin's *The Songlines*, the Tuareg are idealised:

These tall, elegant, light-skinned desert warriors wrap themselves from tip to toe in indigo-dyed robes, however hot it might be ... The dye from the robes rubs off and becomes ingrained in their skin, giving them a blue sheen. The Tuaregs are pure-blooded Berbers, and a remote and mystical race to Arabs as well as Europeans; townspeople speak of them in wonder, in fear and usually with much ignorance.[38]

In Dew's narrative, the Tuareg become something to marvel at rather than disdain, especially as they are 'pure-blooded' others. Unlike the previous others encountered by Dew – the hawking, clamouring, filthy lot in North Africa – the Tuaregs are 'elegant', 'mystical' and romantic. Dew's projection of 'romanticised Africans' is repeated in the travelogue of another modern-day adventuress – Ffyona Campbell's *On Foot through Africa*. During a moment of rest from her trans-continental trek, Campbell contemplates the women who live by the Niger River:

Here I met many Fulani women, exquisitely colourful and poised. They are fine, elegant women bedecked with silver coins on their heads, with necklaces and bracelets. Their legs are shiny mahogany and do not wobble as they walk; even their calves are rigid. The Fulani are such a gentle people; in their presence you feel deeply relaxed, almost sleepy.[39]

However, like Dew, Campbell projects otherness in contradictory ways. Her romantic interpretation of the Fulani women contrasts sharply with her descriptions of the local children who taunt her as she walks through African villages: 'They'd intimidate me, bait me, scream in my ears ... The pressure was on to calm them, but they didn't want to be calmed, not like the ones down south who'd never

---

[38] Dew, *Wind in My Wheels*, p. 178.
[39] Ffyona Campbell, *On Foot through Africa* (London: Orion, 1994), p. 283.

seen whites.'[40] Others are ignorant, threatening and sometimes violent, or they are majestic, calm and beautiful. And it is this juxtaposition that Theroux, Dew and Campbell have in common: they resuscitate the coloniser/colonised framework precisely because it allows them to project difference in such a variety of ways. Others can be located anywhere on the continuum between fear and desire – objects of such ignorance and primitivity that harsh judgements are justified, or objects of such mystery and beauty that a form of idealisation is warranted.

The continuum of fear and desire is transformed in cosmopolitan travel writing that works against the imperial gaze of colonial narratives. Rather than revive the coloniser/colonised framework like Theroux, Dew and Campbell, cosmopolitan travel writers place cultural difference on a plane of equivalence – they locate, administer and celebrate difference within an accepted global order. Travel writers like Theroux who revive the imperial gaze see no change in the generic form of the travelogue, no matter who is doing the writing. However, cosmopolitan travel writers take the democratisation of the genre seriously: it *does* matter who is doing the writing, especially when it comes to resisting the colonial heritage of the genre. Indeed, it is those who have been objectified most by travel writing who must be welcomed into the genre in order to resist its continuing colonial ethos. One of the most intriguing inversions of the coloniser/colonised framework is Tété-Michel Kpomassie's *An African in Greenland* (1983) in which a 'colonised' subject from Togo takes hold of the reins of representation and inhabits the subject position of the travel writer. Many colonial travelogues provide detailed descriptions of the travel writer being the 'first white man' in a foreign country – a sentiment echoed forcefully in Campbell's walk through Africa. But this trope is inverted in Kpomassie's narrative when he describes the reactions of the locals when he arrives in Greenland (see figure 1).[41] While he admits that some of the children were frightened ('others began to scream with

---

[40] Ffyona Campbell, *The Whole Story: A Walk around the World* (London: Orion, 1996), p. 195. *The Whole Story* is a collection of all of Campbell's walks around the world, which includes her trek in Africa.

[41] Kpomassie is not the first African in Greenland. As anthropologist Jean Malaurie explains in the preface to *An African in Greenland*, the first person of African ancestry to visit Greenland was Matt Hensen (Mattipaluk) who accompanied Admiral Peary on the search for the North Pole. As well, Greenland's south-west coast was visited by black soldiers and freed slaves who worked the whaling ships, as well as black soldiers during the Second World War. Malaurie sees Kpomassie as unique because he is 'the first African to choose that country and make his own way there – the representative of a new Africa, eager for discovery and even for expansion': 'Preface', in Tété-Michel Kpomassie, *An African in Greenland*, trans. James Kirkup (New York: Harcourt Brace Jovanovich, 1983), pp. xiv–xv.

Figure 1. Kpomassie with children, *An African in Greenland*, p. 166

fright or to weep'), he is more concerned with expressing the friendli-
ness of the Greenlanders (they thought he was handsome), their
warmth (they were impressed with his height) and their hospitality (he
is accompanied into town by a police escort and a procession of
children).[42] The Greenlanders' fascination with Kpomassie continues
throughout the narrative – at one point he is woken up in the middle of
the night by a bearded man who runs his fingers through Kpomassie's
hair, saying 'Pretty! Pretty!' in Inuit.[43]

Particularly significant in Kpomassie's narrative are the connections
he makes with the indigenous Eskimo of Greenland, and the solidarity
he feels with them in relation to colonial power. For example, recalling
his own education in Togo, he criticises the Danish teachers who favour
teaching European history over native Eskimo culture in the local
schools.[44] As Frances Bartkowski explains, Kpomassie's solidarity with
the Eskimo complicates any simple translation of the coloniser/colonised
framework:

Kpomassie realizes early that in going to the north the indigenous people he will
encounter are, like himself, people of colour whose conditions of existence have
been shaped by white dominance – by Scandinavians, more specifically. And he

---

[42] Kpomassie, *An African in Greenland*, pp. 80–1. See also Frances Bartkowski's analysis
of this passage in *Travelers, Immigrants, Inmates: Essays in Estrangement* (Minneapolis:
University of Minnesota Press, 1995), pp. 73–5.
[43] Kpomassie, *An African in Greenland*, p. 106.
[44] Kpomassie, *An African in Greenland*, p. 119.

will be very attentive to how the cultural practices that are indigenous and therefore seem strange to him resemble aspects of his own culture left behind.[45]

Kpomassie's expressions of solidarity with the indigenous Greenlanders resemble Rushdie's sympathies with the Sandinistas – there is a shared recognition of what it means to live under the 'descending heel' of colonial rule. Because they have first-hand experience of the legacy of Empire, writers like Kpomassie and Rushdie are especially attuned to the continued workings of colonial power. What is more significant, however, is how these writers disrupt the automatic transposition of an identity/difference logic onto a coloniser/colonised framework: they occupy *both* sides of the identity/difference logic. Their first-hand experience of Empire has placed them at the receiving end of colonial power (i.e. they have been produced as subjects marked by difference), but their position as travel writers gives them the power to project their own categories of difference (i.e. their identity is secured by marking out others). And herein lies the difficulty: even in travelogues written by previously colonised others, the projection of difference does not abate. As the preface to *An African in Greenland* explains, he is not above using his position as coloniser of a foreign land: '[Kpomassie] enjoyed giving free rein to certain deep-seated tendencies to dominate, to possess – in short, to play the king a little.'[46] It is both uncomfortable and revealing when Kpomassie escapes his usual confines as a colonised subject, and starts to take on board behaviour previously restricted to colonial powers (e.g. sleeping with local women, moralising about locals, capitalising on his 'natural aristocracy' by 'playing the king a little').[47]

An African in Greenland exemplifies the anxiety caused when travel writers simultaneously occupy *both* positions of the coloniser/colonised framework. But this hybrid position shifts our analysis in an important way: when subjects are no longer contained within specific positions of difference, the category of 'identity' must be re-imagined.

---

[45] Bartkowski, *Travelers, Immigrants, Inmates*, p. 75.
[46] Malaurie, 'Preface', *An African in Greenland*, p. xv; also quoted in Bartkowski, *Travelers, Immigrants, Inmates*, p. 164, n. 3.
[47] The sexual interludes of this text are particularly complex, as Kpomassie does not go looking for sex directly, but instead is offered various women by their fathers, brothers or husbands. More interesting here are the comments by anthropologist Jean Malaurie in response to Kpomassie's 'indiscretions'. As a young researcher, Malaurie 'always refrained' from these sexual offers in Greenland, but he goes on to comment: 'This book is perhaps the proof that two peoples who have both lived under the rule of whites are joined by deep elective affinities. It may be objected that it is a pity to see them expressing themselves here in an orgiastic context, drunk on beer; but ... are we not now witnessing the desperate quest for a lost psychological, cultural, and telluric unity?' ('Preface', *An African in Greenland*, p. xvi).

In other words, we move from external projections of difference (the subjectification of others) to internal constructions of the identity (the subjection of the self). As Kpomassie's narrative reveals, it is not only the depiction of others (e.g. tourists, locals) that is being re-imagined through the democratisation of the genre – it is also the depiction of the travel writer. How then, is the 'democratised' subject position of the travel writer produced as a coherent self in the face of difference?

Securing the self

Solitude and co-dependence

Amidst narratives of escape and transformation, travel writers assure us that even in the most far-flung reaches of the planet, it is possible – and even necessary – to retain a coherent sense of self. In many ways, foreign travel is the ultimate test and affirmation of coherent subjectivity: the logic of identity/difference is so powerful that it regulates us even when we are tempted by the possibilities of becoming someone else when travelling. This gathering of many possibilities into a coherent 'monarch-of-all-I-survey' position is exemplified by the narrative techniques of the travel writer. Todorov argues that modern 'impressionistic' texts indicate that travel writers are 'turning inward' and describing foreign lands in an entirely subjective manner. With the loss of universal standards (for all standards are now recognised as culturally specific) there was nowhere else for the travel writer to go – all observations of cultural difference must be based on personal rather than universal criteria. But Todorov's impressionistic model is particularly limited in its understanding of subjectivity, for contemporary travel writers do not simply conceal themselves behind superficial observations, they also reveal themselves through complicated narrative mechanisms. While Todorov is right to argue that objectivity is lost to contemporary travel writers, this does not automatically produce a wholesale indulgence of subjective, personal anecdotes. In effect, the balancing act between fact and fiction forces the travel writer to manage his/her subject position according to a powerful public/private distinction. Travel writers construct themselves as 'public' figures who form impressions about a place by revealing only selected and strategic aspects of their 'private' selves.

Despite being the principal figure in the text and the character with the most chances to reveal personal information, Theroux offers remarkably little of his life outside his role as a travel writer. His other commitments are only revealed to the extent that they converge with a double purpose: to travel and to write. For example, in *The Great Railway Bazaar*, his 'other life' is positioned as background information, as something he is escaping for a while: 'I was doing a bunk, myself. I hadn't nailed my colours to the mast; I had no job – no one would notice me falling silent, kissing my wife, and boarding the 15:30 alone'.[48] The reader gets little information on his life as a teacher, a husband or a father – these are stories for another genre perhaps, but not for the travelogue. While Theroux's private life is silenced, his public persona is crafted according to the solitude, autonomy and independence that characterised travel writing during the interwar years – what Fussell calls the 'golden age of travel writing'. Fussell's admiration of Evelyn Waugh, Graham Greene, Wilfred Thesiger, Eric Newby and Robert Byron extends to Theroux because he embodies the 'internal freedom and philosophical courage' necessary to undertake a solo journey and express it in writing.[49] At the very beginning of *The Great Railway Bazaar*, Theroux boards the Orient Express and reveals his idea of solitude: 'the conceit of the long-distance traveller is the belief that he is going so far, he will be alone – inconceivable that another person has the same good idea'.[50] In effect, the solo traveller is the ultimate modern subject: alone amongst foreign people, successfully negotiating an unfamiliar environment, ruminating on the condition of exile and ultimately testing the limits of his/her subject position in the face of difference. In this sense, Theroux's 'public' persona is secured not only by his relentless projections of difference, but also by an effacement of his private life. Within his travel writing, Theroux's other 'private' identities (husband, father, and teacher) as well as his personal experiences (growing up in New England) are always subordinate to his identity as a modern travel writer in control of the text.

The coherence of this public identity is ultimately confirmed when the travel writer returns home safely intact – even stronger as a result of

---

[48] Theroux, *The Great Railway Bazaar*, p. 2. Personal information is very scarce in this narrative, for example the reader only works out that Theroux is thirty-two years old when he reveals a childhood memory in Burma (p. 199). Theroux's personal feelings about *The Great Railway Bazaar* are revealed in another generic form, in this case a short essay called 'First Train Journey', *Granta*, Vol. 29, Winter 1989 (*New World*), pp. 167–72. Here we get some more background information about the book (e.g. discussions with publishers, the process of writing, his financial advance), but only brief glimpses of his 'other selves': 'I hated leaving my family behind in London. I had never taken such a trip, I felt encumbered by an advance on royalties – modest though it was; most of my writer friends mocked the idea' (p. 170).

[49] Fussell goes on to describe these heroes at length calling them useful antidotes to the 'pusillanimous' nature of modern man; see *Abroad*, p. 203.

[50] Theroux, *The Great Railway Bazaar*, p. 9.

being tested by the hardships of travel.[51] Travel writers often end their narratives with lessons learnt on the road. This is the case with *Tracks*, Robyn Davidson's critically acclaimed story of her journey across the Australian outback with three camels and a dog (Davidson was the first female winner of the Thomas Cook Travel Book Award in 1980). When she finally reaches the Pacific Ocean, Davidson reveals the lessons she learned on her Camel Trek: 'The two most important things that I did learn were that you are as powerful and strong as you allow yourself to be, and that the most difficult part of any endeavour is taking the first step, making the first decision.'[52] The experience of overcoming hardship on the road makes the travel writer more heroic, more resilient and more confident in his/her judgements of the world. The resolution at the end of Davidson's book is mirrored at the end of Nick Danziger's *Danziger's Travels*. After arduous journeys in difficult places like the Middle East, Danziger returns home to offer the following:

Why have I said all this? Probably just to set the record straight. I have yet to feel any sense of accomplishment. The most important thing for me is the knowledge that I have tried my best, and attempted to stick to my principles and retain my integrity. What I brought back, and what I want to communicate, is the greatest reward travel can give you: understanding.[53]

Danziger's subject position is characterised by predetermined 'principles' and 'integrity' that have passed the test of the journey. Brave in the face of difference, he is the perfect vehicle for transmitting important 'universal truths' to the public — in this case, messages of global understanding. While the subject position of the travel writer is certainly expanded by its encounter with foreignness, it is never disrupted or dislodged from its own parameters of solitude and autonomy. Although Danziger's message of understanding comes at the end of the book, it arises from the 'principles' and 'integrity' that he set off with. So while Danzinger might confront a variety of trials and tribulations en route, and some of those tests might prompt him to question his behaviour, nothing encountered by Danziger will shake his confidence. Travel writers can learn lessons, and they can submit themselves to tests

---

[51] One strategy used by travel writers to prove a coherence to their identities is to confirm their genealogical heritage by following in the footsteps of an ancestor. This strategy characterises the motivations of both Theroux and Chatwin as they travel to Patagonia: Theroux following in his Italian grandfather's footsteps, and Chatwin pursuing the origin of a Mylodon skin sent by his eccentric cousin; see Bruce Chatwin and Paul Theroux, *Patagonia Revisited* (London: Picador and Jonathan Cape, 1985), pp. 12–17.

[52] Robyn Davidson, *Tracks* (London: Picador, 1980), p. 254.

[53] Nick Danziger, *Danziger's Travels*, quoted in Geoff Barton, ed., *Travel Writing: Oxford Literary Resources* (Oxford: Oxford University Press, 1993), p. 121.

(e.g. eating dog, climbing mountains, sleeping with local women), but in order to survive the encounter with difference, the autonomy of the travel writer can never be compromised.

The idea of travel as a rite of passage secures the subject position of the travel writer most explicitly because it dovetails with the narrative structure of travel writing itself. It is easy to see how the subject position of the travel writer goes through a complicated process of unravelling and coming together so that by the end of the narrative, the writer returns home wiser, more knowledgeable and certainly more stable. But that 'unravelling' is carefully controlled by the narrative voice so that the public self of the travel writer is never really dislodged. At the end of *The Great Railway Bazaar*, Theroux carefully stages a brief episode of depression, only to restore it immediately as the journey comes to an end. After days on the Trans-Siberian train, Theroux takes to getting drunk alone in his room and venturing out for the 'greasy stews' of the dining car, arguments about politics and the opportunity to kiss a Russian cook called Nina. But at the end of this brief episode, Theroux quickly restores himself with the thought of home and the resolution of his unhappiness: 'I felt flayed by the four months of train travel: it was as if I had undergone some harrowing cure, sickening myself on my addiction in order to be free of it. To invert the cliché, I had had a bellyful of travelling hopefully – I wanted to arrive.'[54] Like Davidson and Danziger, Theroux's subject position is restored completely by his arrival home:

My book is about my trip, not yours or anyone else's. If someone had come with me and written a book about the trip, it would have been a different book from mine...A travel book, I had discovered, was a deliberate act – like the act of travel itself. It took health and strength and confidence. When I finished a novel I never knew whether I would be able to write another one. But I knew, when I finished my first travel book, that I would be able to do it again.[55]

The resolution and confirmation of the self at the end of the travelogue alleviates Theroux's initial anxieties about switching genres. Travel writing, unlike novel writing, actually strengthens one's identity because the hardships of travel force the writer to hone his/her individuality in the face of difference and unfamiliarity.

But what happens to the confident travel writer who does not reproduce a public/private split? What happens when travel writers are much more open about the negotiation of their public and private selves? Cosmopolitan travel writers resist the public/private split just as

[54] Theroux, *The Great Railway Bazaar*, p. 341.
[55] Theroux, 'First Train Journey', pp. 171–2.

they resist the coloniser/colonised framework: by revealing more information about their private selves, thoughts and imaginings, they are able to re-imagine the logic of identity/difference on more equivalent terms. Instead of the blank canvas of Theroux's private life, many cosmopolitan travel writers are happy to augment their travelogues with personal anecdotes, memories and experiences in the hope of providing a context for their interpretations of cultural difference. Their claims are always relative rather than universal (e.g. '*I* don't like Canadians, but *you* have every right to'), and any subjective commentary is explained and justified with reference to a personal history (e.g. 'I don't like Canadians because their earnest need to be liked is an affront to my notions of autonomy and independence'). In his travelogue *The Place Where Souls Are Born*, Thomas Keneally is open about how his interpretations of the American Southwest are shaped by his Australian identity. In the introduction to the book, travel writer Jan Morris explains Keneally's position: 'he is a New Man in the southwest, bringing to its mountains, deserts, and pueblos comparisons born out of the Outback and the aboriginal encampment'.[56] Indeed, Keneally's references to, and comparisons with, Australia litter the book, and he is intrigued as much by America's physical difference as its 'inveigling similarity' to Australia (e.g. the geological extremities of Colorado and Utah are compared to Ayers Rock, the ski-lift operators at Vail to the surfers Down Under, and the Ute, Navajo, Hopi and Anasazi Indians to the Aboriginals of Australia). But Keneally is not just explicit about his position as an Australian; he is also open about the fact that he is making this journey with his wife and daughter. He discusses his interactions with them throughout the narrative (e.g. 'Aerobics at high and lovely altitudes have a very humanizing influence on a marriage' and 'I found myself frequently confessing to my wife and daughter that certain places in the Southwest produce in me a kind of immensity phobia').[57] While the wife and daughter are never discussed at great length, Keneally's efforts to include them in the narrative remind the reader that he is not overly concerned with projecting an image of solitude and autonomy. In this way, Keneally's subject position is 'open-minded': he is aware of how his Australianness, as well as his personal relationships, shape his interpretation of the American Southwest. Unlike Theroux, Keneally does not conceal his multiple identities, nor does he make lofty claims about truth and objectivity. Having said that,

---

[56] Jan Morris, 'Introduction', in Thomas Keneally, *The Place Where Souls Are Born: A Journey into the American Southwest* (London: Sceptre, 1992), p. xiv.
[57] Keneally, *The Place Where Souls Are Born*, pp. 13, 47.

his 'open-ended' subject position does have its limits. His refusal to let his wife and daughter speak for themselves, let alone really appear in the narrative, suggests an awkward understanding of gender. Does Keneally's position as 'a New Man in the Southwest' include a respect for gender difference as well as cultural difference? Or is there something essentially masculine in Keneally's 'open-ended' persona?

Macho men, honorary men and new men

The public persona of the travel writer is empowered by a masculine, rational and aggressive organising scheme that succeeds to the extent that it writes over feminine characteristics in the self and in others.[58] It is masculinity that marks the travel writer out as independent: it differentiates travel writers from passive groups of tourists, it gives them the objectivity through which they can identify and dominate difference, and it helps them repress any feminine characteristics that might reveal weakness on the journey. To avoid complex and ambiguous encounters with racial and gendered others, many travel writers resort to hyper-masculine adventures in foreign lands to fulfil a predestined 'rite-of-passage'. Perhaps the Amazon has been navigated already, and perhaps even navigated by boat, but not single-handedly in a fibreglass kayak; or perhaps the Sahara has been crossed, and perhaps it has even been crossed in a jeep, but it hasn't been crossed solo, on foot, in less than 'x' number of days. Travel writers can no longer have that treasured moment of being first anywhere, but they can certainly be the first to prove their masculinity by travelling in a dangerous, brave or impossible way.[59] By embracing masculinity, travel writers regain the power to be first, to be tough, to be adventurous in the face of a world already discovered and domesticated. Tim Cahill's book *Road Fever: A High-Speed Travelogue* is an account of his record-breaking 15,000-mile drive from the tip of Patagonia to the tip of Alaska. He and 'professional endurance driver' Garry Sowerby (who has done several high-speed

[58] I have pursued questions of gender, subjectivity, performance and travel writing in much more detail in 'Gender at a Distance: Identity, Performance and Contemporary Travel Writing', *International Feminist Journal of Politics*, Vol. 1, No. 1, June 1999, pp. 66–88. The arguments about gender in this chapter are related to that piece but are more directed to the tensions that arise when masculinity and femininity are translated through a cosmopolitan framework. For a general overview of travel writing and gender, see Susan Bassnett, 'Travel Writing and Gender', in Peter Hulme and Tim Youngs, eds., *The Cambridge Companion to Travel Writing* (Cambridge: Cambridge University Press, 2002), pp. 225–41.

[59] Although he does not address masculinity explicitly, Gary Krist explains how 'real' travel writing depicts the experience of hardship in 'Ironic Journeys', pp. 594–6.

long-distance journeys) aim to drive a souped-up GMC Sierra into the *Guinness Book of World Records*. This modern-day 'buddy' story is all about conquering – the elements, the bureaucracy, the landscape, the fatigue, the machine. As such, it is infused with hyper-masculine passages of battle, competition and strategy on the road. For example, Cahill is constantly pitched against Argentinian drivers who believe themselves to be Juan Fangio, a Grand Prix winner in the 1950s. Trying to deal with the 'macho' local custom of flashing bright headlights into oncoming traffic, Cahill gets himself pumped:

'I'm going to nail the next guy'...The car was less than half a mile away. My fingers tingled at the toggles.
We closed to twenty feet and drew simultaneously.
Die, Fangio.
I had him outgunned. Boom, boom: High beams and Halogens, both at once. I could see two dark heads in the passing car. The night blazed with painful brilliance. They were beaten, fried, and I imagined I could see both their skulls behind the skin, as if in an X-ray.
No mercy as they passed, I hit the sidelights, and then nailed them in the rear high beams.
In the side mirror I saw the car weave across the centre line, then right itself ... I felt I was beginning to master the local customs.[60]

Cahill may not be the first person to conquer the Argentinian roads, but he just may be the fastest, the toughest and the best equipped – in short, the most masculine.[61] The images of competition that run through *Road Fever* illustrate the discourse of masculinity most clearly. Cahill's initial battles against other men (e.g. other drivers who think they are Juan Fangio, other competitors seeking to break the record and even his driving partner Sowerby) are reinforced with his battles against all things foreign. 'Mastering' other men (in this case Argentinian drivers) is therefore accompanied by a 'mastery' of the local customs. To this end, Cahill's masculinity must be reproduced over and over again in different settings: no matter what 'foreign bodies' he encounters, his approach will be, above all, manly.

---

[60] Tim Cahill, *Road Fever: A High-Speed Travelogue* (London: Fourth Estate, 1992), pp. 138–9.
[61] The competitive nature of this passage calls upon other well-known tropes of masculinity, for example the Second World War novel (toggles, outgunned) and sub-literary forms such as men writing about cars (e.g. magazines like *Car & Driver*). Other 'road rage' travelogues include P. J. O' Rourke, 'Third World Driving: Hints and Tips', in *Holidays in Hell* (London: Picador, 1988), pp. 78–82, and his collection of essays entitled 'Drives to Nowhere', in *Age and Guile: Beat Youth, Innocence and a Bad Haircut* (New York: Atlantic Monthly Press, 1996), pp. 140–87.

Framing travelogues through a discourse of masculinity is not to say that only men write these books; indeed, we have already seen how women like Dew and Campbell reproduce a coloniser/colonised framework. We know from Mills and others that women have always written travelogues, but it is only with the recent democratisation of the genre — instigated in part by women writers — that these narratives have been taken seriously. The challenge for women travel writers is how to manage the discourse of masculinity that is so prevalent in travel writing as a whole. Mills explains how the supposedly 'neutral' literary standards used to judge travelogues are actually infused with prevailing assumptions about the travel writer's masculinity. Discussing the annual Thomas Cook Travel Book award, she explains how the judgements are different for men and women authors:

Since 1980, there have been six male winners of the award and one female (Robyn Davidson for her book *Tracks*). In several of the accounts of the male winners, the style and manner of presentation is drawn attention to. However, no such attention is paid to the 'literary' qualities of Davidson's book. It is simply presented as an excellent book since it confounds the stereotypes of the content of women's travel writing: that is, what it is thought possible for a woman to do.[62]

In many ways, Mills's analysis of women's colonial travel writing holds true today: when women travel writers attempt to gain recognition, they must engage with the already established masculine codes of travel writing. As in colonial travelogues, women travel writers only enter the picture when they are rendered doubly extraordinary — first because they have survived the rigorous travels that only men are supposedly capable of, and second, because they have managed to transcend more 'feminine' literary genres (such as diaries or journals) and have somehow accomplished 'real' writing. It is still the case that women must overcome their 'natural' limitations as women and become 'extraordinary' in order to be manly enough to travel and write books about it. In this way, the discourse of masculinity in travel writing continues to install an attending message of '*even women can travel*': even women can travel solo, even women can travel in Muslim countries, even women can walk or kayak around the world — imagine that! One may not be the first person to visit Mali, to kayak up the Nile, to bivouac in the rain-forests of Borneo — but one could certainly be the first woman to do so.

While male travel writers like Cahill are busy pursuing hyper-masculine adventures and reviving colonial adventures, women are busy shedding their negatively coded traits of 'femininity' in an effort

[62] Mills, *Discourses of Difference*, pp. 111–12.

to be taken seriously as travel writers. In effect, women travel writers must become 'honorary men' in order to be recognised within a genre that is shaped so powerfully by a discourse of masculinity. Davidson's *Tracks*, initially published as a story with accompanying photographs in *National Geographic*, presents the most compelling representation of the 'honorary man' and her awkward negotiation of feminine traits. Davidson, like other women travel writers, struggles to represent moments in her journey where being a woman opens up previously uninscribed observations and experiences – but she is continually constrained by the prevailing discourse of masculinity. When journalists initially covered Davidson's story, it was certain 'feminine' attributes that were focused upon, such as her long blonde hair, her 'available' status and her special intuitive connection with both nature and her camels.[63] Reacting to the way that the press continued to focus only on her 'feminine' characteristics, she acutely states at the end of her book: 'And that term "camel lady". Had I been a man, I'd be lucky to get a mention in the *Wiluma Times*, let alone international press coverage. Neither could I imagine them coining the phrase "camel gentleman". "Camel lady" had that nice patronizing belittling ring to it. Labelling, pigeonholing – what a splendid trick it is.'[64] Whereas Cahill can simply get on with his adventures, Davidson bears the burden of proof: before she can 'get on' with her journey, she must demonstrate that she is manly enough to be there in the first place. As the 'regular guy' on a modern adventure, Cahill illustrates how appropriate manliness is the only requirement for the modern adventure. As a woman traveller, Davidson must contend with being categorised as something special, something mythical, something extraordinary in her attempt to complete a journey and write about it. Not only are adventures like Davidson's considered a trivial 'afterthought' to the 'real' travel adventures of men, but being classified as 'extraordinary' works to prevent other women from attempting similar adventures. Davidson expresses her anxiety at the 'myth of extraordinariness' when she reacts to proposed plans for a film of *Tracks*: 'It seems that if anyone does something unusual a whole machine goes into operation to try and make sure that she never does it again. You turn her into a myth, you misinterpret what she's done, and then you turn the film into a love story. There's all sorts of ways of taking the balls off it.'[65] As the last

---

[63] Lyn Hughes, 'The Reluctant Role Model: An Interview with Robyn Davidson', *Wanderlust*, No. 17, Aug./Sept. 1996, pp. 6–7.

[64] Davidson, *Tracks*, p. 237.

[65] Hughes, 'The Reluctant Role Model', p. 6.

sentence expresses, Davidson's narrative doesn't fit neatly with either masculine or feminine codes but is instead the result of a continual and complex negotiation between the two.

Davidson's position as an honorary man is an important disturbance in the subject position of the masculine travel writer. Like the position of post-colonial travel writers, the honorary man alerts us to the fact that subjects do not rest easily within the allotted categories of identity/difference. As Davidson comments, women travel writers can identify the workings of power more keenly because they occupy *both* male and female subject positions, and thus both sides of the identity/difference logic: 'As a woman I had access to both sexes. The woman's world would have been quite closed to a man, whereas I'm allowed into the men's world as an honorary man. I think that gives me more opportunities for seeing how things work than a bloke might have.'[66] The very presence of women in the genre destabilises the masculine gaze of the travel writer. When the author/subject/hero is a woman, she is able to call upon *both* sides of the identity/difference logic in order to authorise her position. In effect, this dual strategy makes her *more* omniscient than her male counterparts, and *more* able to identify how difference and otherness are shaped by power. In this sense, women join post-colonial travel writers at the forefront of transforming the genre along more cosmopolitan lines. As subjects who have experienced colonial and patriarchal power first-hand, they are best able to resist its continued workings because they occupy both positions of the identity/difference logic. But in their efforts to transform the genre, women and post-colonial writers are joined by another subject committed to resisting the past wrongs of colonialism and patriarchy: 'the new man'. Reared on feminism and notions of racial equality, comfortable with the claims of identity politics, progressive in their political affiliations and keen to redress the historical exclusions enacted through colonialism and patriarchy, new men are proving that travel writers are not necessarily chauvinist, racist snobs writing the world through a privileged lens. Keneally's measured assessment of the American Southwest is an example of a new man's contribution to the genre: modest in its aims, sensitive to the plight of American-Indians and keen to distance itself from colonial travelogues that represent America as the other of Europe. But the 'new man' travel writer is a cunning formation of subjectivity, for one cannot be sure how far the commitment to gender and racial equality extends. Many feminists would argue that as long as their own economic, political and social position is secure, new men are happy to

---

[66] Hughes, 'The Reluctant Role Model', p. 7.

promote gender and racial equality. However, once their own positions
are threatened (e.g. by claims of identity politics, by affirmative action,
by 'political correctness', or by 'reverse' discrimination), their commitment to equality wavers. With this in mind, we might ask whether the
new man travel writer is really all that new, or whether he is simply
another version of the same masculine, colonial subject position that has
dominated the genre for so long. One of the problems with the new man
subject position is that his battles against the injustices of colonialism
and patriarchy leave little room for his own individuality to flourish.
In other words, new men travel writers become too political, too serious
and too righteous. The more popular – and indeed more influential –
subjectivity to emerge from the democratisation of travel writing is not
the macho man, the honorary man or even the new man – it is the *joker*.
Rather than educate the reader on the political issues of race and gender
through detailed historical claims and rhetorical argumentation, why not
make them laugh instead?

Self-deprecation and humour

Holland and Huggan are right to argue that many contemporary
travelogues are farcical – travel writers *know* the genre's colonial and
patriarchal judgements are outdated, but they continue to replay these
judgements in ironic and comedic ways.[67] Using Eric Newby's *A Short
Walk in the Hindu Kush* as a model, Holland and Huggan argue that
Bruce Chatwin, Redmond O'Hanlon and Peter Mayle use farce to mask
their inherited feelings of colonial superiority. These travel writers
position themselves as slightly out-of-date *flaneurs* – intrepid dandies
who know they are somehow ridiculous as they pursue their futile
journeys. Unlike Theroux, who finds difference irritating, writers like
Bill Bryson and Michael Palin are more interested in pointing to the
humour that resides in cultural difference. Their knack of 'laughing
with' others is not undertaken in a rude or spiteful manner; rather, it is
accompanied by a healthy dose of self-irony, recognition that the travel
narrative has become 'superficial' in the age of tourism, and deliberate

---

[67] Holland and Huggan, 'Imperial Nostalgia and the English Gentleman Traveler',
Tourists with Typewriters, pp. 274–7. One way to pursue Holland and Huggan's
argument about farce would be to examine travel writing that depicts deliberately
ridiculous journeys as a form of satire, for example, Tim Moore's *Frost on My
Moustache: The Arctic Exploits of a Lord and a Loafer* (London: Abacus, 2000),
Continental Drifter (London: Abacus, 2002) and *French Revolutions: Cycling the Tour
de France* (London: Vintage 2002); see also Tony Hawks's *Round Ireland with a
Fridge* (London: Ebury Press, 1999) and *Playing the Moldovans at Tennis*
(London: Ebury Press, 2001).

attempts to undercut the mythological role of the 'English Gentleman Abroad'. As Tisdale argues, 'to be a foreigner is to surrender somewhat. It requires a certain kind of trust, a willingness to play the fool for a while. There's nothing like a trip to cure a swollen head.'[68] In effect, travel writers use comedic strategies to puncture the 'swollen head' of their own position – they 'play the fool' in order to poke fun at the sense of superiority enjoyed by their colonial predecessors. Holland and Huggan argue that the self-parody of belatedness allows Chatwin et al. to detach themselves from the colonial heritage of the genre. While this may be the case, writers like Bryson and Palin use comedy to present a more hopeful, future-oriented world-view. Rather than looking back on the embarrassment of colonial travel writing, they use humour and self-parody to illustrate that difference is *funny* rather than threatening, and should therefore be respected and celebrated from now on.

The key shift with humorous narratives is that the subject position of the travel writer is opened up – they laugh at themselves as they laugh at others. By actively and self-consciously poking fun at himself, Bryson avoids reproducing the superiority, arrogance and misanthropy of both his colonial predecessors and contemporaries like Theroux. In sending himself up, Bryson makes everybody an available target in his gentle humour – he is teaching the world to laugh at themselves and their national stereotypes. He knowingly exaggerates these stereotypes to the point of absurdity so that both his behaviour, and the behaviour of the locals he meets, is comical and almost cartoonish. In *Neither Here Nor There*, his explanation of why Italians are such bad drivers is exemplary of this type of exaggeration: 'They are too busy tooting their horns, gesturing wildly, preventing other vehicles from cutting into their lane, making love, smacking the children in the back seat and eating a sandwich the size of a baseball bat, often all at once.'[69] Because Bryson's style of comedy is based on exaggeration and hyperbole, difference becomes ridiculous rather than threatening (i.e. his comments on others are so preposterous they cannot be taken seriously). This absurdity underscores his put-downs (e.g. 'I assume the fanatically industrious Swiss don't bury their dead but use them for making heating oil') as well as his self-parody (e.g. 'How many times in recent days had I sat on buses or trains listening to my idly prattling mind and wished that I could just get up and walk out on myself?')[70] Bryson is able to celebrate cultural difference rather than denigrate it because he is not concerned

---

[68] Tisdale, 'Never Let the Locals', p. 68.
[69] Bryson, *Neither Here Nor There*, p. 164.
[70] Bryson, *Neither Here Nor There*, pp. 225–6, 303.

with securing his own superiority. His identity as a travel writer is based on being silly, irreverent and childlike – revealing his own foibles as he points out the foibles of others. At the beginning of his trip through Europe, he wryly states: 'Much as I hate to stand out in a crowd, I have this terrible occasional compulsion to make myself an unwitting source of merriment for the world.'[71] He then proceeds to behave in a childish manner – full of wonder and empty of responsibility – all across Europe. For example, he plays the child to a psychotic couple in Luxembourg, he frolics for hours in the strong winds in Norway, he happily falls asleep on women's shoulders on Italian trains and he wilfully refuses to engage with the complexities of Renaissance painting.[72] Bryson's exaggerated put-downs and wry self-deprecation prove that it is possible to avoid the drudgery of home and work as well as the responsibility of adulthood. As he states at the beginning of his trip: 'I can't think of anything that excites a greater sense of childlike wonder than to be in a country where you are ignorant of almost everything.'[73] Halfway into his trip, he abandons the original itinerary plotted during his 'adult' life in the UK: 'Travelling is more fun – shit, life is more fun – if you can treat it as a series of impulses.'[74] Bryson absolutely *loves* Europe and all its quirkiness, and he maintains his childish enthusiasm until he reaches the edges of Europe (and the end of the book) in Istanbul: 'It was time to go home. My long-suffering wife was pregnant with her semi-annual baby. The younger children, she had told me on the phone, were beginning to call any grown man "Daddy".'[75]

Michael Palin's use of comedy in his travelogues differs from Bryson's in that it is not based on ridiculous exaggerations. Palin is already famous for being funny – he is recognised around the world as a member of *Monty Python's Flying Circus*. But Palin has toned down his earlier comedic overtures and crafted a subtler, more responsible subject position in order to become a respected travel writer and broadcaster. His major journeys – *Around the World in 80 Days* (1989), *Full Circle* (1997), *Pole to Pole* (1992), *Sahara* (2002) and *Himalaya* (2004) – were commissioned and filmed for the BBC and then re-packaged as travelogues. In all of these adventures, Palin's position as a travel writer is marked by his celebrity status as a famous comedian. While much of his narrative is serious, genuine and concerned, he is never that far away from making a joke about himself or the others he encounters.

---

[71] Bryson, *Neither Here Nor There*, p. 28.
[72] Bryson, *Neither Here Nor There*, pp. 16–19, 29, 177, 213.
[73] Bryson, *Neither Here Nor There*, p. 41.
[74] Bryson, *Neither Here Nor There*, p. 161.
[75] Bryson, *Neither Here Nor There*, p. 303.

Nor does he refrain from reminding the reader of his previous life. When meeting some Eskimos in Alaska, he comments:

They may not have fridge-freezers (they bury their food in the permafrost instead) but they do have satellite television and it's not long before word gets around that one of the actors from *Monty Python and the Holy Grail* is on the island. The last thing I have to do before leaving one of the most remote corners of the world is to sign autographs.[76]

Because Palin's fame is what initially attracts viewers and readers to these narratives, he has to strike a balance between being a responsible travel writer and making his audience laugh. Palin understands the colonial heritage of travelling, but he knows that cultural encounters are best translated through a sense of humour rather than a serious polemic. Nowhere is this reliance on humour more apparent than when Palin's fame affords him the opportunity to participate as a 'guest of honour' in local ceremonies and rituals. During a Maori ceremony in New Zealand, he pokes fun at his own position ('[I] will be required to give a short speech, and, horror of horrors, sing a song!'), describes the pantomime intimidation of the Maori challenge ('[their] eyes are rolled, tongues extended, mouths stretched in sneers of disgust and loathing that would make a gargoyle look like Julia Roberts') and participates fully in the *hongi* tradition of rubbing noses ('It's an awfully good use for noses, I think')(see figure 2).[77] This brief encounter with the Maori encapsulates Palin's strategy: make fun of yourself, use that position to poke gentle fun at others and then come together to celebrate cultural understanding.

Palin's travelogues are based on his willingness to be made a spectacle, and to use that position in the name of both humour and cultural understanding. In *Full Circle*, Palin always attracts crowds, but he often becomes a willing spectacle of fun: he dresses in full kimono for the Okunchi Festival in Nagasaki; he judges the 'Miss La Bella Pacifica' beauty contest in the Philippines; he is a guest of honour at the Otago University fun run/mud bath in New Zealand; and he competes in a logging festival in front of hundreds of spectators in British Columbia. All of these episodes endear Palin to his audience because he is so willing to 'play the fool'. This willingness is the key to Palin's popularity, and makes him a highly profitable asset to the BBC and his publishers. As one reviewer explains:

Palin is respectful enough of foreign cultures, but he knows the Difference is Funny. He has a manner – the BBC knows its great value – that lets him

---

[76] Michael Palin, *Full Circle* (London: BBC Books, 1997), p. 15.
[77] Palin, *Full Circle*, pp. 203–4.

Figure 2. 'Maori acceptance', *Full circle*, p. 204, photograph by
Basil Pao

address us at the same time he is addressing someone with strange headgear
standing on a rock; and he does this without slipping into mockery or self-
mockery, without boring us, or seeming impertinent or alien to the man in the
hat. We always expect to see him crushed into the ground by embarrassment,
but he is not.[78]

The point about self-mockery is important here, for while Palin is
certainly willing to poke fun at himself as the traveller, at no point does
that humour threaten the *worthy* enterprise of what he is doing. He does
not slip into 'self-mockery' because that would undercut the purpose
of the entire enterprise. Rather, Palin's efforts to send himself up are
limited by the higher purpose of creating cultural understanding.
This motivation is encoded in the traditional documentary style of his
television programmes: by making the camera and technical crew
invisible, the means of production are hidden and Palin 'appears' to
address the audience directly as he travels alone. I would argue that
the same deception − hiding the means of production − occurs in his

[78] Ian Parker, 'I'm Sorry, I Haven't a Crew', 'Review', *Observer*, 7 September 1997, p. 7.
Mark Lawson argues that Palin's first three travel adventures were so successful for
the BBC that 'only the Director General had the authority to sign the size of the
cheque which accrued to Palin from the royalties of the tie-in books' ('A Farewell
to Charm', *Guardian*, 11 October 1999).

travel writing. Palin's text is unable to call attention to its own conditions of possibility: he can gently poke fun at others and at himself, and he can invite the audience to share in his jokes, but he cannot use humour to question or 'send up' the enterprise of travel itself. To do so would require him to recognise the difficult terrain of cultural difference itself. For Palin assumes that the other – the person with strange headgear standing on a rock – desperately wants to be part of his world where cultural difference is celebrated and ultimately overcome.

The process of 'laughing-with' – of audiences sharing and participating in the humour of a travelogue – tells us something important about the intersubjectivity of Bryson's and Palin's texts. Does a shared sense of humour extend to a shared set of values? By laughing at Bryson's exaggerated stereotypes and Palin's ingratiating efforts, do audiences also take on board the cosmopolitan vision that underscores these travelogues? To what extent does the reader share the travel writer's humorous treatment of difference? The process of 'laughing at ourselves as we laugh at others' is not an end in itself for writers like Bryson and Palin; rather, it is a means to an end. It allows them to achieve their ultimate goal – to overcome deep cultural differences and reveal shared cultural values. Indeed, this 'cosmopolitan sense of humour' is the most *ethical* way to encounter and interpret difference, for it avoids the superiority, romanticism and sexism enacted by colonial travel writers and replaces it with an intersubjectivity based on more equal foundations. I want to argue that the shared values espoused by Bryson and Palin are only shared between the author and his assumed audience – they do not *necessarily* extend to the others being written about. As Simon Critchley argues, humour is often used to enact unequal power relations: 'Humour is a form of cultural insider-knowledge . . . Its ostensive untranslatability endows native speakers with a palpable sense of their cultural distinctiveness or even superiority. In this sense, having a common sense of humour is like sharing a secret code.'[79] In effect, Bryson and Palin use humour to establish a 'secret code' that augments the values they share with their assumed readers, and highlights the differences of cultural others who are ultimately excluded as the butt of the joke.

In the end, Bryson's and Palin's worthy efforts and self-deprecating manner are not enough to avoid being tainted by the colonial and patriarchal heritage they are trying to overcome. In effect, these travelogues are particularly conservative in their efforts to frame difference in a more ethical manner, for they fail to question the dominant

[79] Simon Critchley, *On Humour* (London and New York: Routledge, 2002), pp. 67–8.

order within which certain subject positions are valued by projecting difference onto less-valued others.[80] Particularly upsetting here is the failure of cosmopolitan writers like Bryson and Palin to use humour for more critical ends − not to 'poke fun' at their own foibles or the idiosyncrasies of others, but to rail against a global status quo that reproduces grossly unequal relations of power. The mild self-deprecation of these authors gives the appearance of self-reflexivity and the ability to ethically engage with cultural difference but does nothing to question the privileged network that exists between the author and his assumed audience. But what happens when this humorous approach confronts experiences of violence and atrocity? Bryson simply avoids these areas, choosing to bumble superficially around the museums, hotels and plazas of Europe rather than, say, Auschwitz, Dresden or Dachau. Palin is slightly more engaging here, as he makes an effort to confront the difficult histories of his destinations. In *Full Circle*, he accompanies a survivor of the Soviet Gulags back to the labour camp at Butugyvhag.[81] Immediately Palin's tone becomes sombre and serious: he recites the facts, he condemns the authorities and he takes care to personalise the issue through the survivor's story. But as soon as they are well away from the Gulag, Palin goes back to describing the locals serving him dinner as 'Fawlty-esque' and making hurried plans to leave. While the 'Gulag' section of *Full Circle* (all two and a half pages) seems out of place in an otherwise light-hearted narrative, I want to argue that it works to confirm Palin's status as a good cosmopolitan citizen. By revealing terrible things like Gulags to his audience, Palin not only ushers in the horrors of the past, he also signifies the liberal standards of tolerance that mark a cosmopolitan future. He is prepared to learn about, laugh with and respect different cultures, as long as those cultures do not commit barbarous acts upon their own citizens. Once this line is crossed, his humour disappears.

One could argue that there is nothing wrong with using travelogues to encourage a more cosmopolitan vision where global politics are governed by universal standards of toleration and understanding. In other words, if these texts can help readers understand and respect cultural difference, they are doing no harm. My point is that the cosmopolitan sense of humour used by travel writers like Bryson and Palin produces the same tensions that have always underscored more liberal approaches to cultural difference. There are some cultural practices that are *not* acceptable, and the international community

---

[80] Critchley, *On Humour*, p. 82.
[81] Palin, *Full Circle*, pp. 36–40.

(populated as it is by cosmopolitans from around the world) should do all in its power to stop those practices. But the question of subjectivity here is crucial: *who* gets to be a member of this international community? *Who* gets to decide which cultural practices are acceptable and which are not? *Who*, exactly, is a cosmopolitan? Travel writers like Bryson and Palin are not marginal to these debates: along with diplomats, journalists, commentators, intellectuals and politicians, they are helping to construct the moral architecture of the international community. They participate in the creation of 'universal' standards, they decide what is and is not acceptable practice and they make judgements about cultural difference from an inherited position of privilege. My point is that without interrogating the cosmopolitan subjectivities that wield this power, colonial and patriarchal attitudes will continue to be smuggled into the genre under the guise of uncontested terms like equality, tolerance and universality. Therefore, in order to interrogate the position of the cosmopolitan travel writer, it is necessary to examine critical positions that both refuse colonial and patriarchal nostalgia and question the universality of cosmopolitan dreams.

Decentring the subject: critique, recognition and negotiation

Casey Blanton argues that Bruce Chatwin's indeterminate position as travel writer, nomad and aesthete made him an especially sensitive reader of other cultures:

Chatwin's ability to be decentred or displaced accounts for his open-ended attitude toward not only foreign cultures but truth and history as well. The acceptance of being off centre places one in a position of ignorance and doubt: nothing is sure. If our familiar constructs and sustaining myths can be left at home like Chatwin's very British life, then a world traveller is less likely to import judgemental convictions as he encounters those who are different. Like the nomad, he can travel light.[82]

Blanton believes that Chatwin is the ideal traveller because he is able to 'leave his familiar constructs and myths' at home: in other words, he can jettison his 'very British life' of privilege, education and aesthetic appreciation and wander the world encountering difference. For Blanton, the best travel writers, the 'true' travel writers, are those who are unhindered by their subjectivity (e.g. Chatwin's nomadic wanderings and seductive narratives *have nothing to do* with his privileged middle-class masculinity). The problem, of course, is that Blanton places

---

[82] Blanton, *Travel Writing: The Self and the World*, p. 107.

Chatwin outside of the identity/difference logic and its attending dispersals of power. My point is that all travel writers — even the most 'sensitive' — are enmeshed in that logic. Telling, here, are those travel writers who try to overcome the logic of identity/difference through a cosmopolitan vision. Bryson and Palin employ humour to fulfil the 'worthy' goal of overcoming cultural difference rather than to subvert their own prejudices and those of the audience. In this sense, the comedic self-deprecation used by Bryson and Palin is measured and gentle rather than provocative and demanding. For example, Bryson's projections of difference in the form of national and cultural stereotypes are too exaggerated to cause offence, as if to say 'we know these stereotypes exist, but aren't they silly? And aren't we smart for seeing through that silliness? These are just *jokes* after all.' But the limitations of the cosmopolitan vision are revealed by the questions that go unasked in these narratives. Bryson and Palin can say 'look how silly I am in a foreign country!' but never 'what *right* do I have to pass judgement on these foreigners?' or 'can I ever escape my privileged position in order to understand cultures and peoples radically different from me?' In this way, the cosmopolitan humour used by Bryson and Palin is always contained within a circuit — not too offensive to others, and not too damaging to the self. As one critic argues, it is precisely this liberal approach that middle-class audiences appreciate about Michael Palin: 'he makes them feel better about the way they travel. Palin is not on a quest. He goes here and there; he hopes to be liked by the people he meets (and he is not uninterested in what they have to say), but he is not expecting his life to be turned upside down . . . he is not forever bothering us with epiphanies or personal disclosures.'[83] Palin is popular because he keeps himself contained — he never gets 'too big for his britches', he never emotes in inappropriate ways, and he is polite and charming to the odd people he meets. And it is precisely the *containment* of the author's subjectivity that prevents cosmopolitan travel writers from offering subversive or even critical interpretations of cultural difference. Nothing, not even humorous self-deprecation, can detract from the worthy goal of recognising and overcoming cultural difference in the name of more universal goals. But as Critchley argues, this 'mild-mannered' humour is ill conceived because it does not force a

---

[83] Parker, 'I'm Sorry, I Haven't a Crew', p. 7. Holland and Huggan make a similar argument: 'the most successful travel books are arguably those, like Mayle's or Bryson's or even Chatwin's, that identify a middle-class readership and then pander skilfully to its whims' (*Tourists with Typewriters*, p. viii). In addition, James Duncan and Derek Gregory suggest that modern travel writing is a secular and middle-class form of entertainment; see 'Introduction' in Duncan and Gregory, *Writes of Passage*, pp. 5–7.

confrontation with the dominant order. For Critchley, the most ethical kind of humour is that which reveals

the anxiety, difficulty and, indeed, shame at where one is from ... Humour can provide information about oneself that one would rather *not* have ... as an eager cosmopolitan, I would rather not be reminded of national differences and national styles, yet our sense of humour can often unconsciously pull us up short in front of ourselves, showing how prejudices that one would rather not hold can continue to have a grip on one's sense of who one is.[84]

Critchley's use of 'eager cosmopolitan' is curious here, for it suggests a capacity for critical self-reflexivity in the cosmopolitan citizen. It is worth unpacking Critchley's argument and asking what conditions might encourage a deeper sense of self-reflexivity than cosmopolitan travel writers currently offer. How would a travel writer secure his/her subject position in a condition where subjectivity *itself* could not be guaranteed by the projection of difference, the automatic conferral of power and the confident authorial voice?

Stuart Hall traces how the Cartesian subject, with 'certain fixed human capacities and a stable sense of its own identity and place in the order of things', has been de-centred by advances in social theory such as Marxism, psychoanalysis and post-structuralism.[85] Of particular interest here is the tension Hall identifies between (a) discursively constructed subjects, and (b) subjects empowered by specific identity

---

[84] Critchley, *On Humour*, p. 74.
[85] Stuart Hall, 'The Question of Cultural Identity', in Stuart Hall, David Held and Anthony McGrew, eds., *Modernity and Its Futures* (Cambridge: Polity Press in association with the Open University, 1992), p. 281. Hall starts with Marxist arguments that reject the idea of a 'universal essence' of man and instead point to the structural, historical and material conditions that affect men in particular circumstances. We see these arguments reflected in Todorov's efforts to contextualise both the writer of journey narratives and the others depicted in those narratives. Secondly, Hall argues that the modern subject was de-centred – and indeed split in two – by Freud's discovery of the unconscious. A subject can never be fully conscious to itself and in control if he is always haunted by unconscious desires and repressed fantasies. It is for this reason that difference is understood as a *projection* of the self, which means that the travel writer's effort to secure his/her subjectivity is always governed by fantasy. Indeed, as Behdad explains in *Belated Travelers*, the Oriental other was either feared or desired but was always a projection of the writer's fantasies and anxieties. The third de-centring of the subject is a more general point about the indeterminacy of language and meaning. Using the work of de Saussure and Derrida, Hall makes the point that the subject cannot be guaranteed in language because 'there are always supplementary meanings over which we have no control, which will arise and subvert our attempts to create fixed and stable worlds' (p. 288). We saw this at work in Derrida's essay on the law of genre – generic boundaries are simultaneously exceeded and punctured by meanings that cannot be excluded. The fourth de-centring is Foucault's notion of subjects constructed in discourse; and the final de-centring explains the identity politics of new social movements.

positions within social movements (e.g. 'feminism appealed to women, sexual politics to gays and lesbians, racial struggles to blacks, anti-war to peaceniks, and so on').[86] Hall's succinct outline of the battle between discursive and standpoint positions is particularly significant for this analysis, for it helps us understand how contemporary travel writing — consciously or not — is shaping the battleground of identity politics. We know that the democratisation of the genre means that different types of people from different 'standpoints' are now writing travelogues — women, previously colonised people, new men. But as we have seen, these previously excluded subjects have not necessarily changed the terms in which travel is written about. For example, women writers like Josie Dew and post-colonial writers like Tété-Michel Kpomassie can uncritically reproduce the discourses of gender and race embedded in the generic boundaries of travel writing. Thus, if standpoint accounts of identity politics don't get us very far in politicising the subject position of the travel writer, what about more discursive accounts? If the subject only comes into being through discourse, and if that 'coming into presence' occurs at multiple sites, then the subject is always char- acterised by many different identity formations at the same time (e.g. travel writer, father, friend, husband, intellectual).

The challenge of discursive accounts of subjectivity is that they take away the foundation of identity so needed by subjects who are seeking to redress historical exclusions and gain access to power. Many feminist and post-colonial writers see the developments of post-structuralism as threatening to forms of identity politics that advance the claims of women and racially inscribed others. As Nancy Harstock's famous response to Foucault illustrates, discursive accounts of subjectivity have political consequences:

Why is it that just at the moment when so many of us who have been silenced begin to demand the right to name ourselves, to act as subjects rather than objects of history, that just then the concept of subjecthood becomes problematic? Just when we are forming our own theories about the world, uncertainty emerges about whether the world can be theorized. Just when we are talking about the changes we want, ideas of progress and the possibility of systematically and rationally organizing human society become dubious and suspect.[87]

While those engaged in the debate between feminism and post- structuralism are committed to resisting patriarchy, they are divided

---

[86] Hall, 'The Question of Cultural Identity', p. 290.
[87] Nancy Harstock, 'Foucault on Power: A Theory for Women?' in Linda J. Nicholson, ed., *Feminism/Postmodernism* (London and New York: Routledge, 1990), pp. 163–4.

on strategy: standpoint feminists want to retain a foundation for women, whereas radical and post-structural feminists want to de-centre the subject positions of *all* men and women. The debate over identity politics is also evident in post-colonial circles. The collection '*Race*', *Writing, and Difference* made an effort to deconstruct 'the ideas of difference inscribed in the trope of race, to explicate discourse itself in order to reveal the hidden relations of power and knowledge inherent in popular and academic usages of "race"'.[88] While discursive accounts of racial identity abound in the book, they come together most forcefully in Derrida's essay about apartheid as the 'ultimate racism in the world, the last of many'.[89] The response, by Anne McClintock and Rob Nixon, echoes some of Harstock's arguments that post-structuralism is politically impotent because it fails to guarantee a secure position from which resistance to the dominant order can be formulated. McClintock and Nixon suggest that Derrida's argument is 'of limited strategic worth' because it fails to accompany a linguistic deconstruction of the word 'apartheid' with 'discursive, political, economic, and historical analyses'.[90] In other words, Derrida's obsession with the word 'apartheid' renders the discourses of racism in South Africa 'more static and monolithic than they really are' and leaves no room for a subject position that Africans *themselves* can inhabit in order to resist apartheid. The tension here is familiar: on the one hand is Derrida's all-encompassing deconstruction of words, meanings and the metaphysics of Western presence, and on the other hand is McClintock and Nixon's call for empirical and material strategies to resist racism.

How does this tension between standpoint and discursive accounts of identity play itself out through cosmopolitan travel writers who project difference onto others, *knowing* that this projection carries traces of colonialism and patriarchy? In *Travelers, Immigrants, Inmates*, Frances Bartkowski argues that 'the demands placed upon the subject in situations of unfamiliarity and dislocation produce a scene in which the struggle for identity comes more clearly into view as both necessary and

---

[88] Henry Louis Gates, Jr., 'Writing "Race" and the Difference It Makes', in Henry Louis Gates, Jr., ed., '*Race*', *Writing, and Difference* (Chicago and London: University of Chicago Press, 1986), p. 6. These essays were originally produced in two issues of *Critical Inquiry*, Autumn 1985 (Vol. 12, No. 1) and Autumn 1986 (Vol. 13, No. 1).

[89] Jacques Derrida, 'Racism's Last Word', in Gates, Jr., '*Race*', *Writing, and Difference*, p. 330.

[90] Anne McClintock and Rob Nixon, 'No Names Apart: The Separation of Word and History in Derrida's "Le Dernier Mot du Racisme"', in Gates, Jr., '*Race*', *Writing, and Difference*, p. 353.

also mistaken'.[91] Bartkowski does not resolve the tension between standpoint and discursive accounts of identity because she knows that any resolution would be false. Her work is underscored by post-structural accounts of subjectivity (indeed, she is 'mistrustful of questions of identity' that are anything other than 'fleeting' and 'amalgamated'), but she is aware that contingent identities are always striving for completion in order to make contact with others:

> We must speak, and once we do so we enact an enabling fiction of identity that makes social life possible... We must say 'I', whether in words or some other semiotic system, in order to enter into dialogue with others, and in so doing we necessarily falsify both our fragmented place in the universe of discourse and the place of our interlocutors. The paradox of moving through an experience of cultural dislocation is that we must do violence to ourselves and others to maintain a shred of corporeal standing so that something verging on exchange might occur.[92]

In effect, the fiction of modern subjectivity is necessary because without it we could say nothing at all – but the modern subject is always incomplete, always contingent and always insecure. As Bartkowski argues, we need to dress ourselves with the clothing of identity in order to mask the nakedness of our contingent subjectivities.[93] But if the particular 'identity costume' of cosmopolitanism helps travel writers engage with otherness, can that costume be confidently worn by post-colonial and feminist travel writers?

Post-colonial voyagers: Naipaul, Iyer and Younge

Perhaps the best place to begin unravelling the identity politics of the contemporary travel writer is through the figure of V. S. Naipaul. Because he was born in Trinidad, lived most of his life in London, and has written several travelogues about India, Naipaul's work offers us a useful glimpse of the different relations that develop between dominant and colonised cultures.[94] Naipaul's 'in-between' position – as both West Indian and British – functions as a model for many post-colonial travel writers keen to explore the hybrid subjectivities that have been

---

[91] Bartkowski, *Travelers, Immigrants, Inmates*, p. xix.
[92] Bartkowski, *Travelers, Immigrants, Inmates*, pp. xx, xxiii.
[93] Bartkowski, *Travelers, Immigrants, Inmates*, p. xvi.
[94] Peter Hulme argues that Naipaul's first travelogue, *The Middle Passage* (1962), intersected with both West-Indian debates about the framework for independence and British debates about post-war immigration from the West Indies; see 'Travelling to Write (1940–2000)', in Hulme and Youngs, *The Cambridge Companion to Travel Writing*, p. 89.

foregrounded by the processes of de-colonisation and globalisation.[95] But Naipaul is a notoriously difficult writer to categorise because his elitism prevents him from using his 'post-colonial' status to develop links of solidarity with previously colonised others. Rather, Naipaul has become infamous for his vicious attacks against 'Third World' cultures.[96] As Peter Hulme argues, his three travelogues about India exemplify the contested subject position of the travel writer because the topic at hand is always Naipaul rather than India: 'With the writer's subjectivity centrestage, India usually serves as a backdrop – be it charming, exotic, infuriating, or comic – to the narrator's travels.'[97] Naipaul's ruminations on his own position have both inspired and infuriated other post-colonial writers as they grapple with issues of race and identity. On the one hand, Naipaul claims the identity of exile – excluded from Trinidad because of his Hindu background, excluded from Britain because of his West Indian background and excluded from the India he documents because of his upbringing overseas. On the other hand, Naipaul's conservatism and belief in civilisational standards mean that his travel writing reproduces a particularly English sensibility that cannot help but convey an inherited cultural superiority. As Holland and Huggan argue, 'the chronically displaced Trinidadian Naipaul seems to wish to reincarnate himself as a post-Edwardian Englishman...At times, the persona he projects is wilfully distant and elitist – as if he were trying to wed the rigorous asceticism of Brahminical culture to the class-consciousness and refinement of the gentleman travellers' club.'[98] Indeed, Caren Kaplan argues that it is

---

[95] The most interesting debate over Naipaul's effect on travel writing is the hugely controversial book by Paul Theroux, *Sir Vidia's Shadow: A Friendship across Five Continents* (London: Hamish Hamilton, 1998). Theroux is clear about the influence of Naipaul on his early novels and travel writing and even produced a non-fiction book of criticism, *V. S. Naipaul: An Introduction to his Work* (London: André Deutsch, 1972). But *Sir Vidia's Shadow* is a detailed account of the breakdown in this friendship and, some critics argued, an unnecessary and vindictive public attack on Naipaul. Critic Lynn Barber argues, 'I've never known a book to divide people so strongly, between the Naipaul-is-a-shit and the Theroux-is-a-shit camps. The American critics uniformly took the latter view and Theroux's name in the States is now mud. Theroux believes there was an orchestrated campaign against him, but that's probably his paranoia. Naipaul stoutly maintains that he has never read the book' ('Making Waves', *Observer*, 20 February 2000, p. 40).

[96] Holland and Huggan, *Tourists with Typewriters*, p. 43.

[97] Hulme, 'Travelling to Write (1940–2000)', p. 194; Naipaul's three travelogues on India are: *An Area of Darkness* (London: André Deutsch, 1964), *India: A Wounded Civilization* (New York: Knopf, 1977) and *India: A Million Mutinies Now* (New York: Viking, 1990).

[98] Holland and Huggan, *Tourists with Typewriters*, pp. 6, 43.

precisely this elitism and conservatism that have made him such a popular writer: 'Naipaul has identified with the universalising gestures of mainstream Euro-American literary establishments – in effect, profiting from the very cultures he refuses to affiliate himself with'.[99] By using his 'colonial' heritage (Indian, Trinidadian) as a platform to espouse the 'universal' standards enshrined in Western civilisation, Naipaul has become the ultimate champion of a cosmopolitan vision. Even his experience under colonial rule does not blind him from seeing that the values of cosmopolitanism – even though they derive from Western civilisation – are the best and most persuasive values in the world.

Holland and Huggan describe Naipaul's subject position as both melancholy (for he has lost any clear sense of home and belonging) and misanthropic (for he hates the degradation he witnesses in the Third World). These characteristics abound in his Indian trilogy, which they describe as 'remarkable for its sudden shifts in subject position from outsider to insider, and for the intensity of the pain that comes from the writer's memory of loss'.[100] It could be argued that the shift from outsider to insider characterises all post-colonial subjects and is *the* defining characteristic of the contemporary travel writer. But how does the travel writer – the 'subject-in-transit' – negotiate a position that is simultaneously inside and outside of prevailing discourses? More importantly, if the subject is in transit, how does he/she formulate the discriminations and judgements required by the generic boundaries of travel writing? As Kaplan suggests, 'Some would argue that Naipaul's explicitly conservative politics sever him from the diasporic predicaments explored in a more admittedly progressive writer such as Rushdie.'[101] For Kaplan, some post-colonial writers are more willing than others to explore the emerging and conflicted subject position of exile/traveller/migrant. But as we saw with Rushdie's travel writing, those 'diasporic predicaments' are closed down when he switches from novel to travelogue. As *A Nicaraguan Journey* illustrated, the genre does not implode when previously marginalised others occupy the position of the travel writer – it does not necessarily give way to an examination of the subject-in-transit. Indeed, 'post-colonial' travel writers like Naipaul reproduce the strategies of differentiation that work to secure the position of the travel writer as in control of both the journey and

[99] Caren Kaplan, *Questions of Travel: Postmodern Discourses of Displacement* (Durham and London: Duke University Press, 1996) p. 125.
[100] Holland and Huggan, *Tourists with Typewriters*, p. 43.
[101] Kaplan, *Questions of Travel*, p. 125.

the text.[102] The travel writer – no matter what his/her background or ethnicity – identifies difference, places it in a value-laden hierarchy, and judges it accordingly. I am particularly interested in how Naipaul's contradictory subject position – as cosmopolitan Englishman *and* post-colonial critic – works as a model for two contemporary travel writers who pursue divergent positions with respect to race and identity.

Pico Iyer resolves the conflicted position of the post-colonial travel writer by embracing it. Because his identity straddles Indian, English, American and Japanese cultures (Indian parents, British and American education, Japanese home), Iyer is well positioned to interpret how different local cultures are adapting to the forces and anxieties of globalisation. Specifically, Iyer's work documents the new identities that are forming in this context – hybrid subjects who, like himself, exist between several cultures at once. The travelogue that inaugurated these concerns was *Video Night in Kathmandu and Other Reports from the Not-So-Far East* (1988). *Video Night* examines how various countries in Asia both adopt and adapt to the 'cultural campaign' being waged by America:

I was interested to find out how America's pop-cultural imperialism spread through the world's most ancient civilizations. I wanted to see what kind of resistance had been put up against the Coca-Colonizing forces and what kind of counter-strategies were planned. And I hoped to discover which Americas got through to the other side of the world, and which got lost in translation.[103]

The question of Asia's resistance to American cultural imperialism is significant, for Iyer sees various degrees of it over the course of his travels. The Chinese were pursuing a 'careful courtship' with the West, made apparent in official efforts to prevent ungoverned encounters between visitors like Iyer and the local Chinese population. In contrast, the Filipinos eagerly adopt American popular culture for

---

[102] Holland and Huggan cite Rob Nixon's argument that Naipaul switches between a 'distanced, analytic mode' and an 'emotionally tangled mode' in order to 'maximise the writer's discursive authority' (*Tourists with Typewriters*, p. 11); see also Rob Nixon, *London Calling: V. S. Naipaul, Postcolonial Mandarin* (Oxford: Oxford University Press, 1992).

[103] Pico Iyer, *Video Night in Kathmandu and Other Reports from the Not-So-Far East* (New York: Vintage Departures, 1988), p. 5. Iyer goes on to say, 'if pop culture was, in effect, just a shorthand for all that was young and modern and rich and free, it was also a virtual synonym for America' (p. 7). Holland and Huggan are generally positive about *Video Night* because it focuses on 'the process of transculturation – of mutual exchange and modification – that takes place when different cultural forms collide and intersect': *Tourists with Typewriters*, p. 22. Similarly, John Hatcher sees *Video Night* as 'the first postmodern Asian travel book': see 'Lonely Planet, Crowded World: Alex Garland's *The Beach*', *Studies in Travel Writing*, Vol. 3, 1999, pp. 131–47.

local consumption. Witnessing a karaoke presentation in a 'super-luxury hotel', Iyer comments: 'I absorbed one of the Orient's great truths: that the Filipinos are its omnipresent, always smiling troubadours. Master of every American gesture, conversant with every Western song, polished and ebullient all at once, the Filipino plays minstrel to the entire continent.'[104] While all these countries display some form of cultural hybridity (China cannot completely govern contact with the West, just as the Filipinos can never eradicate their local traditions), it is in India that Iyer discovers the right mix of adaptation and resistance. Rather than refuse America (like China and Burma) or adopt it wholesale (like the Philippines or Hong Kong), India has developed a complex and ambiguous relationship with American culture based on a more equal vision of cultural exchange. On the one hand, India is striving to become Western; as one Indian confesses to Iyer, 'the great dream of every Indian intellectual is to go abroad. He hungers for it. Even I feel more at home in New York or Paris than in Bombay or Delhi.'[105] But on the other hand, Indians refuse to simply adopt American ways of life, and choose instead to create their own versions:

For where Thailand, the Philippines, Nepal and Bali all excelled, in their different ways, at re-creating every rage from the West, India simply naturalised them...India had not imported McDonald's, as most countries had done, but had created instead its own fast-food emporia, Pizza King and Big Bite, which offered hamburgers without the beef...Prodigal, hydra-headed India cheerfully welcomed every new influence from the West, absorbing them all into a crazy-quilt mix that was Indian and nothing but Indian.[106]

The cultural exchange at work in India is key to Iyer's larger argument about globalisation. He ends *Video Night* with quite a polemical statement about the robustness of Asia when confronted by American imperialism (indeed, with a nod to both post-colonial theory and the *Star Wars* sequel, he calls the chapter 'The Empire Strikes Back'). After travelling through Asia and tracking the different reactions to American cultural imperialism, Iyer arrives at the following conclusions: 'the colonials were effectively staging their own takeover...The Orient, then, was taking over the future, a realm that had long seemed an exclusively Western dominion.'[107] It is quite surprising, then, that in much of his subsequent travel writing the polemical voice of resistance disappears. Instead, he begins to project his own subjectivity outward

[104] Iyer, *Video Night in Kathmandu*, p. 153.
[105] Iyer, *Video Night in Kathmandu*, pp. 273–4.
[106] Iyer, *Video Night in Kathmandu*, pp. 280, 358.
[107] Iyer, *Video Night in Kathmandu*, pp. 359–61.

and suggest that his hybrid cultural position is a universal condition. To be sure, Iyer begins *Video Nights* by explaining that home is 'the role and the self we choose to occupy', and admits that 'I left one kind of home to find another: to discover what resided in me and where I resided most fully'.[108] But Iyer moves on from there quite dramatically: he now symbolises a new kind of subject – not just culturally hybrid, but also perpetually in motion. In his most recent book, *The Global Soul*, Iyer develops his ideas about the universal nature of hybridity and homelessness. Citing the work of Emerson, Iyer argues: 'there is a "universal soul" behind us...and shining through us'. Not only does this global soul have a different sense of the self (as he/she is both hybrid and homeless), it also has a different sense of otherness:

our shrinking world gave more and more of us a chance to see, in palpable, unanswerable ways, how much we had in common, and how much we could live, in the grand Emersonian way, beyond petty allegiances and labels, outside the reach of nation-states...the Global Soul would be facing not just new answers to the old questions but a whole new set of questions...His sense of obligation would be different, if he felt himself part of no fixed community, and his sense of home, if it existed at all, would lie in the ties and talismans he carried around with him. Insofar as he felt a kinship with anyone, it would, most likely, be with other members of the Deracination-state.[109]

In *The Global Soul*, Iyer leaves behind the stories of local subjects who resist cultural imperialism and instead argues that the globalised world has become a new home for subjects in perpetual transit. Thus, while each chapter in *Video Night* detailed the variety of national responses to America, each chapter in *The Global Soul* examines the sites where these subjects-in-transit congregate – airports, the global marketplace, the multicultural city, shopping malls and the Olympic games.

The problem, here, is that Iyer's global soul bears significant traces of Naipaul's nostalgic Englishness and superiority. Let us take Holland and Huggan's claim that Iyer inaugurates a new phase of travel writing:

traveller writers such as Iyer, cosmopolitans from mixed cultural backgrounds, are no longer the exceptions they once were; on the contrary, they might yet in time become the general rule. Thus, while their travel books might be seen in a sense as *counter*narratives, insofar as they pit themselves against the various forms of Western cultural imperialism still dominant in the genre, they also

---

[108] Iyer, *Video Night in Kathmandu*, p. 9.
[109] Pico Iyer, *The Global Soul: Jet-Lag, Shopping Malls and the Search for Home* (London: Bloomsbury, 2000), p. 19.

reflect on a world that increasingly accords with their own experience – a diasporic world...[110]

Fair enough, but I see the problem with Iyer as the problem of cosmopolitanism: a refusal to see that his hybrid and homeless subjectivity is in fact saturated with privilege. In *Video Night*, this privilege seeps through every page, as Iyer is guided through Asia by a succession of very wealthy friends from Eton (the famous English public school attended by Princes William and Harry). Although Iyer claims that the ex-pat haven of Hong Kong is 'the world's great community of transients and refugees', the only 'transients and refugees' Iyer associates with are Old Etonians who are now investment bankers, stockbrokers, lawyers, diplomats and businessmen (all men, of course, given that Eton is an all-boys school). While Iyer strives to maintain a certain detachment from the 'clubby' atmosphere of his schoolmates, his associations reveal a great deal about the social circles within which his *particular* experience of hybridity has developed. Iyer's subjectivity is not born of hardship: he is neither transient nor refugee, but a wealthy, privileged and educated man who has all the benefits of travel and cosmopolitan life at his disposal. For Timothy Brennan, *Video Night* can't help but reveal the particular nature of this 'universal' subjectivity: 'from sentence to sentence, this global "we" gives way to a particularist North American and European one'.[111] But by the time he writes *The Global Soul*, Iyer has jettisoned the notion of cultural particularity and transformed his own hybrid identity into a universal condition. Iyer begins to see himself everywhere: 'now when I look around, there are more and more people in a similar state, the children of blurred boundaries and global mobility'.[112] It is no wonder, then, that Iyer's efforts to universalise his own subject position catapult him into a god-like position. Not only does he hope to 'live a little bit above parochialisms', he takes pleasure in the fact that he can 'see everywhere with a flexible eye'.[113] Unlike the Asians who cannily resisted American cultural imperialism, global souls are not interested in the petty struggles of mortals who are encumbered with the baggage of racial and gendered identities (remember, the 'global soul' is a 'he' that lives in a 'de-racinated' state). Rather, global souls gaze at the world and its political struggles from 'the metaphorical equivalent of international airspace' and, like the aloof colonial explorers before them,

---

[110] Holland and Huggan, *Tourists with Typewriters*, pp. 63–4. They go on to argue that the Asia of *Video Nights* is 'a land of surfaces that Iyer composes according to the "laws" of pastiche, collage, the crazy quilt' (p. 164).
[111] Brennan, *At Home in the World*, p. 187.
[112] Iyer, *The Global Soul*, p. 24.
[113] Iyer, *The Global Soul*, p. 24.

make judgements about the world they find below. If we mortals shed our loyalty to traditional identity claims (e.g. race, class, gender, ethnicity), then we too can join the exalted ranks of global souls swirling about in the cosmopolitan heavens. As Brennan argues, Iyer's is a classically cosmopolitan reading of globalisation: the cultural differences exposed by the forces of globalisation are both good and enriching, and if you fail to embrace cultural difference, you will be left out of the game. As he explains, 'the necessary precondition of Iyer's sort of writing is the assertion that the truth of the "global village" is simply unquestionable'.[114] Regardless of the many debates about globalisation that question its novelty, its extent and its reach, Iyer's position as a cosmopolitan global soul leads him to the conclusion that not only is globalisation a generally benign process, but it is a *fait accompli*.

Absent in Iyer's work is the flip side to the global soul – the new 'fundamentalist' identities that are resisting the hegemony of Western values embedded in globalisation in new and often violent ways. The Asia that Iyer visits in 1985 is not just comprised of Filipino karaoke singers, Thai hostesses, Chinese rickshaw drivers and Bombay film stars (for culture is not just about shiny consumer products and celebrity spectacles). Indeed, American cultural imperialism in Asia also takes place amongst longstanding cultural conflicts – between Hindus and Muslims in India, between Tamils and Sinhalese in Sri Lanka, and between Maoists and government forces in Nepal. As Brennan explains, Iyer refuses to see ethnic conflicts in Asia as 'a sign of resistance to the very enforced globalism he is busy constructing'; instead, he ignores those conflicts in favour of an argument about the *lack* of difference between cultures.[115] When Iyer does begin to explore the conflicts and difficulties of globalisation in *The Global Soul*, his tone becomes moralising and judgemental. Global souls like himself and Salman Rushdie are modern, civilised and cosmopolitan, whereas fundamentalists (including those stalking Rushdie) are ancient, backward and parochial. To be sure, fundamentalists use the circuits of globalisation to pursue their 'almost medieval cause', but they are afforded none of the complex and hybrid characteristics that mark out cosmopolitans (indeed, in Iyer's framework it would be impossible for a member of Al-Qaeda or the Taliban to be a global soul). But those complex and hybrid characteristics are also denied to subjects living under authoritarian rule in 'uncivilised' places. Indeed, when Iyer steps off the plane in Haiti, he is as horrified as any pristine Victorian explorer.

---

[114] Brennan, *At Home in the World*, p. 186.
[115] Brennan, *At Home in the World*, p. 187.

His descriptions of the hell he finds there are familiar: rubbish, unemployment, high mortality rates, endemic violence and even women 'relieving themselves along the main streets'.[116]

In the end, I am unconvinced by Holland and Huggan's claim that Iyer writes counternarratives that chart new ground in travel writing. Cosmopolitan travel writers cannot be protected just because they offer a departure from the colonial vision so embedded in the work of writers like Theroux. As Timothy Brennan explains, the 'colonial erotics' of cosmopolitan travel writers like Iyer are not as crude as their predecessors, but the *function* of these narratives remains the same.[117] Holland and Huggan are right to suggest that a text like *Video Night* – which they describe as 'an attractive and superior travel book' – prompts questions about the tension between standpoint and post-structural accounts of identity. And they do not celebrate Iyer's text uncritically; indeed, they make important points about Iyer's obligation to his economic and literary patrons.[118] But my concerns are of a slightly different order – I think *Video Night* and *The Global Soul* are efforts to *overcome* the tensions between standpoint and discursive accounts of subjectivity through an inclusive cosmopolitan identity. The difficulty is that I, like Brennan, see cosmopolitan subjectivities as both provocative and problematic. Iyer's global soul is certainly a complex subject formation – hybrid, fractured, in-transit – but it is also hugely privileged. The central problem here is that cosmopolitans like Iyer define, decide and ultimately erase cultural difference on their own particular terms while claiming to base these judgements on universal criteria.

Gary Younge's book *No Place Like Home: A Black Briton's Journey through the American South* is a more historically oriented travelogue that uses the American civil rights movement to reflect upon trans-Atlantic issues of race, nationalism and ethnic identity. While Iyer is in search of hybrid identities negotiating an increasingly homogeneous global

---

[116] Iyer, *The Global Soul*, p. 32. As Holland and Huggan explain, this moralistic voyeurism is a well-established trope of both colonial and post-colonial travel writers who are 'quick to register distaste for the "degenerate" practices of other cultures, but are less inclined to recognize their enjoyment of the tawdriness those cultures display': *Tourists with Typewriters*, p. 19.

[117] Brennan, *At Home in the World*, p. 185.

[118] Holland and Huggan begin a useful 'political economy' of Iyer's position by explaining how 'his travels – and their literary by-product, his travel writing – are complicit with the very processes of commodification they seek to document and explore'. They go on to lament, 'Iyer's reluctance to come to terms with his own technologies of representation, and to admit their investment in the ideology of consumerism he sets out to critique' (pp. 62–3). As they suggest, perhaps it is the ideology of Iyer's patron and sponsor – *Time* magazine – that prevents him from examining his own complicity in the asymmetrical circuits of both tourism and publishing (p. 165).

culture, Younge is concerned with how the civil rights movement in America has informed the trans-Atlantic black experience. Younge's parents were part of the 'Windrush' generation, West Indians who were enticed to England in the 1950s with the promise of steady employment and new opportunities. His story describes the various forms of racism he and his family encountered while growing up in Britain and compares that with the racial politics that have shaped the American South since the civil rights movement. While Younge covers the same terrain of identity politics as Iyer, he offers a much more nuanced understanding of subjectivity. When he describes how he and his brothers grew up in Stevenage, he articulates a notion of identity that is fractured, hybrid and marked by multiple inflections of difference depending on each social and political context:

> Depending on who we were talking to, we were as likely to say we were Bajan as British... We would pick'n'mix and the answer we gave depended partly on what we thought the motivation for the question was, partly on the fact that nobody gave us the option of being both at the same time and partly on what we perceived our interests to be at any given moment. When it became apparent to me, several years later, that there was more to racial identity than nationality and that, in any case, I didn't have to cement myself in one identity and stay there for the duration of an entire conversation, let along my whole life, it was a great relief.[119]

Younge pursues this theme of strategic subjectivity throughout the book: 'Identities suffocate if trapped in the narrow confines of a definition for too long. But everyone needs a working title.'[120] What makes this book especially provocative are those moments when Younge's complex subjectivity is suspended in the face of racism in both Britain and the South. This is where Younge gets angry and reverts to an essential identity – black – in order to authorise his personal and political statements about racism. In two particular episodes in the book, Younge's 'working title' of black Briton becomes momentarily reified: he is black, he is on the side of the oppressed and he is committed to fighting the structures of power and race that have placed him – and others – in that position. In Orangeburg, South Carolina, Younge makes his way to the All Star Triangle Bowl where three black men were killed in 1968 after their efforts to go bowling instigated a race riot. But he is not prepared when he encounters the original proprietor,

---

[119] Gary Younge, *No Place Like Home: A Black Briton's Journey through the American South* (London: Picador, 1999), p. 12.
[120] Younge, *No Place Like Home*, p. 168.

Harry Floyd, who originally barred the black students from entering his bowling alley:

Professionally I know the right thing to do would have been to go up and ask him for an interview. Politically it would have been the right thing to do, too. I could have asked him if he had a conscience and, if he did, were the lives of three young black men on it? I could have asked whether he had ever thought to apologize to the families of the men who had died . . . But personally, I could not stomach it. The fact that he was still there denoted a lack of progress for me . . . I didn't want to talk to him. I wanted to yell at him, spit in his face and trash all of his vending machines. And since I couldn't do that either, I turned around, put the shoes on the counter and walked out of the door.[121]

Younge is similarly outraged when examining the Civil War memorials in Richmond, Virginia, which openly celebrate racist Confederate heroes. But he is even more dismayed by the attempt to suggest a multiracial society by the addition of tennis player Arthur Ashe's statue at the end of the block. Feeling 'angry and confused' at the fact that these racists were 'honoured and exalted' (and that Ashe's statue needed an explanation whereas the others were self-evidently important), Younge makes a particularly interesting point: 'in the midst of my rage, the slight geographical fact that I am from England and not the American South felt like an irrelevance – they stole my ancestors and just took them somewhere else'.[122] Younge's negotiation here is curious, for in a book that takes great care in outlining the differences between racism in America and Britain, he also expresses solidarity with African-Americans because he is black: 'I resented the fact that on the way to work every day, black people have to look at that.'[123]

What is interesting about Younge's book is his openness about the struggle between standpoint and discursive understandings of subjectivity. He makes no effort to hide the contradictions and difficulties this debate poses for his own position. Younge is strident in his political views on race, and explicit about his commitment to socialist values (the precise qualities that made his book so popular with middle-class *Guardian*-readers), but he is also aware of the difficulties that such a position creates. Certainly, by revealing his anger at the continuing racism in America, his political views are justified. However, by allowing those moments of anger into the text at all, *No Place Like Home* questions the idea that the travel writer maintains an objective distance from his/her subject throughout the text. Indeed, Younge undertook the

---

[121] Younge, *No Place Like Home*, pp. 141–2.
[122] Younge, *No Place Like Home*, p. 67.
[123] Younge, *No Place Like Home*, p. 67.

project precisely because he wanted to work through his own struggles over racial identity: 'I went halfway across the world and actually found out more about myself than I did about where I was going.'[124] This willingness to subject the self to scrutiny is at odds with much contemporary travel writing that, as Todorov suggests, uses the self to convey fleeting impressions of exotic places and people. Younge, of course, is quite aware of this tradition in travel writing:

In terms of affirming identities, it's much easier to pronounce on other people's cultures than to interrogate your own, I think, because you only know the bit of the story that they tell you, and so there is an inbuilt arrogance in all travel writing, which is about: 'Well, I'm going to go there.' If you want to find out about things, stay at home: that is a reasonable argument to make. The number of people that you see travelling around the world who really should stay at home is quite breathtaking![125]

Younge attempts something different in *No Place Like Home*: despite those moments of clarity when he is absolutely sure of his identity (e.g. his anger at continuing racism), he refuses to accept that identities are ever coherent or complete. He knows that every person has a 'fluid' identity, but he also knows that this fluidity does not neutralise politics: 'in a way identity is about labels, a collection of labels and how you use them'.[126]

Younge's awareness of complex subjectivity is rare in a genre that encourages a coherent and stable 'I' — even if, as is the case with Iyer, that identity is itself hybrid. What marks Younge's text off from Iyer's is precisely this measure of awareness: Iyer is unwilling to explore how his own position — hybrid as it might be — is saturated with privilege, whereas Younge is able to illustrate how his changing identity has been informed by both personal experiences (e.g. his mother's racial politics, growing up in a mostly white suburb) and wider structures of power at work during his youth in Britain (e.g. the policies of Thatcher, the rise of skinheads). To what extent, then, does Younge's willingness to interrogate his own position make *No Place Like Home* a radical travelogue, as some critics have argued?[127] Younge himself admits that his subversion of the genre is racial: his identity as a black man automatically disrupts the traditional subject position of the

[124] Tim Youngs, 'Interview with Gary Younge', *Studies in Travel Writing*, No. 6, 2002, p. 104.
[125] Youngs, 'Interview with Gary Younge', p. 104.
[126] Youngs, 'Interview with Gary Younge', p. 106.
[127] Youngs argues that *No Place Like Home* is a radical text because it subverts a particular model of travel writing by augmenting stories of the personal self with a social and cultural self: 'Interview with Gary Younge', p. 105.

travel writer.[128] However, while Younge's own racial politics might be radical, the manner in which he transmits these ideas through the generic form of the travelogue is quite conventional. In effect, Younge does not do anything different with the 'travelling in the footsteps' tradition of travel writing – he follows the Freedom Riders (civil rights activists from the 1960s who famously desegregated buses) and reflects upon how their activities influence contemporary racial politics. In effect, while Younge's complex understandings of race and subjectivity are provocative, they are somewhat contained within the conventional narrative structure of the travelogue. Indeed, the last line – 'I was back home, to a bigotry I understand' – reveals an important absence in the book: how are racial identities formed by the experience of travel and migration? Racial identities do not exist in hermetically sealed locations like 'Britain' or 'America': they are also constructed *in transit* through the circuits of globalisation. Is Younge's own post-colonial identity part of a new black diaspora? Are there new forms of racism being enabled by the forces of globalisation?

In writing *No Place Like Home*, Younge wanted to develop a personal voice capable of revealing his own feelings and experiences about race, and linking those emotions to wider political structures and debates. While he was inspired by socialist writers like Angela Davis, he was frustrated that she evacuated all personal stories and anecdotes from her narratives.[129] What is interesting in Younge's desire to craft a politically engaged personal voice is its feminist heritage – merging the political and the personal has long been a feminist practice. Moreover, Younge's inclusion of personal revelations in *No Place Like Home* means that, for the most part, it avoids the tropes of masculinity that underscore travelogues of even the most committed new men. While Younge is open about his anger, frustration and loneliness while on the road, Iyer's emotions are contained in a serene and objective subject position that is indebted to the English travel writers of the 1930s. Nothing fazes Iyer – even when his house burns down and he is caught in a mudslide, he is never too busy to seek out other displaced global souls and ponder the possibilities of cosmopolitanism. Certainly these two writers differ in their racial politics (Iyer preferring a de-racinated cosmopolitanism, Younge interrogating the endemic structures of racism and oppression), but they also differ in their approach to gender. Iyer is not interested in the gendered characteristics of global souls, whereas Younge employs

---

[128] Youngs, 'Interview with Gary Younge', pp. 103–4.
[129] Youngs, 'Interview with Gary Younge', pp. 98–9.

a feminist merging of the personal and the political because he knows that travel writing has its roots in colonialism *and* patriarchy.

Engendering the travel writer: subjects, bodies and resistance

We know that the production of difference is somewhat arrested by women travel writers who simultaneously occupy both positions in the identity/difference logic. But while the position of the honorary man allows women travel writers to be included in a male-dominated genre, it does not necessarily disrupt the power of representation guaranteed by the masculine gaze. This position is difficult for women travel writers to negotiate: they don't want to fully adopt the hyper-masculine codes of the genre (for this would mean losing their unique status as 'women in a man's world'), but neither do they want to reverse that gaze and end up in a purely 'personal' tale of emotions, sentimentality and everyday detail (for this would disprove that they are tough enough to be included in the travel writing genre in the first place). The limitations of the honorary man position are revealed most acutely when women travel writers have to negotiate difference in foreign lands:

The line between being an 'honorary man' and an available sex object (symbol of the immoral West) is a hard one to negotiate... Often there's an uneasy guilt about identifying with men – who in many cultures are much more likely to approach and entertain passing strangers – and a regret at the barriers that exist in forging closer relationships with women...Being an honorary man might have some advantages, but it can be unsettling to feel excluded as a bad influence or unfit companion for sisters and daughters.[130]

The desire of honorary men to show solidarity with foreign women often ignores the cultural differences at work in the experience of travel. These are complex negotiations: Western women travel writers are patronised and objectified by foreign men, but don't they equally patronise and objectify both men and women of foreign lands when they exoticise them?

On the surface, Dew's *The Wind in My Wheels* appears as an oddly 'genderless' book – which isn't to say there are no messages of masculinity and femininity in the text; it's just that Dew is unwilling and uninterested in dealing with difficult questions that disrupt her superficial and distanced demeanour. As she states herself, 'I prefer to remain "lost within" and throw any self-analysis to the wind.'[131] Dew presents

[130] Natania Janz and Miranda Davies, 'Introduction', in Janz and Davies, eds., *More Women Travel: A Rough Guide Special* (London: Rough Guides, 1995), pp. xiv–vi.
[131] Dew, *The Wind in My Wheels*, p. 172.

herself as a 'genderless' narrator as if her only functions are observer, describer and representer. But the ruse of the 'objective observer' only reinforces the power of masculinity to shape honorary men: what could be more rational, truthful, devoid of sentiment and emotions than 'objectivity'? In short, what could be more masculine? The key function of these 'genderless' texts is the displacement of gendered traits onto local others: masculinity and femininity might not be something that the *writer* exhibits (for she is simply 'objective'), but they can certainly be found in the people being written *about*. During her trips to Egypt, Tunisia and Morocco, Dew's text is filled with descriptions of the pestering and ogling Muslim men who never leave her alone. They are described, at various times, as clamouring, noisy, hawking, relentless, greasy-haired, curious, unceasing, inane, gibbering, hammering, filthy, stalking hustlers and tormentors. And the women, when they are present (which isn't very often given the ubiquitous and pestering nature of the men) don't fare much better. When Dew is invited to dinner by Mohammed in Morocco, she reveals the capacity to displace both masculine and feminine codes away from her own subject position:

His wife could speak no English and sat in a corner smiling shyly, every now and then leaving the room as she obeyed her husband's imperious commands... the evening began to turn sour when he expected payment for his hospitality... All the while his shrew-like little wife sat timidly in the corner, looking embarrassed about the whole affair. It was only because of her mute work-dog role, her poverty, the meal she had prepared for us and her genuine expressions of apology about her husband's aggressive imploring that we handed her some dirhams. Then we left.[132]

As the last sentence illustrates, Dew is able to abandon those awkward negotiations of gender and poverty as if they don't affect her, as if she – as traveller – can step outside of the everyday power relations that are enacted between men and women. Because Dew has swallowed the 'objective' masculine gaze of the travel writer and displaced all negotiations of gender onto those she meets, all she can manage by way of engagement with the other is the temporary salve of hard currency and a hasty retreat.

In neglecting to recognise the gendered *and* privileged nature of her subject position, Dew focuses instead on the values and standards that differentiate her from the locals she meets. Therefore, women in 'unenlightened' places like Morocco are stuck in the traditional gender roles that Western women have already surpassed. In short, Dew is *more emancipated* than the women she encounters in Africa. But this is

[132] Dew, *The Wind in My Wheels*, p. 158.

precisely the difficulty with the honorary man: by displacing gender onto those who are observed, it seems as if the masculine gaze of the travel writer is slightly shifted. But that shift presents its own collusions with power: gender attachments have only moved laterally – from one object (woman) to another (native). What's more, that shift does not disrupt the fact that these women travel writers are still cast as unthreatening figures, 'feminised' to the extent that even the most courageous journeys are placed in the category of myth, eccentricity and abnormality.[133] As Dew's text illustrates, the liberal feminism that underscores the position of the honorary man ends up reinforcing masculine norms and patri- archal structures. Dew's refusal to engage with questions of gender in her travelogue is acceptable within a liberal feminist framework because liberal feminists promote a future of equality when questions of gender will no longer matter. Dew's very position as a travel writer testifies to the success of liberal feminism – the previously male-dominated genre of travel writing has had to make room for her. But once she is on the road, her gender ceases to matter – she is doing what *all* travel writers do, regardless of their gender. In effect, Dew is the ideal liberal feminist, and exemplary of an entire subgenre of women's travel writing that says 'hey look, we can do this too!'

There are, however, more politically engaged travelogues that fore- ground gender as a powerful force shaping the lives of men and women. In these texts, a commitment to feminism doesn't cease just because certain opportunities (like writing about travel) have opened up for women. Davidson's *Tracks* is a particularly good example of this approach, as it addresses both personal and systemic issues of gender politics. Because Davidson is well aware of how gender works to position women negatively in society, she is able to understand why the world's press perceive her camel trek as extraordinary simply because she is a woman. Reflecting upon her new (and unwanted) identity as 'camel lady' at the end of her narrative, Davidson discusses with great clarity the mechanisms by which girls are disciplined into their familiar feminine roles:

The world is a dangerous place for little girls. Besides, little girls are more fragile, more delicate, more brittle than little boys. 'Watch out, be careful, watch.' 'Don't climb trees, don't dirty your dress, don't accept lifts from strange men. Listen but don't learn, you won't need it.' And so the snails' antennae grow, watching for this and looking for that, the underneath of things. The threat. And so she wastes so much of her energy, seeking to break those circuits, to push up the millions of thumbs that have tried to quench energy and creativity and

[133] Lisle, 'Gender at a Distance', pp. 74–6.

strength and self-confidence; that have so effectively caused her to build fences against possibility, daring; that have so effectively kept her imprisoned inside her notions of self-worthlessness.[134]

While Davidson's sentiment applies to a much larger context than travel writing, this passage illustrates how powerful disciplining practices position women in subordinate roles. Her refusal to ignore questions of gender once she is on the road means that *Tracks* presents a hopeful and more explicitly feminist message than Dew's — especially to young girls. *Tracks* certainly suggests that women can travel just like men, but it is also careful to illustrate the different (and often undocumented) experiences that women encounter while travelling. Some of these experiences are difficult and depressing (e.g. sexism, helplessness, exclusion), but some are liberating (e.g. escaping the societal constraints of gender stereotypes). What is compelling about Davidson's narrative is that her experiences are never wholly determined by her identity as a woman. Indeed, like all modern subjects, she is a complex mixture of masculinity and femininity — only in her case, these juxtapositions are worked out primarily in relationship to the camels. After an incident in which one of the camels has a panic attack, she ties him to a tree and 'beat[s] the living daylights out of him'. Once that episode passes, however, she comments: 'If, as Hemingway suggested, "courage is grace under pressure", then the trip proved once and for all that I was sadly lacking in the stuff. I felt ashamed.'[135] These episodes flesh out Davidson's subjectivity: she is constructed in the vacillation between a masculine 'Hemingway' ideal (tough, ruthless, brave) and a more emotional, revealing self (doubtful, questioning, introspective).

Davidson's careful attention to the way gender shapes her own position as traveller, as well as how wider patterns of masculinity and femininity are socially conditioned, means that she goes some way towards disrupting the colonial and patriarchal foundations of travel writing. However, like Younge, Davidson's complex understanding of subjectivity falls silent when she faces the legacies of colonialism and racism in Australia. Davidson is clear on her political position: what Aboriginal communities need is self-determination and independence, and by refusing to support Aboriginal land claims 'we are committing cultural and, in this case, racial genocide'.[136] She spends time with many Aboriginal communities throughout her travels, but she is aware of how her own identity as a white woman traveller conflicts with their desire

[134] Davidson, *Tracks*, pp. 236–7.
[135] Davidson, *Tracks*, p. 123.
[136] Davidson, *Tracks*, p. 167.

for autonomy. While Aboriginal groups are always welcoming – and appreciative of her efforts to speak Pitjantjara – she is careful not to intrude on their culture:

I stayed three days in Areyonga, talking to people and generally getting the feel of the place and living with a schoolteacher and his family. I would have dearly loved to stay down at camp but was too shy to force myself on to people who might not want a whitefella hanging around, poking her nose into their business.[137]

There is something provocative in the juxtaposition of Davidson's cautious regard for Aboriginal communities and her passionate support for their political mobilisation. She is well aware of the legacy of colonialism, and knows that her identity as a white woman prevents her from participating fully within that community. While she refuses simple accounts of subjectivity with respect to gender (she is not only a woman, she is a subject with contradictory masculine and feminine qualities), she accepts that standpoint identity politics are the way forward for Aboriginal communities.

Certainly there are now honorary men and new men who write about travel in more 'gender-sensitive' ways. But those subject positions do not destabilise the *embodied* categories of gender. Despite her masculine behaviour, there is no doubt that at the end of the day Davidson is a woman – her body is the final arbiter of her gender category. While contemporary travel writers are able to represent the vacillation between masculine and feminine behaviour, they are unable to discuss how gender is contained within the more foundational categories of sexed bodies.[138] Certainly, sexual encounters with foreigners have long been

---

[137] Davidson, *Tracks*, p. 120. Given her complex and contradictory understanding of subjectivity, Davidson does not romanticise the Aboriginals like Chatwin does, even when she is advocating their political cause. Despite the liberal credentials of contemporary travel writers, many collude with both patriarchy and colonialism by domesticating, romanticising and patronising the 'Indian' or the 'Aboriginal.' While the writers themselves may be empowered by feminist, post-colonial and cosmopolitan attitudes, the indigenous and Aboriginal groups they encounter are still living a 'false consciousness' under the combined rule of colonialism and patriarchy. This is particularly the case with Monica Furlong's depiction of Aboriginals in *Flight of the Kingfisher*, and Thomas Keneally's representations of the Hopi, Navajo, Zuni and Pueblo Indians in *The Place Where Souls Are Born*.

[138] I use the work of Judith Butler to discuss the embodiment of the honorary man in greater detail in 'Gender at a Distance.' However, given Butler's arguments about the construction of sexuality, I am aware that there is much work to be done on the conjunction of sexuality and travel in contemporary travelogues. For example, a queer analysis of hyper-masculine texts might reveal how travel writers respond to the regulating mechanisms of heterosexuality by repressing their 'forbidden' sexual desires.

part of the travelogue genre (including contemporary women writers who escape their puritanical homes and find sexual liberation abroad), but the embodied categories of gender – the bodies of men and women – are not transgressed in travel writing. The obvious contemporary writer to problematise this question is Jan Morris: soldier and political correspondent James Morris became travel writer Jan Morris after a sex-change operation in 1972. Susan Bassnett calls Jan Morris 'the greatest woman travel writer of the twentieth century' and suggests that in Morris's travelogues 'assumptions about travel writing and gender are most seriously challenged'.[139] For Bassnett, Morris's refusal to rewrite her earlier 'James Morris' travelogues attests to a strong narrative voice that prevails no matter what gendered identity he/she possesses. In other words, Morris is a good travel writer because her texts focus on the 'relationship between the travel writer as individual and the space in which she moves. Everything else is inessential.'[140] I want to argue that Morris's reluctance to discuss matters of gender in her travel writing is absolutely essential because it reveals the power of generic limitations to constrain the subject position of the travel writer. Morris does discuss the ramifications of her gender re-assignment in her autobiography *Conundrum* (1974), which suggests that travel writing does not permit a narrative voice that is sexually ambivalent. Rather, as Holland and Huggan argue, the desexualised and singular narrative voice of Morris's travel writing is used to 'recuperate and imaginatively repossess the British Imperial world'.[141] In other words, admitting an identity that is complex, hybrid and contingent – especially in its sexuality – is unacceptable in a genre so thoroughly governed by colonialism and patriarchy. The generic constraints that prevent Morris from discussing her sexuality in relation to travel work to re-inscribe the public/private split that shapes the coherent subject position of the travel writer: her sexuality is a private matter that has no place in travel writing. The 'self' revealed in her travel writing is a well-constructed public self who is willing to provide impressions of foreign places, but who is not willing to divulge the private desires and contradictions that underscore those personal impressions.

---

[139] Bassnett, 'Travel Writing and Gender', p. 238.
[140] Bassnett, 'Travel Writing and Gender', p. 239.
[141] Holland and Huggan, *Tourists with Typewriters*, p. 119. More interesting for Holland and Huggan are the moments in Morris's travel writing that 'suggest a more conflicted view than the one she wishes to present in her autobiography' (*Tourists with Typewriters*, p. 119); see also Richard Phillips, 'Decolonizing Geographies of Travel: Reading James/Jan Morris', *Social and Cultural Geography*, Vol. 2, No. 1, 2001, pp. 5–24.

Locating privilege: positioning the travel writer

To make sense of the doubled constraints of genre and gender, it is worth going back to Younge's *No Place Like Home* — a text that not only interrogates questions of race and identity but also goes some way to resisting the masculine gaze of the travelogue. Younge's narrative disrupts the public/private split by allowing discussions of emotional and personal revelations alongside well-constructed 'impressions' of the American South. One of the inspirations for Younge's book was Lisa Jones's *Bulletproof Diva: Tales of Race, Sex and Hair*. Jones's book impressed Younge because it took very personal stories and went 'outwards' — it used stories of the self to tell wider and more politically directed stories about America's pursuit of multiculturalism. Jones — like Younge — is clear about her understanding of identity, and she is perplexed when readers don't understand

that I'm a writer whose work is dedicated to exploring the hybridity of African-American culture and of American culture in general. That I don't deny my white forebears, but I call myself African American, which means, to me, a person of African and Native American, Latin, or European descent. That I feel comfortable and historically grounded in this identity. That I find family there, whereas no white people have embraced me with their culture, have said to me, take this gift, it's yours, and we are yours, no problem. That, by claiming African American and black, I also inherit a right to ask questions about what this identity means. And that chances are this identity will never be static, which is fine by me.[142]

In varying commentaries, Jones traces the tension between, on the one hand, a standpoint African-American identity and, on the other hand, a hybrid multicultural position. *Bulletproof Diva* is not a travelogue: aside from a trip to 'liberal' Minnesota, Jones does not travel outside of New York City, and the book is a collection of newspaper articles that Jones wrote for the *Village Voice* under the heading 'Skin Trade'. But *Bulletproof Diva* is useful here, for it reveals the generic constraints that travel writers must negotiate with respect to representing themselves and representing others. This is not a simple argument that black women are the *only* subjects able to successfully launch a critique of both the colonial and patriarchal legacies of travel writing. Rather, I want to suggest that Jones's narrative is challenging because it balances the claims of identity politics on the one hand (especially race and gender),

---

[142] Lisa Jones, *Bulletproof Diva: Tales of Race, Sex and Hair* (London: Penguin, 1995), p. 31.

and the knowledge of contingent subjectivity on the other hand (especially hybrid, multicultural subjects-in-transit).

In citing Jones's work as an inspiration for *No Place Like Home*, and explaining his own motivation to write a travelogue, Younge argues: 'One of the things I dislike most about some travel books is when they have no purpose. Why are you in the Antarctic? If someone can explain to you why they are somewhere that makes all the difference; it's a motivation for people to be in a certain place.'[143] This highlights the difficulty of travel writing in a context of globalisation: why should readers care about journeys they could potentially make themselves? In many ways, the travelogue is the ultimate self-indulgence: it is based on the assumption that what travel writers have to say about the world is somehow more interesting, more exciting, more thought-provoking, more educational and more vivid than what anyone else has to say about it. Even Paul Theroux acknowledges this aspect of the genre: 'I had always somewhat disliked travel books: they seemed self-indulgent, unfunny and rather selective. I had an idea that the travel writer left a great deal out of his books and put the wrong things in... The travel book was a bore. A bore wrote it and bores read it.'[144] Of course, Theroux believes that *his* travel writing is of a different order − it avoids the clichés of travel writing by recording the truth: 'Travel had to do with movement and truth: with trying everything, offering yourself to experience and then reporting it.'[145] Theroux's conceit here is simply another form of self-indulgence − an arrogance that *he alone* can find, translate and report the 'truth' of travel. In Theroux's case, the 'special status' that grants him the privilege to write travelogues is his reputation as a successful novelist. But with the democratisation of the genre, there are a multitude of 'special-status' positions that allow travel writers to justify why *their* musings are more important than the average tourist's: previously marginalised others (e.g. the first woman/black/disabled person to make this journey); an already acquired 'celebrity' personality (e.g. Michael Palin); or simply a talent for humorous writing that appeals to the middle classes (e.g. Bill Bryson). What is particularly interesting in travel writing is that *all* these 'special-status' positions still require a coherent subject capable of describing, organising and

---

[143] Youngs, 'Interview with Gary Younge', p. 100; earlier on in the interview, Younge argues, 'In a lot of newspapers now you get people who just write about their lives and what's in their fridge and all that kind of stuff, and I think it's fine to write just about your life, so long as your life is more interesting than mine because otherwise why would I read that? I've got a life of my own...' (p. 98).
[144] Theroux, 'First Train Journey', p. 167.
[145] Theroux, 'First Train Journey', p. 168.

translating difference. So Theroux can be misanthropic when surveying other cultures, Dew can be silent about herself but judgemental of others, Iyer can project his own hybridity into the world, Bryson can be self-deprecating when faced with the childishness of what he is doing, and Palin can be ironic when encountering difference – but none of these travel writers are able to confront the contingency of their own subject positions during the experience of travel. In effect, the genre that offers the most opportunity to explore intersubjective relations between the self and the other is paralysed by literary conventions that protect the subject position of the travel writer. To be sure, meta-discussions of the author-function occur in literature and autobiography, but they are rare in the travelogue.[146] This lack of reflexivity means that when new subjectivities – new 'special-status' categories – emerge in travel writing, they are soon assimilated into literary conventions that insist upon either a 'monarch-of-all-I-survey' subjectivity keen on reviving colonial and patriarchal visions, or a cosmopolitan subjectivity keen on encountering cultural difference only to overcome it in the name of universality.

---

[146] As Holland and Huggan explain, 'It is worth noting here that travel books – particularly those that declare themselves as generic – do not generally exploit opportunities for textual play and reflexivity. Such play might perhaps threaten the different kinds of authority the traveller claims, including that of truth telling, itself dependent on the fiction of a centred self', *Tourists with Typewriters*, p. 174. They explore this 'centred self' through autobiographies written by travel writers, such as Paul Theroux's *My Other Life – A Novel* (London: Penguin, 1997) and Jonathan Raban's *Hunting Mr Heartbreak* (London: Picador, 1991), pp. 174–8.

4   Civilising territory: geographies of safety and danger

I'm not that comfortable about writing about the third world.
I find it hard to make jokes when people are sleeping under bridges
and don't have enough to eat.

Bill Bryson[1]

After publishing successful travelogues about America, Europe, the UK and Australia, Bill Bryson was approached by the charity CARE International to write a book about some of their development projects in Kenya. The result was a carefully orchestrated eight-day trip and a 56-page travelogue – *African Diary* – which was published just before Christmas 2002. The whole point of the endeavour was that all profits from Bryson's *African Diary* went directly to CARE International. While the book was an entirely worthy effort to eradicate poverty and underdevelopment, its worthiness reveals something important about the limitations of Bryson's cosmopolitan vision. *African Diary* tries to squeeze Kenya into Bryson's well-established comedic formula of 'ordinary guy abroad': he continues to be self-deprecating (he is afraid of flying, afraid of snakes, afraid of catching a disease); he embellishes his romantic notions of Africa (gleaned largely from 'Jungle Jim' movies of the 1950s); he gushes about the Rift Valley ('startlingly sumptuous in its beauty'); and he carefully contrasts himself (scared, timid, innocent, naïve) with the brave and committed workers in CARE International.[2] Initially, Bryson's reactions to Kenya are a familiar blend of innocence and incredulity: for example, he is dumbfounded by the statistics of poverty in Nairobi's largest slum: 'Really?... That's amazing!... Truly?' His childlike wonder begins to take on a more judgemental tone when he learns about corrupt Kenyan officials: 'In one year, according to

---

[1] Fiachra Gibbons, 'Bryson to Turn Over the Maple Leaf', *Guardian*, 2 June 2003, p. 11.
[2] Terence Blacker argues that 'Bryson is a master anecdotalist, recounting his adventures, mishaps and encounters of an ordinary guy abroad in a relaxed fireside manner', 'Bill's Awfully Big Adventure', *Sunday Times* (Culture), 11 June 2000, p. 33.

the BBC, ten billion dollars of public funds went missing in Kenya. Ten billion dollars! In one year! And it didn't even top the list!'[3] As the narrative develops, Bryson's usual comedic formula begins to disappear, and by the time he visits a Somali refugee camp at Dadaab, he appeals to the reader directly: 'They were just normal people like you and me who wanted to be somewhere where they could have a life.'[4] This direct mode of address culminates on the last page of the book when Bryson congratulates the reader's charitable intentions: 'I don't know if you are fully aware of it, but in acquiring this slender volume you didn't actually buy a book. You made a generous donation to a worthy cause and got a free book in return, which isn't quite the same thing. It's much nobler. On behalf of CARE, thank-you.'[5] It is easy to see why Bryson chose to combine his usual comedic formula with a direct mode of address in *African Diary:* his previous travelogues were successful precisely because this narrative combination allowed readers to identify directly with the 'ordinary guy' persona of the author, foibles and all. But Bryson's travelogues do not offer equivalence; rather, they flatter the reader by encouraging a paternal attitude towards the author. In other words, Bryson's form of direct address does not say 'I'm just like you', it says 'you are much less shambolic and childish than I am'. This rather cosy relationship relies on sharing 'light-hearted' opinions (e.g. the French are rude, the Americans are stupid), but it also allows Bryson to offer more 'political' observations (e.g. destroying the environment is bad, eradicating poverty is good). Bryson's cultivation of a middle-class Anglo-American audience is successful for two reasons: (a) his 'serious' political opinions never intrude on his comedic observations (i.e. the books never get too 'preachy'), and (b) his political opinions are uncontentious (i.e. he never calls for anything radical that would upset the status quo).

What makes *African Diary* so interesting in this context is Bryson's failure to appeal to his loyal readership. Despite his established success and his good intentions, *African Diary* was badly received by readers and critics alike. As the opening quotation suggests, there is something about Bryson's usual approach that does not work in Africa – there is something wrong about recycling hyperbolic stereotypes and exaggerated caricatures in the face of more pressing concerns. Reflecting on this failure, Bryson commented: 'It is much, much easier for me to make fun of people in wealthy countries like Canada. I have a problem writing my

---

[3] Bill Bryson, *African Diary* (London: Doubleday, 2002), p. 49.
[4] Bryson, *African Diary*, p. 39.
[5] Bryson, *African Diary*, p. 56.

kind of book about Third World countries... the response to the book made it clear to me that reviewers would not let me write seriously.'[6] Embedded in this observation is a crucial assumption: that Bryson's self-deprecation, hyperbole and 'poking fun' only work in wealthy countries. Indeed, he has successfully mocked eccentric Britons (*Notes from a Small Island*), fat Americans (*The Lost Continent*) and idiosyncratic Australians (*Down Under*). Why, then, can he not poke fun at Africans? Is it because Africans are not funny? Certainly not – the satirical works of Sembene Ousemane, Wole Soyinka and Emmanuel Dongala point to a diverse and healthy tradition of African comedy. Is it because Bryson is not funny? Certainly not – even if his style is not to everyone's liking, there is no doubt he has a talent for observational comedy. I want to argue that *African Diary* fails because it disrupts the geopolitical assumptions that sustain the genre of travel writing. Telling, here, is Bryson's comment that reviewers would not let him write 'seriously': what critics and readers did not like was the comedic treatment of a 'serious' subject like poverty.[7] Africa *can* be the object of 'serious' travel writing, political journalism, news reports and charity appeals because these cultural forms invoke pity, concern and guilt on the part of the reader. But Africa *cannot* be the object of comedy because laughter contravenes deeply entrenched expectations of how one is supposed to react to a place that is only ever represented as poverty-stricken, war-torn, corrupt and devastated. What reviewers, critics and readers found difficult about *African Diary* was its juxtaposition of pity and laughter: the former is acceptable in the context of Africa, but the latter is not. We are familiar, and therefore comfortable, with the prevailing discourse of development that routinely places Africa in an abject position to be pitied, governed and ultimately controlled. We know how to react when the appropriate cultural forms (e.g. Sunday supplements, photojournalism) reproduce this abjection – we feel pity, we feel sorrow, we feel anger and we may even donate money. But we feel anxious when 'inappropriate' cultural forms like comedic travel writing try to represent places like Africa because the privilege of our usual – and easy – compassionate response is exposed.

For me, *African Diary* is particularly significant because it shows how readers, writers and critics have become attached to a world that is

---

[6] Vanessa Thorpe, 'Bryson Books a Wry Look at the Arabs', *Observer*, 1 June 2003, online only at http://www.observer.guardian.co.uk/uk_news/story/0,6903,968258,00. html.

[7] Slavoj Zizek makes a similar argument about the regulation of humour in his review of *La Vita Bella*, a comedy film about the Holocaust; see 'Camp Comedy', *Sight and Sound*, Vol. 10, No. 4, April 2000, pp. 26–9.

'naturally' divided into civilised and uncivilised regions. With that in mind, this chapter explores how contemporary travel writing – both serious and comic – reproduces powerful assumptions about geopolitical space. It is not enough to ask about the subjectivities attached to travel writing (i.e. *who* travels, *who* an author encounters on the journey, *who* reads these texts), it is also necessary to ask *where* these subjects are located, and how those spaces are saturated with conflicting relations of power. Therefore, this chapter argues that the logic of identity/difference is secured by spatial divisions between home and away, here and there, somewhere and elsewhere. I am interested in pursuing Islam's claim that space is the ontologically primary category of travel writing by examining how the subjects and objects of these texts are located according to a prevailing geopolitical discourse.[8] For example, travel writers repeatedly differentiate themselves from others by situating their authority in a stable, superior and unquestioned home. While the author is not actually at home for the duration of the narrative, home provides the geographical anchor from which he/she can make observations and judgements about foreign people and places. In other words, travel writing delivers 'us' and 'them' most successfully when it locates those identities in the differentiated spaces of 'home' and 'away'. What is politically significant about this spatialisation of subjectivity is the way destinations are produced, evaluated and judged according to the supposedly universal categories of civilisation and security that characterise the travel writer's home. Thus, I am interested in how home/away distinctions are always bolstered by the attending binaries of civilised/ uncivilised and safe/dangerous. This is precisely why travel writers should be situated at the front lines of global politics: they venture out into the dangerous world in order to portray the terrors that lurk elsewhere and remind readers of the security and comfort of their homes. This chapter examines how travel writing reproduces a *discourse of modern cartography* by bolstering the distinctions between here and there with familiar binary oppositions between a safe, civilised home and a dangerous, uncivilised elsewhere. Of particular interest here is how the production of space, like the production of otherness, is framed by the juxtaposition of colonial and cosmopolitan visions. That is to say, oppositional spaces are either resuscitated through a colonial map where old empires have transformed into a devastated Third World governed and controlled by powerful Western nations, or they are projected onto a cosmopolitan map where new coalitions of civilised states are united by core values of equality, democracy and justice.

---

[8] Islam, *The Ethics of Travel*, pp. 5–6.

Mapping the global imaginary: the discourse of modern cartography

Space is a central feature of all travel – there must be a journey from one point to another for travel to really count. Underscoring this claim is an assumption that space can be measured accurately – distances may be great or small, but one is always able to *map* a proposed journey from here to there. Our desire to control space through its accurate measurement has been fulfilled by the Enlightenment practice of cartography and symbolised most effectively in the Mercator map of the world. But maps – whether textual or pictorial – are always discursive: they make sense only to the extent that they are bolstered by already circulating myths, messages and meanings about the world. The discourse of modern cartography, then, refers to a much larger set of mapping practices – mental, textual, physical – that produce modern space according to Enlightenment notions of objectivity, accuracy and universality. To apply Derek Gregory's useful phrase, mapping practices are never just about signs, they are about the production of meaning and the creation of a *geographical imagination*.[9] Moreover, Gregory points out that the architecture of the Enlightenment geographical imagination is founded on the power relations of Empire. With this in mind, it is not difficult to see how travel writing has become a vital part of this geographical imagination: these are textual reproductions that mimic cartography's desire to represent the world accurately. Indeed, Mary Louise Pratt argues that Enlightenment travel writing took its lead from natural science by reinforcing an emerging 'planetary consciousness' that either silenced or justified the less palatable effects of colonial rule.[10] Following Pratt, this chapter argues that when travel writing reproduces spatial divisions between here and there *as if* these cartographies were unproblematic or somehow neutral, it willingly reproduces the prevailing discourse of modern cartography. Of course, this is not all that travel writing does – it also documents the *crossing* of established spatial boundaries and thus reveals moments when the discourse of modern cartography fails to arrange, organise and harness our geographical imaginations. As Gregory explains: 'Not only can conventional cartographic discourse be turned against itself, for example; not only can the mapping metaphoric be used ironically or

---

[9] As Gregory argues, 'historians have usually presented cartography as the Survey of Reason, a narrative journey of progress from darkness to enlightenment, in the course of which maps become supposedly more "accurate" and more "objective"'; see Derek Gregory, *Geographical Imaginations* (Oxford: Basil Blackwell, 1994), p. 7.

[10] Pratt, *Imperial Eyes*, pp. 15–37.

parodically; but it is also possible to envisage other more open forms of cartographic discourse.'[11] To continue with Gregory's metaphor, contemporary travel writing not only reproduces a discourse of modern cartography, it also reveals important moments of *cartographic anxiety*.

Critical geographers like Gregory have taken inspiration, in part, from Foucault's work.[12] Although direct concerns about geography remain in the background of Foucault's thinking, an important understanding of space is central to his notion of discourse. As he explains, 'space is fundamental in any exercise of power'.[13] Foucault provides important links between subjectivity, space and power because he not only asks *which* subjects are enabled and constrained by power, but *where* these practices take place – which territories, which institutions, which societies. Although his specific observations about the organisation of modern space (what he calls 'structural space') focus on the emergence of geography as an institutionalised object of knowledge in the nineteenth century, he provides a sustained engagement with the relationship between space and power in all of his work: 'to decipher discourse through the use of spatial, strategic metaphors enables one to grasp precisely the points at which discourses are transformed in, through and on the basis of relations of power'.[14] For Foucault, power does not exist in a vacuum; rather, it is always felt *somewhere*, in *some place* (e.g. courts, hospitals, schools, states, families and other social institutions).[15] Gearóid Ó Tuathail builds upon Foucault's analysis by

---

[11] Gregory, *Geographical Imaginations*, p. 7.

[12] Along with Gregory's work, the following texts offer a discursive and critical approach to geography: Marcus A. Doel, *Poststructural Geographies: The Diabolical Art of Spatial Sciences* (Edinburgh: Edinburgh University Press, 1999); James S. Duncan and David Ley, eds., *Place/Culture/Representation* (London and New York: Routledge, 1993); David Harvey, *The Condition of Postmodernity: An Enquiry into the Origins of Social Change* (Oxford: Blackwell, 1989); Frederic Jameson, *The Geopolitical Aesthetic: Cinema and Space in the World System* (London: BFI Publishing, 1992); Doreen Massey, *Space, Place, Gender* (Cambridge: Polity Press, 1994); David Sibley, *Geographies of Exclusion* (London: Routledge, 1995); and Nigel Thrift, *Spatial Formations* (London: Sage, 1996).

[13] Michel Foucault, 'Space, Knowledge and Power', in Paul Rabinow, ed., *The Foucault Reader* (New York: Pantheon Books, 1984), p. 252. Foucault's concerns with geography are most explicit in this piece, as well as in 'Questions on Geography', in *Power/Knowledge: Selected Interviews and Other Writings* (New York: Pantheon Books, 1980), pp. 63–77, where he argues that *'Territory* is no doubt a geographical notion, but it is first of all a juridico-political one: the area controlled by a certain kind of power', p. 68.

[14] Foucault, 'Questions on Geography', p. 70.

[15] While critical geographers like Gregory have taken inspiration from Foucault, they have also made several important extensions to his arguments about geography, space and power. For example, David Harvey uses Foucault to develop his argument about the accumulation of cultural capital and the reorganisation of social power: 'If space,

arguing that *global* space is just as discursively constructed as any other space and thus helps to illustrate how the asymmetrical relations of power embedded in the discourse of modern cartography are globalised: 'Geography was not something already possessed by the earth but an *active writing of the earth by an expanding, centralizing imperial state*. It was not a noun but a verb, a *geo-graphing*, an earth writing by ambitious endocolonizing and exocolonizing states who sought to seize space and organize it to fit their own cultural visions and material interests.'[16] Ó Tuathail makes two important points here: firstly, that territory is only understood to the extent that it is written, represented and inscribed (i.e. geo-graphy or earth-writing), and secondly, that our received understandings of global space have been shaped by imperialism.[17]

as Foucault would have it, is always a container of social power, then the reorganization of space is always a reorganization of the framework through which social power is expressed' (*The Condition of Postmodernity*, p. 255). Harvey provides a compelling historical account of how modern time—space compression has reorganised social power: because the mechanical clock globalised time, space was effectively annihilated (pp. 240–59). In a different direction, Henri Lefebvre deconstructs the modern spatial ontology by re-classifying 'natural' space into experienced, perceived and imagined spaces: see *The Production of Space* (Oxford: Basil Blackwell, 1991). However, the most far-reaching critique of modern cartography is Gilles Deleuze and Felix Guattari's formulation of deterritorialisation and re-territorialisation; see *A Thousand Plateaus: Capitalism and Schizophrenia*, trans. Brian Massumi (Minneapolis: University of Minnesota Press, 1987).

[16] Gearóid Ó Tuathail, *Critical Geopolitics: The Politics of Writing Global Space* (Minneapolis: University of Minnesota Press, 1996), p. 2. The best introduction to the critical geopolitics literature is Gearóid Ó Tuathail and Simon Dalby, eds., *Critical Geopolitics: A Reader* (London: Routledge, 1998); see also Ó Tuathail, *Critical Geopolitics*; Andrew Herod, Gearóid Ó Tuathail and Susan M. Roberts, eds., *An Unruly World: Globalization, Governance and Geography* (London and New York: Routledge, 1998); Simon Dalby and Gearóid Ó Tuathail, eds., *Rethinking Geopolitics* (London and New York: Routledge, 1998); Simon Dalby, 'Critical Geopolitics: Discourse, Difference and Dissent', *Environment and Planning D: Society and Space*, Vol. 9, No. 3, 1991, pp. 261–83; Klaus-John Dodds and David Atkinson, eds., *Geopolitical Traditions: A Century of Geopolitical Thought* (London and New York: Routledge, 2000); John Agnew, *Geopolitics: Re-visioning World Politics* (London and New York: Routledge, 1998); and Klaus-John Dodds, 'Geopolitics and Foreign Policy: Recent Developments in Anglo-American Political Geography and International Relations', *Progress in Human Geography*, Vol. 18, No. 2, 1994, pp. 186–208.

[17] Derek Gregory echoes Ó Tuathail's concern with the relationship between geography, writing and travel: 'I have chosen to speak of a "scripting" precisely because it accentuates the production (and consumption) of spaces that reach beyond the narrowly textual, and also because it foregrounds the performative and so brings into view practices that take place on the ground' (p. 116). He goes on to explain that travel writing 'stages' particular places, records the passage of bodies through material landscapes and exemplifies the process by which routes are shaped by 'powerful imaginative geographies': 'Scripting Egypt: Orientalism and the Cultures of Travel', in Duncan and Gregory, *Writes of Passage*, pp. 116–17.

How, then, can travelogues be understood as practices of 'earth-writing' that entrench the asymmetric power relations of Empire? Because travelogues functioned as important documents of statecraft during the colonial period, their geopolitical currency helped to foster the popular imagination of foreign spaces as both threatening (which justified colonial intervention) and desirable (which objectified difference and brought it into the orbit of the imperial gaze). But the contemporary projection of fear and desire onto the global terrain is more difficult to grasp. Certainly, travel writing benefited from the post-war boom in tourism, in other words, 'more travel = more travelogues'. But in the face of a world so accessible to anyone with the means to travel, contemporary travel writing has been forced to recalibrate its geographical imagination to ensure the survival of exotic destinations. I want to argue that this recalibration takes two forms: either contemporary travelogues *preserve* certain destinations for travel writers to repeat the judgements and adventures of their colonial predecessors, or they *homogenise* the world as a single destination within which travel writers can frame cultural difference through universal categories. What happens in this preservation and homogenisation of global space is a territorialisation of the tourist/traveller binary. We know that travel writers distinguish themselves from tourists by claiming that their independent encounters with difference are *more* authentic than the mediated experience of tourists. But in making this distinction, travel writers categorise certain areas for banal tourist consumption, and certain areas for their own daring adventures. This re-mapping is not a simple colonial repetition where passive tourists are located in central spaces like London and Paris and intrepid travel writers are located in exotic places like Lagos and Patagonia. Because the entire globe has been opened to mass tourism, the creation of inaccessible space is extremely difficult – which is why Holland and Huggan argue that travel writers 'must labour to extract novelty and excitement from frontiers that once existed'.[18] When travel writers cannot find inaccessible space, they must reinvent and rediscover places that have already been commodified by the tourist gaze. Holland and Huggan go on to suggest that these efforts of re-imagination have made travelogues important documents of globalisation: 'As popular compendiums to different kinds of disciplinarity – history, geography, politics, anthropology – travel books offer comprehensive and informed commentary, a route along which travellers, whether armchair or field, can become knowledgeable

---

[18] Holland and Huggan, *Tourists with Typewriters*, p. 68.

and open-minded about the contemporary world.'[19] This statement is provocative: it suggests that the travelogue's process of mapping offers an 'open-minded' engagement with difference. For Holland and Huggan, then, travel writing is at the forefront of a new geographical imagination – one that both celebrates the multiple spaces still available for consumption, and reinvents familiar spaces by highlighting their foreign characteristics.

Regardless of whether travel writers resuscitate a colonial map or develop a cosmopolitan one, they all organise global space into a 'route': they have detailed itineraries, they have plans, they have maps, they have timetables. As Holland and Huggan go on to say, travelogues confirm the difference of foreign space by mapping it through a 'preassigned generic path'.[20] This suggests that the spatial contours of the travelogue are determined by the literary regulations of the genre *before* the text is even written – all the travel writer must do is territorialise foreign space in accordance with already established generic rules. For Islam, the co-dependence of space and genre in travel writing has two important consequences. Firstly, it creates a 'vantage point from which to represent the other' so that the objective, omniscient position of the travel writer who marks others through codes of difference is reinforced.[21] Secondly, all travelogues remain 'within the grounded enclosure of home' because they cannot encounter spatial difference through anything other than familiar categories.[22] The point here is that travel writing cannot escape an Enlightenment geographical imagination that requires an already structured vantage point and an already planned route. In this sense, Islam is right to argue that the genre is not about travel at all, but is in fact rather sedentary.[23]

The travel writer's itinerary: marking space in *The Great Railway Bazaar*

The Great Railway Bazaar is indicative of how the discourse of modern cartography shapes the travel writer's production of foreign space. From the very outset, the reader is given two complementary itineraries that

---

[19] Holland and Huggan, *Tourists with Typewriters*, p. 69.
[20] Holland and Huggan, *Tourists with Typewriters*, p. 69.
[21] Islam, *The Ethics of Travel*, p. viii.
[22] Islam, *The Ethics of Travel*, p. 56.
[23] Islam's main concern in *The Ethics of Travel* is the dialectic between sedentary travellers (who write travelogues) and nomadic travellers (who write other kinds of stories about travel). The former cannot shake loose the spatial ontology of modernity, while the latter critique the assumption that space is something pre-given outside of language and discourse.

reveal Theroux's territorialisation of Asia. The first is the 'Table of Contents' that lists each separate train journey as a chapter (there are thirty in total) and outlines the circuitous route he takes through Asia. The second, and more instructive, is the two-page cartographic map (see figure 3) that plots Theroux's route by rail, plane and ship from London to Japan and back again: these two points of reference illustrate Theroux's itinerary, or, as he calls it, 'my original route, the one I had marked out on my map before I left London'.[24] Commenting on the planning stages of his trip, Theroux reveals how and why he settled on this particular itinerary:

I was determined to start in London, and to take the Orient Express. My route would take me through Turkey, into Iran, into Baluchistan, and after a short bus ride I could catch a train in Zahedan, go into Pakistan and more or less chug through the rest of Asia – to Hanoi, through China, Mongolia and the Soviet Union. Much of this, on closer examination, proved impractical or impossible. The Chinese Embassy in 1972 simply hung up when I said I wanted a visa to take trains through China. I had to wait fourteen years before I was able to make that trip. There was a war in Baluchistan – I rerouted myself through Afghanistan. I decided to include Japan and the whole of the Trans-Siberian. I didn't mind where I went as long as it was in Asia and had a railway system and visas were available. I saw myself puffing along from country to country, simply changing trains.[25]

All of Theroux's intricate planning is simply distilled on the first page of his travelogue: 'It was my intention to board every train that chugged into view from Victoria Station in London to Tokyo Central'.[26] While Theroux appears to be flexible in terms of when he will catch a particular train (for example, he will remain in a town if he wishes to look around), his flexibility has more to do with *when* he leaves rather than *if* he will leave at all. When confronted with seductive spots like Istanbul, his predetermined itinerary rears its head: 'I had a train to catch; so I poked in a few corners and satisfied myself that this was a city I would gladly return to.'[27] The relationship between flexibility and rigidity in Theroux's itinerary is instructive: his flexibility reassures readers that he is a modern traveller with the freedom to make up his own mind, and that he has successfully escaped the pressures, tight schedules and deadlines that plagued him at home. But that freedom is

---

[24] Theroux, *The Great Railway Bazaar*, p. 65.
[25] Theroux, 'First Train Journey', pp. 169–70.
[26] Theroux, *The Great Railway Bazaar*, p. 1.
[27] Theroux, *The Great Railway Bazaar*, p. 35. A similar sentiment emerges in Pakistan: 'Peshawar is a pretty town. I would gladly move there, settle down on a verandah, and grow old watching sunsets in the Khyber Pass' (p. 78).

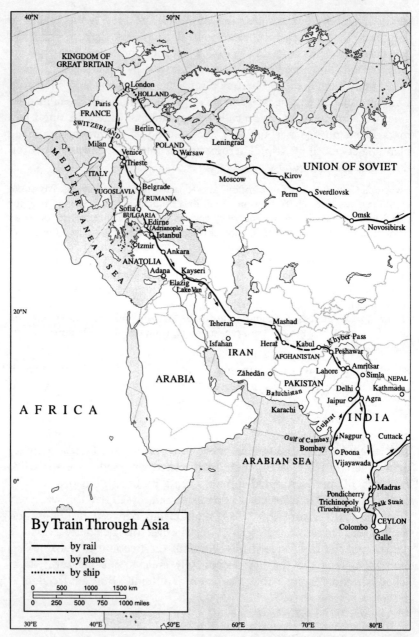

Figure 3. 'By Train Through Asia', itinerary map, Paul Theroux, *The Great Railway Bazaar*.

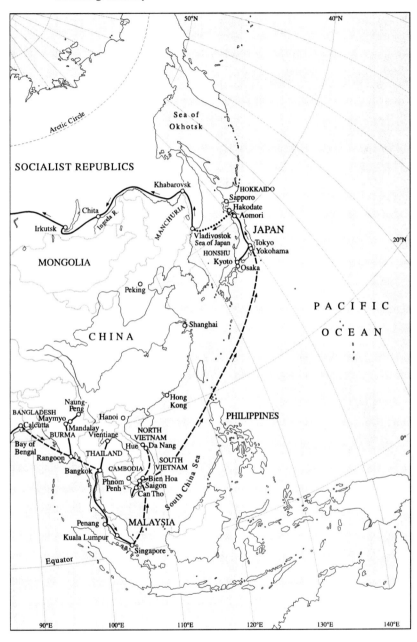

always handcuffed to the predetermined itinerary set out at the beginning of the book: the reader never loses confidence in Theroux's ability to *complete* the proposed journey. Theroux's itinerary gives the reader a sense that although he will engage with foreign cultures along the way, this is a man with a purpose, an intention, and a goal that he will accomplish without significant delay. So while Theroux is 'free' in his travels compared with the confinements of home, his decisions are always curtailed by a pre-established itinerary.

The Great Railway Bazaar reinforces what Holland and Huggan call the 'preassigned generic path' of travel writing: it convinces the reader that the home-away-home structure of Theroux's journey will be contained within the beginning-middle-end structure of his narrative. This is a careful production of space — nothing in the narrative will detract Theroux from completing the route he planned before he left London. More importantly, Theroux has chosen rail travel to achieve this objective because he thinks trains are the *best* way to navigate foreign territory: 'Train travel animated my imagination and usually gave me the solitude to order and write my thoughts: I have travelled easily in two directions, along the level rails while Asia flashed changes at the window, and at the interior rim of a private world of memory and language. I cannot imagine a luckier combination.'[28] Trains may not be the most modern, the most efficient or even the fastest means of transportation, but trains allow Theroux the time to be alone, to gather his thoughts and to write in the glow of the landscape he is passing. This means, of course, that Theroux frames his encounter with foreign landscapes primarily from train windows. Looking out of the Orient Express, 'the scene was composed like a Flemish painting...The train, the window frame holding the scene for moments, made it a picture.'[29] Just as Theroux is distanced from the local others he observes (cocooned as he is in the role of narrator), so too is he distanced from the landscape these others inhabit (cocooned as he is in his train compartment). The train windows in *The Great Railway Bazaar* function as an important filter for foreign territory: they allow Theroux to maintain his distance from Asia and simultaneously to produce it as either devastated or beautiful. Given Theroux's misanthropic state of mind, it is no surprise that foreign landscapes in *The Great Railway Bazaar* are often judged negatively. This process starts immediately in Turkey, which is 'changeless and harsh...a landscape of unheeding devastation' that becomes 'bigger, drier, emptier with repetition...[the hills] so sunlit and empty they made my

---

[28] Theroux, *The Great Railway Bazaar*, p. 166.
[29] Theroux, *The Great Railway Bazaar*, p. 28.

eyes ache'.[30] These judgements do not abate throughout the journey, and on his last leg through the Soviet Union he describes the coast as 'brown, flat, and treeless, the grimmest landscape I had ever laid eyes on, like an immense beach of frozen dirt washed by an oily black sea'.[31]

The most intense descriptions of devastated landscape emerge in Vietnam, where 'the roads were falling to pieces and cholera streamed into the backyards'.[32] Quite apart from the 'natural' ugliness witnessed in other areas, Vietnam is unique because it is a man-made disaster. As he journeys from 'beleaguered' Saigon to the war-ravaged Hué, Theroux focuses on the remnants of this violence:

[I] could see and smell the war: it was muddy roads rutted by army trucks and people running through the rain with bundles, bandaged soldiers tramping through the monsoon slime of the wrecked town ... few houses were without a violent gouge and most had a series of ragged plugs torn out of their walls. The whole town had a dark brown look of violation, the smirches of raids among swelling puddles.[33]

Certainly the timing of Theroux's journey (December 1973) provided the perfect opportunity for him to comment on the war before America began its cultural campaign to rewrite that experience.[34] While he is mostly concerned with how the war will affect his predetermined itinerary (e.g. 'Do you think it's safe to take the train to Bien Hoa?'), he makes his position on the conflict clear: 'The tragedy was that we had come, and, from the beginning, had not planned to stay.'[35] Theroux disagrees that the Americans invaded Vietnam to establish a long-term imperial presence, and sees the war instead as a botched attempt to offer short-term military support against a Communist threat.[36] In this way, he is not critical of the American decision to intervene in Vietnam; rather, he is critical of the decision to pull out and abandon the

---

[30] Theroux, *The Great Railway Bazaar*, pp. 51, 53, 114.
[31] Theroux, *The Great Railway Bazaar*, pp. 307–8. This vision is only strengthened further along the Trans-Siberian route at the city of Chita: 'a satanic city of belching chimneys and great heaps of smoking ashes dumped beside the tracks' (p. 325).
[32] Theroux, *The Great Railway Bazaar*, p. 250.
[33] Theroux, *The Great Railway Bazaar*, p. 252.
[34] The American rewriting of Vietnam is an interesting process of cultural production that has taken place across cinema, literature, photography and art; see Linda Dittmar and Gene Michaud, eds., *From Hanoi to Hollywood: The Vietnam War in American Film* (New York: Rutgers University Press, 1990); Michael Anderegg, ed., *Inventing Vietnam: The War in Film and Television* (Philadelphia: Temple University Press, 1991); Jim Neilson, *Warring Fictions: Cultural Politics and the Vietnam War Narrative* (Mississippi: University of Mississippi Press, 1998); and Lucy Lippard, *Different War: Vietnam and Art* (Seattle: Real Comet Press, 1994).
[35] Theroux, *The Great Railway Bazaar*, p. 259.
[36] Theroux, *The Great Railway Bazaar*, pp. 250–1, 255–6.

Vietnamese. This position is not revealed in lengthy political discussions, but in Theroux's depictions of the Vietnamese landscape. Indeed, much of the devastation that Theroux describes is the result of the American evacuation, and while he feels sympathy for the American soldiers who fought the war, he feels 'even sorrier for the inheritors of all this junk'.[37] Theroux describes Vietnam as a 'ruined' country littered with the debris of America's 'brutal adventure'. But the enormity of that devastation is magnified when Theroux encounters the beauty of the Ashau valley:

> no picture could capture the complexity of the beauty ... Of all the places the railway had taken me since London, this was the loveliest...I had been unprepared for this beauty; it surprised and humbled me in the same degree the emptiness had in rural India ... we should have known all along that the French would not have colonized it, nor would the Americans have fought so long, if such ripeness did not invite the eye to take it.[38]

The Ashau Valley is symbolic here: not only is this what Vietnam looked like *before* the American intervention, its beauty allows Theroux to explain and justify years of imperial adventure. For Theroux, the tragedy of Vietnam is aesthetic rather than political – he is primarily concerned with how Vietnam's beautiful landscape has been devastated by warfare.

The oppositional readings of Vietnamese territory – as either devastated or beautiful – are central to *The Great Railway Bazaar* because they function as the outer limit of Theroux's spatial production. All the landscapes he encounters in Asia are made to fit within the aesthetic register of horror/beauty that he constructs in Vietnam. But the catalogue of spatial difference that abounds within that register – exciting, boring, grim, stunning, frightening – does not emerge spontaneously in the moment of encounter. Rather, what is important in *The Great Railway Bazaar* is the spatial anchor that underscores Theroux's itinerary – his home. The West more generally, and America more specifically, continually serve as stable points of comparison during his journey. England may be where he lives (which gets a brief mention at the beginning and end), but as Theroux's page-and-a-half treatment of Laos exemplifies, it is his American home that is central to the narrative:

> Laos was really Ruritania, a slaphappy kingdom of warring half brothers, heavily mortgaged to the United States ... it was one of America's expensive practical jokes, a motiveless place where nothing was made, everything imported; a kingdom with baffling pretensions to Frenchness. What was surprising was that

---

[37] Theroux, *The Great Railway Bazaar*, p. 261.
[38] Theroux, *The Great Railway Bazaar*, p. 258.

it existed at all, and the more I thought of it, the more it seemed like a lower form
of life, like the cross-eyed planarian or squashy amoeba, the sort of creature that
can't die even when it is cut to ribbons.[39]

Even Theroux's mild criticism (that Laos was America's practical joke)
does not detract from the spatial framing here: Laos only makes sense to
the extent that it can be compared to more civilised places like America.
As this passage makes clear, Theroux consolidates his 'secure vantage
point' in *The Great Railway Bazaar* by territorialising foreign space and
offering wide-ranging judgements about the inability of other places to
manage even the essentials of proper (i.e. American) governance. In
addition to Laos, neither the Vietnamese nor the Pakistani governments
have a basic understanding of political geography or effective government, and Theroux is quick to criticise their inexperience and compare
them unfavourably to America.[40]

Luckily, Theroux never has to leave the comfort of the train carriage
to prove the anarchy and disorganisation of Asia because for him, the rail
network is the key to national character:

The trains in any country contain the essential paraphernalia of the culture: Thai
trains have the shower jar with the glazed dragon on its side, Ceylonese ones the
cars reserved for Buddhist monks, Indian ones a vegetarian kitchen and six
classes, Iranian ones prayer mats, Malaysian ones a noodle stall, Vietnamese
ones bulletproof glass on the locomotive, and on every carriage of a Russian train
there is a samovar. The railway bazaar, with its gadgets and passengers,
represented society so completely that to board it was to be challenged by the
national character. At times it was like a leisurely seminar, but I also felt on some
occasions that it was like being jailed and then assaulted by the monstrously
typical.[41]

While the railway tells him everything he needs to know about the places
he visits, it also provides him with the opportunity of *moving on* once he
has successfully judged a particular destination (e.g. 'I will flee Tehran
on the next available train'; 'I was determined to deal with Afghanistan
swiftly and put that discomfort into parenthesis'.)[42] Because Asia is
seen primarily through the train window, and because the mode of
transportation makes it possible for Theroux to move on whenever he
wants, his confident pronouncements about 'national character' are
never challenged, let alone jeopardised. By the time he reaches the
farthest point in his journey – Kyoto – his ability to judge foreign space
becomes crystallised:

[39] Theroux, *The Great Railway Bazaar*, p. 208.
[40] Theroux, *The Great Railway Bazaar*, pp. 247, 77.
[41] Theroux, *The Great Railway Bazaar*, p. 209.
[42] Theroux, *The Great Railway Bazaar*, pp. 65, 72.

Travelling over a long distance becomes, after three months, like tasting wine or picking at a global buffet. A place is approached, sampled, and given a mark. A visit, pausing before the next train pulls out, forbids gourmandizing, but a return is possible. So from every lengthy itinerary a simpler one emerges, in which Iran is penciled over, Afghanistan is deleted, Peshawar gets a yes, Simla a maybe, and so on.[43]

Theroux never has to face the practicalities and complexities of a place – he never has to live there, or grow up there, or work there, or come from there. Nestled in his train compartment, he is always comforted by his reassuring Mercator maps of Asia, and his belief that his Anglo-American viewpoint is ultimately superior. *The Great Railway Bazaar* shows us that Theroux's physical movement through space is super-fluous because his encounters with difference are *already contained* by a modern spatial ontology. In this sense, Islam's argument makes perfect sense: despite an extensive journey through Asia, *The Great Railway Bazaar* is a 'sedentary' text. It fails to question or disrupt the spatial anchor of home, and it fails to reflect on how that anchor produces and regulates foreign space according to a Western geographical imagination.

Texts of security in an insecure world: locating safety and danger

And much as he/she would wish it otherwise, the travel writer's 'alternative route' invokes the same geographical imagination as the tourist's beaten track. Both 'routes' confront and homogenise foreign space through a simple equation of 'same = home' and 'difference = elsewhere'. But as Martha Rosler suggests, this bounding of space in the service of travel has political consequences: 'the beaten path beats down that which it managed to reach with such difficulty. Erasure of difference always leads to efforts by the colonizer to "preserve" it, but as a depoliticised, aestheticised set of cultural practices – as a "destination".'[44] Travelogues enable this simultaneous erasure and preservation of difference because all destinations are produced and written over from the stable (but portable) vantage point of the travel writer. Travel writing, then, is an act of spatial confirmation – it is another cultural product that confirms the differences between us and them, here and there. But Rosler's argument is more acute – it suggests that the

---

[43] Theroux, *The Great Railway Bazaar*, pp. 293–4.

[44] Martha Rosler, 'In the Place of the Public: Observations of a Traveller', in Ole Bouman and Roemer Van Toorn, eds., *The Invisible Architecture* (London: Academy Editions, 1994), p. 435.

simultaneous erasure and preservation of difference is de-politicising because it covers over the complex relations of power that are reproduced by the discourse of modern cartography. This is what Islam means when he argues that travelogues are sedentary – travel writers are locked within a world-view that locates, interprets and translates foreign territory according to a home that remains forever unquestioned. I want to argue that the discourse of modern cartography is reproduced most effectively in contemporary travel writing through the mapping of safe homes and dangerous destinations.[45] In this way, travelogues can be understood as texts of security in an insecure world: they reassure readers that their civilised homes are contrasted to (and must be protected from) various foreign places that cannot peacefully govern their own territory. Moreover, the production of safety and danger reifies the traveller/tourist distinction – while *all* of us are governed by a geographical imagination that distinguishes between home and away, tourists and travellers are separated by contrasting organisations of safety and danger. Both want to go somewhere *different* from home, but because the tourist circuit must guarantee the security of its subjects, the tourist's destination must be both special *and* safe. When danger appears on the horizon of tourism, questions of security always prevail: if the safety of the tourist cannot be ensured, then a site will be excised from the circuit of global tourism no matter how exotic, different or coveted it is. Conversely, because danger provides a guarantee that tourists will be absent, it works like a magnet for travel writers. Dangerous places are the *only* places that travel writers can be sure to avoid the ubiquitous tourist industry and encounter the authenticity they so desire. It is no surprise, then, that many travelogues have carved out a new generic path akin to political journalism by travelling to the most remote and dangerous parts of the world.

By territorialising spaces of danger as wholly other to civilised homes, contemporary travel writers reproduce colonial space in their belated encounters with Empire. Indeed, it is no coincidence that the devastated and dangerous parts of the world coveted by intrepid travel writers were previously under colonial rule. For example, foreign space continues to be an object of both fascination and repulsion: travel writers are captivated by the devastation they encounter (and they need that devastation to stay in business), but they are also disgusted by the unspeakable horror and depravation they witness. Having said that,

---

[45] I have used this mapping of safety and danger to discuss the relationship between war and tourism; see 'Consuming Danger: Re-Imagining the War-Tourism Divide', *Alternatives*, Vol. 25, No. 1, Jan./Mar. 2000, pp. 91–116.

the production of danger in contemporary travel writing is not simple mimicry – travel writers do not reproduce a colonial cartography without question. In this sense, travel writers who document dangerous places reveal particular linkages and contradictions between colonial and cosmopolitan visions. The cosmopolitan travel writer's aim of finding common ground between different cultures in order to encourage universal standards of equality, justice and tolerance is extremely difficult in spaces of danger and devastation. How can there be any common ground between the poverty and disease-ridden slums of a Third World capital (the travel writer's destination) and the civility and security of America or England (the travel writer's home)? When faced with such 'extreme' sites, the cosmopolitan dream gives way to familiar colonial reasoning – only this time around, devastation, poverty and underdevelopment are not solved by a virtuous and benign imperial power but by the promises of liberal democracy. In effect, cosmopolitan travel writers are modern-day missionaries: they open up 'uncivilised' spaces and make them available (and receptive) to the evangelising forces of liberal democracy – whether those forces are welcome or not.

The edge of the world: escape, danger, and dystopia

In her book *Dangerous Places: Travels on the Edge*, American writer Rosa Jordan documents four decades of travelling in Central and South America. Aside from a few journeys with her daughter and her various partners, she prefers to travel alone. For Jordan, travelling solo – especially to dangerous places – is the only way to sort out her problems:

> This is how it has always been: me, running. I've always thought of it as running away. But the light has shifted. I see that what started with running away has become, or perhaps always was, running toward something. Toward danger, my friends would say, and they may be right ... what I once knew instinctively and now know from experience is that when faced with real or imagined danger, truths about life, other people, and myself are revealed; truths that remain hidden from me as long as things are predictable and I feel safe.[46]

Dangerous Places is explicit in its understanding of global security – certain forms of violence exist everywhere, but the structural violence of war is always found in Central America. The numerous trips that Jordan

---

[46] Rosa Jordan, *Dangerous Places: Travels on the Edge* (Lawrencetown, Nova Scotia: Pottersfield Press, 1997), p. 14. While this passage retroactively articulates Jordan's desire for danger, she is usually unwilling to explain her motivations when on the road. Walking from Costa Rica into Nicaragua at the end of the 1970s, she is asked by Sabina, a 17-year-old Sandinista guerrilla, why she is courting such danger: 'I don't know. I just want to see the end of the war' (pp. 167–8).

makes to war-torn Nicaragua, El Salvador and Guatemala reveal interesting contradictions in her production of space. While Jordan's own subject position is multifaceted (she is a journalist, an aid-worker, a volunteer, a poet and a director of the NGO Earth Trust), she is very clear that she is *not* a tourist and does not adhere to the tourist circuit. Indeed, *Dangerous Places* has many passages lamenting the rise of tourism in Latin America, and expressing her own delight at discovering places that are 'untouristed jewels'. So far, not that different from any number of other travelogues about Central America. But *Dangerous Places* presents a gendered reading of space that requires further exploration. Jordan does not present her travels as remarkable simply because she is a woman, nor does she think it extraordinary that many of the guerrilla fighters she encounters are women. Rather, it is her *genderless* identity that enables her to encounter the 'real' Latin America behind the headlines and tourist brochures, and behind the gender stereotypes that constrain cultural encounters between men and women. For example, Jordan is judgemental when gender stereotypes almost prevent her from discussing 'real' issues like housing and poverty with Mexican politicians. During a press junket with the Mexican president, she distances herself from the women in the entourage because they are excessively feminine 'with makeup melting down their faces', and obsequious in relation to their powerful husbands. Instead, Jordan becomes an honorary man who interacts with the male politicians on their terms – at one point wearing a man's silk shirt to a dinner party where the male guests toast her 'unisex look'.[47] She is even aware of her own reproduction of gender stereotypes; for example, she is ashamed when a guerrilla soldier corrects her assumptions: 'Stupid *gringa*...Don't you know what it means to be a revolutionary? The women are our comrades, our equals! Revolutionaries aren't *macho* pigs! We have respect for women!'[48] In many ways, *Dangerous Places* can be read as a feminist book: Jordan cites well-known feminist authors like Gloria Steinem; she expresses the concerns particular to women solo travellers (e.g. walking alone at night); she respects female guerrilla fighters; and she admits to feeling safer when travelling and living with local women.

However, Jordan's position as an honorary man is contradicted by her reliance on emotional mapping. Despite efforts at objectivity (e.g. listing facts and statistics), Jordan depicts her encounter with war-torn Central America primarily through an emotional register. This comes out clearly

---

[47] Jordan, *Dangerous Places*, pp. 154, 157–8.
[48] Jordan, *Dangerous Places*, p. 176.

in her refusal to reproduce masculine bravado in the midst of a civil war (she often expresses fear and insecurity); in her willingness to express emotion (she is forever breaking down in tears); and in her relationship with her daughter. While Jordan's 'feminine' emotional mapping contrasts with her position as an honorary man, these gendered negotiations are not the primary feature of the book. Rather, *Dangerous Places* is driven by Jordan's attraction to danger and her efforts to escape the constraints of her 'bourgeois' life in North America. However, when she actually confronts the danger and violence of Central America, she wants to go back home immediately. The reader is never allowed to forget that Jordan always has the capacity to board a plane home: 'I leave El Salvador glad to be going, away from the madness of a nation making war upon itself, a nation of Rambos who believe that they are its reality and its future. It is hopeless'.[49] In this sense, *Dangerous Places* is less about the negotiations of gender and more about how Jordan's subjectivity is forged between two poles – the danger of Central and South America and the safety of North America. Indeed, her home (first California and then British Columbia) is the anchor for her adventures and gives her the opportunity to develop 'expert' knowledge about Latin America (at one point she takes a research position as an area specialist at the right-wing Rand corporation). Jordan is clear that her 'expert' position enables her to confidently territorialise the foreign space of Central America: 'Like most North Americans I travel with the assumption that I know where I am going and, unlike my earlier travels, am now well-informed enough to know what to expect when I get there'.[50] It is Jordan's confidence as an 'expert', and the anchor of her 'safe' North American home, that are tested in the dangerous places she visits. At times, as, for example, when she is in the company of Nicaraguan guerrillas, she is able to recognise her privileged position:

I see something which has been in other gazes that have followed me all day. In a moment as desolate as I have ever known, I suddenly understand what it is. I am passing through a nation where perceptions of 'us' and 'them' have been honed by war. They are the 'us' and I am the 'them'. It shows now in the captain's eyes as it has in others, a kind of curiosity mingled with indifference. My throat constricts as if touched by a knife.[51]

In the end, however, this recognition only goes so far. While she is mostly critical of American intervention in the region, she grows weary of the anti-American sentiment she encounters: 'It's true that I travel for

---

[49] Jordan, *Dangerous Places*, p. 197.
[50] Jordan, *Dangerous Places*, p. 181.
[51] Jordan, *Dangerous Places*, p. 178.

pleasure. But what is the joy when every trip opens onto a new vista of violence, and not even in the jungle do I find anyone who admires the nation of my birth?'[52]

Dangerous Places is centred around the axis of safety and danger and the freedom Jordan discovers in danger:

Eventually this travelling to the edge of predictability and stepping off into events I cannot even imagine will become a habit, a way of life. I am sometimes inclined to call it a dangerous addiction. But more often it comes to me like a gift, and with it a feeling that some part of me, long caged by named and unnamed fears, is free.[53]

By the end of the book, Jordan comes to realise that the freedom she enjoys in her travels is not afforded to the locals in war-torn Central America. At this point, she asks a different question – 'is there something I should be doing?' – and the narrative focuses on her efforts to help the ordinary men and women she has encountered on her travels (i.e. as a volunteer in a refugee camp in El Salvador). In this way, *Dangerous Places* details Jordan's transformation from a traveller and part-time journalist to an activist – her most recent travels have been as the director of social justice programmes for Earth Trust. By the end of the book she does not despair at the devastation of war in Central America but instead foregrounds a 'human spirit' that unites us all: 'If I hadn't travelled so far afield I would not know what I know about courage, wouldn't know that this quality of the human spirit lives in the soul of so many ordinary people. I would not have seen how many ways and for how many reasons it emerges to take a stand against what Camus called "the human order of terror".'[54] Jordan's earlier journeys are solipsistic mappings of space: Latin America is simply a backdrop for Jordan to test herself in the face of danger and sort out her emotional problems. But her more recent journeys temper that solipsism with political commitment. As she sorts out her own emotional life (and moves to Canada with her new partner), she is able to pay more attention to the structural and material needs of Central Americans. To be sure, Jordan is always central to the narrative, but her commitment to the 'backdrop' of Central America slowly comes into focus. She starts out horrified at the devastation of Nicaragua, El Salvador and Guatemala but gradually becomes hopeful as she witnesses the generosity and courage displayed by local people. After leaving El Salvador in its 'hopeless' state, she claims: 'Yet I take with me bits of hope: memories of individuals who refuse to submit to terror and defy the purveyors of it, people whose

---

[52] Jordan, *Dangerous Places*, p. 186.
[53] Jordan, *Dangerous Places*, p. 14.
[54] Jordan, *Dangerous Places*, p. 203.

courage has created another reality.'[55] Her book suggests that this 'other reality' lies in the simple things that connect people across continents – shared experiences, laughter, common insights (of women for example), late-night conversations and feelings of hope in the face of terror.

Ultimately, however, the universalising gestures in *Dangerous Places* are hollow and awkward, not least because they reproduce a 'hippie' mentality, a romantic vision of Central America, and yet another example of a privileged Westerner working out his/her personal problems at the expense of locals. Like many contemporary travel writers, Jordan pursues authenticity – she believes that she has access to the 'real' Central America that most people miss. This is what allows her to chastise her friends for travelling 'improperly' in Mexico: 'Where I wanted to be was in the "real Mexico" – a place I failed to find in San Miguel's trendy expatriate community. Not until this trip . . . had I began to touch realities, remote from my own life, that were truly Mexican.'[56] But Jordan's production of the 'real' Central America is always framed in advance by her own location: she always has a stable home to return to and venture out from. She has never faced the death squads or state terror that millions of Central Americans have faced – she is only ever a voyeur on their situation, a 'terror' tourist with an ever-present escape route. In the end, her noble intentions and her gestures of solidarity with Central Americans are smothered by a solipsistic emotional narrative that says more about her own identity and her ideas of civilisation than it does about the terror she is attracted to.

The same sentiments of authenticity underscore Robert Kaplan's 1996 travelogue *The Ends of the Earth: A Journey at the Dawn of the Twenty-first Century*. Kaplan's book is an account of his travels across parts of Africa and Asia, and makes efforts to resuscitate travel writing through political journalism: 'Though many landscapes are increasingly sullied, that need not spell the decline of travel writing. It does mean that travel writing must confront the real world, slums and all, rather than escape to an airbrushed version of the more rustic past. This book, which folds international studies into a travelogue, is an attempt at that.'[57] When Kaplan suggests that his book will 'confront the real world' rather than romanticise about a 'rustic past', he has a particular image in mind. The 'real world' that Kaplan encounters is simply a catalogue of disasters – economic, demographic, colonial, medical, environmental, political, social and cultural – located and contained *far away* from

---

[55] Jordan, *Dangerous Places*, p. 197.
[56] Jordan, *Dangerous Places*, p. 152.
[57] Kaplan, *The Ends of the Earth*, p. ii.

the civilised world within which both Kaplan and his readership live. Like *Dangerous Places, The Ends of the Earth* suggests that it is only in spaces of danger that the 'real', the 'true' and the 'authentic' can be located. Both books suggest there is something *more real* in the presence of danger that strips away the artifice and superficiality that tourists *mistake* for the real in their highly managed enclaves. While Jordan was concerned with the tourists she saw wrecking the authenticity of Mexico, Kaplan is more concerned with the independent travellers who populate his off-the-beaten-track 'real-world' itinerary. At a restaurant in Central Asia, Kaplan patronises the 'hippies', 'drop-outs' and 'charlatans' he so despises: 'The clientele were hippie backpackers and Western travellers. It was like a Greek island in August. Though here, rather than the sex-and-beer-get-together, small groups composed mostly of males kept apart, as if each group of travellers was determined to believe that it – and no one else – had discovered Kashgar.'[58] The irony here is tricky. Although hippies and backpackers believe they are encountering the real Kashgar, Kaplan's pejorative comments suggest that these travellers are incapable of that kind of 'authentic' encounter. Although Kashgar is surrounded by some dangerous places, it is too populated by Western travellers to count as *really* dangerous. As Kaplan goes on to say, 'Kashgar was still a nexus, if not of the Silk Route, then of this 1990's hippie route.'[59] Perhaps backpackers now venture outside of the more obvious tourist circuit (Kashgar rather than the Taj Mahal), but none are able to encounter the 'real world' that Kaplan seeks to document. Elusive to all but the most courageous travel writers, the 'real world' is only to be found in areas of extreme danger and devastation.

The geographical imagination that underscores *The Ends of the Earth* is made manifest in Kaplan's vision of the 'Last Map': 'Henceforward, the map of the world will never be static. This future map – in a sense the "Last Map" – will be an ever-mutating representation of cartographic chaos; in some areas benign or even productive, and in some areas violent.'[60] As comments on the back cover of Kaplan's book testify, this 'Last Map' clarifies precisely where danger is located:

The Ends of the Earth offers an intimate portrait of the devastated parts of the world, whose cultural disasters – like those in Bosnia, Chechnya and Rwanda

---

[58] Kaplan, *The Ends of the Earth*, p. 308.
[59] Kaplan, *The Ends of the Earth*, p. 308. An excellent satire of this hippie/backpacking/poverty tourism in India is William Sutcliffe, *Are You Experienced?* (London: Penguin, 1998).
[60] Kaplan, *The Ends of the Earth*, p. 337. This is taken (almost verbatim) from p. 75 of his earlier essay 'The Coming Anarchy', *Atlantic Monthly*, No. 273, 2 February 1994, pp. 44–76.

today – will dominate our attention and remake the world of tomorrow... It describes, in haunting detail, the abyss on which so much of the world now teeters ... Kaplan's dark prognosis for the future will be recognized by anyone who has travelled the unfashionable regions of the third world.[61]

Kaplan's prognosis is not a good one. The 'Last Map' is a dystopian vision involving heady mixtures of crime, disease, overpopulation and tribalism that Western states must protect themselves from. In this way, *The Ends of the Earth* functions as an important cultural corollary to 'official' documents (e.g. security profiles, consular warning sheets, news bulletins) that translate geopolitical aims by carving the world into safe and dangerous places. The problem, of course, is that these geopolitical divisions further entrench the idea of a 'civilised' West and an 'uncivilised' rest.[62] Thus, *The Ends of the Earth* territorializes the world through a resuscitated imperial gaze that reproduces ideas of Western superiority, progress and enlightenment. It confirms 'our' civilisation by telling apocalyptic stories about the uncivil, intolerable and barbaric conditions of 'their' cultures. By attaching the devastated areas of Africa and Asia to an already circulating colonial cartography, Kaplan is able to contain danger, violence and degradation within spaces that are *already understood* to be uncivilised. In effect, the litany of devastation described by Kaplan's 'Last Map' mimics the 'dangerous' Orient presented in colonial travelogues. Indeed, the same threatening adjectives are repeated (e.g. Africa is 'seething with fecundity') and the same descriptions used (e.g. this is the 'terrifying face' of the other). Only now, Kaplan's 'Last Map' provides a much clearer taxonomy of contemporary devastated/backward/uncivilised areas: all of West Africa, Cambodia, most of India and parts of the Middle East.

Kaplan's resuscitation of a colonial cartography shapes both his personal observations and his more generalised explanations. His personal disgust is most prominent in West Africa, especially when he observes a neighbourhood in Abidjan:

It is a slum in a bush – a patchwork of corrugated-zinc roofs and walls made of cardboard, cigarette cartons, and black plastic wrap (the kind we use for trash

---

[61] Kaplan, *The Ends of the Earth*, back cover comments by editor William Shawcross and travel writer Peter Matthiessen.

[62] This is Simon Dalby's central claim in 'The Environment as Geopolitical Threat: Reading Robert Kaplan's Coming Anarchy', *Ecumene*, Vol. 3, No. 4, 1996, pp. 472–96. Gearóid Ó Tuathail makes similar claims in *Critical Geopolitics* in the section on Samuel Huntington, pp. 240–9; see also Ó Tuathail's 'At the End of Geopolitics? Reflections on a Plural Problematic at the Century's End', *Alternatives*, Vol. 22, No. 1, Jan./Mar. 1997, pp. 33–56 (especially pp. 49–50).

bags), located in a gully choked with coconut and oil palms ravaged by flooding. There is no electricity, sewage system, or clean water supply. Children defecate in a stream, filled with garbage and grazing pigs, droning with mosquitoes ... Babies were everywhere, as intrepid as the palm trunks sprouting out of the sand or orange lizards. You couldn't help noticing the number of pregnant women.[63]

This is primitive, barbaric poverty of the worst kind. These places can't even manage the veneer of civilisation – and this scene is only the start of Kaplan's odyssey into festering Third World life. What is telling in *The Ends of the Earth* is Kaplan's unwavering vantage point in the face of all this devastation: even in the most catastrophic parts of the world, his own civilisational values remain unsullied (e.g. in this particular passage, Kaplan's cultured, objective, Western masculinity is poised against the hyper-fertile women living in the cesspit of West Africa). But Kaplan's personal observations in *The Ends of the Earth* are supported by facts: he strives for objectivity in an effort to rescue travel writing from its origins in sentimentality: 'My impressions might be the "wrong" ones to have, but they would be based on what I saw. And what I saw turned out to be consistent with what the statistics reveal.'[64] Kaplan draws on a variety of sources to support his personal observations, from economic statistics to previous travelogues. But as Holland and Huggan suggest, when Kaplan's personal observations fail to find the 'causes' of this devastation, he 'returns addictively to – largely undeveloped – general theories' which serve as 'a kind of shorthand for Western traveller-observers whose accounts of the countries through which they move substitute easy myths for hard analysis'.[65] While Kaplan presents himself as a traveller in search of answers, *The Ends of the Earth* is simply an act of confirmation: Kaplan *already knows* that these places are disaster areas, but his decision to 'go and see for himself' suggests that Kaplan might change his mind if confronted with contradictory evidence. Surprise surprise – what he sees 'turns out to be consistent with what the statistics reveal'. In other words, his prejudices about Africa and Asia are confirmed by the sources he consults prior to his trip, the statistics he cites, his personal observations and the generalisations he develops in the narrative.[66]

[63] Kaplan, *The Ends of the Earth*, p. 19.
[64] Kaplan, *The Ends of the Earth*, p. 11. Kaplan frames his book against the tradition of travel writing inaugurated by Laurence Sterne's eighteenth-century *A Sentimental Journey*.
[65] Holland and Huggan, *Tourists with Typewriters*, pp. 211–12.
[66] Indeed, Holland and Huggan would categorise *The Ends of the Earth* as a 'programmed travel account': 'The Western commentators in these accounts most frequently find their encounters confirming ideological biases and prescribed knowledge' (*Tourists with Typewriters*, p. 213).

The problem, as Simon Dalby explains, is that Kaplan tries to present his geographical imagination as truth:

If one reads it as a cultural production of considerable political importance it is fairly easy to see how the logic of the analysis, premised on 'eye-witness' empirical observation, and drawing on an eclectic mixture of intellectual sources, leaves so much of significance unsaid. But the impression, as has traditionally been the case in geopolitical writing, generated from the juxtaposition of expert sources and empirical observation is that this is an 'objective' detached geopolitical treatise.[67]

Kaplan does not prove anything other than what he already knows in *The Ends of the Earth*. He makes a series of ideologically motivated assertions that reveal more about Kaplan's 'political angst about the collapse of order' than they do about the places he encounters. The central failure of Kaplan's text is that it uncritically reproduces an understanding of global security that allows the West to ignore its responsibility to, and complicity in, spaces that are deemed insecure and dangerous. For example, if we are to believe Kaplan's 'objective' analysis, Africa's problems are its own fault – and not, as Dalby rightly argues, a complicated mix of historical factors (e.g. centuries of colonial rule) and external interventions (e.g. economic structures imposed by Western institutions like the IMF).[68] This point is crucial, for it allows Kaplan to argue that the West should 'abandon Africa to its fate' since its problems are all self-imposed. Africa is hugely symbolic in *The Ends of the Earth*, as it is the most deprived, wretched and dangerous place in the world – a 'grand festering threat to the non-African world'.[69] As the 'limit case', it serves as a warning to the other 'hot spots' he visits and justifies his decision to ignore many other dangerous places in the world (however, some areas like Bosnia were such disasters that they warranted their own book).[70] But even if one accepts Kaplan's statistical 'indicators' and his general theories of poverty, overpopulation, disease and environmental decay, the absence of the whole of Latin America seems flawed (especially given the political situation of places like Guatemala and São Paulo). Similarly, there are no discussions of Indonesia, Japan or the Philippines – and one begins to understand that within Kaplan's geographical imagination, a place is especially dangerous and uncivilised if it doesn't aspire to the liberal democracy and

---

[67] Dalby, 'The Environment as Geopolitical Threat', p. 480.
[68] Dalby, 'The Environment as Geopolitical Threat', p. 482.
[69] Nuruddin Farah, 'Highway to Hell: The Travel-Writing of the Disaster', *Transition*, Issue 70, Vol. 6, No. 2, Summer 1996, p. 68.
[70] Robert Kaplan, *Balkan Ghosts: A Journey through History* (New York: St Martin's Press, 1993).

capitalism so successful in the West. South Africa and Kenya do not fit into Kaplan's apocalyptic dystopia of Africa because they remain within territory that, however falteringly, has embraced Western modes of liberal democracy and capitalism. This criteria is made clear when he reaches Thailand and explains that even a failed attempt at Westernisation is better than capitulating to military rule: 'Thailand provides evidence for Francis Fukuyama's "End of History" argument that democratic capitalism operating in the context of an economically developed, civil society is the best political system, and while it may not take hold everywhere, people will be happiest where it does.'[71] The citation of Fukuyama here reveals Kaplan's geographical imagination most clearly – for it was Fukuyama's argument that popularised a clear demarcation between the West (who have reached the end of history) and the rest (who are still mired in struggle and conflict). All we can do in the West by way of response to the 'danger' lurking out there is to secure our own territorial boundaries and protect the civilisation, democracy and capitalism we have worked so hard to achieve. Hopefully, in time, the devastated parts of the world will come to understand that they will be 'happiest' if they embrace Westernisation.

After reading the litany of devastation in Kaplan's narrative, one gets the feeling that he derives some kind of pleasure from gazing upon horror – indeed, the more horrific the better. In effect, *The Ends of the Earth* is not fuelled by objectivity, but by a series of desires and fantasies about the other. Although commenting on his earlier book *Balkan Ghosts*, Ó Tuathail's observation holds equally true for *The Ends of the Earth*:

Kaplan's whole project is framed as an adventure journey through an exotic past as present ... the result is yet another postmodern 'colonial *New York Times*' correspondent's perspective on a region of the world, this one unconsciously revelling in the raw hatred and slaughter stories of a region supposedly overwhelmed by its history.[72]

Kaplan takes pleasure in the atrocity he confronts because it confirms his geographical imagination: 'our' civilisations must be secured from the barbaric others who live in uncivilised and dangerous countries. But the combination of 'objective' travel writing, international politics and war-reportage in *The Ends of the Earth* fails to silence the ever-present fantasies that underscore this text. As Nuruddin Farah argues, '[Kaplan] plunges further and further into the interior of Africa, stalked by his

---

[71] Kaplan, *The Ends of the Earth*, p. 378; see Fukuyama's review of Kaplan's book in *Commentary*, Vol. 101, No. 4, 1996, pp. 70–1.
[72] Ó Tuathail, *Critical Geopolitics*, p. 297, n. 70.

disorienting fears'.[73] Kaplan is not the brave investigator searching out the truth of 'devastated' areas in order to reinforce current strategic thinking – he is an ignorant creature both tormented and fascinated by 'horrified and horrific visions' of otherness. Like a paranoid security guard in charge of Western values, Kaplan patrols the perimeters of the civilised world and makes forays into the devastation that lurks outside 'our' borders. The more 'facts' he gathers about the devastated parts of the world, the more Western civilisation will be able to protect itself from the threat of contamination. As Farah explains, Kaplan's vigilance only reveals his arrogance: 'Robert Kaplan is tremendously skilled in the art of solipsism. His opinion of himself is enormous, threatening to turn history itself into a footnote to his autobiography.'[74] In the end, this book is not about Africa or Asia, but about Kaplan's production and perception of these places and how they align with American foreign-policy objectives. Africa only functions as the backdrop to Kaplan's 'doomsday messages' which were formulated in America before he departed. The Africans themselves, whenever they are encountered, do not speak with any authority about their own situation – those voices are given to Kaplan's Western informants, 'who, we are made to believe, dispense the genuine stuff of which history is made'.[75] Finally, at the end of an odyssey propped up by the myth of objectivity, Kaplan finally reveals who the book is about:

Nevertheless, many of the problems I saw around the world – poverty, the collapse of cities, porous borders, cultural and racial strife, growing economic disparities, weakening nation-states – are problems for Americans to think about. I thought of America everywhere I looked. We cannot escape from a more populous, interconnected world of crumbling borders.[76]

It is *America* that must address the problems that Kaplan identifies, *America* that symbolises a utopian territory capable of guiding Kaplan through foreign peril, and *America* that needs to be protected from 'the coming anarchy' – the dangerous world that is threatening its borders.

While Holland and Huggan agree that *The Ends of the Earth* is deeply flawed in its reproduction of colonial power and its myth of objectivity, they also argue that it is better than most: 'it is perhaps unfair to pass harsh judgement on Kaplan's book, probably the most ambitious and broadly defined of a clutch of popular "political" travelogues'.[77]

[73] Farah, 'Highway to Hell', p. 67.
[74] Farah, 'Highway to Hell', p. 63.
[75] Farah, 'Highway to Hell', p. 66.
[76] Kaplan, *The Ends of the Earth*, p. 436.
[77] Holland and Huggan, *Tourists with Typewriters*, p. 213.

I disagree – I think it is *absolutely fair* to pass judgement on Kaplan's book, and indeed, it is politically necessary. Certainly, *The Ends of the Earth* is no different from other 'political' travelogues in that it confirms Kaplan's ideological biases – in this Holland and Huggan would agree. But what they fail to examine is Kaplan's influence outside of his assumed middle-class readership: his work *directly* influences American foreign policy. Dalby argues that Kaplan's text has been easily mobilised into an ethnocentric foreign-policy discourse that justifies continuing repression of developing nations, and offers 'modernisation' as the only possible solution to entrenched global inequality. This framework justifies the isolation and containment of Africa as a *cordon sanitaire* of disaster, and excludes Africans from the 'larger scheme of power and economy'.[78] I don't think Kaplan's work should be 'let off the hook' simply because it is 'ambitious'. As Farah explains, its mask of ideological neutrality must be exposed, and its influence on American foreign policy traced:

Why should I take Kaplan's travel writing so seriously, debating its merits? Because he represents the new face of an old breed, the war reporter as moralist: Murrow and Marlow and Montesquieu all mixed together, plowing in and out of the heart of darkness. Also, because he is so patently ill informed, his prose filled with the most lurid fantasies, especially concerning Africans and Muslims. And because, despite all this, Robert Kaplan is one of the most influential journalists in America, a reporter-cum-policy wonk whose previous book, *Balkan Ghosts*, found favour with President Clinton himself.[79]

In terms of cultural and political influence then, Kaplan's work *must* be interrogated for its explicit ideological bias and its complicity in recent American foreign-policy decisions. There is nothing 'unfair' in revealing how *The Ends of the Earth* reproduces a problematic geographical imagination that secures the West as safe and civilised and produces the rest of the world as dangerous and uncivilised. And there is nothing 'unfair' about arguing that this geographical imagination aligns with the one circulating in the minds of policy makers in Washington. But there *is* something 'unfair' about allowing *The Ends of the Earth* to reproduce its geographical imagination without comment. This is a profoundly irresponsible book – it is popular precisely because it does not challenge its readers to reflect upon how their privilege comes at the expense of the

[78] Dalby, 'The Environment as Geopolitical Threat', pp. 485–6.
[79] Farah, 'Highway to Hell', p. 62; Dalby agrees: 'Kaplan was taken seriously in the White House, given his track record as a travel writer and war correspondent with a knack of getting into conflict areas. In particular, his book *Balkan Ghosts* reportedly had considerable influence on President Clinton's policies in Bosnia' ('The Environment as Geopolitical Threat', p. 474).

developing world. In effect, the book simply confirms Western privilege, morality and civilisation by convincing its readers that places like Africa are so dangerous and uncivilised that they are best left alone. As Dalby explains, the geopolitical vision shared by Kaplan and the Pentagon is not neutral:

> This geographical imagination has been frequently coupled with assertions of cultural superiority and ideological rectitude in the form of various articulations of moral certainty. The dangers of ethnocentrism, when coupled to geopolitical reasoning, are greatest precisely where they assert strategic certainty in ways that prevent analysis of the complex social, political and economic interactions that might lead to assessments that in at least some ways 'the problem is us'.[80]

When 'political' travel writing like Kaplan's reproduces a cartography of safety and danger that is fuelled by imperial notions of civilisation and progress, we are prevented from seeing how safety and danger always exceed a world divided into 'the West vs. the rest'. While travelling to dangerous places allows writers like Kaplan to avoid tourists, it does not allow him to examine the dangers that have *already* contaminated the supposedly secure spaces of his home. It is not the 'Last Map' that Kaplan fears, but rather its 'ever mutating' character − the threat that, for example, Africa's 'wall of disease' will travel across the Atlantic and infect his home. Kaplan wants to reify the Last Map by implementing Fukuyama's civilisational borders, even if it means resuscitating an imperial vision and the strategies of colonial rule.

Getting away from it all: escape, utopia and emptiness

Many cosmopolitan travel writers are not interested in reproducing the colonial relations that underscore Kaplan's work and are well aware of the political consequences of a world divided into 'the West vs. the rest'. While they still want to avoid tourism, they have no pretensions to war-correspondence and are thus driven by a desire for emptiness.

---

[80] Dalby, 'The Environment as Geopolitical Threat', p. 489; Dalby directs the question of responsibility to Kaplan's readers as well: 'What ultimately seems to matter in this new designation is whether political disorder and crime will spill over into the affluent North. The affluent world of the *Atlantic* advertisements with their high-technology consumer items is implicitly threatened by the spreading of "anarchy"…What cannot be found in this article is any suggestion that the affluence of those in the limousine might in some way be part of the same political economy that produces conditions of those outside. This connection is simply not present in the text of the article because of the spatial distinctions Kaplan makes between "here" and "there". He notes the dangers of the criminals from "there" compromising the safety of "here" but never countenances the possibility that the economic affluence of "here" is related to the poverty of "there"' (p. 484).

These narratives are an excessive version of 'getting away from it all' – not to a tropical beach to be waited on by a Third World tourist industry, but to a place so remote and empty that *nothing happens*. By fetishising abandoned and empty places, many travel writers seek to avoid the colonial baggage that comes with coveting danger zones. The geographical imagination at work here creates an oppositional relationship between remote spaces where nothing happens, and centred spaces that are too much to bear. This kind of territorialisation inverts the tourist's desire for something extraordinary – in this case, what distinguishes a destination from home is its inactivity, its quietness, its remoteness. Empty zones cannot become tourist sites because they have nothing extraordinary to offer – large spaces, boredom and life lived at a snail's pace will hardly attract tourists who require *some* form of excitement in their chosen destination. This explains why many travel writers have been attracted to remote places like Patagonia: places with nothing in them – no civilisation, no infrastructure, no culture – certainly won't be overrun by souvenir shops and organised tours. In this kind of territorialisation, it is the *absence* of any form of civilisation (rather than its failure) that guarantees an omission from the tourist gaze.

Pico Iyer's book *Falling Off the Map: Some Lonely Places of the World* (1993) is an account of his journeys to places that are geographically isolated. Iyer argues that geographic isolation – whether by mountains (like Bhutan) or by sea (like Iceland) – leads to 'quirky' behaviour, and often political isolation:

In the half-unnatural state of solitary confinement, Lonely Places develop tics and manias and heresies. They pine, they brood, they molder. They gather dust and data, and keep their blinds drawn around the clock. In time, their loneliness makes them stranger, and their strangeness makes them lonelier. And before long, they have come to resemble the woman with a hundred cats in a house she's never cleaned, or the man who obsessively counts the names in the telephone book each night. They grow three-inch nails, and never wash, and talk with the artificial loudness of someone always talking to himself.[81]

With this in mind, many of Iyer's choices make sense: North Korea's mania is characterised by its leader Kim Il Sung (and continues with his son Kim Jong Il); Iceland is isolated, melancholy and covered in darkness half the year; Bhutan suffers from collective oxygen depletion; nothing ever happens in Paraguay; and Australia is 'five thousand miles from anywhere'. Much like Kaplan's strategy, Iyer chooses his empty

---

[81] Pico Iyer, *Falling Off the Map: Some Lonely Places of the World* (London: Vintage Departures, 1994), p. 6.

spots before he starts travelling. However, while Kaplan's observations simply confirm his already formulated ideas about uncivilised creatures in dangerous places, Iyer must engage in a more proactive writing of space. Kaplan's strategy is simple: what he finds confirms what the statistics tell him. But Iyer's strategy is more difficult: he must first construct a place as empty, and then fill it up with the quirky behaviour expected of places as remote as Iceland. We know that every travelogue is about *writing over* space according to preconceived ideas about home and away. But there is a difference between travel writers like Kaplan who believe they are objectively *documenting* what is there, and travel writers like Iyer who, because they aspire to fiction, offer a more *creative* account of foreign space. Both write over space according to the prevailing geographical imagination, but Iyer's strategy does not depend on 'social scientific' and 'factual' authorities like Kaplan's. Rather, Iyer's account of emptiness is a twofold strategy designed to create maximum room for his creative endeavours – first he evacuates foreign space, and then he fills it up again with the 'epidemic oddness' of loneliness.

This does not mean that Iyer's 'geo-graphy' is any less problematic than Kaplan's. Indeed, as Iyer's description of Australia illustrates, he too reproduces a colonial vision. In this case, Iyer repeats a version of *Terra Nullius*, the practice by which land was classified as empty in order to justify its occupation:

And as the night begins to descend, it seems as if the land is reclaiming itself, and Australia is more than ever a place emptied out of people, some dark, elemental presences awakened behind the placid surfaces of its newborn world. The light in Australia is like nothing else on earth – as befits, perhaps, a country that feels as if it has fallen off the planet …. Australia is, of course, the definitive – perhaps ultimate – *terra incognita*… And even today the world's largest island seems to occupy a huge open space in the mind, beyond the reach of our sights. Australia, for one thing, borders nothing and is on the way to nowhere. It feels, in every sense, like the last place on earth.[82]

In short, if a space is not empty, it can be *made* empty. These destinations work like a 'blank canvas' for Iyer, simply waiting to be inscribed, shaped and brought to life by the creative force he possesses. But this desire for lonely places is also a desire to ease the process of creative writing. Writers of all sorts desire quiet places to organise their thoughts – indeed, *Falling Off the Map* was completed in a religious retreat in Big Sur that offered Iyer 'peace beyond measure and the perfect place in which to think about loneliness and space'.[83]

---

[82] Iyer, *Falling Off the Map*, pp. 174–5.
[83] Iyer, *Falling Off the Map*, p. ix.

By travelling to remote destinations, by facing immense emptiness, by conjuring up a story out of nothing, Iyer stands heroic in the success of his creation. In refusing the titillation of danger that attracts travel writers like Kaplan, Iyer creates a new form of *'Terra Incognita'* – a 'blank canvas' that can be filled up with creative and witty accounts of how quirky people behave at the edges of the world. The problem, of course, is that there *are* no empty places in the world – even barren stretches of Antarctica are populated by international scientists, and the supposedly 'uninhabited' Sahara is perpetually criss-crossed by nomadic groups and trade routes. In effect, Iyer's production of empty space is part of the same colonial vision that Kaplan employs in describing Africa and Asia as dangerous, uncivilised and threatening. It is the ultimate process of writing over difference – by emptying foreign space of its inhabitants, travel writers don't have to confront others who might confound their expectations. The *Terra Nullius* metaphor is apt here: the travel writer's production of empty space is the literary equivalent of colonial powers clearing Australia of its Aboriginal inhabitants in order to possess and construct a 'new' land. This idea of novelty is crucial, for within the process of evacuating space is the longstanding desire to be first to colonise it. For example, when Iyer arrives in the land already made famous by Bruce Chatwin and Paul Theroux, he comments not on the literary fame now granted to Patagonia as a result of these books, but on the barrenness and emptiness of the landscape: 'I could see nothing but miles of nothingness. Occasionally, an eagle circling above a carcass. A hut. The rusted shell of an abandoned car. A flock of ostriches. Around them all, stretching everywhere, miles and miles of nothingness.'[84] Not only does Iyer fail to recognise the travellers, geographers, scientists and diplomats who preceded him to Patagonia and produced it as a space of imagination and fantasy long before he arrived, but he ignores the literary tourists who descend on Tierra del Fuego every year 'clutching tattered paperback copies of *In Patagonia'*.[85]

For Iyer, *Falling Off the Map* is a snapshot in time – he is well aware that these lonely places will not remain so for much longer, and that 'loneliness itself may become extinct'. What results, then, is a book of secrets. These quirky out-of-the way places are actually charming, unique and 'authentic' pockets of civilisation, and Iyer's book is an effort to catch these moments before they inevitably become commodified by the tourist circuit. This is very much in line with his arguments in both

[84] Iyer, *Falling Off the Map*, p. 45.
[85] Shakespeare, *Bruce Chatwin*, p. 301.

Video Night in Kathmandu and *The Global Soul* – that signs of a 'global' civilisation can be found in the most unlikely places. For example, Buenos Aires 'has a kind of café society cosmopolitanism that could put New York to shame', and Iceland 'boasts the largest number of poets, presses, and readers per capita in the world'.[86] Iyer is both surprised by signs of a global culture in such lonely and remote places, and delighted that he managed to experience their soon-to-be-exposed charm. He is not concerned with being the first traveller to any of these places, but he definitely thinks he is one of the last – for tourists are quickly catching on to the fact that lonely places are ideal spots to 'get away from it all'. For example, Australia is starting to capitalise on the popularity of its emptiness:

the greatest reason of all for Australia's sudden appeal is, in the end, the very thing that has outlawed it for so long: the tyranny of distance. Suddenly, people are realizing that Australia is so far from the world that it is the ideal place for people to get away from the world, do nothing, and watch others do the same.[87]

By claiming that the popularity of emptiness is sudden, Iyer confirms to both tourists and readers that he is the last person to see these places in their 'natural' state of emptiness. But by the time readers have finished his book, these places will already be the newest destination on the tourist circuit.

No such conceit is apparent in Bill Bryson's account of Australia in *Down Under* (2000), for, as ever, he is quite content to be 'just another tourist'. He happily goes sightseeing, potters around museums and marvels at the friendly and open Australian character. Bryson is under no illusion that he is the first travel writer to document Australia, and he gladly cites previous travelogues by Jan Morris, Tim Bowden and Thomas Keneally alongside many historic, scientific and political texts. Bryson's entire book is an effort at convincing his readers that Australia is far from empty and boring:

Australians can't bear it that the outside world pays so little attention to them, and I don't blame them. This is a country where interesting things happen, and all the time...This is a country that is at once staggeringly empty and yet packed with stuff. Interesting stuff, ancient stuff, not readily explained. Stuff yet to be found. Trust me, this is an interesting place.[88]

Down Under methodically unveils a secret – we may think Australia is a vast stretch of empty land at the edge of the world, but Bryson wants to

---

[86] Iyer, *Falling Off the Map*, pp. 27, 67.
[87] Iyer, *Falling Off the Map*, p. 175.
[88] Bill Bryson, *Down Under* (London: Black Swan, 2001), pp. 17, 22.

prove that it is teeming with life. This is Bryson at his most earnest – he *really* wants to convince the reader that Australia is not empty at all, but abundantly interesting and lively. The uncompromising image that starts the book, 'Australia is the driest, flattest, hottest, most desiccated, infertile and climactically aggressive of all the inhabited continents', is soon followed by a narrative that invokes this 'hostile' image only to work against it.[89] In other words, *Down Under* reproduces the 'boundless blank' of the Australian outback as a stretch of emptiness, but it also *fills up* this space through positive accounts of history, nature and culture.[90]

In *Down Under*, Bryson is fascinated by the successive attempts by nineteenth-century explorers to find a way through the Australian outback. Historical figures like John McDougall Stuart and Ernest Giles are everywhere in the text, as Bryson describes the irresistible pull of this emptiness: 'It is an environment that wants you dead, yet again and again in the face of the most staggering privations, for the meagrest of rewards, explorers ventured into it.'[91] He retells these tales with his characteristic hyperbole, childishly obsessing about explorers drinking their own urine and eating raw baby wallabies 'fur, skin and all'. But Bryson reserves some of this awe for the people he meets in the 'miles of stubbled nothingness'. He is shy and reverent around the labourers who drink in the outback bars, and constantly astonished at hoteliers, bar owners and shop workers who live in the 'forbidding Never Never' all year round. How can Australia be empty when it has remarkable people like this? Bryson is similarly awe-struck by Australian animals – especially the poisonous snakes, lethal spiders, hungry crocodiles and toxic jellyfish. He gleefully presents himself as an urban scaredy-cat, hideously out of his depth in a country teeming with such danger. While he tries to prepare himself for his inevitable encounters with nature, he finally admits: 'it isn't possible in a single lifetime to read about all the dangers that lurk under every wattle bush or ripple of water in this wondrously venomous and toothy country'.[92] He is paralysed by fear of sharks and jellyfish, he freaks out at spiders (even dead ones), and generally – though exuberantly and certainly deliberately – behaves like a total sissy. But his histrionics are surpassed by his respect for the

---

[89] Bryson, *Down Under*, p. 20.
[90] Bryson's contradictory account of the outback is central to the book: this 'vast and baking interior, the boundless void that lies between the coasts' is, for Bryson, the 'real Australia'. He goes on to say 'I have never entirely understood why, when people urge you to see their "real" country, they send you to empty parts where almost no sane person would choose to live, but there you are. You cannot say you have been to Australia until you have crossed the outback' (*Down Under*, pp. 24–5).
[91] Bryson, *Down Under*, p. 320.
[92] Bryson, *Down Under*, p. 82.

diversity and robustness of Australian animals, and not just the 'obvious' candidates like the platypus, koala or kangaroo. Bryson is fascinated by the sturdiness of Australian animals in the face of such a harsh climate, and against the rules of normal evolutionary progress. He gleefully recounts the discovery (and laments the disappearance) of bizarre creatures long thought extinct − yellow ants, rat kangaroos, pig-footed bandicoots and the frog that gives birth through its mouth. How can Australia be empty when it has such remarkable biodiversity? Bryson is not just fascinated by Australia's history and nature; he also makes great efforts to extol its cultural and urban virtues. For Bryson, Australia is not only similar to where he lives, it is *better*:

Let me say right here that I love Australia − adore it immeasurably − and am smitten anew each time I see it. One of the effects of paying so little attention to Australia is that it is always such a pleasant surprise to find it there... This is comfortable and clean and familiar... these people are just like you and me. This is wonderful. This is exhilarating. This is why I love to come to Australia... Life doesn't get much better than this.[93]

He spends much of his time in the 'safe and clean' cities along the south-east coast − he sips coffee, reads local papers, visits friends, goes for walks and wanders through museums. For Bryson, Sydney has the best of everything: it is a 'safe and fair-minded city', has a climate that makes you 'strong and handsome', and boasts a perfect balance of culture (e.g. the famous Opera House) and nature (e.g. its many parks). Observing the commuting office workers during weekday rush hour, he states: 'No wonder they looked so damn happy.'[94] How can Australia be empty when it is so perfect?

While *Down Under* pleased Bryson fans once again, many critics were getting tired of his childish enthusiasm and his usual gags. As one critic put it, 'as he writes more and more of these books on the basis of less and less travel, the humour wears thin... the result is deeply tedious'.[95] More importantly, reviewers criticised Bryson for not spending enough time in Australia, suggesting that his four separate trips resulted in a superficial and 'aimless' book. As Australian writer Kathy Lette argued: 'Any decent publisher would have ordered the author to spend another six months with his subject − but hey, this is Bill Bryson.'[96]

---

[93] Bryson, *Down Under*, p. 24.
[94] Bryson, *Down Under*, p. 78.
[95] Charles Saumarez Smith, "Upside-Down View of Down Under: Two Outsiders Get Funny Peculiar Ideas about Australia", *Observer*, 2 July 2000, p. 14.
[96] Kathy Lette, *Sunday Telegraph*, as quoted in Stephen Moss, '*Down Under* by Bill Bryson', *Guardian*, 5 July 2000, online only at http://www.books.guardian.co.uk/critics/reviews/0,5817,340067,00.html.

Critics argued that much of the narrative in *Down Under* – the historical accounts, facts about the natural world, the cultural life of Sydney and Melbourne – could have been written without ever going to Australia. For Mark Sanderson, this lack of authenticity undermines the book: 'He is not really a travel writer at all. He prefers bookshelves to backpacks; he goes in search of clichés rather than new experiences. With an ego the size of Ayer's rock, he seems to think God's Own Country needs the help of a patronizing American'.[97] What Bryson fails to grasp is that Australia has been written over so many times – not least by travel writers – that it is already familiar to an Anglo-American audience. His earnest pleading on behalf of Australia's 'interesting' character falls on deaf ears – his readers and critics *already know* that Australia is interesting, and indeed, many of them have already visited. As Terence Blacker argues,

The problem is that, after a few pages, one finds oneself looking forward to the moments when Bryson takes us back to the library. The rich fascination of Australia's history and ecology, as seen by other writers, points up the thinness of our author's first-hand version of the country. From its defiantly dreary title onwards, *Down Under* feels like a journey taken at too great a speed on a road well-worn by other, more intrepid travellers, not to mention millions of ordinary, non-writing tourists.[98]

To be sure, Bryson cites many other authors who have written about Australia – and even includes a bibliography of sources – but these admissions don't alleviate the sense that Bryson's narrative is both superficial and derivative. Indeed, one gets the sense that Bryson spent more time reading about Australia than he did travelling through the country. As a result, he relies on an outdated literary stereotype of Australia as an empty and barren place in order to launch what he thinks is an original argument – that Australia is, in fact, an exciting and lively place.

While I disagree with the suggestion that there is a 'real' Australia that Bryson failed to engage with, I think the idea that Bryson's stereotype of Australia is outdated is a useful one to pursue. If Bryson's image of Australia was gleaned from previously written travel accounts, does it also reproduce an imperial gaze? It is not difficult to see how Jordan and Kaplan reproduce a colonial cartography by securing their 'civilised' homes through oppositional productions of danger in 'uncivilised'

---

[97] Mark Sanderson, as quoted in Stephen Moss, '*Down Under* by Bill Bryson'.
[98] Terence Blacker, 'Bill's Awfully Big Adventure', *Sunday Times* (Culture), 11 June 2000, p. 33.

foreign places. My point is that the desire to 'get away from it all' reproduces the same cartography through different strategies. Both Iyer and Bryson have a sense of what counts as civilised, central and cosmopolitan space, and this assumption frames their subsequent positioning of lonely and empty spaces. Iyer invokes the colonial strategy of evacuating foreign space in order to fill it up with his own preconceptions of oddity, whereas Bryson's entire book is premised on the literary stereotype that Australia is empty and his job is to convince us otherwise. My point is that all these travelogues – Jordan's, Kaplan's, Iyer's and Bryson's – uncritically reproduce the prevailing discourse of modern cartography and fail to interrogate how and why certain places are considered dangerous and others are considered safe and, indeed, empty. Moreover, these travelogues do not question how our prevailing understandings of security – *where* is safe and *where* is dangerous – are themselves framed by a geographical imagination inherited from colonial rule. While this cartography may be easier to spot in Jordan's and Kaplan's narratives, the pursuit of emptiness is not a solution. Neither Iyer's rendition of rapidly disappearing lonely places nor Bryson's depiction of a simultaneously empty and full Australia resolves the fact that our preconceptions of *what a place is like* are derived from colonial narratives. The bigger question underscoring Iyer's and Bryson's narratives is 'just where are these places remote *from*?' Travelogues about Antarctica, Iowa and Australia do not subvert the global placement of safety and danger – they simply reinforce it from the other end.

The conceit of these travel writers is the belief that they are somehow not influenced by wider circulations of geopolitical discourse – that they produce *original* and *individual* accounts of chosen destinations, even if those places have already been written about. While the geographical imagination of these authors is the same, their styles and strategies differ: Jordan offers a holistic and 'new age' account of how individuals from different cultures can connect in dangerous circumstances; Kaplan offers an objective argument about why the world is falling apart and how we can stop it; Iyer offers a nostalgic journey that waves good-bye to 'quirky' places soon to be devoured by tourism; and Bryson offers an enthusiastic (if superfluous) rebuttal to the idea that Australia is empty and remote. The point is that none of these writers recognise or acknowledge that the criteria by which they have chosen their destinations rests upon a *colonial* geographical imagination of safe places (i.e. civilised homes) and dangerous places (i.e. threatening destinations).

Extreme satire: middle-class anxiety and libertarian aggression

While not necessarily offering an alternative to this geographical imagination, P. J. O'Rourke's *Holidays in Hell* and Mark Lawson's *The Battle for Room Service* use satire to expose the impossibility of containing safety and danger within recognised geopolitical boundaries. Both suggest a critical cartography that opens global space to more heterogeneous and conflicting interactions between safety and danger. To be sure, satire is a complex political strategy that requires a shared understanding between the writer and the audience about *which* prevailing values are being lampooned.[99] While their pursuits are different, both O'Rourke and Lawson target the conceit and arrogance of those who believe that clear geopolitical distinctions between safety and danger result in a more secure world. O'Rourke uses excess in *Holidays in Hell*: he depicts dangerous places as so completely beyond all hope of civilisation that they become absurdities. Lawson plays off of O'Rourke by using inversion in *The Battle for Room Service*: he sends up the stereotype of the intrepid traveller by deliberately choosing boring and safe destinations. These satirical strategies produce a self-reflexivity that differentiates Lawson and O'Rourke from Jordan, Kaplan, Iyer and Bryson. For the satirist, the self must be as available for ridicule as everyone else. Kaplan and Iyer provide no personal information and show no signs of self-reflexivity, whereas Jordan is consumed by new age musings on emotions, holism, spiritual connections and 'finding peace'. Indeed, these are humourless books and full of the 'liberal twaddle' that O'Rourke takes such delight in ridiculing. While O'Rourke and Lawson have more in common with Bryson's approach, there is a significant difference here. Bryson is certainly self-deprecating, and *Down Under* continues his strategy of being childlike and incompetent when travelling. But Bryson's travelogues are not satire in the strictest sense, for they fail to ridicule prevailing social values or the conditions of possibility for his own subject position as a travel writer. In effect, Bryson's self-deprecations (e.g. his endless mugging to the camera with 'isn't this great!' and 'look at the mess I've gotten myself into!') are efforts of self-preservation – it is as if he thinks such self-controlled

---

[99] For further reading on the political effect of satire, see Frederic V. Bogel, *The Difference that Satire Makes: Rhetoric and Reading from Jonson to Byron* (Cornell: Cornell University Press, 2001); Linda Hutcheon, *A Theory of Parody: The Teachings of Twentieth-Century Art Forms* (Champaign, IL: University of Illinois Press, 2000); Dustin Griffin, *Satire: A Critical Reintroduction* (Lexington: University of Kentucky Press, 1994); and Charles A. Knight, *The Literature of Satire* (Cambridge: Cambridge University Press, 2004).

parody will deter others from questioning his authority as a travel writer. In contrast, O'Rourke and Lawson take every opportunity to ridicule the values inherent in their own positions as middle-class tourists and professional travel writers. Unlike Bryson's mock self-deprecation, their satiric strategies *do* allow them to ask difficult questions about how they end up where they do, and what criteria they construct to make judgements about foreign places and people.

This suggests another way in which O'Rourke and Lawson differ from Jordan, Kaplan, Iyer and Bryson: both go one step further in engaging with difficult political questions that most travelogues avoid. To be sure, the dangerous destinations visited by Jordan and Kaplan are overflowing with obvious political problems – war, conflict, overpopulation, environmental damage, poverty, starvation, disease. Likewise, the destinations chosen by Iyer and Bryson seem apolitical – places like Iceland and Australia have less pressing problems than Central America and Africa (and we remember what happened when Bryson tried to engage with 'serious' problems in Africa). My point is that the satire of O'Rourke and Lawson is *politically directed* because it reveals the difficulty of encountering, representing and offering solutions to global problems. They recognise their own complicity in these problems, and are under no illusions – like Kaplan is – that their observations will make any difference whatsoever. With this in mind, there is a particularly telling moment in *Down Under* that reveals the reluctance of conventional travel writers to engage with difficult political questions. In keeping with Bryson's liberal subjectivity, he is duly horrified by the racist attitudes of the white Australians and their ability to ignore 'the Aboriginal question'. But after 350 pages, he makes a startling revelation about his inability to provide snappy answers when faced with difficult issues such as this. As he sips a coffee one morning and watches the 'shadowy Aborigines' amble by, he offers the following admission:

I realized that I didn't have the faintest idea what the solution to all this was, what was required to spread the fruits of general Australian prosperity to those who seemed so signally unable to find their way to it. If I were contracted by the Commonwealth of Australia to advise on Aboriginal issues all I could write would be: 'Do more. Try harder. Start now'. So without an original or helpful thought in my head, I just sat for some minutes and watched these poor disconnected people shuffle past. Then I did what most white Australians do. I read my newspaper and drank my coffee and didn't see them anymore.[100]

At least Bryson has the sense to end a chapter on such a note – when, in fact, he should have ended the entire book. What O'Rourke and Lawson

---

[100] Bryson, *Down Under*, p. 355.

provide that Bryson does not is a collection of these moments where the travel writer comes up against intractable and complex political problems that cannot be passed over in a glib or superficial manner.

In contrast to the dangerous places visited by Jordan and Kaplan, Mark Lawson's *The Battle for Room Service: Journeys to All the Safe Places* is a satirical version of prevailing geopolitics. Rather than danger zones or remote sites, Lawson creates an itinerary based entirely on boredom and safety. Because he desires 'tranquillity, stability, and conventionally civilized values', his route includes New Zealand, Middle America, Canada, Luxembourg and Milton Keynes. Rather than tracing a cartography of 'hot spots', Lawson focuses on the forgotten areas of calm that never appear in our newspapers or on our television screens: 'All those places which the great travel writers ignored with a yawn would call me as Kashmir called them.'[101] This 'beaten track' of safety defines Lawson in direct opposition to writers like Jordan and Kaplan who covet danger zones. He already knows that international affairs are violent and dangerous – they are the stuff of war correspondence, political journalism and intrepid travel writing rather than the nice middle-class cultural criticism he usually practises. But Lawson is unapologetic about his lack of courage and explains his cowardice as a 'wimp illness'. Indeed, *The Battle for Room Service* questions why anyone would want to put themselves in harm's way when they could have a nice safe holiday in a boring place. Nonetheless, Lawson's examination of areas usually forgotten by the frenzied world of international conflict still reproduces a distinction between 'the tourist zones and the terrorist zones'.[102] In effect, one reinforces the other: 'My map would be of the quiet world, tourist not terrorist ... My object was to visit those places most unlikely to be subject to bloody insurrection.'[103] The difference here is that Lawson positions prevailing geopolitics as an object of satire. Borrowing from a taxonomy used by business travellers, he provides a clear picture of the world divided into four 'zones' – the first relatively safe, and the fourth extremely dangerous. Admitting that 'the genre of travel writing is, these days, mostly practised on Level Four nations', he promptly develops and describes his own category: 'Level Zero (Nonchalance)': 'There is almost no serious crime. Politically, one right-wing monetarist government is occasionally replaced by another, but this leads only to minor

---

[101] Mark Lawson, *The Battle for Room Service: Journeys to All the Safe Places* (London: Picador, 1993), p. 8.
[102] Lawson, *The Battle for Room Service*, p. 2.
[103] Lawson, *The Battle for Room Service*, p. 7.

traffic hold-ups on polling day or during a royal or religious procession.'[104]

What emerges in *The Battle for Room Service* is a much more nuanced understanding of what counts as safe and dangerous, and where those places are situated in the world. For all its sarcasm, *The Battle for Room Service* is highly politicised: in his efforts to avoid anything obviously dangerous, Lawson can't help but point out the social and political struggles that engulf supposedly boring places – especially the consequences of globalisation and economic recession. He starts his journey in 1991 in New Zealand where the landscape is like 'the scene in a nuclear holocaust movie in which the survivors venture out on to the burned, unpeopled, eerie Earth'.[105] When he eventually gets to Timaru (the 'Mecca of the non-event, an oasis of stasis, the world centre of the early night') he witnesses a place squeezed by economic recession, awash in gang violence and coping with a recent teenage murderer.[106] Lawson's experience of Timaru's underbelly shapes the rest of the book: he discovers that while quiet places might be out of the way, they experience the same social tensions and difficulties that characterise more urban settings. For example, as the forces of globalisation break up New Zealand's old trading patterns (e.g. lamb and butter to the UK), economic recession deepens and reveals entrenched social and political cleavages about race and ethnicity. But rather than reorganise their economic base in conjunction with South East Asia and Australia, the Kiwis revert to a nostalgia for 1950s England (especially the royal family), a suspicion of the Japanese and patronising, demeaning and often violent attitudes towards the Maori. What Lawson discovers on his first stop in New Zealand is that the 'borders of the quiet world are pervious'. New Zealand – like other boring places in the early 1990s – is full of threats and fears: 'Everywhere you went in the quiet world at that time, you saw the same warning initials on posters: UV and HIV. Sex was death and sun was death. And the money was running out.'[107]

As Lawson makes his journeys in 1991–2, he is witnessing the initial phase of post-Cold War globalisation. What he notices is that even boring places are transforming in line with geopolitical upheaval: 'In the

---

[104] Lawson, *The Battle for Room Service*, p. 4. While Iyer and Bryson are keen to make lonely and out-of-the-way places exciting for the reader, Lawson is more circumspect. Admitting that his itinerary is dictated by the stereotypes about boring places already in circulation, he holds out the hope that the evidence will contradict his preconceived ideas: 'Perhaps Canada would dazzle, and Switzerland dizzy' (p. 10).

[105] Lawson, *The Battle for Room Service*, p. 33.

[106] Lawson, *The Battle for Room Service*, p. 18.

[107] Lawson, *The Battle for Room Service*, p. 24.

quiet world that year, the countries were reshuffling, more peacefully but no less seriously than in the wreck of Eastern Europe'.[108] While he comments on the obvious indicators of globalisation (e.g. 'McDonalds, Coca-Cola, CNN and Andrew Lloyd Webber'), Lawson is always alert to the less palatable consequences of that homogenisation. For example, he reveals how the quiet world is turning desperately to tourism in order to alleviate economic recession; he traces how Japanese economic influence is rearranging traditional power blocs of North America (and affecting North American workers as a result); he suggests that economic globalisation is quashing separatist notions like those in Quebec; and he notices that there is increased 'foreigner-hostility' in peaceful places like Belgium due to the reorganisation of Europe. *The Battle for Room Service* is a significant early document of the effects of globalisation because it reveals how economic restructuring exacerbates social and political cleavages in the unlikeliest of places, but also produces dissent and resistance. To be sure, Lawson focuses on the boring and banal characteristics of 'second-tier' suburban cities like Peoria, Normal and Bloomington, Illinois, but he also detects the rumblings of discontent in Middle America. In effect, the economic recession of the early 1990s fuels anger and resentment in a variety of disaffected groups: 'For years, everyone had prophesied that anarchy in America would come from black anger. Perhaps Los Angeles proved that it would. But a new possibility was brewing: that the anarchists might be the middle-class whites. What was stronger? The anger of never having had or the anger of losing what had been?'[109] As the tectonic shifts of globalisation and economic recession take hold, Lawson realises that even the safest, most boring, banal places in the world are awash with violence, anxiety and fear. As he realises in Brussels, 'There was an undertow of menace on the streets, so that, in a comparison I would never have thought possible, Brussels reminded me, at times, of Detroit.'[110]

At the end of the book Lawson visits Milton Keynes, Thatcher's ideal 'planned town' that was supposed to reduce crime, unemployment and violence through the rational organisation of urban space. Lawson discovers that despite its spatial regimentation and governance, Milton Keynes displays all the usual markers of modern urban living: 'As for safety, there was a high rate of car crime – theft from the parks, joy-riding on the estates... There was also a series of rapes and assaults on

---

[108] Lawson, *The Battle for Room Service*, pp. 188–9.
[109] Lawson, *The Battle for Room Service*, p. 98.
[110] Lawson, *The Battle for Room Service*, p. 198.

the Redways...Dream town? Dream on.'[111] In effect, *The Battle for Room Service* presents an intriguing contradiction. On the one hand, Lawson is scathing about the banality of certain places: Winnipeg is 'shorthand for Canadian drabness'; Canberra was like 'political tofu', Alaska is deeply tedious, Vancouver is 'germless', and it is not even worth being rude about Luxembourg. But on the other hand, Lawson is careful to reveal the underbelly of these places: children are routinely abducted at EuroDisney, there is a dramatic increase of 'assaults, rapes and robberies' in Australia, and he relays the frightening story of an 11-year-old girl raped on her way to school in Milton Keynes. At the end of the narrative, Lawson concludes:

Only a fool or a neurotic would deny that it was still better to be born in any of these destinations than in Bosnia, Somalia, Beirut, or one of the other horror spots that kept CNN and the UN in business. But it was equally apparent that the borders of the safe zones were receding. There were no islands any more. There was no easy opt-out anywhere from poverty, joblessness, or – and this more strikingly – some variety of violence.[112]

What *The Battle for Room Service* does is reveal that the geographical imagination dividing the world into safe zones and danger zones is a myth. Unlike Kaplan who wants to fortify the borders of the 'safe' world against the tyranny and anarchy outside, Lawson acknowledges that the 'safe world' is already characterised by new forms of violence and disorder.

Lawson writes his book in direct opposition to another popular travelogue: 'P. J. O'Rourke called a book *Holidays in Hell*. This, perhaps, was *Holidays in Purgatory*. He had pioneered macho travel. Here was wimp tourism.'[113] O'Rourke's 'frat-boy' image is miles away from Lawson's cultivated aesthete, and yet both share the aim of satirising the same geographical imagination – albeit from opposite directions. *Holidays in Hell* is a particularly interesting moment in O'Rourke's development as a satirist and political commentator. While much of his journalism describes his own transformation from a 'left-wing hippie' to a committed libertarian, *Holidays in Hell* is written in the 1980s before his more conservative views take hold. As such, there are particular moments when O'Rourke's own confusions and difficulties surface and prevent him from reproducing the unquestioned arrogance of a political

---

[111] Lawson, *The Battle for Room Service*, p. 240. Redways were the bricked walkways through the town – their dips and bad lighting made them perfect hideouts for criminals during the 1980s.
[112] Lawson, *The Battle for Room Service*, p. 288.
[113] Lawson, *The Battle for Room Service*, p. 7.

travel writer like Kaplan. Whereas *The Ends of the Earth* is full of assured policy suggestions – Kaplan's answers to world problems are based on 'truth', and are therefore untainted by political bias – O'Rourke makes no claims of neutrality or objectivity. Rather, his approach to the 'troubled' areas in the world is an excessive and exaggerated version of Pax Americana:

So-called Western civilization, as practised in half of Europe, some of Asia and a few parts of North America, is better than anything else available. Western civilization not only provides a bit of life, a pinch of liberty and the occasional pursuance of happiness, it's the only thing that's ever tried to... We are fools when we fail to defend civilization... To extend civilization, even with guns, isn't the worst thing in the world... The trouble in Lebanon, South Africa, Haiti and the occupied territories of Palestine should, simply, be stopped by the military intervention of civilized nations.[114]

O'Rourke is not travelling to the ends of the earth to *test* whether or not Western civilisation is the best on offer – he already *knows* its worth and takes every opportunity to extol its virtues. Not only does he think American democracy should be exported to the Third World and the former USSR, he also thinks that 'left-wing Europe' should take notice as well. When O'Rourke is unable to get a visa to cover the American bombing of Libya in 1986, he gets stuck in Europe for a month and writes 'Among the Euro-weenies' to counter growing anti-American sentiment on the continent. His snide comments about these 'stinky little European countries filled with Commies and Nazis and creepy-looking Greens' offset his unbridled enthusiasm for America's general greatness and its welcome decision to 'take a punch at the Libyans'.[115] His hyperbolic patriotism finally manifests itself in a long rant to the British at the end of his stay: 'We're the big boys, Jack, the original, giant, economy sized, new and improved butt kickers of all time... We eat little countries like this for breakfast and shit them out before lunch.'[116]

O'Rourke's excessive jingoism is crucial to the satire at work here, for while *Holidays in Hell* covers many 'hot spots' and laments their lack of democratic freedoms, he is equally critical of America. This is precisely what differentiates O'Rourke from Kaplan – for all his bluster about the greatness of America, O'Rourke interrogates his beloved 'civilisation' just as carefully as he examines the 'troubled spots' of the world. Along with the usual Third World horror destinations, O'Rourke takes hellish

---

[114] P. J. O'Rourke, *Holidays in Hell* (London: Picador, 1988), p. 13.
[115] O'Rourke, *Holidays in Hell*, pp. 275, 194.
[116] O'Rourke, *Holidays in Hell*, pp. 209–10.

holidays in Europe, Australia, the USSR, Disneyland, Harvard, North
Carolina and Florida as well. Often, he compares the squalor of the
Third World with certain urban zones in America: 'it's a mess over there.
To tell the truth, it isn't a worse mess than the Brownsville section of
Brooklyn or downtown Detroit. But it's a different mess.'[117] Moreover,
he provides a historical explanation for the different colonial legacies in
North and South America. He argues that 'farm colonies' led to nice
civilised places, whereas 'exploitation colonies' did not: 'New England,
Canada, Costa Rica and parts of Argentina are reasonably nice places,
while Mississippi, Jamaica, Mexico and most other sections of our
hemisphere are shit holes.'[118] O'Rourke's satire works because it
deconstructs the expectations readers have about *both* troubled spots
and safe places – Costa Rica civilised? Mississippi uncivilised? In effect,
his ironic mapping turns the global arrangement of safety and danger
inside out and rewrites the cartography of civilisation. Despite his
patriotism, O'Rourke does not reproduce an easy equivalence between
America and civilisation. For example, instead of praising the rich and
powerful alumni at the 350th anniversary of Harvard University,
O'Rourke lists the atrocities they have perpetrated in the supposed
'national interest' (e.g. the Vietnam War, the 'demagoguery' of FDR,
and JFK's Bay of Pigs fiasco). At the 'Heritage USA' theme park he
laments the stupidity of a nation so overweight and so enthralled by
'refried Jesus-wheezing TV preachers' that they have become effectively
lobotomised. Covering the 1988 Democratic Party Convention,
O'Rourke laments the lack of political discussion in America:

And the real political debate – debate that could change anybody's mind or put
anything in that mind to change – wouldn't fill out a T-shirt slogan. Party
platforms are as bland as Perrier soup, vague as a TV commercial for
condoms... bumper stickers [are] as close as American political parties come
to argument of hypothesis by logical reference.[119]

Although O'Rourke is passionate about the civilised values at the heart
of America, he is highly critical of its corruption, violence, idleness,
stupidity, boredom and government interference. *Holidays in Hell* is
significant because O'Rourke manages to sustain a number of contradictions and uncertainties about America's relationship to civilisation.
By the end of the book, he offers a more humble vision of his beloved
homeland: 'Maybe our Disney World mindlessness is... like
a McDonald's Big Mac. It's mushy and tasteless and made out of

---

[117] O'Rourke, *Holidays in Hell*, p. 240.
[118] O'Rourke, *Holidays in Hell*, p. 143.
[119] O'Rourke, *Holidays in Hell*, pp. 269, 274.

disgusting parts of things. But, when you come right down to it, everybody wants one'.[120] America may not be in the kind of trouble one finds in Central America or Africa, but it is in danger of wasting the opportunities that come with being a global superpower. And it is precisely this disappointment and boredom with America that leads O'Rourke into places that are more dangerous.

As his journeys take place during the last days of the Cold War, O'Rourke goes to Warsaw in 1986 to document life in the shadow of the USSR. Playing on the expectation that the Eastern Bloc is awash with espionage and Communist efforts to brainwash its populace, O'Rourke comes to the following conclusion: 'Communism doesn't really starve or execute that many people. Mostly it just bores them to death. Life behind the Iron Curtain is like living with your parents forever.'[121] These cartographic inversions in *Holidays in Hell* work by sending up the geopolitical expectations of a middle-class, Anglo-American, 'holiday-going' audience. In 'A Ramble through Lebanon', he draws upon the travel experience of his audience through 'guidebook' language:

West Beirut can also be toured on foot. You'll find the city is full of surprises – a sacking of the Saudi embassy because of long lines for visas to Mecca, for instance, or shelling of the lower town by an unidentified gunboat or car bombs several times a day. Renaults are the favoured vehicles. Avoid double-parked Le Cars. Do not, however, expect the population to be moping around glassy eyed. There's a lot of jewellery and make-up and the silliest Italian designer jeans on earth. The streets are jammed. Everyone's very busy, though not exactly working.[122]

The chapter on Lebanon provides the satirical architecture of the book: the juxtaposition of tourism and danger. O'Rourke is doing what any travel writer would do – he is telling the audience what is worth seeing and what is not. The problem is that he is doing it *in the wrong place*. Being a tourist in Lebanon disrupts the prevailing geopolitical arrangement of safety and danger – tourists can only ever be located in safe destinations, and not in places like Beirut where bombs are going off. The juxtaposition of *Holidays in Hell* only works because O'Rourke portrays himself as a tourist rather than an intrepid travel writer or war correspondent. In fact, the tourist/traveller dichotomy is heavily

---

[120] O'Rourke, *Holidays in Hell*, p. 275.
[121] O'Rourke, *Holidays in Hell*, p. 98.
[122] O'Rourke, *Holidays in Hell*, p. 26. O'Rourke's multi-layered satire of guidebooks, the holiday-going audience, the situation in Lebanon in the mid 1980s, and the geopolitical binary of safety/danger were too much for the commissioning editors of *Vanity Fair* in 1984 – they thought it 'much too weird to publish' at the time; *Holidays in Hell*, p. 22.

parodied in this book. With tourists pitching up in Central America, Iran and Afghanistan, it is clear that the prevailing geographical imagination no longer prevents the tourist gaze from commodifying danger zones:

> Also at present in Angola, Eritrea and God-knows-Where are the new breed of yuppie 'experience travellers'. You'll be pinned down by mortar fire in the middle of a genocide atrocity in the Sudan, and right through it all come six law partners and their wives, in Banana Republic bush jackets, taking an inflatable raft trip down the Nile and having an 'experience'... Then there's squalor. That hasn't changed since 1867, but once tourists tried to avoid it. Now they seek it out. Modern tourists have to see squalor so they can tell everyone back home how it changed their perspective on life. Describing squalor, if done with sufficient indignation, makes friends and relatives obligated to listen to your boring vacation stories. (Squalor is conveniently available, at reasonable prices, in Latin America.)[123]

Intrepid travel writers have been squeezed out of the danger stakes not only by increasingly popular war correspondents, but also by increased opportunities for adventure travel. Danger zones have become the new coveted destination, with Fielding's *The World's Most Dangerous Places* providing a guidebook and rating system for those seeking the adrenaline rush of civil war, drug running, revolution, armed insurrection and human rights violations.[124] The skill of *Holidays in Hell* is that it parodies the prevailing geopolitical imagination of safety and danger by revealing its obsolescence.

The juxtaposition at the heart of O'Rourke's 'terror tourism' is revealed most clearly in Central America where the safety/danger binary begins to break down. Whereas Kaplan spends over 400 pages detailing the myriad of dangers lurking outside of the civilisational boundaries of America (and provides policy suggestions to keep those dangers at bay), O'Rourke is not as naïve about the sanctity, security, or indeed success of those civilisational boundaries. He knows that America has its problems, and more importantly, he knows that America is complicit in the problems faced by Central American countries. His month spent along the Mexican/American border is enough to convince him of the complexity and difficulty of maintaining civilisational boundaries. While travelling with a border patrol agent, O'Rourke inadvertently captures three illegal Mexicans trying to cross the border at Laredo – and immediately wishes he hadn't. His regret prompts him to reflect on the

---

[123] O'Rourke, *Holidays in Hell*, pp. 17, 20. O'Rourke uses 1867 as an origin point here because that is the year Mark Twain published *The Innocents Abroad*.

[124] Robert Young Pelton, Coskun Aral and Wink Dulles, *Fielding's The World's Most Dangerous Places*, 3rd edition (Redondo Beach, CA: Fielding Worldwide Inc., 1998).

overwhelming asymmetry in the Mexico–America relationship: 'A walkabout on the border raises all the big, ugly, stupid questions of the twentieth century. What makes a Mexico a Mexico? What makes a United States a United States? And what the hell are we supposed to do about it?'[125] O'Rourke then asks different people on both sides of the border about the 'moral quandary' of the immigration problem and receives no satisfactory answers. When he travels along the Mexican side of the border looking for 'obligatory squalor', his anxiety is even clearer: 'The overfed white reporter goes around stuffing his microphone – or, in my case, pencil – in people's faces. "Just how poor are you?" "Mind if I look around in your hovel?" "Say, you wouldn't happen to have any kids that are a little more crippled or anything, would you?"'[126] What O'Rourke succeeds in doing is making the reader both laugh at their geopolitical assumptions but also feel uncomfortable about them.

While there is something funny about O'Rourke rambling through Lebanon and unwittingly capturing illegal aliens at the Mexican border, there is also something awkward in the kind of voyeurism required by these adventures. But what makes O'Rourke different from Kaplan is that he recognises this anxiety and *uses* it to pose difficult questions to both himself and his readers. Unlike Kaplan's need to *prove* his authorial position with statistics and social science indicators, O'Rourke is much more explicit about his attraction to the role of heroic war correspondent: 'What I've really been is a Trouble Tourist – going to see insurrections, stupidities, political crises, civic disturbances and other human folly because... because it's fun.'[127] He continually contrasts himself with the 'important' political journalists of 'Punditry Inc'. by attending the same events (e.g. the Reagan/Gorbachev summit) and refusing to report them properly. He falls asleep at important speeches; he misses important events, he prefers talking to locals in pubs and bars rather than offices, and he spends a great deal of his time being drunk with other disillusioned and misanthropic journalists. His withering gaze also extends to other travel writers; for example, he describes Joan Didion's critically acclaimed *Salvador* as 'something of an in-country laughing-stock'. Instead of the seriousness invoked by political travel writers like Kaplan, O'Rourke is more interested in having a good time: 'Some people are worried about the difference between right and wrong. I'm worried about the difference between wrong and fun.'[128]

---

[125] O'Rourke, *Holidays in Hell*, p. 233.
[126] O'Rourke, *Holidays in Hell*, p. 240.
[127] O'Rourke, *Holidays in Hell*, p. 11.
[128] O'Rourke, *Holidays in Hell*, p. 125.

This 'frat-boy' persona animates much of the satire of the book precisely because O'Rourke is so willing to send himself up. For example, when he finally gets arrested in Warsaw, he steels himself against the policemen by behaving like James Bond: 'They weren't going to break me...I was determined to let no emotion show. I fancied they'd rarely dealt with as cool a customer as I.'[129] But, as O'Rourke sullenly admits, he was not arrested for espionage as he had hoped – it was only a $2 fine for jaywalking.

To be sure, *Holidays in Hell* works because O'Rourke knows what readers expect of the intrepid travel writer, and he parodies that role with such precision. But the more interesting moments in the book occur when his 'frat-boy' persona falls away completely to reveal anger, confusion and impotence in the face of devastation. Sometimes these are brief glimpses before the joking returns. For example, he drinks his way through the Americas Cup in Perth in order to stop thinking about 'how many starving Ethiopian kids you could feed with just one of these twelve-metres' – but then he immediately disregards his sentimentality: 'Of course, that's ridiculous. You can boil *Kookaburra III* for as long as you want, and starving Ethiopian kids still won't eat it.'[130] But O'Rourke is at his best when he is angry in the face of injustice, violence and oppression. When he tours a Palestinian hospital in Gaza city, he reacts to the young boys who have been wounded by Israeli soldiers: 'This is bullshit. This is barbarism, I've covered a lot of rioting and pushes-comes-to-shoves, and there is no excuse for this kind of civilian-hammering by soldiers and police.'[131] When O'Rourke is shocked by the horrors of war – as he is when confronting the work of the death squads in El Salvador – his jocularity is silenced:

I walked fifty or sixty feet out into the cinders and saw a pair of skeletons, rib cages intermingled .... The bones weren't hard to look at. They were clean from the birds and the sun – theatrical really... And then I was sick and shocked. And scared too. I had to keep myself from running. I got us out of there as fast as I could and off to look at some dumb Maya Pyramid... How can these things happen in a place that looks like Santa Barbara? A place that's just a quick jaunt down the Pan American Highway? A place that was settled by Christian Europeans a full ninety-five years before the Massachusetts Bay Colony?[132]

O'Rourke's revulsion at these scenes of horror expresses not just a shock at the sign of death, but a more general concern that these events are

---

[129] O'Rourke, *Holidays in Hell*, p. 98.
[130] O'Rourke, *Holidays in Hell*, p. 156.
[131] O'Rourke, *Holidays in Hell*, p. 255.
[132] O'Rourke, *Holidays in Hell*, pp. 141–2.

taking place in America's backyard – and possibly with American support. When the humorous deflation of our prevailing geopolitical expectations suddenly becomes serious, O'Rourke's voyeurism is exposed and left wanting, and readers are forced to recognise their complicity in his gaze. *Holidays in Hell* is the most provocative of O'Rourke's books because he leaves these moments open to interpretation – frat-boys can ignore his sentimentality just as 'thoughtful-type readers' can agree with his indignation. The book is full of contradictory and ambiguous moments when O'Rourke questions his belief in the values of civilisation and becomes anxious at his own voyeurism. As a result, there is little of the problem solving and libertarian evangelising that characterise his later books. For example, when he returns to Manila to cover the progress of democracy in the Philippines, he cannot bring himself to go back to Smokey Mountain, the 'ski-slope-size pile of rotting, burning trash' that provides sustenance for a thousand people:

I never want to go back there. There are some kinds of desolation that leave you impotent in the fucking that's life. I could turn my pockets out for the Smokey Mountain residents but that wouldn't go far. I could throw up, but I don't see how that would help. I could pester the dump-pickers as I had in '86 and write it up in a colourful way and make a buck off the thing, which is what I guess I'm doing anyway.[133]

With scenes like those in El Salvador and Manila, O'Rourke's frat-boy persona is silenced by human atrocity. For all its satire, *Holidays in Hell* makes a serious point that we are all impotent in the face of this kind of violence.

Holidays in Hell is a fantastically contradictory text – offensive statements about American power and Third World squalor are followed by insightful commentary about global injustice and the West's complicity in continuing poverty and underdevelopment. But it is O'Rourke's willingness to include himself and his values in the satire that reduces the hypocrisies that populate much political travel writing. When O'Rourke's 'frat-boy' image recedes in front of horrific violence, he is able to pose deeply reflexive and difficult political questions – and even when these are followed by more frat-boy antics, his self-reflexivity is never totally buried within the narrative. In effect, *The Battle for Room Service* and *Holidays in Hell* are important vehicles for social critique – they reproduce the prevailing geopolitical imagination in order to parody, satirise and ultimately deconstruct it. Moreover, Lawson and O'Rourke do not shy away from critiquing their own values and the

---

[133] O'Rourke, *Holidays in Hell*, p. 111.

deeply problematic position they find themselves in when confronting social and political struggles in foreign space. One can only hope that Bill Bryson takes note when he comes to write his planned travelogue about 'the lifestyle and culture of the Middle East'.[134]

Travelling through heterotopia: alternative orderings of space

The satirical writing of Lawson and O'Rourke offers a provocative inversion of the dominant geopolitical cartography. While Lawson covets safety and O'Rourke covets danger, both end up with the same conclusion: that safe places are often dangerous, and that dangerous places are full of people carrying on the mundane activities of everyday life. Neither develops this conclusion, but their agreement is significant: embedded in these satirical texts is the kernel of a critical cartography and a sense that our inherited maps of the world are inadequate at expressing the complex ways in which space is produced and understood. I want to push the insights of Lawson and O'Rourke in order to draw out the possibilities of resistance embedded in the prevailing geopolitical discourse. Is it possible for travel writing to critique the fundamental distinctions between home and away? Can these texts acknowledge the asymmetries of power that circulate between here and there? Attempts to critique the spatial ordering of travelogues have analysed how certain texts produce prevailing spatial categories. So, for example, *The Cambridge Companion to Travel Writing* provides an analysis of the genre by dividing the world into recognised sites, and then tracing how travel writing has produced and maintained those sites over the years (e.g. The Middle East/Arabia; South America/Amazonia; The Pacific/Tahiti; Africa/The Congo; The Isles/Ireland; India/Calcutta; and The West/California).[135] While authors illustrate how these sites are written, mediated and culturally produced by travelogues, they never really disrupt the prevailing discourse of modern cartography. In the end, the critical potential of *The Cambridge Companion* is limited because its spatial organisation simply reinforces prevailing cartographies of power. Holland and Huggan suggest a more sophisticated cartographic arrangement by arguing that the destinations covered by travel writers are 'textual zones' which must be understood 'in ideological and mythical, rather than merely geographical terms'.[136] They are

---

[134] Thorpe, 'Bryson Books a Wry Look at the Arabs'.
[135] Hulme and Youngs, *The Cambridge Companion to Travel Writing*, pp. 105–222.
[136] Holland and Huggan, *Tourists with Typewriters*, p. 68.

concerned with how particular zones are over-determined – how they are repeated over and over again in successive travelogues such that the destination itself is displaced by its rigorous textuality. However, in a remarkably similar taxonomy to *The Cambridge Companion*, Holland and Huggan analyse 'The Tropics', 'The Amazon', 'The Orient', 'The South Seas' and 'The Arctic'. To be sure, their analysis is more critically directed, and they provide compelling accounts of the genre's writing and rewriting of space, but I wonder whether the categorisation of space into 'zones' does the work of adequately critiquing the discourse of modern cartography. Isn't the 'zone' simply another way of reproducing modern spatial categories as measurable, divisible and immutable?

Helpful in this respect is Mary Louise Pratt's *Imperial Eyes*. Although she focuses mainly on colonial texts, Pratt suggests an alternative understanding of space that goes some way to disrupting the discourse of modern cartography. Because Pratt refuses to reduce colonial encounters to simple binaries of power between subjects (e.g. coloniser/colonised) and spaces (e.g. centre/periphery), she is able to illustrate how indigenous and local people continually resisted their representation by imperial powers. Two especially innovative theoretical concepts in Pratt's work create the possibility for understanding space, power and subjectivity differently. The first is the 'contact zone', which Pratt explains as 'the space of colonial encounters, the space in which peoples geographically and historically separated come into contact with each other and establish ongoing relations, usually involving conditions of coercion, radical inequality, and intractable conflict'.[137] Pratt's emphasis on 'contact' within asymmetrical colonial power relations (instead of absolute domination, repression or control) creates the possibility for resistance to totalising accounts of the colonial encounter. In effect, the unequal power structures of colonialism work both ways: 'To speak of travel in contact zones shifts the focus away from the traveller's experience of discovery and towards his (or, less frequently, her) dependency on established routes and relationships, indigenous and colonial.'[138] What Pratt foregrounds are the *complex spaces* within which the colonial encounter takes place. Rather than lock the participants into a coloniser/colonised relation, Pratt situates both subject positions within an already ambiguous and over-determined spatial area. The 'contact zone' is where competing knowledge

---

[137] Pratt, *Imperial Eyes*, p. 6.
[138] James Clifford, 'No Innocent Eyes: Western Travellers as Missionaries of Capitalism', *Times Literary Supplement*, 11 September 1992, p. 4.

claims about the world – the most obvious being indigenous and European – encounter each other. For example, Pratt explores how transnational love affairs within the contact zone were meetings of desire, power and gender that led to the emergence of a new 'creole' subjectivity. Her framework provides room for subjects to move and negotiate the space of encounter within which they find themselves – activities which are expressed through Pratt's second term of resistance: transculturation. Pratt explains that within the contact zone, subordinated groups selectively appropriate and utilise cultural images, materials and influences that have been transmitted to them by the dominant colonial power. Transculturation does not deliver strict relations of domination and control; rather, it expresses the practice of negotiation through reading, reception, appropriation and interpretation. In other words, subjects can manipulate the ordering of power and space in ways that resist the prevailing discourse of modern cartography.

'Contact zone' and 'transculturation' are useful terms because they make it possible to detect alternative orderings of space in travel writing. While Pratt draws on Foucault's earlier work, I think his later work on geography – especially his essay 'Of Other Spaces' – is a better starting place to deconstruct the discourse of modern cartography and resist structural, delimited and formalised space. The spatial concerns of Foucault's earlier work (symbolised most effectively by the panopticon of *Discipline and Punish*) enabled him to trace various conjunctions of power, space and subjectivity in particular sites like prisons, states and homes. While this early work argued that space could be controlled in the service of power, Foucault's later work examines various possibilities of resistance to the modern organisation of space. No matter how rigorous the discourse of modern cartography might be, it can never completely order space – there are always alternative spatial orderings within any given territory supposedly outlined and overrun by power. To explain this reworking, Foucault introduces the notion of 'heterotopia', or spaces that have 'the curious property of being in relation with all other sites, but in such a way as to suspect, neutralize, or invert the set of reflections they happen to designate, mirror, or reflect'.[139] Foucault places heterotopia in relation to utopia – perfected and 'unreal' spaces that are never realised but always desired. In contrast, heterotopia are the 'counter-sites' of utopia – 'real spaces of otherness' that puncture the totalising goals of utopian spatial production.

---

[139] Michel Foucault, 'Of Other Spaces', *Diacritics*, Vol. 16, Spring 1986, p. 24.

There are two principles of heterotopia that resonate specifically within travel writing. The first is Foucault's suggestion that a heterotopia 'is capable of juxtaposing in a single real space several spaces, several sites that are in themselves incompatible'.[140] The destination of the travel writer is such a collection of sites. No matter what the encountered landscape offers, travelogues work according to already formed 'utopian' visions of what will be available upon arrival. Therefore, the mobile vantage point of the travel writer allows him/her to measure the spatial encounter to see if it meets, or fails to meet, the utopian spatial ideal governing the narrative. To re-imagine the destination of the travel writer as heterotopian, the utopian ideal must be punctured by the always present 'other' visions of territory that challenge and contest prevailing expectations. The destination then becomes a site that is over-determined, over-written, and over-coded with 'several sites that are themselves incompatible'. If one spatial vision operates as the utopian ideal, there are always 'other' spatial visions present that offer alternative geographical imaginings of the same territory. The second principle of heterotopia has to do with the discursive regulation of space. As Foucault explains, 'Heterotopia always presuppose a system of opening and closing that both isolates them and makes them penetrable. In general, the heterotopian site is not freely accessible like a public place.'[141] For Foucault, the spatial boundaries that require any given territory to be governed and policed (closings) are always situated in relation to *other* possible orderings of space (openings). Discursive openings and closings might suggest marked territory, but they also create the opportunity for transgression. As Islam explains, 'the passages through which power goes out, and the passages through which the outside intrudes, are also passages of travel'.[142] In travelogues, the perfectly ordered utopian ideal is never closed off from alternative mappings that take place within the very boundaries that the authorial vantage point marks out. This is what makes heterotopia such a useful concept: it is not that these 'other' spaces exist elsewhere, rather, they exist within, through, around and in relation to space that is already mapped. What remains to be seen is how the vantage point of the travel writer continues to produce utopian visions of landscape in the face of competing geographical imaginations.

A common misunderstanding of heterotopia is that 'alternative orderings of space' exist on the margins of society, whereas more

---

[140] Foucault, 'Of Other Spaces', p. 25.
[141] Foucault, 'Of Other Spaces', p. 26.
[142] Islam, *The Ethics of Travel*, p. 37.

rational, efficient and productive space characterises sites that are central to the functioning of modern society. By analysing central spaces that are heavily scripted by power, Kevin Hetherington clarifies Foucault's argument that heterotopia exist even in spaces of total control and spaces of total freedom. To divide space into centre (utopia) and margin (heterotopia) suggests that the two extremes of total control and total freedom somehow exist outside of the social ordering of space. Hetherington is right to point out that even the most legalised site (extreme control) or debaucherous site (extreme freedom) is made possible by *some form* of spatial ordering. What Hetherington stresses is that where space is ordered (even hyper-ordered), it is also disordered – where there is a utopian vision of space, there are also territorialisations that unwork the governance of that vision. As he explains,

Heterotopia are spaces in which an alternative social ordering is performed. These are spaces in which a new way of ordering emerges that stands in contrast to the taken-for-granted mundane idea of social order that exists within society... [heterotopia] insist on a compulsion to order, and that ordering derives from a utopian view of modernity as an exercise in both freedom and control in all its ambivalence.[143]

There is no place, no margin, no outside where social ordering does not occur. Practices of social ordering, or territorialisations, are the very conditions of possibility for a space to be designated *as* a space – as bounded, named and subject to governance. Recovering the concept of heterotopia from its common misunderstanding means arguing that heterotopia are *not* romanticised spaces that exist elsewhere on the margins. Rather, heterotopia are integral to modernity, crucial to the discourse of modern cartography and at the heart of our prevailing understandings of space. Otherness and difference are never spatially eradicated – they are always juxtaposed upon and within the cartographies that are most familiar to us. This misunderstanding of 'heterotopia as marginal' is the basis for Hetherington's title 'The *Badlands* of Modernity' – because, as he argues, 'the badlands of modernity are not all that bad'. In other words, there is no *other* place, no 'wrong side of the tracks', no terrifying marginal space where counter-hegemonic resistance occurs without its *own* territorialisations and social orderings. By refusing to romanticise the margins, Hetherington suggests that spatial ordering happens whenever there is

---

[143] Kevin Hetherington, *The Badlands of Modernity: Heterotopia and Social Ordering* (London: Routledge, 1997), p. 40.

territorialisation and whenever space is called into presence by a prevailing geographical imagination.[144]

When we identify alternative orderings of space – territorialisations that do not take hold and vantage points that are unstable – it becomes possible to disrupt the discourse of modern cartography. As Hetherington argues:

> It is the juxtaposition of things not usually found together and the confusion that such representations create, that marks out heterotopia and gives them their significance ... as sites – and these can be textual sites just as much as geographical ones – they bring together heterogeneous collections of unusual things without allowing them a unity or order established through resemblance.[145]

If we take spaces of safety and spaces of danger as the 'unusual things' to be juxtaposed, then their separation (as dictated by the discourse of modern cartography) can never be realised. Following Hetherington's argument that even spaces of total freedom and total control constitute heterotopia, it is possible to argue that spaces of total safety and spaces of total danger (the extreme points of the geographical imagination of travelogues) are also heterotopia. However, moments of resistance to the hegemonic vantage point of the travel writer are difficult to tease out of travelogues. The stable/mobile vantage point is precisely what allows travel writers to settle territory: it gives them the authority to speak *from* this place and *about* that place. But with the concept of heterotopia, 'this' place and 'that' place are no longer distinct – they are juxtaposed upon the same territory. When we re-imagine the cartography of safety and danger in light of the juxtaposed spaces of heterotopia, the vantage point that bolsters the 'civilised traveller' becomes vulnerable to the 'other spaces' it tries unsuccessfully to expel. The vantage points can no longer territorialise at will by calling forth already understood and secure locations of safety and danger – these have been unfastened from the discourse of modern cartography and let loose in a world of multiple, heterogeneous and hybrid spatial orderings. It is not that the practices of

---

[144] In reaction to the romanticisation of difference, Hetherington's 'case studies' are detailed 'heterotopographies' of sites *within* the very centre of modernity in the eighteenth century (e.g. British factories, Masonic lodges and the *Palais Royale* in Paris). Hetherington sees modernity as a series of utopian visions, which, despite the impossibility of being realised, aim to order society by setting down various 'spatial arrangements'. This draws on Foucault's suggestion that heterotopia are 'effectively enacted utopia' – the key here is that in the interpretation and enactment of utopia, difference can never be eradicated; see especially chapters 3 and 4 of *The Badlands of Modernity*.

[145] Hetherington, *The Badlands of Modernity*, pp. 42–3.

territorialisation disappear once the safety/danger binary has been re-imagined – indeed, this would suggest a 'romanticisation' of the margins as a utopian space free from the play of power and control. Rather, reading the destinations of travel writing as heterotopia opens the territorialising practices of the text to difference: while 'space' is still ordered, that ordering never completely evacuates alternative territorial imaginings.

Expectant cartographies: the seduction of utopian space

To be sure, carving the world into safe and dangerous places betrays the travel writer's desire to maintain prevailing cartographies of power. But I want to argue that even within the most rigorous spatial and textual mappings, it is possible to identify alternative orderings of space where power does not align completely with the discourse of modern cartography. To use Pratt's terms, all destinations are potential contact zones – they contain within them alternative spatial coordinates that subjects utilise in their resistance to prevailing cartographies of power. Regardless of the travel writer's efforts to settle foreign territory, they are always confronted with subjects who question, resist and critique their expectations – subjects who map their world through alternative spatial arrangements. The difficulty here is that even in travel writing that seeks to document 'alternative' destinations away from more familiar sites, the seduction of modern cartography is still so powerful. Even travel writers who portray cultural intersections like borders, ports and trading posts find it extremely difficult to illustrate the heterotopian character of these contact zones. When confronted with alternative spatial orders, travel writers too often take comfort in recognisable spatial categories such as safety and danger. The process is as follows: when travel writers encounter heterotopian space that does not correspond to the prevailing discourse of modern cartography, they retreat back into a utopian ideal and set about re-ordering their destination accordingly. I am particularly interested in the disjuncture between the travel writer's increasingly desperate efforts to contain foreign space within a utopian ideal, and the alternative orderings of space practised by local subjects.

In *Sparring with Charlie: Motorbiking down the Ho Chi Minh Trail*, Christopher Hunt maps Vietnam through the trope of 'adventure travel' and thus positions the travelogue alongside popular cinematic interpretations of the Vietnam War (e.g. *Apocalypse Now* (1979), *Platoon* (1986) and *We Were Soldiers* (2002)). However, rather than indulge in cinematic narratives of guilt, tragedy and defeat, *Sparring with Charlie* uses the non-fiction status of travel writing to document the effects of the Vietnam War twenty-five years on. To access the 'real' Vietnam, Hunt chooses to motorbike along the infamous supply route the Viet Cong used to defeat the Americans. What is particularly interesting about *Sparring with Charlie* is its spatial juxtaposition: the cinematic space of Vietnam functions as a utopian cartography that is increasingly at odds with Hunt's experience travelling along the Ho Chi Minh Trail. That Hunt's encounter with Vietnam is mediated by cinematic images is not surprising, but what *is* surprising is his inability to question, let alone disrupt, the conventional mythologies that underscore these cinematic visions. Therefore, his 'purely academic' (i.e. non-fiction) interest in the war is constantly shaped by what films like *Platoon* have told him — that Vietnam is *still* governed by violence, warfare and danger. Hunt is obsessed with the idea that Vietnam in 1997 is the same as Vietnam in 1967, and that he — as hero of the narrative — will encounter unforgiving Viet Cong: 'Still, I found it hard to believe that twenty years would dull every taste for revenge. Odds were that somewhere there lurked a rice-paddy Rambo looking to take a pot-shot at a lone American.'[146] Venturing out from Laos with a local guide, Hunt reveals his expectations that danger and warfare still lurk on the Ho Chi Minh Trail: 'The way would be littered with fossilized jeeps and tanks. Time permitting, he could also show me the remains of American helicopters and jets.'[147]

Hunt is concerned with documenting the complete route of the Ho Chi Minh Trail in order to illustrate the remaining effects of the war. But his desires are constantly diffused by, on the one hand, the utopian vision of Vietnam he has gleaned from Vietnam War films and, on the other hand, the elusiveness of the Ho Chi Minh Trail itself. Because he is continually disappointed that the Vietnam he confronts bears no resemblance to what he has seen on movie screens, he rewrites the landscape through familiar generic tropes such as the war film and the espionage thriller. For example, Hunt portrays himself as a mercenary soldier like Rambo in order to convey to the reader that his solo wanderings are 'threatening national security'. As the title suggests, Hunt refers to the Vietnamese as 'Charlie' (as in 'Charlie had me surrounded'), which equates Hunt with cinematic heroes like Chris Taylor in *Platoon* or Captain Willard in *Apocalypse Now*. Lest the reader

---

[146] Christopher Hunt, *Sparring with Charlie: Motorbiking down the Ho Chi Minh Trail* (London: Bantam Editions, 1997), p. 2.
[147] Hunt, *Sparring with Charlie*, p. 158.

think that Hunt dwells in the fantasy world of Col. Kurtz, Hunt is careful to ground his soldier and spy fantasies in 'real-life' experience:

Being followed wasn't new to me...Thus ignited, my paranoia invented dangers. How long had that green jeep been parked outside my guest house? Should I have avoided American veterans? Was I under suspicion for mingling with the MIA team? The cloak and dagger games weren't just in my mind ... One night I had dinner with an American investor living in Hanoi. 'Did you notice the three spies outside?' was his greeting.[148]

Hunt wants us to believe that his adventures are *more* believable than those offered in Vietnam War films because the dangers he faces are *real* as opposed to fictionalised. In this sense, the generic ambiguity of the travelogue serves Hunt well in his re-territorialisation of Vietnam: its fictional aspirations allow him to draw on well-established myths of the Vietnam War film (e.g. heroism, moral responsibility, humanitarianism, individuality) while its factual status lends empirical *gravitas* to his 'real' adventures in a still dangerous Vietnam.

Hunt's re-territorialisation of Vietnam is at its most intense when he tries to construct an 'authentic' route along the Ho Chi Minh Trail in order to align his North-to-South journey with a beginning-middle-end story. However, these efforts are continually spoiled by his failure to locate the Trail itself. Before he sets off from Hanoi, Hunt is frustrated that he cannot get any 'correct' information about the Trail from the locals: 'I was ready to break some rules. My failure to organize a sanctioned expedition still smarted. I wanted to show the Hanoinkers that they couldn't stop an American with a will. Stupid? I wouldn't know how stupid it was unless I tried to see the trail on my own.'[149] By hinting at elaborate revenge-fuelled conspiracy theories about why the Vietnamese don't want a lone American on the Trail, Hunt becomes more determined to complete his motorbiking odyssey. However, what Hunt fails to comprehend is that the Ho Chi Minh Trail itself has never been a singular route, but rather a network of smaller interconnected pathways that were constantly moving and shifting during the war. This, of course, makes any 'final' mapping of the Trail impossible. For all its claims about 'real' adventure in a dangerous place, *Sparring with Charlie* is built upon an imagined cartography: the landscape that supposedly ties the story together from beginning to end has never existed within the modern spatial ontology that governs travel writing. Not only does the Trail resist the grid-like mapping of both

[148] Hunt, *Sparring with Charlie*, p. 210.
[149] Hunt, *Sparring with Charlie*, p. 44.

strategic analysis and tourist itineraries, it also frustrates Hunt's efforts to regulate it and frame it within a conventional travel narrative.

For me, *Sparring with Charlie* is interesting because it unwittingly reveals an example of heterotopia: the Ho Chi Minh Trail is a series of mobile interconnecting channels that offer alternative spatial orderings of Vietnam and resist any efforts to construct a final cartography. More telling, of course, is Hunt's inability to engage with, let alone accept, this alternative organisation of space. When he realises he is failing to conquer the Trail, Hunt begins to panic. After a fraught journey from Hanoi, he makes increasingly desperate efforts to connect the utopian cinematic vision of Vietnam with the confusing landscape he experiences. Hunt's answer to this disjuncture is revealing: when he fails to locate a single traversable Ho Chi Minh Trail, he starts to *produce* its location in opposition to the 'beaten track' of the new tourists – the 'unshowered backpackers who, having come to Asia to be near "the people" spent most of their time comparing hotel prices lest too much money pass from West to East'.[150] As the story unfolds, Hunt starts to define the Trail against the coastal 'tourist' road of Highway One that the backpackers and tourists follow. With this decision, Hunt finally has a concrete space to work against, a territory that can help him define the Ho Chi Minh Trail as any jungle or mountain route that is *not* Highway One. This strategy of negation also helps him differentiate himself from the backpackers he despises: he constructs the Trail as *inaccessible* for those who stick to the main route. Of course, this solution doesn't stop Hunt from re-territorialising Vietnam through various fantasies and projections. When he is searching vainly for the Trail in the middle of the jungle, he dreams of nothing more than a clear journey on a smooth patch of highway. But when he is actually forced to travel down Highway One (as the Trail often intersects with the Highway), he yearns for his mythological Trail: 'the coastal route had its own, more subtle, obstacles. Boredom was one. None of Vietnam's "places of beauty" held my interest for more than thirty minutes. Playing it safe, staying out of the mountains and off the Ho Chi Minh Trail, I was likely to fall asleep at the wheel.'[151] Hunt's dissatisfaction is unsurprising – although his spatial opposition between the elusive Ho Chi Minh Trail and the boring Highway One is clever, it ultimately fails to align with his preconceived understanding of a cinematically dangerous Vietnam.

Given Vietnam's recent economic performance in South East Asia and its popularity with tourists, Hunt's attempts to replay the Vietnam

---

[150] Hunt, *Sparring with Charlie*, p. 43.
[151] Hunt, *Sparring with Charlie*, p. 212.

War twenty-five years on seem absurd. His lack of attention to present-day Vietnamese life reinforces the disjuncture between his utopian vision of Vietnam as 'dangerous territory' and the heterotopian space exemplified by the elusive Ho Chi Minh Trail. Not only is Hunt's geographical imagination twenty-five years out of date, his entire journey comes across as a futile attempt to encounter a romanticised and dangerous Vietnam. In effect, *Sparring with Charlie* is not about Vietnam at all – it is yet another cultural artefact that tries to find consensus over *America's* experience in the Vietnam War.[152] Hunt has no desire to engage with Vietnam at all; rather, he is more interested in using the conventions of the travelogue to contribute to cultural debates about the role of the Vietnam War in American identity formation. While Vietnam may indeed be a heterotopian contact zone available for complex negotiations of space and subjectivity, *Sparring with Charlie* is not interested in these questions. Hunt's geographical imagination is so fixed, so driven by the utopian vision of Vietnam represented on film, that all he can provide are banal, belated and impotent re-territorialisations. More importantly, *Sparring with Charlie* offers nothing new or critical to America's continuing cultural resassessment of the Vietnam experience. It recycles tired clichés about a dangerous landscape, wily and untrustworthy locals, a threatening jungle terrain and a heroic figure that will rescue the good name of 'America' from its infamous military defeat.

If Vietnam is a space that is over-determined in the cultural sphere, what happens when travel writers deliberately seek out a more oblique itinerary? Thornton McCamish's *Supercargo: A Journey among Ports* is a narrative about port cities around the Mediterranean and the east coast of Africa. McCamish wants to discover if there is anything common to port cities of the world regardless of their cultural location and history. 'Places' or 'zones' already documented by travel writers (e.g. Vietnam, Patagonia, the Congo) hold no interest for McCamish – he wants to locate something universal in ports no matter where they are situated. As spaces, ports are explicitly heterotopian: not only are they sites of exchange and interaction where different subjects and cultures come into contact, they are also sites of mobility where goods, information and subjects participate in wider networks of exchange

---

[152] *Sparring with Charlie* is also a narrative of disaffected and disillusioned American 30-somethings in search of a valued identity within post-Cold War American culture in the 1990s. Many members of this 'Generation X' community chose the experience of global travel over more traditional career paths, and Hunt places himself in this category when he decides to quit law school and write pulp fiction; see *Sparring with Charlie*, pp. 3–10.

and circulation. Surely, then, a travelogue like *Supercargo* should foreground the notion of heterotopia and show how networks of mobility, subjectivity and power arrange and order space in different ways? Unfortunately, *Supercargo* does no such thing. In fact, it tells us more about the discursive regulations of modern cartography than it does about potentially complex, provocative and heterotopian port cities. Just as Hunt fails to discover the mythical Vietnam made famous in film versions of the Vietnam War, McCamish fails to discover the mythical ports recounted in historical naval literature and travel writing. Like *Sparring with Charlie*, *Supercargo* is structured by a particular tension between McCamish's utopian vision of 'ancient port culture' and the heterotopian space he confronts upon arrival. Unlike the implicit nature of Hunt's utopian visions, McCamish is up-front about the mythologised port culture he is searching for. Indeed, McCamish is clear that *Supercargo* is 'a sentimental quest':

I didn't want to follow in anyone's footsteps, particularly; I didn't want to re-enact any great sea journeys. I had a simpler mission. In my mind's eye, I saw myself holding forth in a series of dockside dives between London and Malacca. I would keep company with dissipated missionaries, exiled Anglophiles, sea dogs, pimps and saints. The whiskey would be vile rotgut. There would be a piano in the corner with keys sticky from spilt absinthe on which I might, if the mood was right, play 'Bound for South Australia' or the theme from *ET.* It would be a purely whimsical trip, an attempt to find a culture that may have already disappeared.[153]

McCamish develops his fantasies about port cities through the novels of Joseph Conrad and Evelyn Waugh, famous 'naval' accounts from the 1930s, and more recent travelogues by Jack Kerouac and Jonathan Raban. But McCamish's itinerary is more constrained than those pursued in the interwar years: his dream of booking passage on freighters as he goes along is no longer possible because ports everywhere have increased their immigration, passport and border controls: 'travellers ought to be able to talk their way onto freighters, for a fair price. But they can't. Not on a freighter that has any kind of insurance policy, anyway, which includes all but the most pitiful rust buckets afloat. The world is getting smaller and travel is getting smaller-minded.'[154] Thus, McCamish is forced to plan and arrange his entire itinerary in London before he leaves.

---

[153] Thornton McCamish, *Supercargo: A Journey among Ports* (Footscray: Lonely Planet Publications, 2002), p. 10.
[154] McCamish, *Supercargo*, pp. 210–11.

Undaunted that ports have become 'less receptive to wanderers' like himself, McCamish embarks on his journey and begins to trace the remnants of 'ancient port culture'. Despite his best efforts, McCamish cannot connect his fantasies of sea life and port culture with his experience on working freighters or in the waterfront cities he visits. By travelling on freighters, McCamish enters a hyper-masculine world of modern shipping that does not sit particularly well with his liberal middle-class values. For the most part he is rebuffed by the sailors who resent his status as a tourist and passenger in their space of work (especially the ship captains who see McCamish as a bureaucratic hassle). Much of his first freighter journey in the Mediterranean is spent with another passenger, a photographer called Nadia, who is compiling a coffee-table book of famous port cities. During this journey, the gendered nature of the ship's space becomes apparent: both passengers are feminised by the crew, prohibited from the masculine areas of work and confined to passive activities in regulated areas like the passenger deck (e.g. looking through binoculars, scanning the horizon, playing cards). Their presence on the ship is managed and controlled: they mostly come in contact with officers rather than sailors, they eat at separate times and they have their own safety drills. While McCamish initially welcomes Nadia's companionship (and admires her cosmopolitan lifestyle), he is increasingly dismayed at his status as 'feminine by association' and seeks to distance himself accordingly. Nadia is quickly presented as neurotic (e.g. she refuses the ship's food), manipulative (e.g. she encourages the affections of certain sailors), ambitious and rude (e.g. she badgers locals in port cities so she can get better photographs). By the time he is on his second freighter – this time without Nadia – he is determined to break through the barrier of masculinity that kept him feminised and isolated in the Mediterranean. McCamish's efforts at friendship include trying to beat the sailors at table-tennis and snooker, offering them endless cigarettes and trying to join them on their bar crawls in various port cities. Although he claims to have a 'grip on the mariner's globe' (e.g. best prostitutes in Brazil, cheapest prostitutes in Africa, best clothes in Turkey, cheapest computers in Syria), the world of the sailor is perpetually closed to him.[155] The codes of masculinity are either too misogynist (e.g. he refuses to procure prostitutes himself but won't condemn the sailors for doing so) or too radical (e.g. he is baffled when these 'manly' men grope each other while flirting and dancing at ship parties). Unsurprisingly, McCamish's exclusion from the masculine space of the ship confines

---

[155] McCamish, *Supercargo*, p. 110.

him to hours and days of solitude, often spent in his small cabin enjoying old travel stories from the 1930s.

McCamish's inability to manoeuvre in the confined space of the ship is equalled by his inability to encounter the 'cosmopolitan range of scoundrels' he dreams about. His utopian cartography begins to unravel in the first port of call where he becomes 'desperate to find something resembling the Marseilles of legend', but fails to locate any of the 'scurvy-ridden old sea dogs' he has read about.[156] By the time he arrives in Sardinia, he realises that the closest he gets to this 'elusive port ambience' is eating in gentrified waterfront restaurants. Moreover, when he steps out of that tourist circuit and confronts working ports like Gioia Tauro in Italy (one of the largest container ports in the Mediterranean), McCamish is overwhelmed and afraid:

The docks were an astonishing sight. A desolate plateau of dusty concrete during the day, the wharf at night looked like a John Wyndham dystopia, an out-of-date vision of the future. Dwarfed by the scale of it, we scuttled back to the safety of the ship among towering cranes, fifteen-metre forklifts and charging shadows thrown by the eerie halogen glare of the floodlights.[157]

In order to 'tame' these dystopian visions, McCamish offers formulaic descriptions of port cities: he arrives, recounts the history of the port, occasionally visits some ruins or a museum and then focuses on the evenings he spends with sailors in various dockside bars and restaurants. By using conventional narrative strategies to align modern port cities with his pre-existing utopian image, McCamish fails to see the heterotopian networks and economies at work in these sites. To be sure, he introduces some of these economies (e.g. the spread of disease, the practice of stowaways, the organisation of prostitution, the development of tourism, the work of missionaries), but only in the most cursory fashion. His failure to analyse how these networks shape the cultures and practices of contemporary ports reveals the profoundly apolitical nature of *Supercargo*. As McCamish realises that he will never encounter the 'brigands, thieves, slave-traders, desperate refugees, corrupt officials, cut-throats and chancers' of his utopian dream, he gets further and further away from asking provocative questions and instead retreats into an air-brushed literary version of port culture.[158] McCamish's geographical imagination – driven as it is by a utopian cartography – can do nothing but romanticise ports and express disappointment when they don't live up to his expectations. Revealing, in this respect, are the

---

[156] McCamish, *Supercargo*, p. 23.
[157] McCamish, *Supercargo*, pp. 93–4.
[158] McCamish, *Supercargo*, p. 181.

absences in the text: just as McCamish fails to explain the complex economies at work in specific port cities, he also fails to pursue more significant questions about shipping in general (e.g. who owns the freighters, how do the multicultural crew communicate, what cargo is carried by the ships, what are the effects of the development of container shipping and how is air transport affecting the shipping industry). In short, McCamish doesn't care about these questions – all he cares about is continuing his futile search for pirates and sea dogs, and indulging his disappointment when these creatures cannot be found.

In effect, *Supercargo* is a book about colonial nostalgia. Rather than engage with the heterotopian space on offer in ports – for these are 'contact zones' of complex economic, political and cultural exchange – McCamish continues to interpret these sites as relics of a lost age. *Supercargo* is therefore underscored by disappointment that these 'dockside dives' are being transformed into efficient industrial transfer stations:

All around the world, docks were falling into disrepair or being turned into loft apartments, cinemas and generic fish cafés... Perhaps modern globalism is the final insult to old-fashioned ports, by-passed by air travel and reduced to gross functionality by efficient, high-volume trade. Modern docks are unsightly and, being unsightly, are usually tucked out of sight on cheap industrial land. They seem tacked on to the backsides of cities which try to look the other way.[159]

Surely this is the interesting question – how cities manage the competing forces of global trade and tourism? But McCamish is uninterested: all he wants to do is wax nostalgic about a romanticised, utopian vision of port culture. Towards the end of the book, McCamish reveals his motivation to an American ex-pat in Zanzibar: 'I told Diane I thought the only way you could get away from the disappointment of travelling to imagined places was to try to travel to the past instead, where the tour groups couldn't go.'[160] And this is the key to *Supercargo*: its utopian cartography is reproduced only to the extent that it can be located in a romanticised colonial past. McCamish ends his book with the hope that it will find its way to the bookshelves of 'Ceylon and Abyssinia, and all the other places that no longer exist.'[161] The point here is that those places *have never existed*: they are products of a mythologised colonial past that has been reproduced over and over again through a variety of cultural artefacts including travelogues.

---

[159] McCamish, *Supercargo*, pp. 12, 46.
[160] McCamish, *Supercargo*, p. 216.
[161] McCamish, *Supercargo*, p. 268.

What this tells us about travel writing is that the prevailing geographical imagination at work in these texts – the imagination that signifies which places are civilised and uncivilised – has an important historical component.

The past is a foreign land: historicising cartographic power

The spatial dimensions of travel writing are crucial in any discursive analysis of the genre because they are its most obvious markers of difference: foreign territory signifies otherness. These markers guarantee the spatialisation of identity/difference by ensuring that others are located in different geographical coordinates from authors, critics and readers. Increasingly, these placements dovetail with prevailing arrangements of power and security in global politics: contemporary travelogues reinforce preconceived ideas about which places are safe and which places are dangerous by repeatedly banishing danger elsewhere in order to secure safe and civilised homes. But as we know, the writing of space is also a *production* of space that fulfils circulating myths about superiority, civilisation and progress. That these are colonial mythologies does not matter, for travel writing is able to translate these desires into a contemporary vernacular – it offers spaces that either adhere to cosmopolitan values (and are thus safe), or do not adhere to these values (and are thus dangerous, and available for a variety of actions from exclusion to intervention). But the travel writer's relationship with his/her destination has always been a strange mixture of fear, desire, ambivalence and parody. Even in the most rigorous efforts to map foreign space – and Kaplan is exemplary here – fissures in the prevailing geographical imagination emerge. Whether by conscious intention or unconscious revelation, travel writers produce heterotopian spaces that do not align with preconceived understandings of global territory. Heterotopia are revealed when satirical writers like Lawson and O'Rourke deliberately rearrange our understandings of safety and danger, transgress cartographic boundaries and reveal a juxtaposition of spatial ordering. However, it is more common for contemporary travelogues to arrange foreign territory in much simpler ways through *utopian ideas of space*. The problem, of course, is that when travel writers like Hunt and McCamish are confronted with complex, unexpected and heterotopian spaces which contradict their preconceived utopian ideals, they retreat back to an imaginary colonial map of how the world *used* to be (e.g. the exciting jungles of the Vietnam War, the ports alive with colonial trade). Even when itineraries offer a potential engagement with heterotopia – either through culturally saturated space (e.g. Hunt's Vietnam) or space that is shot through with competing networks and economies (e.g. McCamish's ports) – destinations are framed through a *nostalgic* geographical imagination. It is the disappointment of travel writers, those unscripted moments when their utopian fantasies of elsewhere are unrealised, that reveals the *temporal* framing of the genre's spatial ontology. When the prevailing geographical imagination fails to deliver the utopian dream – when heterotopia are revealed – practices of temporalisation emerge to help reorganise the globe in terms of historical progress rather than spatial integrity. In other words, the spatial coordinates of travel writing make little sense without the historical narratives of progress that help us distinguish between civilised homes and dangerous elsewheres.

5 Looking back: utopia, nostalgia and the myth of historical progress

> *More than space, then, it is in time that Lonely Places are often exiled, and it is their very remoteness from the present tense that gives them their air of haunted glamour. The door slams shut behind them, and they are alone with cobwebs and yellowed snapshots, scraps of old bread and framed photographs of themselves when young.*
>
> Pico Iyer[1]

Iyer's argument that Lonely Places are forever backward looking repeats Lowenthal's famous claim that the past is a foreign country. Indeed, Iyer goes on to say that 'you wind back the clock several decades when you visit a Lonely Place', and thus locates countries like Paraguay, North Korea and Argentina outside of the modern 'MTV and CNN circuit'.[2] While Iyer caricatures Lonely Places in terms of their eccentricity (they are 'dotty' and 'queer'), his argument dovetails nicely with the spatial assumptions of travel writing; indeed, geographical hierarchies (e.g. home/away; safe/dangerous; civilised/primitive) make no sense without their attending historical dimensions. This chapter analyses how the geographical imagination reproduced by contemporary travel writing is shaped by a particular – and problematic – understanding of history. Because contemporary travel writing maps global territory through a historical timeline that is linear, evolutionary and progressive, certain destinations are located father back in time than others. The most helpful way to think about this conjunction of space, time and travel is through Doreen Massey's image of the 'historical queue'.[3] She argues that to write a 'true' and 'full' account of another

---

[1] Iyer, *Falling Off the Map*, p. 7.

[2] Iyer, *Falling Off the Map*, pp. 7, 9; see also David Lowenthal, *The Past Is a Foreign Country* (Cambridge: Cambridge University Press, 1985).

[3] The historical queue underscores much of Massey's critical geography, but she discussed it in detail at a seminar entitled 'Thinking about Space' in the Department of Geography at Keele University, 10 March 1998. In this talk, Massey drew on her previous work about space, power and identity in order to frame some emerging contradictions in the discourse of globalisation; see 'Imagining Globalization: Power-Geometries of Time-Space', in Avtar Brah, Mary Hickman and Mairtin Ghail, eds.,

place, one must be situated at the front of an evolutionary historical queue. In other words, it is only the most historically 'evolved' – the most sophisticated, civilised and experienced subjects – who are able to map their own progress retroactively, and judge the progress of others through a linear, plotted history. As Massey argues, this is precisely how power operates here: space, time and identity are all mapped according to Western notions of progress and evolution – which means that Western subjects are always at the front of the queue. More importantly, Massey argues that the historical queue is one of the most powerful mechanisms through which colonial relations are established in the contemporary cultural sphere. What makes travel writing so significant in this respect is its explicit reproduction of the historical queue: travel writers do not choose their destinations simply because the landscape is different, or because it is located on the other side of the world, they choose destinations that will allow them to go *back in time* as well as far away. Indeed, the more the world is discovered – not just by travel writers but also by tourists – the more travel writing provides an opportunity to escape the forces of modernity and globalisation and retreat back into a Golden Age of discovery, exploration and Empire. In other words, one can avoid the anxieties of a modern cosmopolitan global order by withdrawing into an imagined past where everyone knew their place within the hierarchies of Empire.

Iyer's travel writing is particularly interesting because he frames the evolutionary historical queue through 'present-tense' values of multi-culturalism and cosmopolitanism. He might come from a place farther back in the historical queue (India) but now he freely inhabits the most 'modern' places at the front of the queue (America, England, Japan). Because Iyer has moved up that queue himself, his descriptions of variously evolved places are considered *more authentic* because of his personal experience. Particularly revealing here are Iyer's discussions about Burma in *Video Night in Kathmandu* which in turn inspired his full-length study of Lonely Places in *Falling Off the Map*. For Iyer, Burma functions as the limit case: it occupies the most backward and 'infantile' position in the historical queue:

Burma's sins were so original, its freedom from self-consciousness so absolute, that it was indeed tempting to believe that it languished in some pre-fallen age

Global Futures: Migration, Environment and Globalization (Basingstoke: Macmillan, 1999), pp. 27–44; 'Spaces of Politics', in Doreen Massey, John Allen and Phil Sarre, eds., *Human Geography Today* (Cambridge: Polity Press, 1999), pp. 279–94; and 'Space-Time, "Science" and the Relationship between Physical Geography and Human Geography', *Transactions of the Institute of British Geographers*, Vol. 24, No. 3, 1999, pp. 261–76.

of the world's infancy; by the limited standards of the world, Burma had never grown up. It was, I thought, a lost world in both senses of the word: a remnant of the past, but also a baffled child trying to make its way about an adult universe.[4]

By infantilising Burma, Iyer confirms the relative progress not only of his chosen homes in America, England and Japan, but also of the surrounding Asian countries scrambling their way forward along the historical queue. Burma's innocence locates it *behind* other countries: less modern, less Western, less evolved. And this is the key to Iyer's particular vision of the historical queue: countries can only evolve to the extent that they embrace modern Western values. Therefore, Asian countries that accept and incorporate the forces of American cultural imperialism move further up the historical queue – Hong Kong and India are *more evolved* than Burma which has spent the last three decades resisting all foreign influence. As Iyer explains, 'Almost alone among the countries of the Third World, it seemed not to seek more Western sophistication, convenience and flash, but less.'[5] So while countries like India and Hong Kong lead the way in the new hybrid 'Amer-Asia', Burma is located at the rear of the historical queue – doomed to last place because of its innocence and its wilful refusal to Westernise.

Iyer argues that Burma's post-war isolationist policies effectively 'put the entire country to sleep' and forced it to look backwards for reassurance. The problem, of course, is that Burma's history cannot be disentangled from the British Empire:

Burma had long lived in the past tense, I suspected, because Burma had long been preserving the memories of an Empire that had itself been built on memory... in locking the modern world out, Burma had mostly succeeded in locking in the fading legacy of the long-ago outside world. By now, as a result, Rangoon had been turned into a sepia-coloured daguerreotype of the Raj.[6]

The layers of nostalgia here are complicated. The British Empire was itself a nostalgic institution: 'home' was always a distant place, and despite Herculean efforts at verisimilitude, it could never quite be replicated in the colonies. All subjects in colonial outposts – from colonial administrators to local merchants – were constrained by the ideals of a romanticised 'motherland' on the other side of the world.

---

[4] Iyer, *Video Night in Kathmandu*, p. 215. I have chosen to repeat Iyer's use of Burma here, rather than the more appropriate Myanmar, to remain consistent with the *Video Night in Kathmandu* text. However, Iyer's semantic choice is significant in that it reveals the extent to which he values the legacy of the British Empire.

[5] Iyer, *Video Night in Kathmandu*, p. 203.

[6] Iyer, *Video Night in Kathmandu*, pp. 217, 202; fittingly, Iyer's title for the chapter on Burma is 'The Raj Is Dead! Long Live the Raj!'

Whether replicated, dreamed about, longed for, fought against, or resisted – the home of 'Great Britain' occupied the centre of the colonial imaginary. Iyer's point is that Burma added yet another layer to that powerful sense of nostalgia. Since its independence in 1947, Burma's refusal to engage with the outside world meant that it turned to its own past and became nostalgic for a time when it was an esteemed colonial outpost in the British Empire. Thus, Burma's wilful isolation from the modern world produced a more complex form of nostalgia: 'Burma offered, in the end, a double romanticism: the nostalgic continuation of an age of nostalgia.'[7] Rather than confront the new cultural imperialism of America, Burma comforted itself with 'the sweet ache of nostalgia' and 'elegiac' memories of its time as a valued British colony. Iyer's narrative of Burma's complex nostalgia is accompanied by his own form of fantasies and projection. In its infantile, isolated and nostalgic condition, Burma is depicted as 'quirky', 'beguiling', 'wistful' and 'alluring' rather than as a country that has, since independence, been systematically oppressed by an often violent ruling elite. Because this 'presentable' face of colonialism fits with Iyer's own romantic sensibility, *Video Night in Kathmandu* silences the more unpalatable aspects of Burma's 'half monk and half misanthrope' identity. What results is an entirely benign description of the Burmese government as 'a malfunctioning guinea pig of fundamentalist socialism' that offered a 'winning blend of merriment and strictness'.[8] Indeed, Iyer conveniently overlooks the government's oppressive practices, especially towards Aung San Suu Kyi's burgeoning pro-democracy movement that was mobilising during Iyer's two visits in the mid 1980s.[9] Moreover, in suggesting that Burma had abdicated from the 'rough and tumble of world affairs', Iyer implies that it was somehow untouched by the social and political issues that were engulfing other South East Asian countries at the time (e.g. continuing ethnic conflicts, the beginning of the AIDS epidemic, a growing narcotics trade, the onset of 'backpacker tourism' and global economic restructuring). By imagining Burma through its 'ruined grandeur' and its 'picturesque decay', Iyer wilfully turns away from the complex political and material struggles that characterise contemporary Burma. It is only at the very end of the chapter when he is reminded of the 'reality' of Burmese life (i.e. its run-down hospitals and intense poverty) that Iyer's own nostalgic visions come up short. He realises that

---

[7] Iyer, *Video Night in Kathmandu*, p. 218.
[8] Iyer, *Video Night in Kathmandu*, p. 206.
[9] For a chronology of the pro-democracy movement in Burma, see http://www.dassk.org/index/php?id=127.

he too has created a 'fabulous fiction' of Burma, and admits that nostalgia is 'the ultimate Western luxury'. What is revealed in that brief but poignant conclusion is Iyer's own incarceration in an outdated and romanticised vision of Empire.

This chapter argues that the drive for nostalgia currently fuelling contemporary travel writing is shaped by two temporal projections – on the one hand, dreams of a future multicultural utopia, and on the other hand, nostalgic memories of innocent and uncorrupted destinations. It is through these simultaneous forward and backward projections that contemporary travel writers are able to embed a historical queue and judge the comparative evolution of their destinations. What makes Iyer's travel writing significant is that the end point of his historical queue is a multicultural and diverse society where 'global souls' intermingle in a cosmopolitan public sphere. For Iyer, Western liberal democracies have come closest to achieving the cosmopolitan ideal because they are able to manage their multicultural, ethnically diverse and plural populations through modern political institutions. Conversely, societies that are unable to 'modernise' and 'Westernise' by implementing liberal democratic institutions are considered less evolved. The problem, here, is that Iyer's nostalgic longings and utopian fantasies cover over the colonial legacy embedded in his vision of a cosmopolitan future. In effect, his historical queue rests upon outdated claims about who counts as 'evolved' and who counts as 'backward'. My point is that Iyer's cosmopolitan community of global souls does not exist in the present tense at the front of the queue: it exists in the future as an endlessly deferred utopia. For Iyer, this cosmopolitan fantasy has not been achieved in the present because even the most sophisticated and modern societies are plagued with the struggles of identity politics (e.g. tensions over ethnicity, religion, culture, race and gender). By projecting this multicultural utopia into the future, Iyer suggests that it is possible to escape the difficulties of the present as long as we continue along the evolutionary path of modernisation and Westernisation. *One day* we will reach the Promised Land – *one day* all of us will be well-travelled global citizens intermingling in a cosmopolitan nirvana. Of course, Iyer's utopian vision of a cosmopolitan future works most effectively when it is coupled with nostalgic visions of the past. As we saw with his depiction of Burma, there was a time *before* our modern conflicts over identity began – an innocent time, a primitive time, a time of Empire where both subject positions and relations of power were clearly defined. In places like Burma, it is possible to experience a time before the onset of modernity – an isolated and innocent place filled with an 'autumnal sense of yesterday' and untouched by the difficulties of present-day identity politics. What Iyer manages to do is retroactively shape the various stages of evolution through nostalgia for lost innocence, which in turn allows him to secure a utopian future and alleviate the anxieties of the present tense. In effect, Iyer projects backwards to explain how we got into the difficulties of the present, and projects forward to provide a solution for those difficulties. By projecting a sense of 'anywhere but here' and 'any time but now', Iyer's travelogues are best understood as escapist texts – not about lonely places at all, but about past memories and future dreams.

The problem, here, is that Iyer's escapism avoids the struggles of the present tense and fails to disrupt or critique the power relations of Empire embedded in his evolutionary understanding of history. In Iyer's multicultural utopia, current conflicts over identity politics are alleviated because everyone agrees upon the stages of historical progression required to gain entrance into the future. So while multiple identities and relationships are permitted in Iyer's travel writing, competing accounts of time and history are not. The historical queue is *singular* – one either moves forward towards the utopia, or slides backwards into innocence. And it is precisely this singularity that prevents alternative accounts of history from emerging. For example, Iyer cannot represent Burma as modern, progressive or radical in any sense, and consequently marginalises Burma's democratising forces, silences its continuing ethnic, political and social struggles, and ignores the increasingly vocal Burmese Diaspora.[10] Likewise, Iyer cannot represent powerful cities such as London, New York and Los Angeles as anything other than cosmopolitan, progressive and diverse – which silences the entrenched struggles over racism, crime, violence, immigration and security that characterise all modern urban spaces. While Iyer offers a compelling argument in favour of a diverse and heterogeneous future, his claims are limited by his conventional and singular understanding of history. This chapter argues that Iyer's teleological account of history and his reproduction of the evolutionary historical queue exemplify a more general trend in contemporary travel writing. Just as generic founda-tions, subject positions and geographical imaginations are discursively regulated in travel writing, so too is the genre's temporality. Reproducing a progressive historical queue allows travel writers to locate their destinations according to particular evolutionary stages, and judge those destinations according to Western values of civilisation and

---

[10] For more information on the political mobilisations of the Burmese Diaspora, see 'Burma Campaign UK', a leading advocate of human rights and democracy in Burma, http://www.burmacampaign.co.uk.

enlightenment. Moreover, the singularity of the historical queue allows only *one* account of the past (which is then preserved as a Golden Age) and attaches all future projections to a singular utopian vision. Even the most cosmopolitan and progressive travel writers – and surely Iyer is exemplary here – cannot help but repeat the sentiment that while the past is a foreign country, we have yet to reach our future destination of cosmopolitan diversity. The problem in all of this is that the present anxieties currently shaping travel writing are left unexamined.

Nostalgia: it's not what it used to be

This chapter examines how the geographical imagination of travel writing is secured by practices of *temporalisation* that locate global space upon a progressive and evolutionary historical queue. In depicting foreign space as *past* and domestic space as both *present* and *forward looking*, contemporary travel writers are able to replay the adventures of colonial exploration that the forces of globalisation have nullified. In other words, travel writers use strategies of temporalisation to perpetuate the myth that certain places are 'stuck' in the past and untouched by modernity – undiscovered places that are simply awaiting documentation by travel writers. Their job is to illustrate the different stages of historical progress: foreign countries represent *previous* stages along the trajectory of enlightenment that have *already* been achieved by civilised countries back home. By augmenting their spatial journeys with an even more powerful temporal journey from the present (enlightenment, civilisation, sophistication) to the past (ignorance, barbarity, backwardness), travel writers reassure themselves and their readers of their highly evolved status at the front of the historical queue. Unevolved foreign destinations work as a poignant warning: sticking to the evolutionary path of modernisation and Westernisation will secure one's position at the front of the historical queue and prevent the dreaded 'backslide' into a primitive past. In this way, backward destinations are framed by a powerful *discourse of nostalgia* that convinces us there was once a Golden Age when things were simpler, when conflicts were fewer, when needs were basic and when everybody knew their place. The problem, of course, is that nostalgia is the perfect way to avoid engaging with and taking responsibility for the conflicts, struggles and challenges of the present day. Had enough of asylum seekers and refugees? Never mind – read Redmond O'Hanlon's *Congo Journey* (1996) and be assured that there is still a 'heart of darkness' where these primitive savages belong. Tired of news reports of ethnic cleansing and genocide? Never mind – read Robert Kaplan's *Balkan Ghosts* (1993) and be assured that it is 'ancient' and 'primordial' hatred between primitive European groups that continually propels them into conflict.

With this in mind, this chapter examines how a *discourse of nostalgia* functions in contemporary travel writing. By that I do not simply mean the strategies by which travel writers look back and rearrange the world according to a teleological understanding of history; rather, I also mean the strategies by which travel writers construct a mythical and utopian future in order to secure a difficult present. What becomes clear in this analysis is that contemporary travel writing is shaped by a temporal framework of a 'present-yet-to-come' and a 'past-as-it-never-happened'. Moreover, I use nostalgia rather than utopia in order to foreground the power relations of Empire that are embedded in the historical queue. Utopian visions can develop in a variety of ways and provide a variety of escape routes from the present, but try as they might, nostalgic visions cannot avoid the experience of Empire. To puncture these colonial imaginings, this chapter re-imagines the inscription of the present through alternative formations of history. To this end, Foucault's genealogical method is invaluable because it goes some way towards disrupting notions of progressive, evolutionary and teleological time. For Foucault, genealogies are detailed accounts of the workings of power and knowledge *in specific historical periods*. For example, in *The History of Sexuality* Foucault explains how bodies and attitudes towards sexuality were disciplined, repressed and shaped during the Victorian era. In revealing the organising principles of particular epochs, the genealogical method exposes the limits of what it is possible to be, do and think under certain historical regimes of power/knowledge. In articulating this 'alternative' history, Foucault's genealogical critiques 'give new impetus, as far and wide as possible, to the undefined work of freedom'.[11] The abundant historical detail of Foucault's genealogical research, and his ability to uncover alternative and previously hidden accounts of the past (e.g. stories of patients, criminals, prisoners and the sexually excluded), are powerful interventions in the 'official' historical record. They show how 'official' accounts of the past are always complicit in time-bound articulations of power and knowledge. However, genealogies also reveal how any historical account is always *also* a history of the contemporary moment within which the account is being constructed. For example, Foucault's observations about sexuality during the Victorian era were undertaken as a way of exploring and commenting upon the *continuing* repression and regulation of desire still at work in our current attitudes towards sexuality. What this means is

---

[11] Michel Foucault, 'What Is Enlightenment?', in Rabinow, *The Foucault Reader*, p. 46.

that while genealogical work is historically detailed, it is never divorced from the present-tense context within which it is written.

Given Foucault's careful attention to detail and his commitment to uncovering hidden narratives, he opposes historians who 'invoke objectivity, the accuracy of facts, and the permanence of the past'.[12] Any simple chronology of events – any narrative that reifies a past–present–future timeline – is precisely the kind of account that covers over the workings of power/knowledge in particular historical epochs. But as Foucault explains, getting under the historian's habit of telling the chronological 'truth' of what happened is very difficult: 'Truth is undoubtedly the sort of error that cannot be refuted because it was hardened into an unalterable form in the long baking of history.'[13] To counter this reified production of truth, Foucault's genealogical method refuses any clear or grounded origin point for a historical account. Once the *contemporary* agenda of any historical account is revealed, its 'secure' origin point in the past disappears – which makes it very difficult to construct a 'truthful' narrative about the past. In effect, all Foucauldian genealogies are histories of the present because all accounts of the past are products of contemporary concerns and anxieties.[14] As he explains, a genealogy 'does not pretend to go back in time to restore an unbroken continuity', but instead makes efforts to uncover the 'impure and confused' nature of any discursive origin point: 'What is found at the historical beginning of things is not the inviolable identity of their origin; it is the dissension of other things. It is disparity.'[15] Because it foregrounds the present-day agenda of all historical accounts and deconstructs the notion of a time-bound origin point, Foucault's genealogical method allows us to interrogate the progressive, evolutionary and teleological notion of history embedded in the discourse of nostalgia. As Foucault explains, the discourse of nostalgia operates by locating truth in the past and lamenting its disappearance: 'The origin lies at a place of inevitable loss, the point where the truth of things corresponded to a truthful discourse, the site of a fleeting articulation

---

[12] Michel Foucault, 'Nietszche, Genealogy, History', in Rabinow, *The Foucault Reader*, p. 91.

[13] Foucault, 'Nietszche, Genealogy, History', p. 79.

[14] As Foucault argues, 'I would like to write the history of this prison … Why? Simply because I am interested in the past? No, if one means by that writing a history of the past in terms of the present. Yes, if one means writing a history of the present': see Foucault, *Discipline and Punish*, pp. 30–1.

[15] Foucault, 'Nietszche, Genealogy, History', pp. 81, 79. The editor's note to this passage explains that by 'disparity', Foucault also means discontinuity, division and difference.

that discourse has obscured and finally lost.'[16] Chronological historical accounts alleviate contemporary anxieties by encouraging us to recall the days when truth and discourse 'corresponded' in a stable origin point. In this way, nostalgia is always twinned with loss – it is an effort to recover a distant point in time when truth and discourse corresponded.

With this in mind, it is not that difficult to see how the lost time currently being recovered in contemporary travel writing is the time of Empire. In arguing that contemporary travelogues are *primarily* anachronistic texts, Holland and Huggan illustrate how this nostalgia for Empire functions within the genre. They are particularly interested in the resilience of the genre – why, despite various post-war claims that we are witnessing the 'final age' of travel writing, the genre continues to thrive and even grow. For Holland and Huggan, nostalgia for Empire is one of the most powerful strategies by which contemporary travel writers combat the always-immanent obsolescence of the genre within a globalised world:

> Imperialist nostalgia comes in handy for contemporary travel writers, who can deploy it to mystify their own economic motives, as well as to yearn for the 'simpler' ways of life – often rural, premodern, preindustrial – that they, and their metropolitan readers, persuade themselves they need ... it describes a more generalized, pastoral mode of wistful reminiscence that seeks control over, but not responsibility for, a mythicized version of the past ... it attempts the restoration of Empire's former (imagined) glories, and the resuscitation of Empire's erstwhile (imaginary) 'subordinate' subjects.[17]

By keeping the question of Empire at the forefront of their analysis, Holland and Huggan illustrate the different ways in which contemporary forms of nostalgia rely on colonial power relations. Indeed, they argue that a majority of contemporary travelogues are nothing more than supplements to earlier travel accounts – supplements that cling desperately to the 'mythic' and 'glorious' world of Empire.[18] More importantly, Holland and Huggan begin an analysis of how the relationship between travel writing and globalisation works to animate the discourse of nostalgia. Indeed, Roland Robertson argues that nostalgia is the *direct result* of the forces of globalisation: by inaugurating a shift from modernity to an indeterminate 'post-modern' era, globalisation marks a profound transformation in the way humans relate to their own history.[19] Going

---

[16] Foucault, 'Neitszche, Genealogy, History', p. 79.
[17] Holland and Huggan, *Tourists with Typewriters*, pp. 29–30.
[18] Holland and Huggan, *Tourists with Typewriters*, p. 67.
[19] Roland Robertson, 'After Nostalgia? Wilful Nostalgia and the Phases of Globalization', in Bryan S. Turner, ed., *Theories of Modernity and Postmodernity*, (London: Sage, 1990), pp. 45–61.

even further, Bryan S. Turner argues that nostalgia is so intrinsic to the post-modern condition that it has taken on ontological significance:

The nostalgic mood is of particular importance in contemporary cultures in association with the loss of rural simplicity, traditional stability and cultural integration following the impact of industrial, urban, capitalist culture on feudal social organization. Within a broader perspective, it has been suggested that the theme of alienation in human societies represents a form of ontological nostalgia which perceives human beings, because of their consciousness, as alienated from the life-world of the human species.[20]

For Turner, our contemporary social alienation is augmented by forms of nostalgia that take us away from the present tense. Whether to the future or to the past, we want to escape the difficulties of the present and avoid 'the impact of industrial, urban, capitalist culture'.

The ontological significance of nostalgia makes itself felt most clearly in the destabilisation of home. As Caren Kaplan argues, 'nostalgia is rooted in the notion that it is "natural" to be at "home" and that separation from that location can never be assuaged by anything but return'.[21] *This* is why nostalgia has become so important: we long for the territorial distinctions of Empire where everyone understood how the structures and practices of colonial power separated home and away. But as the home is penetrated and re-imagined by foreign subjects and cultures, it becomes a space of ambivalence that is no longer secured by the borders of Empire. But it also becomes a *time* of ambivalence: globalisation makes it increasingly difficult to locate a sanctified home at the front of the historical queue (and therefore in the present) and everywhere else farther behind in different stages of evolution (and therefore in the past). Nostalgia, then, becomes the cure for spatiotemporal ambivalence: by looking back to a time when the territorial claims of Empire were sacrosanct, readers and writers are

---

[20] Bryan S. Turner, 'A Note on Nostalgia', *Theory, Culture and Society*, Vol. 4, No.1, 1987, pp. 152–3. I am using Turner here because of his specific focus on globalisation, however, my argument is informed by more general studies of nostalgia including Christopher Shaw and Malcolm Cross, eds., *The Imagined Past: History and Nostalgia* (Manchester and New York: Manchester University Press, 1989); John Frow, 'Tourism and the Semiotics of Nostalgia', *October* 57 (1991), pp.123–51; Christopher Lasch, 'The Politics of Nostalgia', *Harper's Magazine*, November 1984, pp. 65–70; Fredric Jameson, 'Nostalgia for the Present', *South Atlantic Quarterly*, Vol. 88, No. 2, 1989, pp.517–37; Georg Stauth and Bryan S. Turner, 'Nostalgia, Postmodernism and the Critique of Mass Culture', *Theory, Culture and Society*, Vol. 5, No. 2–3, 1988, pp.509–26; and Susan Stewart, *On Longing: Narrative of the Miniature, the Gigantic, the Souvenir, the Collection* (Baltimore: Johns Hopkins University Press, 1984).

[21] Kaplan, *Questions of Travel*, p. 33.

assured of the *natural* distinctions between civilised and uncivilised, modern and primitive, evolved and backward. But as Turner suggests, that nostalgic longing for home is always coupled with a utopian vision: 'home is located in a lost place in a lost time and thereby assumes a Utopian dimension, since that home is free from the conflicts of multiculturalism, political pluralism, and ethnic conflict'.[22] What makes travelogues particularly significant in this context is their promise of escaping the pressures and anxieties of globalisation by locating an idealised home outside of the space and time of the present. More than any other genre, travel writing can either project us back to an era when the coordinates of Empire and modernity were sacrosanct, or project us forward into a utopia where contemporary conflicts and struggles have been effectively resolved.

The three stages of nostalgia: utopia, authenticity and lament

How then, does the discourse of nostalgia work? What are its coordinates, its regulations and its limits? Looking back from their 'advanced' position, travel writers use the discourse of nostalgia to construct post-hoc narratives of progress that locate different cultures at different stages on the path to enlightenment. As well, they continue that evolutionary historical queue by connecting the most advanced position of the present tense to an imagined and not-yet-attained future. These simultaneous projections are shaped by three discursive stages: the creation of utopia, the testing of authenticity and the onset of lament. The travel writer's decision to choose a particular destination emerges from a series of *already-held* assumptions about global territory – what I have called the prevailing geographical imagination. Prior to physically encountering the destination, the travel writer will imaginatively construct it as a utopian space. In this way, the chosen destination becomes remote in both space and time: it is a faraway 'Shangri-La' awaiting discovery. This is not to say that the destinations of travel writers are *always* located in the past; indeed, many travelogues about metropolitan cities suggest that urban spaces are *of the future* – sophisticated, ultra-modern, efficient and

---

[22] Turner, 'A Note on Nostalgia', p. 154. Turner explains the loss embedded in nostalgia in four ways: because of our failure to meet rational goals we have lost the progression of history, because of increased fragmentation we have lost a sense of wholeness, because of bureaucratic and institutional success we have lost our ability to be spontaneous and expressive, and finally, because of global homogenisation we have lost our individual autonomy (pp. 150–1).

exciting.[23] However, I am particularly interested in how the nostalgic dreams of travel writers function through powerful utopian fantasies. Travel writers who wish to alleviate the difficulties of the present by retreating into a mythic past are also projecting a utopian future: they may write about a foreign country languishing in a pre-modern idyll, but that destination is shaped *a priori* by an implicit utopian vision. What connects the space of nostalgia with the space of utopia is the evolutionary historical queue: no destination exists outside of that temporal continuum, and all destinations remain outside of the present tense of the travel writer. This makes it impossible to discuss travelogues according to timeless notions of 'reality' or 'truth', for all destinations are shaped by prevailing fantasies, myths and projections which have *already been temporalised* through the evolutionary historical queue. Authors, readers and critics *already know* these unfamiliar destinations at some level, they have already seen cultural images of the place and they have already made a decision as to where it is located on the historical queue. Helpful here is Frances Bartkowski's argument that the prevailing fantasies, myths and projections of travel writing are either instances of nostalgia (when the imagination is directed backwards) or forelonging (when the imagination is directed forwards).[24] The key here – and Bartkowski would agree – is that both forward and backward projections are governed by an *a priori* utopian vision that secures a progressive, evolutionary and teleological sense of time.

Once the utopian fantasy has been constructed, all that remains for the travel writer to accomplish is leaving the present tense of home and travelling to a destination that is spatiotemporally remote. And this is the second stage of the discourse of nostalgia: when travel writers arrive physically at their chosen destination. Once there, travel writers invoke a number of strategies and techniques through which they 'test' the authenticity of their utopian fantasies (i.e. it really *is* quite primitive) and 'prove' the historical position of their chosen destination (i.e. it really *does* languish in the past). But these practices of authentication always fail: as soon as they arrive, travel writers confront the inevitable incongruity between their utopian fantasies and the *present tense* of the destination. I do not mean that travel writers jettison fantasy in favour of reality – for we know that both fantasy and reality are mediated by competing discourses. Rather, I mean that travel writers are forced to

---

[23] Pico Iyer's *The Global Soul* is a good example of what these future spaces might be like – urban spaces like the multicultural city of Toronto, or more universal spaces like airports and Olympic villages.

[24] This argument emerges in Bartkowski's discussion of André Gide, Roland Barthes and Michael Butor; see Bartkowski, *Travelers, Immigrants, Inmates*, p. 19.

negotiate the disjuncture between the fantastical and the real – *neither* of which contains the 'truth' or 'reality' of the destination in question. As travel writers begin to test the authenticity of their expectations, the disjuncture between their utopian fantasy and the material condition of their destination begins to grow. Assaulted by the very symbols of modernity they have just escaped – the golden arches of McDonald's, large hotel chains, bank machines, Western media, consumer culture, the tourist industry – travel writers find it impossible to re-attach their destination to a backward position in the historical queue. Signs of modernity are reminders that the travel writer has failed to create a destination that is spatiotemporally remote – a failure that only augments their sense of being out-of-time. How can you prove that a destination is primitive when it is saturated by the colourful neon of modern technology?

It is precisely in reaction to these markers of modernity that travel writers rearticulate the third and most significant stage in the discourse of nostalgia. Dissatisfied at being too late to see the 'real' thing, travel writers quickly invent a previous time of cultural authenticity for their destination. In other words, they locate it *even further back* on the evolutionary historical queue. *At one time*, this place was full of all the dreamed-about exoticism that fulfilled the travel writer's utopian fantasy. In this way, authors comfort themselves with the knowledge that they are simply too late to encounter the signs of a bygone era so vividly imagined. They may have failed to access the 'Shangri-La' of their dreams, but they can certainly create a temporal utopia that remains untouched by the forces of modernity and globalisation. Once the imagined destination is locked in an even more temporally remote past, it is gazed upon, imagined and dreamed of once again as an object of desire – only this time, it is an object of *loss* rather than an object of potential future encounter. This is where nostalgic reverie reaches its full potential: travel writers mourn the loss of the exotic, they lament the dilapidated condition of the present, and they console themselves with memories of the glory days when their chosen destination was more beguiling in its authenticity. As Heather Henderson argues, the 'climate of expectation' that underscores contemporary travel writing guarantees the proliferation of loss, melancholia and disappointment to such an extent that it has become 'virtually a convention of the genre itself'.[25] This expression of lament has a significant etymological foundation; as Caren Kaplan explains, nostalgia combines the Greek terms *nostos*

---

[25] Henderson, 'The Travel Writer and the Text', p. 235.

(a return home) and *algos* (a painful condition).[26] The key here, as with the previous two stages, is the role of disappointment, loss and melancholy in securing the evolutionary historical queue. The initial encounter with foreign space is hugely disruptive to the established timeline: overwhelming signs of modernity lift a destination out of its past tense and send it crashing into the present tense of the travel writer. However, by repositioning the destination even further back in time through repeated expressions of loss, the timeline is restored to its original linearity. With a rueful shake of the head, travel writers can say, 'it's not like it used to be ... but oh, what it used to be like!'

As these three stages illustrate, the discourse of nostalgia creates a very comprehensive system of regulation in travel writing. So comprehensive, in fact, that it is able to govern the previous discourses of genre, subjectivity and space – all of which get attached to, and regulated by, an evolutionary historical queue. First of all, establishing a linear timeline prevents travelogues from transgressing their status as non-fiction texts. Chronological historical accounts do not allow any fictional embellishments to alter the linear voyage from past to present – after all, it is nothing short of *the truth* that is at stake in the 'proper' progression of history. While fictional devices may help make the truth more meaningful, they cannot be allowed to change the facts of 'what really happened' in the past. And the delivery of those facts can be made seamless when the home-away-home/beginning-middle-end structure rests upon a past-present-future timeline. Secondly, travel writing attaches its formulations of identity and difference to particular historical stages of development. For example, 'other' subjects (those being written about) move from barbarity to civility, from darkness to light and from primitive to enlightened. What is crucial in this temporalisation is the distinction between the present tense of the travel writer and the past tense of those being written about. In this way, travel writing functions in the same way as traditional anthropological texts in which the 'modern' researcher is distinguished from the 'pre-modern' social and cultural groups under scrutiny. With this in mind, Johannes Fabian's critique of anthropology can be fruitfully applied to travel writing:

The Other's empirical presence turns into his theoretical absence, a conjuring trick which is worked with the help of an array of devices that have the common intent and function to keep the Other outside of the Time of anthropology.... By this I mean a persistent and systematic tendency to place

---

[26] Kaplan, *Questions of Travel*, p. 34.

the referent(s) of anthropology in a Time other than the present of the producer of anthropological discourse.[27]

Just like anthropologists, travel writers reproduce the identity/difference logic by distancing themselves temporally from others who are situated elsewhere. Thirdly, prevailing understandings of modern cartography (e.g. which places are safe and which are dangerous) are underscored by a progressive, linear and teleological understanding of history. In other words, places are dangerous and uncivilised because they are *not as historically evolved* – they remain somewhere behind enlightened Western democracies in the historical queue. And it is precisely through the temporalisation of global territory that popular debates in global politics are animated most clearly (e.g. Francis Fukuyama's thesis in which Western liberal democracies (safe, enlightened, civilised) have reached the 'end of history', whereas other places (dangerous, conflict-ridden, barbaric) are 'stuck' in the struggles of the past). The temporal regulation of genre, subjectivity and space through a progressive and linear account of history suggests that the discourse of nostalgia is the most far-reaching in contemporary travel writing.

Disappointed travellers: Theroux's solitude and Bell's Paradise

Henderson argues that many contemporary travel writers 'employ a variety of self-insulating strategies designed to keep the contemporary world at a distance; they consciously perform contortions in order to keep their romantic visions alive.'[28] By taking comfort in a Golden Age, travel writers create an important temporal distance between their factual observations and their imagined destinations, between their own subject position and that of locals, and between their 'civilised' homes and 'backward' destinations. In Paul Theroux's *The Great Railway Bazaar*, this distance is governed by a utopian fantasy about the Golden Age of train travel. It is this same fantasy that drives many of his subsequent travelogues: by train through the Americas (*The Old Patagonian Express*, 1979); by train through China (*Riding the Iron Rooster*, 1988); and by train through Africa (*Dark Star Safari*, 2002). Anxious that the automobile and aeroplane are making modern travel more accessible, efficient and affordable, Theroux wants to experience the romance of train travel before it disappears altogether. For Theroux,

---

[27] Johannes Fabian, *Time and the Other: How Anthropology Makes Its Object* (New York: Columbia University Press, 1983), pp. xi, 31.
[28] Henderson, 'The Travel Writer and the Text', p. 237.

trains produce *better* journeys – calmer, more peaceful, less hectic, quieter and more authentic:

Railways are irresistible bazaars, snaking along perfectly level no matter what the landscape, improving your mood with speed, and never upsetting your drink. The train can reassure you in awful places – a far cry from the anxious sweats of doom aeroplanes inspire, or the nauseating gas-sickness of the long-distance bus, or the paralysis that afflicts the car passenger... the notion of travel as a continuous vision, a grand tour's succession of memorable images across a curved earth – with none of the distorting emptiness of air or sea – is possible only on a train.[29]

As this passage makes clear, Theroux's romantic image of train travel does not derive from efficient modern trains, but from the hey-day of rail travel during the nineteenth century. However, because Theroux cannot access nineteenth-century rail travel in the modern spaces of America and Europe, he travels to Asia where the Golden Age of rail travel can still be experienced. To the extent that trains remain a primary mode of long-distance travel in previously colonised places like Asia, Theroux is able to *travel backwards in time* along the colonial railways.

This utopian fantasy about nineteenth-century train travel shapes *The Great Railway Bazaar* on two levels: firstly, it romanticises the general railway itself (i.e. that trains are the best way to travel); and secondly, it romanticises the specific form of rail travel in Asia (i.e. that Asia is one of the only places left where Theroux can experience the hey-day of train travel). This dual structure inserts an unbridgeable distance between Theroux and his destination – he is not interested in discovering the 'real' Asia as much as he is interested in waxing nostalgic about the last remaining form of 'real' train travel. This distance is mediated in both material and imaginary ways – he only encounters the 'real' Asia from his train compartment, and his understanding of the 'real' Asia is derived from nineteenth-century literary descriptions. Theroux's understanding of Asia is generated within the sleeping car which allows him to focus his imagination in complete solitude: 'The romance associated with the sleeping car derives from its extreme privacy, combining the best features of a cupboard with forward movement. Whatever drama is being enacted in this moving bedroom is heightened by the landscape passing the window.'[30] However, because Theroux travels alone, the only drama being played out in his sleeping car is the process by which he shapes the passing landscape through previously established literary stereotypes. In effect, it doesn't matter what passes in front of the

---

[29] Theroux, *The Great Railway Bazaar*, p. 1, 82.
[30] Theroux, *The Great Railway Bazaar*, p. 82.

window of Theroux's sleeping car, for it will automatically be translated through the 'imagined Asia' he has already derived from great works of literature. Theroux's utopian fantasy of Asia is contained within a closed circuit: he is isolated in his solitary sleeping car, and his narrative is isolated within an Orientalist literary canon in which Asia is always subordinated to colonial powers.

The sleeping car – 'the most painless form of travel' – functions as an objective home for Theroux. From this solitary position he can make succinct, unfettered and informed judgements about how far the Asia seen from his window departs from the Asia depicted by great writers. Theroux is hermetically sealed off from the space and time of Asia because his *presence* in the sleeping car is also always a *present tense*. In other words, the sleeping car is a portable time capsule that allows Theroux to maintain his position at the front of the historical queue while repeatedly placing the countries of Asia at previous stages of historical development. Thus, Theroux temporalises his journey in the following way: he travels from present-day civilisation (London, Paris) to primitive places (Afghanistan, Sri Lanka), to the most backward places where time stops (Burma, Southern India), to the increasingly modern (Japan) and then back to the present tense again (London). This temporalisation is accompanied by appropriate judgements: while the reasonably civilised Turkey continues to languish in 1938 (the year of Atatürk's death), it is still much more evolved than Southern India where 'people were running around in drooping loincloths'.[31] As Theroux tests his utopian fantasy of Asia, he draws his 'evidence' not from his surroundings, but from the Western literary canon. In Lahore, for example, it is Kipling who gives him guidance:

My image of the Indian city derives from Kipling, and it was in Lahore that Kipling came of age as a writer. Exaggerating the mobs, the vicious bazaar, the colour and confusion, the Kipling of the early stories and *Kim* is really describing Lahore today, that side of it beyond the Mall where processions of rickshaws, pony carts, hawkers, and veiled women fill the narrow lanes and sweep you in their direction. The Anarkali Bazaar and the walled city, with its fort and mosques, have retained the distracted exoticism Kipling mentions, though now, with a hundred years of repetition, it is touched with horror.[32]

Because Lahore is both exotic and horrific, it offers only a limited fulfilment of Theroux's utopian fantasy. The 'horror' here – like the

---

[31] Theroux, *The Great Railway Bazaar*, pp. 37, 148.
[32] Theroux, *The Great Railway Bazaar*, p. 85; for a more specific discussion of Kipling's participation in colonial discourses, see Patrick Williams, 'Kim and Orientalism', in Patrick Williams and Laura Chrisman, eds., *Colonial Discourse and Post-Colonial Theory: A Reader* (New York: Columbia University Press, 1994), pp. 480–97.

original Conradian metaphor – is crucial to the narrative, for it
reinforces Theroux's argument that Kipling's Lahore is irretrievably lost.
While it might still display 'authentic' signs of exoticism (e.g. rickshaws,
mosques), Theroux is dismayed that the Pakistanis want to 'ruin'
Lahore by modernising it. Throughout *The Great Railway Bazaar*,
Theroux is irritated at the presence of the present – at signs of
modernity in what he assumes to be backward places (e.g. modern
movie ads in Delhi, skyscrapers in South East Asia). Not only do these
signs disrupt his implementation of the historical queue, they also
contaminate his position as the *most* modern subject looking back and
surveying the historical progress of other countries. As Henderson
argues, 'The fear of being let down leads the traveller to employ bizarre
devices in an attempt to salvage the moment.'[33] Thus, in the early stages
of his journey, Theroux confronts the irritating signs of modernity by
dismissing them. For example, he describes Iran's prolific efforts at
modernisation as fake: 'It is an old country; everywhere in the gleaming
modernity are reminders of the orthodox past – the praying steward, the
portraits, the encampments of nomads, and, on what is otherwise one of
the best-run railways in the world, the yearning for *baksheesh*.'[34] Despite
its efforts to move forward in the queue of history by installing a
'gleaming modernity', Iran cannot mask its status as more traditional
and less evolved than Western nations. This is indicated especially in
Theroux's anger that Asian railways cannot manage even the most basic
consumer transactions of 'modern' capitalism without resorting to
'traditional' forms of economic exchange (e.g. bribery). Significantly,
while Theroux wants his utopian fantasy of nineteenth-century rail
travel to be 'traditional', he also wants it wrapped in the 'modern'
amenities of Western consumerism.

Despite Theroux's continual judgements of Asia as less evolved than
the West, his inability to dismiss the signs of modernity proves that his
utopian fantasy is just that – a fantasy. And it is at this point that a
significant spatiotemporal shift occurs in the narrative. Rather than
continue to suggest that the space of Asia is less evolved (and thus the
best place for his fantasy to be fulfilled), he accepts that Asia has been
'contaminated' with signs of modernity and thus relocates his fantasy of
Asia even further back in time. The signs of modernity constantly
remind him of the disjuncture between his fantasy of Asia derived from
nineteenth-century literary tropes and the present tense of Asia creeping
forward on the historical queue. By relocating his utopian vision of Asia

---

[33] Henderson, 'The Travel Writer and the Text', p. 235.
[34] Theroux, *The Great Railway Bazaar*, p. 57.

even further back in time, Asia continues to occupy a protected and privileged position that can be endlessly dreamed about, romanticised and eulogised. And this is where feelings of loss begin to dominate the text. To be sure, *The Great Railway Bazaar* mourns the loss of nineteenth-century European rail travel from the very beginning. But Theroux's realisation that he cannot even capture that experience in less-evolved places like Asia instigates another layer of mourning – his utopian fantasy derived from great works of literature is now truly lost. When Theroux cannot find his Kipling-inspired fantasy at the famous Punjab club in Lahore, the cycle of expectation – realisation – disappointment begins to take hold:

I had imagined a crowded bar, a lot of cheerful drinkers, a snooker game in progress, a pair in the corner plotting adultery, waiters with trays of drinks, chits flying back and forth. This could have been a clinic of some kind; there was not a soul in sight, but it had the atmosphere – and even the magazines – of a dentist's waiting room ... the lighted empty rooms depressed me. The place was abandoned.[35]

For Theroux, the alienating condition of the Punjab club is symbolic of how the Indian subcontinent has changed since its departure from colonial rule. To be sure, he stops short of suggesting that the Empire should be reinstated, but he finds great sadness in the loss of the grand, imperious and romantic institution that built such magnificent railways.

Theroux's expressions of mourning and loss become even more acute when he leaves South East Asia and travels to Japan. Because Tokyo is the most 'modern' city on Theroux's itinerary, it begins to seem familiar – its commercial economy, futuristic trains and efficient social order present a serious challenge to Theroux's utopian fantasy. As ever, the railways symbolise this challenge. The 'railway bazaar' of the title refers to the slow and winding trains of India, so when Theroux boards the 'Express' from Butterworth to Singapore, his utopian fantasy begins to disintegrate. By the time he catches the bullet train from Tokyo to Kyoto, Theroux makes sense of the modernity of Japan by locating the 'lazy' trains of India further in the past. By doing so, his utopian fantasy of train travel is protected from the onslaught of 'gleaming modernity', and preserved for his nostalgic imagination:

Lacking the traditional features of the railway bazaar, the Japanese train relies on aircraft comforts: silence, leg room, a reading light ... Speed puts some people to sleep; others it makes breathless. It doesn't enliven conversation. I missed the slower trains with the lounge cars and the rackety wheels. Japanese train journeys were practical, uncongenial transitions from city to city: only

[35] Theroux, *The Great Railway Bazaar*, p. 88.

the punctual arrival mattered. The frseeeeeeefronnnng trains of Asia were behind me.[36]

This is a complex expression of nostalgia. In part, Theroux is nostalgic for the London he left behind – a London that is reflected in the modern, urban landscape of Tokyo. But in part, he is nostalgic for the slow trains and 'railway bazaars' of India that he has just left behind. Thus, it is in Japan that Theroux's confident placement of Asia begins to falter. Because Japan has effectively marched along the queue of history and caught up to the modern position occupied by Theroux, it is increasingly difficult for him to situate it within a teleological and progressive understanding of time. All Theroux can do is offer an unconvincing disappointment that Japan has been unable to properly maintain its 'appropriate' historical position behind the West. His loss here is tinged with frustration; indeed, he is vitriolic about the Japanese because they have inappropriately ambitious desires to become modern and Western. The chapters on Japan reveal Theroux at his most anxious – desperate to locate Japan behind his position at the front of the historical queue, and equally desperate to preserve it alongside other Asian countries as an object of nostalgic desire. It is only by securing that evolutionary progression that Theroux can savour the lingering romance of Empire and use the literary canon to stave off the emptiness of modernity.

Some of the most popular contemporary travelogues enact nostalgia by following in the footsteps of great literary or historical figures. Not only does this automatically structure the spatial itinerary of the contemporary journey (for all the author has to do is follow the exact footsteps of the predecessor), but it also gives the past-to-present framing of the narrative even greater significance. By providing historically informed discussions of the famous figure and his/her original visit, the following author simply explains how a destination has, or has not, changed since that time. As Henderson argues, 'The pleasure of imagining scenes from the past on the spot where they took place is often greater than the pleasure of witnessing scenes of today.'[37] With this in mind it is not difficult to see how 'follow-in-the-footsteps' narratives rely heavily on the discourse of nostalgia: not only does the contemporary author long to *be* the famous literary or

---

[36] Theroux, *The Great Railway Bazaar*, p. 290.
[37] Henderson, 'The Travel Writer and the Text', p. 232; she goes on to argue that the original literary figure in these texts provides both motivation for contemporary travel writers within a context of globalisation, and a simple narrative structure that is based on the original itinerary (pp. 242–3).

historical figure, but he/she also longs to have the *original* experience of being one of the first Westerners in foreign lands (for inevitably, contemporary travel writers use this experience to both escape the banality of modern life and judge it negatively against the glories of the past).[38] Foreign correspondent and travel writer Gavin Bell chose to follow Robert Louis Stevenson's journeys to the South Seas in order to capture the spirit of the man who had written *Treasure Island*. Using Stevenson's Polynesian name that means 'teller of tales', Bell produced *In Search of Tusitala* which won the 1995 Thomas Cook Travel Book Award. As Stevenson's original journey involved a number of stops and starts throughout the Pacific, *In Search of Tusitala* repeats the cycle of utopia, authentication and lament several times over. The central anchor for this formation of nostalgia is Bell's special affinity with Stevenson:

> Here was a man I could admire and for whom I felt a strong empathy. A fellow Scot, traveller, writer, and francophile, he was a romanticist whose spirit flew above Victorian conventions, Calvinism and chronic illness . . .. By the time RLS enticed me to the South Seas with his tales of ruffians, wizards, and cannibals, he was summoning an inveterate wanderer.[39]

Very simply, Bell wants to explore his empathy with Stevenson by re-living his nineteenth-century adventures in a twentieth-century context. To give his book a sense of authenticity, Bell intersperses his own narrative with the prose and letters of Stevenson himself, as well as anecdotes, letters and comments from other relevant sources (e.g. J. M. Barrie, Conan Doyle, Gauguin, and Stevenson's wife Fanny). In addition, the geography of the South Pacific is usually first framed by a Stevenson quotation, and then followed up by Bell's contemporary descriptions and comparisons.

Because the itinerary for Bell's narrative has already been decided by Stevenson's route, the space of the South Seas is always encountered by Bell *looking backwards* to the time of Stevenson's journey. In other words, Bell secures his literary affinity with Stevenson by continually reproducing a timeline that connects him to his hero in the common space of the Pacific Islands. This longing for the past is made easier for Bell because Stevenson is part of a significant cultural and literary tradition that continues to reproduce the Pacific Islands as Paradise on

---

[38] One of the most popular travelogues in this vein is Redmond O'Hanlon's *In Trouble Again: A Journey between the Orinoco and the Amazon* (London: Penguin Books, 1989) in which he follows scientist and explorer Alexander von Humboldt's journey through South America between 1799 and 1804; see Holland and Huggan's discussion of this text in *Tourists with Typewriters*, pp. 76–81.

[39] Gavin Bell, *In Search of Tusitala: Travels in the Pacific after Robert Louis Stevenson* (London: Picador, 1994), pp. 5–7.

earth.[40] Therefore, Bell does not have to work hard at securing his destination farther back in the evolutionary historical queue – a powerful 'Paradise' mythology has already done that for him. From the first moments when Bell gets on the 'silver time capsule' aeroplane in Glasgow to the last moments at Stevenson's grave in Samoa, the reader is in no doubt that Bell is journeying backwards into 'The Land that Time Forgot'. For example, at Butaritari, Bell agrees with Stevenson that 'he had wandered into a scene from the *Arabian Nights*' and describes his surroundings as 'having slipped back in Pacific dreamtime to become a sleepy outpost of fishermen and vegetable farmers happily remote from the stresses of the twentieth century'.[41] Central to the Paradise mythology that drives both Bell and Stevenson is the possibility of finding a 'tropical Garden of Eden', a utopian fantasy that is brought home to Bell as he walks through the remains of Stevenson's property in Samoa: 'Not another soul was to be seen. I felt like Adam waiting for God to produce Eve, and content to admire His other creations in the meantime.'[42] As is appropriate in a Garden of Eden, the Pacific Islands contain the 'purest' form of nature, and are populated by the most 'innocent' native people. Often mesmerised by the 'savage beauty' of the Pacific, the following passage, at the village of Keuea, is typical of Bell's rapture over nature:

I strolled a few steps to the shore, and caught my breath at the view. Warm golden tones of the setting sun radiated over a long stretch of spotless beach, on which brightly painted canoes were drawn up. Three children were punting a raft in the shallows, dark silhouettes of happiness on a sparkling sea. The sky was a magnificent deep blue etched with piles of cumulus tinged with rose and gold. I stood there for a long time, drinking in the aching beauty of it all.[43]

As the presence of these frolicking children suggests, the awesome nature of Paradise is equalled by its innocent, generous and uncomplicated population. Using literary metaphor and anthropological observation in equal measure, Bell represents the people of the Pacific as the 'purest' form of humanity. Although the men are 'strong and handsome' and the young girls 'exceedingly beautiful', Bell concludes that 'their beauty came from within; an inherent good nature and happy

---

[40] For a cultural analysis of the South Seas mythology in travel writing see Neil Rennie, *Far-Fetched Facts: The Literature of Travel and the Idea of the South Seas* (Oxford: Clarendon Press, 1995); for an overview of how this myth has been sustained in the genre, see Rod Edmund, 'The Pacific/Tahiti: Queen of the South Sea Isles', in Hulme and Youngs, eds., *The Cambridge Companion to Travel Writing*, pp. 139–55.

[41] Bell, *In Search of Tusitala*, p. 230.

[42] Bell, *In Search of Tusitala*, pp. 289–90.

[43] Bell, *In Search of Tusitala*, p. 255.

disposition twinkling from mischievous eyes'.[44] While on the leper colony in Molokai, Bell's utopian framing of both land and people is at its clearest. Comparing it to 'an American village of the 1940s', Bell experiences the colony as a 'living museum...the village was a haven of tranquillity. There was an air of timelessness, and of profound peace.'[45] In effect, Bell has to travel back in time as well as across the Pacific in order to encounter a land and a people in their purest, most innocent form. These ideas of purity, goodness and innocence – not to mention the search for Eden in the Pacific – reinforce the spiritual character of the book. Bell's quest for traces of Stevenson is also a quest for redemption: Bell needs to find paradise on earth to cure him from all the strife he has seen as a foreign correspondent. Luckily, redemption is on offer from three different sources in *Tusitala*: in the 'spirit' of Stevenson that governs the narrative (e.g. it is Stevenson rather than another deity who receives Bell's prayers during dangerous inter-island flights); in the refreshing and restorative power of nature (e.g. Bell is swarmed by butterflies, he sees beautiful rainbows, he swims in empty lagoons, he watches magnificent storms); and in the 'essence of Christianity' that anchors the 'benign code of life' on the Polynesian islands.

Bell's entire narrative is an account of how much these islands have changed since Stevenson's time and whether it is still possible to encounter Stevenson's spirit in such a spatiotemporally remote location. To remain true to this quest, Bell sticks as close to Stevenson's original itinerary as possible, which fills the narrative with 'coincidental' examples of Bell experiencing the same thing a century later: as Stevenson addressed a community feast in Kiribati, Bell addresses their descendants; as Stevenson wrote his novels in a shack on Butaritari, Bell writes up his notes on the same spot; as Stevenson spends a week at the leper colony at Molokai, so too does Bell. To the extent that Bell agrees with Stevenson, his utopian fantasy remains intact: yes, much of the landscape is 'as daunting as the wildest regions of northern Scotland'; yes, Atuona still expresses a 'menacing gloom'; yes, the Polynesians are still great storytellers; no, the Kariatebike are not as friendly as the Butaritari; yes, the native dancing on Samoa is still 'enchanting'; and yes, there are still a lot of spider plants on the walk to Hookena. By agreeing with Stevenson's observations, it is easier for Bell to connect himself with a previous era and convince himself that nothing has

---

[44] Bell, *In Search of Tusitala*, p. 232.
[45] Bell, *In Search of Tusitala*, pp. 196–7.

changed in the intervening hundred years. So, when he is asked to address a community feast, Bell reports the following: 'As I rose to speak, I saw Stevenson's lean frame standing before a similar gathering a century before. Lacking the man's eloquence, I made a brief speech about being gratified to see that the passage of time had not altered the beauty of Tuatira or the kindness of its people.'[46]

The problem, of course, is that Bell is unable to mimic Stevenson's nineteenth-century world-view in the late twentieth century because he cannot hold off the surrounding signs of modernity. In effect, *Tusitala* depicts an on-going struggle between Bell's efforts to maintain a utopian vision of the Pacific islands that connects him to Stevenson, and the realisation that his fantasy has disappeared with the onset of modernisation, Westernisation and mass tourism. Try as he might, Bell fails to relive Stevenson's romantic life in the Pacific islands and is often discouraged that he is unable to find signs of Stevenson's legacy in the Pacific. After his first stop in the Marquesas, he reveals his disappointment: 'I felt lonely and depressed by the rude landscapes and the sultry weather. The spirit of Stevenson had eluded me.'[47] Not only is Bell angry at the inadequacy of the few 'Stevenson' plaques, he is frustrated that the houses Stevenson stayed in and built were either disappearing or sinking into ruin. For example, the site of the Tahitian house where Stevenson lived and wrote *The Master of Ballantrae* 'was now occupied by two ramshackle dwellings owned by elderly Chinese. The buildings were squalid, and the garden was overgrown with weeds.'[48] More alarmingly, the Vailima mansion that Stevenson built on Samoa was in a terrible state. Subsequent wealthy owners had altered the original design, and it was being 'restored' by two wealthy American businessmen who were rumoured to be turning it into a Stevenson theme park. Bell's reaction to the state of Vailima is revealing: he had imagined a 'quiet stroll around the grounds' visualising Stevenson at work and play, but he was confronted by a structure 'falling to pieces . . . a derelict house from which his "spirit intense and rare" had long departed'.[49]

Bell's disappointment is palpable here: he feels the locals have failed to commemorate Stevenson properly because they have been seduced by

---

[46] Bell, *In Search of Tusitala*, p. 135.
[47] Bell, *In Search of Tusitala*, pp. 79–80.
[48] Bell, *In Search of Tusitala*, p. 126.
[49] Bell, *In Search of Tusitala*, p. 286. Much to Bell's pleasure, Vailima was not turned into a theme park and has been restored 'properly' and 'authentically' as a Stevenson museum; see William Murtagh and Delta Lightner, 'Robert Louis Stevenson in the Pacific', *Cultural Resource Management*, 19 August 1998, p. 44; http://crm.cr.nps.gov/archive/19-8/19-8-15.pdf.

consumer culture, modern technology and the potential revenue from mass tourism. In other words, the Pacific Islanders have lost their 'authentic' culture (and their respect for people like Stevenson) because they have been pursuing a course of modernisation and Westernisation since the Second World War. Because Bell cannot ignore or condone these processes, he chooses to focus on what has been lost in the drive to modernity. In this way, *Tusitala* is best understood as a long elegy to Stevenson's era – an evocation of all that has disappeared and a lament at the modernising forces that have 'not been kind to Oceania'. Consequently, the narrative is littered with disappointment at the encroaching presence of modernity: that ugly modern architecture is replacing traditional Polynesian housing; that communities sit passively in front of modern videos rather than gather around the fire for traditional legends; that locals would rather earn more money working for a French nuclear power company than protect their atolls from atomic testing; that traditional languages are disappearing as everyone speaks English or French; that Papeete and Waikiki are leading the descent as 'hideous' money-making tourist traps; that traditional singing and music are being replaced by modern keyboards and karaoke; that sustainable aquaculture is being supplanted by short-term and environmentally destructive industries like black pearl farming; and that even traditional Polynesian tattooing is now done with disinfected mechanical needles rather than the traditional bone implements. In short, the *authenticity* of the Pacific islands that Stevenson encountered has been lost to the rampaging juggernaut of modernity. When Bell realises that he has missed the opportunity to experience the Pacific as it was in Stevenson's era, he offers a curious moment of reflection:

There were times in my travels when I was discouraged, and this was one of them. I was trying to span a century in which the world had been convulsed by wars, automobiles, air travel, and the insidious cult of television. How could I hope to relive Stevenson's adventures in islands where fishermen had abandoned their villages to build highways and nuclear bombs?[50]

Highways, satellite dishes, military bases and nuclear bombs symbolise a time completely at odds with Bell's expectations of what the Pacific is supposed to be – a place *exactly* like it was when Stevenson was there. Therefore, whenever Bell's utopian fantasy is under threat from the signs of modernity, he relocates the *real* South Pacific back in Stevenson's era so it can function as an object of nostalgic reflection. Indeed, Bell's disappointment is mitigated when he 'communes' with

[50] Bell, *In Search of Tusitala*, p. 168.

Stevenson's spirit, but he is only able to do so in sites and moments where his utopian fantasy of a pre-modern and Edenic Pacific is confirmed (e.g. in quiet spaces of natural beauty). In this way, *Tusitala* is a cyclical tale of disintegration and restoration: Bell protects his utopian fantasy of communing with Stevenson in the Paradise of the Pacific; when those moments are threatened by the ever-present signs of modernity, Bell responds by repositioning his fantasy back in Stevenson's nineteenth century in order to mourn its passing. This cycle of disintegration and restoration reaffirms the precious link between Stevenson and Bell by securing the historical queue once again – the *real* Pacific exists, but it is far away in both space and time, and can be accessed only by nostalgic reverie.

The problem with Bell's account is its simple and uncritical temporal judgement: Stevenson's nineteenth-century experience in the South Pacific was *better* than Bell's twentieth-century mimicry. Stevenson's Paradise was peaceful, beautiful, innocent, authentic – Bell's Paradise is spoiled, damaged, barren and fraudulent. *Tusitala* makes no effort to reveal the unsavoury colonial relations that underscored Stevenson's nineteenth-century voyage, nor does it examine how the modernisation of the South Pacific in the intervening years has actually *improved* the material existence of local people. In the end, I am not concerned that Bell fails to replicate Stevenson's nineenth-century experience in the twentieth century (indeed, the failure is itself compelling), but I am concerned that the narrative does not question, let alone problematise, the assumptions behind its nostalgic and elegiac fantasies. With this in mind, Bell's failure, as well as Theroux's anxiety and isolation, require some unpacking. To be sure, both Bell and Theroux produce problematic assumptions about both Asia and the Pacific islands; principally, that they exist far back on the historical queue where they languish in a colonial and pre-modern state. But no matter how hard they try to occupy an antecedent time – in both cases by retreating into colonial literatures – neither can escape their present tense. The inability of travel writers to maintain their presence (and present tense) at the front of the historical queue while keeping others locked in the past reveals that the discourse of nostalgia cannot ultimately secure a progressive, teleological and evolutionary account of history.

Arresting the timeline: deconstructing the teleology of travel writing

As the work of Theroux and Bell illustrates, the home-away-home/ beginning-middle-end structure of travel writing is fertile ground for nostalgia – for the creation of utopian fantasies, the construction of authenticity and the onset of lament. And as we have seen, the political significance of nostalgia is its ability to reproduce a teleological understanding of history and temporalise difference according to reconstructed power relations of Empire. While contemporary travel writers may enthuse about the *equality* of cultural differences, those differences are placed on an *unequal* historical queue that is controlled and led by Western powers. Indeed, travel writing installs a progressive, linear and evolutionary timeline in order to secure the cartographic hierarchies of global politics (e.g. here/there; home/away; safe/dangerous; civilised/uncivilised). Contemporary travel writers work to reposition their destinations *behind and before* the present tense, even when those 'backward' destinations show abundant signs of modernity. The point, of course, is that the genre's teleological understanding of history equates cultural difference with a *lack* of civility, modernity and progress. Thus, Theroux positions Asian countries at different historical stages behind his own Anglo-American culture (e.g. Turkey is less evolved than England or America, but more evolved than India), whereas Bell contrasts the innocent and pre-modern Pacific with the vulgar consumer culture of the West.

Deconstructing the genre's teleological understanding of history requires thinking further about the relationship between history and narrative. Here, I mean the narrative accounts of history common to the genre of travel writing, but also the more general problem of how we narrate and interpret historical facts. Certainly Foucault's genealogical method helps us reveal the linear timeline at work within the discourse of nostalgia. But his method requires more than a simple illustration: a genealogy reveals the political effects of leaving an 'official history' unquestioned but also begins to deconstruct the teleological character of that historical narrative. Along with calling attention to the continuing existence of power relations, a genealogy also carefully draws out its discontinuities, ruptures and temporal breaks. As Foucault argues, to employ a genealogical method

is to identify the accidents, the minute deviations – or conversely, the complete reversals – the errors, the false appraisals, and the faulty calculations that gave birth to those things that continue to exist and have value for us; it is to discover that truth or being does not lie at the root of what we know and what we are, but the exteriority of accidents.[51]

Foucault's understanding of history as contingent and accidental runs in direct opposition to teleological understandings that encourage objective

---

[51] Foucault, 'Nietszche, Genealogy, History', p. 81.

and progressive accounts of the past. Following on from Foucault, it is worth coming back to Hayden White's point that 'official history' claims to be 'neutral' and 'objective' because it attaches time-space-specific events (e.g. wars, inventions, disasters, births, deaths) to an unquestioned and ontologically secure historical record. This is why history is traditionally understood as an objective account of 'what really happened'. White, of course, refutes these claims of neutrality, objectivity and ontological security by illustrating that history is a *narrative formation* – it is a story rather than a truth claim. White's argument that there is nothing inherent in the historical record that encourages us to narrate it in one way or another introduces much more fundamental questions about the nature of the historical record itself. We get a hint of these questions when White insists that the 'raw material' of history – the stuff that exists before chronological arrangement and narration – is not legible or linear, but rather chaotic, contingent and indeterminate. His analysis shows that this 'raw material' is temporalised and arranged upon a linear timeline only with the introduction of power. In this respect, White's arguments build on Foucault's claim that the world does not turn a legible face towards us, rather, we 'do violence' to the world every time we seek to represent it. In White's framework, *the historical record* does not turn a legible or indeed a linear face towards us, and *historians* 'do violence' to the chaotic past by arranging it into a past–present–future chronology.

In *Metahistory*, White argues that the main narrative structures of history (i.e. metaphor, metonymy, synecdoche and irony) are chosen through *random* decisions rather than rational designs, and thus calls attention to the political, social and cultural reasons why historians might choose to represent time-space-specific events according to certain narrative structures. In this way, White places the observer (the historian) squarely in the centre of his/her research and calls attention to the ways in which a historian's particular agency shaped his/her subsequent historical account. His argument suggests that history is not *better* when historians pursue more 'accurate' representations of reality; rather, history is *better* when historians recognise how their preconceptions and expectations not only shape their research, but also shape the world their research claims to describe. When historians fail to reflect on how political agendas of the present shape our reconstructions of the past, their historical narratives are driven by a conservative political orientation. By this, he means that the supposedly 'factual' claims of history reinforce the status quo of the present and the belief that the 'Now' is the culmination of a natural evolution towards a more progressive, emancipated and mature social arrangement.[52] Even in critical traditions such as Marxism, any claim to represent the 'correct' history (e.g. a Marxist might seek to uncover the 'real' history of exploitation underneath bourgeois oppression) is equally guilty of imposing a linear timeline that uses fictional strategies to animate the historical record. Indeed, White's revelations of how historians produce and secure a conservative status quo critique *any* political movement that seeks to resolve present difficulties by appealing to a supposedly unquestionable historical record (i.e. 'this is how we got here') and promising a brighter future (i.e. 'this is where we are going').[53] For White, placing the historical record beyond question is politically dangerous because it justifies the prevailing status quo and prevents critical interrogations of the past. It says 'we have arrived at the present by moving through the *natural* progression of historical stages'. In other words, when an historical account suggests that the present tense was *inevitable*, it closes the door to alternative narratives that suggest the trajectory of history *could have been otherwise.*

White's arguments are crucial to the study of contemporary travel writing because struggles over which history becomes the 'official' history take place primarily on the terrain of culture. Representations like travelogues either secure the present by reproducing hegemonic accounts of the historical record (e.g. 'this is what really happened'), or reveal the complexities and difficulties of the present by providing alternative accounts of the past (e.g. 'it could have happened otherwise'). My point is that the genre's reproduction of a teleological understanding of history allows a conservative political orientation to flourish and thus restricts the critical potential of these texts. Very simply, contemporary travel writing tends to claim 'this is what really happened' rather than ask more difficult questions such as 'who is telling this history?', 'who is being left out of that telling?', and 'how have these events been arranged so as to make the present situation seem like an inevitability?' For me, this critical questioning is especially significant at the moment, as much post-Cold War travel writing has willingly accepted and reproduced Francis Fukuyama's conservative political vision. With his publication of 'The End of History?' (1989) and the subsequent book *The End of History and the Last Man* (1993), Fukuyama revitalised linear, progressive and teleological understandings of history and placed them once again beyond

---

[52] White, *The Content of the Form*, pp. 58–82.
[53] White, *The Content of the Form*, p. 73.

question.[54] Not only did he make the progressive character of the historical queue explicit, he also made it seem natural and indeed beneficial to all humanity. If we recall, the cartography of Robert Kaplan's *The Ends of the Earth* was underscored by Fukuyama's teleological framework in which Western countries have reached 'the end point of mankind's ideological evolution'.[55] Fukuyama argues that by embracing liberal democracy, the West has emerged from the darkness of ideological struggle and embraced 'the final form of human government'. As such, the world is now divided in half between Western liberal democracies which have reached the end of ideological struggle, and those unfortunate places still 'mired' in history. Travelogues like Kaplan's that test out Fukuyama's thesis in the 'devastated parts of the world' have been crucial in popularising his bifurcated cartography and evolutionary account of history. In effect, post-Cold War travel writing has been reinvigorated by Fukuyama's thesis because he has made the 'devastated' half of the world visitable and exotic once again. Travel writers no longer have to worry about their obsolescence in a globalised world: to the extent that Fukuyama's thesis prevails, there will always be 'dangerous' and 'less-evolved' destinations available for rediscovery, exploration and documentation.

The championing of Fukuyama by contemporary travel writing is revealed most clearly by a shared discourse of nostalgia. Like many travel writers, Fukuyama longs for a time gone by – a time that continues to be experienced by other parts of the world as they slowly move up the historical queue. As he explains at the end of his argument, previous ideological conflicts called forth heroic forms of 'daring, courage, imagination, and idealism', whereas those of us who have reached the end of history are consigned to the banality of economic calculation and consumerism. Thus, it is with a measure of sadness that Fukuyama makes the following conclusion:

I can feel myself, and see in others around me, a powerful nostalgia for the time when history existed. Such nostalgia, in fact, will continue to fuel competition and conflict even in the post-historical world for some time to come ... Perhaps this very prospect of centuries of boredom at the end of history will serve to get history started once again.[56]

---

[54] Francis Fukuyama, 'The End of History?' *The National Interest*, No. 16, Summer 1989, pp. 1–18; *The End of History and the Last Man* (London: Penguin Books, 1993). For a good synopsis of the critical responses to Fukuyama's argument, see Gearóid Ó Tuathail, 'New World Order Geopolitics: Introduction', in Gearóid Ó Tuathail, Simon Dalby and Paul Routledge, eds., *The Geopolitics Reader* (London and New York: Routledge, 1998), pp. 103–13.

[55] Fukuyama, 'The End of History?', p. 4.

[56] Fukuyama, 'The End of History?,' p. 18; see also Robertson, 'After Nostalgia?', p. 55.

Indeed, as Fukuyama goes on to say, the only activity left in a post-historical world is the 'perpetual caretaking of the museum of human history'. Embedded in Fukuyama's nostalgia is a supposedly 'universal' assumption that the ideal social arrangement (liberal democracy) can be achieved after periods of struggle and conflict. Thus, the *temporality* of Fukuyama's thesis (historical progression) is wedded to a *teleological* structure (the 'end' of history and the achievement of liberal democracy). The linear progression of this argument is clear from the very beginning: because states must go through different stages of development, some are 'stuck' in history, while others have moved up the historical queue and now rest in a future-oriented phase of post-history. But Fukuyama's Hegelian liberalism is not an innocent conjunction of temporality and teleology. To be sure, it justifies the continuation of violence in those places still mired in history because violence is seen as a 'necessary evil' that all societies must journey through on their way to liberal democracy. But what is most objectionable about Fukuyama's 'coherent and directional history of mankind' is its depoliticising effect. Any kind of ideological or political struggle is evacuated from those places that have reached the end of history, which means that Western liberal democracies are portrayed *without* conflict, antagonism and violence. Likewise, those places stuck in history − 'strange' places like Albania and Burkina Faso − are always engulfed in political struggle, economic strife and ethnic conflict and therefore show no signs of modernity or enlightenment. By combining a divided global cartography with an evolutionary temporality, Fukuyama de-legitimates any beneficial, innovative or emancipatory political solutions suggested from those on the margins − especially from those subjects participating directly in the struggles of history. In effect, these actors cannot participate *fully* in global politics because they have not fulfilled the sufficient criteria required to make sober and mature contributions to the progress of international society.

Fukuyama's argument emerged in response to the momentous political upheavals that marked the end of the Cold War (e.g. the fall of the Berlin Wall, the collapse of the Soviet Union). His claim about the triumph of liberal democracy rested upon what he saw as the 'total exhaustion of viable systematic alternatives to Western Liberalism'.[57] For Fukuyama, the main opponents that had been defeated by this triumph were Marxism and Communism. But this so-called 'death' of the Left has been contested by those scholars committed to the spirit of critique embedded in Marxism. One such response that directly

[57] Fukuyama, 'The End of History?', p. 3.

addresses Fukuyama's thesis is Derrida's 'Conjuring Marxism'.[58] Derrida argues that the end-of-history thesis is a 'tireless anachronism'. He seems perplexed that the public sphere, the media industry and intellectual circles have accepted Fukuyama's argument so willingly, considering that forty years ago arguments about the end of history, the last man and the end of Marxism were 'our daily bread'. As Derrida argues, Fukuyama is seeking to catch the last train after it has already departed – he has come late to the end of history.[59] Significantly, Derrida's sarcasm towards Fukuyama is replicated in Mark Lawson's travelogue *The Battle for Room Service*. Unlike Kaplan's willing acceptance and evangelical zeal about Fukuyama, Lawson is much more critical:

After the fall of the Berlin Wall in 1989, an American academic called Francis Fukuyama had become rich and famous with a thesis called *The End of History*, which boasted that capitalism had triumphed unequivocally in the century's conflict of ideas. We were all, he had said, free marketeers now. It was now increasingly clear that he had held the party too soon. History didn't end anywhere, not even at the borders of the boring world.[60]

As we recall, Lawson illustrated that the boring world is also a dangerous world. In doing so, he offered not only an important disruption to Fukuyama's equation between cartography and temporality, but also a much more complex vision of global political life. Taking our cue from Lawson's argument, it is worth thinking further about Derrida's critique of Fukuyama and how it might be used to disrupt the genre's uncritical reproduction of the 'end-of-history' thesis.

Derrida argues that we have not reached the end of history as such, but rather, that Fukuyama's thesis exemplifies the end of a certain *conception* of history. *Spectres of Marx* uses the enduring spirit of Marxist critique to deconstruct the teleology embedded within Fukuyama's conception of history. In doing so, the cartography, temporality and teleology of Fukuyama's argument are unhinged, and a more critical understanding of history, time, memory and tradition begins to take shape. Derrida is concerned with how Fukuyama's end-of-history thesis forms a hegemonic discourse that involves political, cultural, media and

---

[58] Jacques Derrida, 'Conjuring Marxism', in *Spectres of Marx: The State of the Debt, the Work of Mourning, and the New International*, trans. Peggy Kamuf (London: Routledge, 1994), pp. 49–75. Another significant, although more general, response to questions about the end of history is Jean Baudrillard's *The Illusion of the End*, trans. Chris Turner (Cambridge: Polity, 1994). Baudrillard argues that history has not ended, but rather, has disappeared into simulation and spectacle.

[59] Derrida, *Spectres of Marx*, pp. 14–15.

[60] Lawson, *The Battle for Room Service*, p. 289.

intellectual spheres in the triumphant 'good news' of the arrival of liberal democracy. What makes this triumphalism so worrying for Derrida is that it is framed by Fukuyama's Christian eschatology. Not only does this 'neo-evangelism' bind cartography, temporality and teleology together, it repeats a Hegelian vision of God and augments it with biblical images of a future Promised Land.[61] According to the utopian and messianic character of Fukuyama's argument, the teleological progression of history ends up in the Promised Land of liberal democracy currently exemplified by Europe and America. In Fukuyama's understanding, the Promised Land either has been achieved now (by post-historical Europe and America), or will be achieved in the future (by those countries still stuck in history but struggling to improve their lot). What Derrida finds most intriguing about this 'noisy new gospel' is its manic character and its paranoid celebration of victory: 'This triumphant discourse seems relatively homogeneous, most often dogmatic, sometimes politically equivocal and, like all dogmatisms, like all conjurations, secretly worried and manifestly worrisome ... this triumph has never been so critical, fragile, threatened, even in certain regards catastrophic, and in sum bereaved.'[62] It is as if the triumph of liberal democracy cannot seem to shake off those it has vanquished – those 'other' viable systematic alternatives that are always waiting in the wings. This secret worry, this tacit recognition of a lingering threat amidst the celebration, is what Derrida uses to prise open Fukuyama's teleological account of history. Derrida's critique of liberal democracy's victory focuses on its inability to provide the much-vaunted Promised Land it evangelises about. Fukuyama's end-of-history thesis falls apart in the gaping distance between its utopian vision of liberal democracy and the numerous empirical realities that contradict this goal. Although Fukuyama admits that disasters and wars have characterised the West in the twentieth century, he does not believe that they compromise or detract from the basic *principles* of the liberal democratic state. For Fukuyama, these Hegelian principles cannot be improved upon.[63] Citing the kind of events that contradict

---

[61] Derrida, *Spectres of Marx*, pp. 59–61.

[62] Derrida, *Spectres of Marx*, pp. 56, 68.

[63] Fukuyama, 'The End of History?, p. 5. In making this critique, Derrida (like White) is not suggesting that the Marxist alternative to liberal democracy/market capitalism does not also employ a teleological understanding of history. Indeed an 'emancipatory promise' is at the heart of the Marxist project (i.e. after the revolution there will be a utopia where the equal distribution of wealth will prevail). This is why Derrida is concerned to distinguish between 'the spirit of Marxist critique' (which he uses) and the specific concepts of Marxism (which he does not use): *Spectres of Marx*, pp. xv–xx, 3–48.

these principles (e.g. Nazism, Stalinism, the Second World War, Pol Pot's regime), Derrida explains Fukuyama's refusal to acknowledge, let alone engage with, any counter-examples:

Their accumulation would in no way refute the *ideal* orientation of the greater part of humanity toward liberal democracy. As *such*, as *telos* of a progress, this orientation would have the form of an ideal finality. Everything that appears to contradict it would belong to historical empiricity, however massive and catastrophic and global and multiple and recurrent it might be.[64]

By banishing these examples to an empirical level, Fukuyama is able to protect the ideal finality – or utopian position – of his precious liberal democracy. What Derrida is concerned about is that by situating this Promised Land at the end of a teleological historical progression, the always-imminent arrival of the ideal finality (liberal democracy) ends up justifying all the atrocities (contradictory empirical facts) accrued along the journey.

In his typical fashion, Derrida pushes at Fukuyama's intransigent position between the ideal and the empirical. By highlighting where Fukuyama gets stuck, Derrida begins to expose and unravel the teleology embedded in the end-of-history thesis. His argument begins at an obvious level: because conflict and violence still characterise liberal democracies, it is impossible for Fukuyama to claim that the ideal finality has been achieved:

Even though he believes in its effective realization (that is the 'important truth'), Fukuyama does not hesitate all the same to oppose the *ideality* of this liberal democratic *ideal* to all the evidence that bears massive witness to the fact that neither the United States nor the European Community has attained the perfection of the universal State or of liberal democracy, nor have they even come close.[65]

To cover over this failure of actualisation, Fukuyama must arrange all these contradictory empirical elements, 'all the *evil*, all that is *not going well*', into a story based on the promise that liberal democracy is sure to be realised *very soon*. By pointing out the discrepancy between the ideal of liberal democracy and its material failures, Derrida suggests that Fukuyama's thesis fails to guarantee its telos or ideal finality. And that gap between materiality and ideal finality is what allows Derrida to question the fundamental desirability of this Promised Land. He goes on to argue that the *'as yet inaccessible'* utopia of liberal democracy functions as a *regulating ideal* that allows Fukuyama to go about 'certifying the

[64] Derrida, *Spectres of Marx*, p. 59.
[65] Derrida, *Spectres of Marx*, p. 63.

finally final defeat of the so-called Marxist States and of everything that bars access to the Promised Land of economic and political liberal-isms'.[66] Fukuyama can tell such a convincing story because these regulating mechanisms appeal to transhistorical criteria – *natural* standards of right and wrong that 'help us evaluate the goodness or badness of any regime or social system'.[67] And because these standards *transcend* the normal flow of history, their realisation is positioned at the end of historical progression – they are always imminent, always deferred and always in the future.[68] In effect, Fukuyama's teleological understanding of historical progress actually 'locks up, neutralizes, and finally cancels historicity'. In other words, *what counts* as history is already provided through transhistorical criteria (the principles of liberal democracy), and the *direction* of that history is already determined (as linear, progressive, teleological).

By approaching Fukuyama's thesis through the spirit of critique inherited from Marxism, Derrida casts even more doubt on the telos of liberal democracy.[69] He takes apart the temporality at work in the end-of-history thesis by questioning the discrete time periods upon which Fukuyama's narrative of historical progression rests (e.g. past–present–future). Thus, *Spectres of Marx* gives us a specific example of how temporality always exceeds its linear cage: despite the triumphalism of liberal democracy and its desire to exorcise Marxism, the political commitments of the Left refuse to go away. Derrida represents Marxism as a spectre here to illustrate how it haunts the ideal finality that liberal democracy encourages.[70] This concept of the spectre encapsulates many of Derrida's more general concerns about the connections between cartography, temporality and teleology, and is best understood in conjunction with his better known discussions about traces, infections, contaminations and impurities. In order to avoid the 'program or design' that accompanies Fukuyama's teleological understanding of history, Derrida invokes his earlier work on the metaphysics of presence to illustrate how all discrete temporal moments contaminate each other.[71] Derrida is concerned with how hegemonic understandings of time give

---

[66] Derrida, *Spectres of Marx*, p. 69.
[67] Fukuyama as quoted in Derrida, *Spectres of Marx*, p. 67.
[68] Derrida, *Spectres of Marx*, p. 67.
[69] Derrida, *Spectres of Marx*, pp. 54–5.
[70] In *Spectres of Marx*, Derrida develops this concept of 'hauntology' and poses it against 'ontology' to explain the lingering power of Marxist critique.
[71] Derrida's earliest concerns with temporality appear in his work on the phenomenology of Husserl, but they are crystallised in his critique of the 'metaphysics of presence' in *Of Grammatology*, trans. Gayatri Chakravorty Spivak (Baltimore: Johns Hopkins University Press, 1976).

'full-presence' and power to the 'Now' of the present.[72] Because the moment of 'Now' can never be entirely blocked off either from what comes before it or what comes after, Derrida argues that the present 'Now' is *always* shot through with other times, and with an infinite number of 'not-Now' moments. Given this contamination, the present cannot maintain its fullness, discreteness or purity. More importantly, this temporal haunting works retroactively to shape the past, just as it works in anticipation to shape the future. If there was ever a pure moment in the past that can be considered a 'true' origin point, then it becomes retroactively contaminated by its representation and dissemination in future moments. Likewise, in anticipating the future of the 'Now-about-to-come' and holding open a place for it, the present moment of 'Now' is contaminated by all the 'not-yet-Now's of tomorrow. Rather than understand 'Now' as an 'intemporal kernel of time' situated on an infinitely divisible continuum (as Husserl does), Derrida sees the present as only existing through its 'constitutive outsides' – through all the infinite 'not-Now's that surround and contaminate the 'Now'.[73] Derrida goes on to explain how the historical progression of past–present–future is undone by the failure of the 'Now' to repeat itself in a pure or original form. When temporality and teleology are forged together, the meaning of 'Now' sustains its currency by being repeated along a temporal continuum: 'Now' retains the meaning of 'just-past-Now' but also carries forward this meaning to the 'Now-about-to-come'. But Derrida argues that all repetitions of 'Now' are slightly different each time they emerge: because there is never a 'pure' originary moment, it can never be retained as such across time. This slight difference is what further disrupts the teleology of history, for how can we rationally move towards a concrete ideal when that ideal changes with each iteration?

Derrida's specific critique of Fukuyama and his more general critique of the metaphysics of presence pose radical questions to traditional accounts of history. To go back to Hayden White, deconstruction is a way to represent the 'raw material' of history, not in its 'authentic' state, but in narratives that do not necessarily reinforce the hegemony of linear history. The *impurity* of the past–present–future timeline that deconstruction reveals prevents any ideal finality from being imposed. Keeping in mind how Foucault, White and Derrida problematise our

---

[72] This framing of Derrida's temporality as 'Now' and 'not-Now' is taken from Henry Staten, *Wittgenstein and Derrida* (London and Lincoln: University of Nebraska Press, 1984) especially pp. 19–20, 50–3.

[73] Staten, *Wittgenstein and Derrida*, pp. 19, 48–53.

traditional ways of telling and understanding history, the question arises as to how this critique might apply to contemporary travel writing. In terms of how it conceives of its own historical development, the distance between contemporary travel writing and colonial travel writing is suddenly truncated. To use Derridean language, contemporary travel writing is haunted by its colonial heritage – it cannot banish the Empire 'back in time' but instead must continually confront the ways in which the imperial gaze is maintained and rearticulated. In terms of how the genre conceives of the historical development of others, travel writers can no longer act as unreconstructed anthropologists who situate foreign subjects back in the queue of history to be gazed upon and documented. There is no 'pure' position along an evolutionary historical queue, just as there is no protected authorial vantage point at the front of the queue that remains uncontaminated by other subjects, spaces and times. What the critical revisions of Foucault, White and Derrida show us is that despite its many efforts, the genre of travel writing fails to secure a past–present–future timeline and thus cannot fully govern its nostalgic visions.

Complex temporality and memory: Ritchie's Empire and Diski's America

Far more critical understandings of history and nostalgia are employed in Harry Ritchie's travelogue *The Last Pink Bits: Travels through the Remnants of the British Empire*. Because Ritchie exposes the cycle of nostalgia from the start, there is no utopian fantasy to drive the narrative and secure a linear timeline. Very simply, Ritchie argues that there is nothing to be nostalgic about when it comes to the British Empire: 'it is undeniable that the "Pax Britannica" was often brutally imposed, that it involved slavery, disease, prostitution and all manner of destruction'.[74] With this in mind, Ritchie argues that any nostalgic reverie for the days of Empire betrays a conservative morality, a paternal and often racist attitude towards others and an unwillingness to comprehend the political complexities of Britain's remaining colonies. Conversely, Ritchie is intrigued by the contradiction of these outposts: if the horrors wrought by the British Empire are well known, then why do places like Bermuda, the Falklands and Gibraltar still wish to remain British? What he discovers is that these places are not characterised by 'a farcically inappropriate Britishness'; rather, 'instead of finding them out of touch,

---

[74] Harry Ritchie, *The Last Pink Bits: Travels through the Remnants of the British Empire* (London: Sceptre, 1997) p. 8.

tune, or step with Britain or the rest of the world, I soon appreciated that the people in each country entertained no delusions about themselves or the supposed motherland'.[75] In fact, Britain's remaining colonies are 'extraordinary, fascinating, perplexing countries' negotiating their own social, political and economic difficulties. *The Last Pink Bits* is Ritchie's effort to expose, satirise and critique any nostalgia for 'the motherland' by suggesting (a) that the British Empire was a violent, racist and exploitative institution not worth being nostalgic about, and (b) that any form of nostalgia for Britain's past reveals its continuing 'delusion of importance' on the world stage. For Ritchie, Britain is not 'Great' in any respect, but rather a 'fairly ridiculous' country that 'matters very little in global politics and tends to inspire not respect but derision'.[76] With this, Ritchie inverts the teleological character of the historical queue: Britain is no longer the *most* evolved country but is in fact at the same evolutionary stage as its colonial possessions. And it is this equivalence that destroys the myth of Britain's greatness – how can Britain be superior to its colonies when both places are confronting the *same* social, economic, political and cultural difficulties?

By inverting the historical queue and making it impossible to locate Britain's colonies back in time, Ritchie prevents the discourse of nostalgia from taking hold. There is no assumed reading of history in *The Last Pink Bits* – no linear timeline that is secured with either utopian dreams or nostalgic longing. Ritchie's determination to read his destinations as modern rather than backward lends his writing a political edge that is missing in the work of other 'humorous' travel writers like Redmond O'Hanlon and Tim Moore. Because Ritchie is well aware of the limitations imposed by nostalgia, he represents his destinations through a *complex temporality* rather than a simple linear timeline. Thus, for example, he does not wallow in Bryson's utopian fantasies (e.g. 'isn't Australia great!'), but instead seeks out the difficult issues that disrupt the usual fantasies of travel writing. For example, had Ritchie written about Australia, he would have engaged directly with the thorny issue of Aboriginal land claims rather than shy away from it like Bryson does. Indeed, Aboriginal land claims exemplify the complex temporality Ritchie is interested in: here is an 'ancient' culture using 'modern' institutions to pursue 'universal' issues of justice, equality and recognition. To be sure, Ritchie's writing resembles Bryson's in tone and style (e.g. the self-deprecations, the comedic turns, the exaggerated

---

[75] Ritchie, *The Last Pink Bits*, p. 5.
[76] Ritchie, *The Last Pink Bits*, p. 6.

adventures), but it far exceeds the conservative political orientation underscoring Bryson's nostalgic framework.

Ritchie starts out in Bermuda, determined to 'spot the snake in the lawn' and destroy its image as a happy, sunny and prosperous country. In fact, Ritchie has no interest in visiting Bermuda at all, and he readily admits to his own prejudices: 'Everything I'd read about the place had confirmed my notion that it was not so much a country as a country club, enjoyed only by rich Americans.'[77] But what he discovers by the end of his trip – to his dismay – is that Bermuda does not have a 'hidden, hideous flaw'. Certainly, there are wealthy and snobby people living there, and it does suffer all the usual setbacks of being a tourist destination (namely, too many tourists), but for the most part, Bermuda is a prosperous, well-run, democratic and cosmopolitan country. Given that Ritchie is especially keen on exposing the racist legacy of the British Empire, he does his best to uncover examples of discrimination and exploitation. After visiting the 'ghetto' (one block, a few wizened drunks) and speaking to locals in a popular bar ('good-looking, well-dressed, joyful customers, black and white'), Ritchie concludes that Bermuda is 'as colour-blind as locals claimed', and that the only 'convincingly oppressed' people were the white British guest workers. What Ritchie manages to do is equate Bermuda's situation with that in Britain: while certainly not as severe, Bermuda does suffer from similar social and economic problems (e.g. an increase in crime, unemployment dictated by the global market, a growing drug culture). Ritchie reveals that Bermuda *does not* celebrate its colonial ties to Britain because of some misplaced nostalgia for the 'motherland'; rather, it maintains its status as a colony because its ties to Britain foster a hugely profitable offshore financial industry. Bermuda does not want independence from Britain because that would disrupt its dominance of the 'captive management' market (i.e. underwriting parent companies). Currently, Bermuda is able to secure this market through a well-established *British* system of financial and legal regulation. Not only does Bermuda's offshore banking industry have an untarnished reputation, but it also benefits many British companies which take advantage of Bermuda's minimal taxation, highly dedicated and educated workforce, and sophisticated telecommunications network.[78] In the end, Ritchie discovers that the myths of the British Empire do not exist in Bermuda, and in fact 'Britain was reluctantly pitied in wealthy, sunny Bermuda'.[79] Ritchie is forced to concede that

[77] Ritchie, *The Last Pink Bits*, p. 15.
[78] Ritchie, *The Last Pink Bits*, pp. 43–4.
[79] Ritchie, *The Last Pink Bits*, p. 5.

Bermuda is nothing like the refuge for public school, colonial racists he had predicted, but rather, a charming country with a 'strangely urbane, semi-tropical tranquillity'.

In Gibraltar, Ritchie continues to equate the social and political issues at work in 'the last pink bits' with similar difficulties in Britain. Rather than confront a group of nostalgic ex-pats who are 'more British than the British', Ritchie discovers something altogether different:

> Gibraltar has had a markedly cosmopolitan population ever since the Spanish inhabitants were replaced by an eclectic mix of British soldiers, chancers from different parts of Spain, merchants and sailors from Portugal, Malta and Genoa, Jews and Moors . . . locals now enjoy citing such phenomena as the town's kosher restaurant employing a Muslim head waiter.[80]

But Ritchie is not convinced that Gibraltar is a harmonious cosmopolitan place, and soon uncovers an 'ethnic pecking order': the bottom rung is occupied by Moroccan guest workers who are refused citizenship, live in poor housing, and face deportation if they lose their jobs; the middle tier is occupied by 'Spanish speaking colonial types'; and the elite position, of course, is occupied by the 'pale faced' English speakers who 'tend to think of themselves as a cut above the rest'.[81] For Ritchie, this racial hierarchy does not condemn Gibraltar to a position at the back end of the historical queue; rather, it is a more explicit version of the institutional and structural racism at work in most modern European cities (e.g. London, Berlin, Paris). Gibraltar's complex temporality – as both colonial outpost and modern city – is entrenched in its economic activities. While Gibraltar might operate within a sophisticated European financial industry, its local economic transactions are governed by a 'frontier' mentality. Unlike Bermuda's well-regulated industry, Gibraltar's offshore banking has a decidedly 'unsavoury reputation' due in part to its expertise in money laundering. So while it may claim membership in a modern financial industry, its local operations are much more parochial, often illegal, and certainly dodgy. In addition, Gibraltar's image as 'begrimed by crime' comes from a well-established smuggling industry. As Ritchie argues, 'Let's be realistic – this is a frontier town and a port and so temptingly situated, what with Morocco just across the water and lots of secluded coastline spots next door to Spain . . . I think it can reasonably be said that more than a few Gibraltarian families can boast a long and happy tradition of criminal activity.'[82] Indeed, Ritchie explains that Gibraltar continues to transfer contraband goods between Britain, Gibraltar,

[80] Ritchie, *The Last Pink Bits*, p. 141.
[81] Ritchie, *The Last Pink Bits*, p. 141.
[82] Ritchie, *The Last Pink Bits*, p. 150.

Spain and Morocco, including 100 million packets of cigarettes across the perimeter fence and into Spain, and at least 500 tonnes of hashish transported via super-fast speedboats from Morocco to the Costa del Sol.[83] Again, Ritchie confronts a mixture of temporal conditions here: an 'ancient' activity (smuggling) aided by 'modern' technology (speed-boats). Moreover, the security, tradition and sophistication Gibraltar accrues from being a British colony has always existed alongside a less-than-savoury reputation as a frontier state where the usual rules do not apply. In effect, Gibraltar is *out of time*: it is modern and backward, sophisticated and ancient. Given that Gibraltarians consistently vote to remain a part of Britain, its contradictory temporal status as both an 'upstanding' colony and a 'frontier' town must be beneficial. What Ritchie concludes is that Gibraltarians are not 'backward' ex-pats waxing nostalgic about Britain − they have simply made a pragmatic decision to secure the continuation of their double life.

The curious juxtaposition of Gibraltar's modern and pre-modern temporality exemplifies Ritchie's disruption of the historical queue. As such, none of his destinations are wholly attached to their status as colonial outposts lagging behind the 'motherland' and waxing nostalgic about Britain's global dominance. Ritchie is more interested in revealing their *contemporary* political significance by asking about the everyday struggles that occupy these British citizens. Thus, for example, the Falkland Islands are occupied with their own social and political issues: their plans to upgrade the main road from the airport; their uncertainty over the discovery of offshore oilfields; their concerns over rising crime rates; their efforts to jump-start an indigenous wool industry; and their investments in a newly built state-of-the-art school. Despite his assumption that the Falkland Islands are desolate, Ritchie has an enjoyable time hiking, drinking with the locals, looking at the stars, visiting the smaller islands and taking an aeroplane tour. He discovers that the Falkland Islanders' desire to remain British is not born out of nostalgia, but rather, out of the legacy of the 1982 conflict. In effect, the war frames Ritchie's visit − initially he avoids mentioning it, but gradually he reveals his anti-Thatcher position, provides a potted history of the war's key events and starts talking to locals about their experiences. What he discovers is not the simple patriotic devotion that Thatcher encouraged and relied upon in the early 1980s, but rather, a complex formation of memory, grieving and obligation. As Ritchie listens to the Islanders' stories, he becomes even more convinced that the war must be re-imagined outside of any nostalgia for Britain's

---

[83]   Ritchie, *The Last Pink Bits*, p. 149.

military greatness. For Ritchie, the Falklands War – like the British Empire – is a shameful incident in the nation's past that must be revealed as such, and not glossed over as a patriotic example of British 'courage, resolve, self-sacrifice, a sense of duty, of decency, of fair play'.[84] He soon realises that the war is still present in the minds of both locals and soldiers, and that these memories are painful rather than wistful or nostalgic. This becomes clear when the Falklands' newspaper editor barely manages to hold it together while explaining how he witnessed the death of three civilians who were killed by misguided British bombs. Another woman reluctantly and awkwardly tells how she risked her life to save a British soldier who was drowning after the Argentinians shot down his helicopter. For Ritchie, these traumatic stories suggest a profound contradiction in how the locals are dealing with the legacy of the war. On the one hand, the Falkland Islanders still feel a terrible debt and obligation to the 255 British soldiers who died on their behalf. On the other hand, they also remember the scared and ill-equipped young Argentinian soldiers who occupied Port Stanley during the conflict. Ritchie is told by several people that 'compassion had driven them to smuggle food to such starving, barely teenage boys'.[85] These war stories are not shaped by the easy work of nostalgia – they do not hearken back to a Golden Age, glorify 'Pax Britannica' or reproduce the patriotic fervour of British military greatness. Rather, these memories reveal a tightly knit community still traumatised by their role in a global conflict that was fought over abstract notions of sovereignty, security and colonialism.

As the survivors of the Falklands War illustrate, memory seldom maps nicely onto a past–present–future structure and is more appropriately understood through cycles, repetitions and interruptions. Indeed, as many of the Falkland Islands veterans have experienced, the trauma of war refuses to be locked into the past and continues to erupt and repeat itself in the present tense.[86] A more recent travelogue that pursues the disruptive quality of memory is Jenny Diski's *Stranger on a Train: Daydreaming and Smoking around America with Interruptions*.[87] While

---

[84] Ritchie, *The Last Pink Bits*, p. 6.
[85] Ritchie, *The Last Pink Bits*, p. 92.
[86] For a political account of post-traumatic stress disorder (PTSD) see Patrick J. Bracken and Celia Petty, eds., *Rethinking the Trauma of War* (London: Free Association Books, 1998); for a more general account of trauma and memory in the political sphere, see Jenny Edkins, *Trauma and the Memory of Politics* (Cambridge: Cambridge University Press, 2003); for a soldier's account of his own experiences of PTSD in the Falklands, see Tony McNally, *Cloudpuncher* (Liverpool: Pharaoh Press, no date).
[87] Jenny Diski, *Stranger on a Train: Daydreaming and Smoking around America with Interruptions* (London: Virago, 2002).

Diski's narrative covers a range of provocative issues, it is her complex arrangement of temporality that is most challenging to the reader. *Stranger on a Train* recounts two rail journeys that Diski made around the perimeter of America trying to make sense of her competing desires for solitude and social interaction. For Diski, this balance is found in the strangeness of being an Englishwoman in America: 'Strangerhood seems to be what I need in order to see people clearly and be touched by them.'[88] But Diski does not explain her condition of estrangement by recourse to nostalgia – she focuses instead on how her identity is shaped by the complex temporality of memory rather than the linear timeline of experience. Diski's subjectivity as a stranger is *temporalised* through a variety of strategies that slow down, speed up, elongate, interrupt and repeat the passage of time. In many ways, her need to disrupt linear time is a deliberate resistance to the efficiency of modern travel and the desire to get from point A to point B in the shortest amount of time. This resistance is made clear in her decision to travel in a circle around the perimeter of America. Not only does this upset the idea of a straight line from beginning to end, it allows Diski to recall her past as a depressed teenager in London when she used to skip school and ride the Circle line all day long. Indeed, it is this circular understanding of time and travel that holds Diski's narrative together. She makes a passionate case – via Bertrand Russell – that the cyclical nature of history is more gratifying than the 'whistling vacancy' of straight lines and neat endings. But it is her mode of travel, as well as the structure of her journey, that reinforces her disjointed sense of time. By choosing the unpredictability, erratic timing and comparative slowness of long-distance trains (instead of the efficiency and regularity of aeroplanes), Diski already marks herself out as falling behind mainstream experiences of travel. Furthermore, since American passenger trains are less profitable and thus a lower priority than freight trains, Amtrak does not stick to its schedules and timetables. This gives Diski and her fellow passengers the feeling of always lagging behind where they should be; indeed, Diski hears many horror stories of trains arriving hours and even days later than expected. As she explains, once you decide to travel by train, 'you have given yourself up to Amtrak time, which has a delightfully eccentric relation to US time'.[89] This is just as well for Diski, as she has no particular destination or timetable in

---

[88]   Diski, *Stranger on a Train*, p. 67.
[89]   Diski, *Stranger on a Train*, p. 71. She goes on to say 'The accomplished long-distance train traveller understands the futility of holding on to a time outside their temporary universe. In transit it doesn't matter' (p. 73).

mind and is happy to allow the disjointed and unhurried nature of train travel to shape her simultaneous commentary on memory.

One of the most compelling aspects of the book is Diski's representation of the relationship between subjectivity, time and memory. The passage that sets the tone for the book is Diski recalling a time when she was nine years old and having great difficulties imagining herself at fifty. As Diski is fifty when she is writing the book, this memory is especially jarring, for she remembers exactly how she dealt with this difficulty:

I send a message out into the future, etching into my brain cells a memo to the other person, who will be me grown to be fifty, to remember this moment, this very moment, this actual second when I am nine, in bed, in the dark in my room, trying to imagine being fifty... There is a sense of vertigo, something quite dizzying about having arrived at the unimaginable point she reached out towards, at recalling her message and being in a position – but not able – to answer her question: here I am, it's like this.[90]

Diski does not produce a sense of nostalgia for her childhood, but rather a sense of herself as two completely different people. She doesn't want to be nine again, and, despite living in a culture that privileges youth and beauty, she is quite happy being fifty. This exemplifies Diski's ability to recall her past and weave it into a present-tense narrative without any sense of nostalgic longing. In other words, she does not try to alleviate the anxieties of the present by retreating into an imaginary past. Perhaps this is not surprising, considering that her childhood was spent in a repressed household, in foster homes or in psychiatric care. But throughout the journey, Diski uses the complexities of memory to examine the anxieties of the present and illustrate how lives are not easily contained within progressive and linear accounts of history. This approach began, for Diski, in the psychiatric unit of a London hospital where she became attached to a man with no memory: 'I felt as unconnected with my life, as unhinged from my past, as he was with his. We were outlaws together. Uncluttered and new'.[91] Because memory guarantees the self by providing a coherent back-story, the opportunity to vanquish all memory was like starting fresh – like becoming a new person. However, her subsequent battle with depression made her realise that she could not rid herself of her memories if she hoped to stay alive, nor could she ignore unpleasant or difficult memories when they emerged. At one point, Diski describes apologising to an old childhood friend whom she had once bitten on the cheek in a fit of rage. There is

[90] Diski, *Stranger on a Train*, pp. 41–2.
[91] Diski, *Stranger on a Train*, p. 51.

a sense of ambivalence in Diski's description, for not only does the friend remember their past very differently (which casts doubt on Diski's own memory), but Diski is not sure how valid her apology is, forty-five years later. What comes out of descriptions such as this is Diski's understanding that memory functions with a complex temporality: it does not obey regulations, it does not stay contained until a more appropriate moment, it changes over time, it differs from other interpretations and it absolutely will not be repressed or handcuffed to a linear trajectory. Memory is *inherently* disruptive of both time and subjectivity, and Diski's life and her writing are sustained efforts to engage with those disruptions.

During her train journeys, time and memory go through various permutations. The most common is the slowing down of time whenever Diski smokes: 'Cigarettes and my desire to smoke them formed the humming rails of my train of thought as I travelled.'[92] Her journey takes on a different quality in the smoking car: the time of the outside world is superseded by the slow, languid and relaxing time it takes to light, smoke and extinguish a cigarette. And it is during these times that Diski's memories are most often triggered by a seemingly random comment, personality, story or image. The slow time of her smoking sits in juxtaposition with the speeding landscape outside of her window. Either in her sleeping car or in the observation car, Diski often wishes the train would go slower to allow her to take in this foreign landscape. Nonetheless, she realises that everything witnessed from her train window is fodder for her ever-expanding collection of memories:

Our thought processes work more slowly than the speed of the train or the eye. There's as much relief as frustration in that...The eyes look and take in the fleeting images, absorb them into the processor inside the head which transforms them into a memory: the recollection of a split second gone by which will become a memory of something seen yesterday, a week ago, a decade past, somewhere back in the mists of time. The flashing pictures remain, but they settle in beside other related images.[93]

Diski is mesmerised by these speeding glimpses of America not only because they become new memories, but also because they provoke memories long forgotten. She is perplexed at how something so fast sutures itself into the more permanent process of building a self. However, unlike Theroux, Diski is aware that what she sees outside her window is *already mediated*. She has encountered these landscapes thousands of times before on the cinema screen, and she admits to

[92] Diski, *Stranger on a Train*, p. 46.
[93] Diski, *Stranger on a Train*, p. 98.

certain confusions: was that image from a train window or from a movie? No matter how spectacular the scenery she witnesses, she is under no illusion that it is anything original. This same sentiment shapes her understanding of the depressing stories told by her fellow passengers. No matter how heart-rending, she knows that all of their narratives conform to certain generic principles: 'It was as if each story illustrated the old cliché that there are no more than ten set pieces about how lives are lived. What discouraged me was the similarity of the stories, the repetition of the basic forms.'[94] If the landscape she sees is mediated through the cinema, and the stories she hears are mediated through literary tropes, Diski realises that these images and stories are *infinitely repeatable*. In this respect, Diski's story is quite Derridean: 'what interests me is repetition, intensification, moreness'.[95]

By insisting on the unruliness of memory, and the infinitely repeatable nature of images and narratives, Diski goes some way to puncturing the linear nature of the beginning-middle-end/home-away-home structure of travel writing. This disruption is enabled by Diski's knowledge that *things could be otherwise*. In fact, she actually lives several lives in the midst of her narrative by entertaining a number of different possibilities with the other passengers on the train. Her alternative imaginings are spurred on by a sense of guilt at not being as adventurous as other travel writers. She knows she should be more spontaneous but can't face the difficulties that spontaneity offers: 'There was still that lurking sense of how one ought to be a travel writer, free to make detours, when detours were the last thing I wanted.'[96] Thus, she imagines alternative possibilities – and alternative selves – that do not disrupt her balance of solitude, sociability and strangeness. These flights of imagination first began for Diski in her relationship with the memoryless man in the psychiatric ward: 'We talked a lot, he wondered who he might be, and we imagined a variety of lives for him. It was a game in which he would accept or reject my suggestions according to whether he fancied the idea or not.'[97] This tendency to conjure up alternative lives – to continually hold open the possibility that life could be otherwise – is a crucial part of Diski's writing. Given that she is a woman travelling on her own, these moments for pondering another life are most often presented by men. For example, she enjoys the entertaining stories of a 'shameless new-world/old-world flirt' called Big Daddy, who, after teaching her the dance routine from *The Sound of Music*, asks her to spend a few days

[94] Diski, *Stranger on a Train*, p. 146.
[95] Diski, *Stranger on a Train*, p. 153.
[96] Diski, *Stranger on a Train*, p. 158.
[97] Diski, *Stranger on a Train*, pp. 49–50.

with him in Montana. While contemplating this option, she comments, 'I was quite tempted by the spontaneity and irregularity of the idea — until I remembered how many hours there are in even a single day let alone two, and how easily charm turns sour.'[98] She declines the offer 'with something like genuine regret' and retreats into her memories of the sixties when everyone was into 'grabbing experience' in the most spontaneous of ways. However, when she meets the middle-aged widower Eugene, she permits herself an even more full-fledged future living in Rochester and enjoying a 'civilized and mature relationship'. Reflecting on this possible future, she comments:

> Once again an unlooked-for change of direction in my life beckoned; sort of picked me up and played with me the game of unconsidered possibilities ... I slipped into the possibility of a new existence as, in the changing room of a frock shop, I would try on a dress of the kind I would never wear, just to see who I would be if I wore such a thing.[99]

Diski's ability to imagine things otherwise is more awkward when she promises an alcoholic called Raymond that she will visit him in LA if he ever sobers up. The difficulty here is that Raymond takes her in two simultaneous directions: one, imagining a future possible life with him on North Beach, and two, re-imagining her own experiences with alcohol, drugs and trying to maintain relationships with addicts. As Raymond laments why he hadn't met her sooner so she could have prevented his slide into alcoholism, Diski is angered: 'I didn't like his appropriation of my alternative past. That story was mine to play with.'[100] Indeed, Diski's ability to 'play' with her own story while leaving it open to different possibilities and interpretations is what makes her narrative so compelling. While not as critical of nostalgia as *The Last Pink Bits*, Diski's travelogue is instructive in that it uses memory to puncture the easy trajectory of utopia, authenticity and lament. In this sense, both Ritchie and Diski go some way to deconstructing the teleological understanding of history embedded in travel writing. However, the complex understandings of time, memory and history in their books are not matched with a similarly complex narrative structure, Indeed, these are quite conventional beginning-middle-end/home-away-home accounts. Given the critical understanding of genre at work in this book, what kind of travelogue could simultaneously disrupt linear temporality *and* formal generic boundaries?

[98] Diski, *Stranger on a Train*, p. 196.
[99] Diski, *Stranger on a Train*, p. 228–9.
[100] Diski, *Stranger on a Train*, p. 120.

In an Antique Land: double histories, co-presence and 'discrepant cosmopolitanism'

Amitav Ghosh's *In an Antique Land* combines travel writing, anthropology and history to tell a series of complex narratives about travel, trade and cultural encounter.[101] The reflexive and complex understanding of time that underscores Ghosh's text suggests that it is possible to creatively translate the issues of history, narrative and deconstruction raised by Foucault, White and Derrida. Because Ghosh tells a story of the present simultaneously with a story of the past, he is able to foreground the difficulties and ambiguities of providing an accurate account of history. *In an Antique Land* is told from the point of view of the author, an Oxford-trained anthropologist, who recounts his recent fieldwork in Egypt. Alongside this contemporary narrative, Ghosh presents another story about a Jewish merchant called Ben Yijû and his slave Bomma who participated in the Indian Ocean trading economy during the twelfth century. While travel is a constant theme in Ghosh's story, these two narratives are shaped by more direct and critical encounters with academic literatures. The contemporary story of Ghosh in rural Egypt picks up on the recent critical turn in anthropology and addresses the complicated issue of how one can pursue ethnographic research without necessarily imposing an imperial framework. However, in the historical narrative of Ben Yijû and Bomma, Ghosh turns his anthropological gaze 'back' in time and comments on the highly speculative, incomplete and interpretative nature of all historical accounts. Of course, there are many other stories woven into Ghosh's book, but this 'double history' challenges the conventional reproduction of an evolutionary historical queue embedded in most travelogues, and immediately distorts and resists any simple past–present–future timeline (especially as the chapters flip-flop between the two eras).

In setting these two stories beside one another, Ghosh is trying to resist hegemonic understandings of the world divided into discrete cultural, religious, ethnic and national groups. Rather, Ghosh is more interested in revealing the religious networks that connect Judaism, Islam, Christianity and Hinduism, and also the national and ethnic networks that connect urban and rural Egypt, India, Europe, America and the Middle East. While doing his fieldwork in rural Egypt, it is difficult for Ghosh to maintain his focus on these networks because he is constantly hassled by Muslim villagers who are simultaneously horrified, awed and disgusted that in India people 'worship cows' and 'burn

[101] Amitav Ghosh, *In an Antique Land* (London: Granta Books, 1992).

their dead'. Once this 'blasphemous' news gets around the village, Ghosh is repeatedly pestered by people asking him questions about Hindu rituals, culture and religion. While these are not violent encounters, Ghosh contrasts the homogeneous categories of cultural difference (e.g. that Muslims and Hindus are separate and different) with the complex cultural, national and religious networks that flourish in the twelfth-century trading economy. Ghosh uses the livelihood of the Indian Ocean merchants to argue that numerous co-operative and prosperous trading networks *have always* characterised this part of the world. For example, in his descriptions of the Malabar coast, Ghosh describes the cosmopolitan city of Mangalore where the diverse community of foreign merchants (approximately 4,000 of them) routinely welcomed ships from China, Sumatra, Yemen and Iran.[102] In this way, Ghosh re-imagines the historical period of the Middle Ages as being *more* civilised than the current reifications of cultural difference that characterise much of the Middle East. By repositioning cosmopolitan civilisation in the twelfth century, Ghosh is able to resist the idea that history necessarily moves in a linear, progressive direction. Indeed, the situation of peace, co-operation and tolerance that existed in the Indian Ocean so many centuries ago is actually *more desirable* than the divided cultural, ethnic and religious communities that currently populate the Middle East. What's more, by focusing on the *global* character of this ancient trading network Ghosh also refutes the idea that globalisation has only recently occurred in the twentieth century.

What makes Ghosh's re-imagination of temporality significant is that it reveals how history is usually told within the temporal cage of teleology. In choosing to trace the story of Bomma the slave (only known as MS H.6 until the mystery of his name is unravelled), Ghosh works against the traditional assumption of *who* counts in a historical narrative. But he also comments on *what* counts: Ghosh is explicit about how his story is cobbled together from scraps and fragments of information rather than from any coherent and complete historical record. After he comes across the first reference to the slave, Ghosh explains his re-imagination of the *who*, *what* and *how* of historical representation:

the reference comes to us from a moment when the only people for whom we can even begin to imagine properly human, individual, existences are the literate and the consequential, the wazirs and the sultans, the chroniclers and the priests − the people who had the power to inscribe themselves physically upon time. But the slave of Khalaf's letter was not of that company: in his instance

---

[102] Ghosh, *In an Antique Land*, pp. 242−4.

it was a mere accident that those barely discernible traces that ordinary people leave upon the world happen to have been preserved. It is nothing less than a miracle that anything is known about him at all.[103]

While uncovering the people that history 'forgets' is an increasingly common narrative device in fiction, it is not considered a 'proper' method of historical accounting in non-fiction work. And this is the important point for Ghosh. By painstakingly tracing the story of the slave Bomma through his master Ben Yijû's correspondence, Ghosh introduces the reader to the insufficiencies of archival historical documentation and the gaps in the supposedly complete historical record. These observations are symbolised in Ghosh's depiction of the Geniza archive where the story of Bomma is first discovered. The Geniza was a repository library for the Jewish community in ancient Egypt, and was attached to the main synagogue at the edges of Cairo. Any document that referred to God was placed in the Geniza for safe-keeping – including such things as marriage deeds, poetry, insurance documents and letters of trade. This massive archive was undiscovered for many centuries until the British occupation of Egypt in the nineteenth century. As archaeologists, historians and entrepreneurs discovered the potential worth of the Geniza documents, they were haphazardly distributed and sold around the world to universities, museums and private collections. It is in one of these fragmentary collections, in a library in Oxford, that Ghosh first comes across a reference to the slave.

The position of the Geniza in Ghosh's tale is crucial. Alongside the particular example of how Bomma's life is pieced together by scraps and fragments, Ghosh is able to comment on how all history, even when gathered together in an archive, only ever consists of scraps of information, missing documents and damaged or incomplete items. While Ghosh's real interest is unearthing Bomma's story, his efforts to trace the Geniza documents illustrate a much wider point about the incompleteness of the historical record. And this is why Ghosh is so explicit about the speculative nature of his story: his reliance on words like 'possibly', 'maybe', 'could be' and 'perhaps' are hardly the active grammar of solid historical accounting that tells us 'what really happened'. This tension between speculation and documentation is best symbolised in his representation of the master and the slave. Because Bomma is only ever mentioned in the letters of his master Ben Yijû, the brief snapshots of the slave are often eclipsed by a *better-documented* tale of the life of a wealthy merchant. But even that story is

---

[103] Ghosh, *In an Antique Land*, pp. 16–17.

constrained – the documentation of Ben Yijû's life is already restricted to letters about trade with only brief scribbles about his personal life. This tension between the official and the personal is another important aspect of Ghosh's story, for he is constantly trying to fill in the former with speculations about the latter. For example, in tracing Ben Yijû's almost twenty-year residence in Mangalore, Ghosh cannot uncover the overriding reason why the merchant married a woman both outside his religion and outside his class. As all cultural norms at the time went against this decision, Ghosh is unsure of how to interpret Ben Yijû's decision: 'If I hesitate to call it love it is only because the documents offer no certain proof.'[104] In this respect, Ghosh does not shy away from the absences, hiccups and inconsistencies in the historical record. He does not hide the fact that his representations of Bomma and Ben Yijû are full of his own imagination. But in refusing to pursue celebrated and popular subjects for historical documentation (e.g. heads of state or great warriors), Ghosh is released from the stranglehold of 'fact' and allowed to 'fill in' those absent spaces between the scraps of information he has acquired. In this way, Ghosh favours the creative role of the travel writer over the restricted role of the historian.

Ghosh's focus on the personal nature of historical narrative extends from his representations of twelfth-century merchant trading to his more contemporary stories of rural Egypt. Although the official reason he goes to the villages of Lataîfa and Nashâwy is to do anthropological fieldwork, the reader is never treated to long descriptions of the indigenous social arrangements and cultural rituals that usually characterise anthropological texts. Instead, Ghosh provides a collection of character sketches that cannot be maintained within the simple identity categories of self and other that form the bedrock of traditional anthropology. Ghosh's refusal to represent the people he encounters as ignorant, backward or primitive is accompanied by a careful self-analysis – he doesn't exempt his own position from personal, cultural and ethical interrogation. Rather than observe others from a safe distance, Ghosh makes friends with those who are supposed to be his subjects – the elder Shaikh Musa in Lataîfa, Zaghloul the weaver, Ustaz Sabry the teacher in Nashâwy, and Khamees the Rat. In doing so, he places the categories of self and other in the same temporality and introduces a *co-presence* of subjectivity. Whether he meets peasants, religious leaders, shop owners or respected elders, Ghosh describes them all as complex and rich characters in their own right – these people are very aware of their position in an unequal world and aware of how various forms of power shape their daily lives

---

[104] Ghosh, *In an Antique Land*, p. 230.

(e.g. Western media, governmental bureaucracy, military agendas and urbanisation). Very simply, all the people in the text – even those in the twelfth century – are represented with fullconsciousness and with an awareness of their own historical circumstances. This is not to say that Ghosh's text is overtly romantic about those he meets; indeed, there are *both* reflexive and narrow-minded people in contemporary Egypt as well as in twelfth-century trading circles.

By refusing to locate others 'back' in the queue of history as primitive, innocent and uncivilised, Ghosh disrupts the omniscient power and presence of the authorial vantage point. *In an Antique Land* disorganises the queue of history by representing others with as much sophistication as the writer – a shift that takes away the privileged position of the author at the front of the historical queue. What is striking about *In an Antique Land* is the author's self-reflexive commentary about his own ambiguous position in Egypt. Ghosh is well aware of the damage that anthropology does when it locates its subjects back in time, and consequently understands his own authorial vantage point as complex, ambiguous and contingent. Ghosh is painfully shy, often awkward, sometimes temperamental and at times inadvertently offensive to members of the Muslim community (moments that cause him great shame). Although the reader gets little information about Ghosh's personal life outside of research and writing, his encounters with the villagers in Egypt reveal more than enough about his own character. He is patient, curious, easily embarrassed, solitary, thoughtful, bewildered and playful – hardly the characteristics of a hard-nosed anthropologist, rigorous historian or intrepid travel writer. Moreover, as a citizen of Bangladesh, a scholar of Oxford and a visitor to Egypt, Ghosh's identity disrupts the conventional subject positions of travel writing: he is both author and other. In this way, Ghosh's own subject position symbolises the complex temporality of the book: he comes from one 'primitive' country (Bangladesh), travels to a 'civilised' country for education (England), and then moves on to another 'primitive' place for research (Egypt). Which time, then, does Ghosh belong to? Is he a 'primitive' colonial subject, or has he moved up the historical queue to a more 'modern' and evolved position?

Ghosh's own ambiguous position makes *In an Antique Land* especially attuned to the power relations of Empire sequestered in the teleological understanding of history and the automatic location of places like India, Pakistan and Egypt at the back end of the historical queue. During a particularly upsetting argument with the Imam of Nashâwy (who is outraged by the barbarity of Hindu customs), Ghosh is forced to prove that India, Pakistan and Bangladesh are modern – that they possess both science and the technology of modern warfare. In order to establish its more advanced position on the 'ascending ladder of Development', Ghosh cites examples of India's nuclear capability and military might – its most obvious signs of Westernisation. The problem here is that instead of finding common ground with the Imam (e.g. through the experience of colonial oppression), Ghosh resorts to a teleological understanding of history to prove his point that India is *more* advanced and Westernised than Egypt. Ashamed at his lack of solidarity with the Imam, Ghosh has a poignant revelation:

At that moment, despite the vast gap that lay between us, we understood each other perfectly. We were both travelling, he and I: we were travelling in the West ... in the end, for millions and millions of people on the landmasses around us, the West meant only this – science and tanks and guns and bombs. I was crushed, as I walked away; it seemed to me that the Imam and I had participated in our own final defeat, in the dissolution of the centuries of dialogue that had linked us: we had demonstrated the irreversible triumph of the language that has usurped all the others in which people once discussed their differences.[105]

Despite his careful rendering of both modern Egypt and twelfth-century merchant life as both cosmopolitan and modern, even Ghosh is seduced by the idea that the West occupies the most advanced position in the historical queue. In this moment of realisation, Ghosh expresses an *ambivalent* relationship with the West that is central to his narrative: he participates in its hegemonic culture (e.g. by leaving his home in Bangladesh to inhabit Western centres of knowledge) while also resisting it (e.g. by looking for common ground between his own colonised heritage and the Egyptian experience). This ambivalence allows Ghosh to critique the conventions of anthropology, history and travel writing and invert the evolutionary historical queue.[106] It allows him to argue that modern Egypt is *co-present* with twelfth-century trading routes, and that both of these destinations are *co-present* with the West. In other words, Ghosh is able to argue that history does not involve an orderly march along an evolutionary queue; rather, it involves a complex temporality in which 'backward' sites exist in the same time and space as 'modern' sites.

[105] Ghosh, *In an Antique Land*, p. 236.
[106] James Clifford explains how important the position of ambivalence is for critical anthropologists: 'Their cultural comparisons need not presuppose a Western/university home, a "central" site of theoretical accumulation. And while their research encounters may involve hierarchical relations, they need not presuppose "white" privilege. Their work may or may not crucially depend on colonial and neocolonial circuits of information, access and power' (*Routes: Travel and Translation in the Late Twentieth Century* (Cambridge and London: Harvard University Press, 1997), p. 79).

While Ghosh's narrative offers a powerful antidote to stereotypical visions of the Middle East and Asia, he is not immune from the seductions of nostalgia. Unlike Theroux and Bell who pursue romantic visions of Empire that reify a linear timeline, Ghosh is nostalgic for something altogether different – for the 'discrepant cosmopolitanism' expressed by twelfth-century Indian Ocean trading routes and contemporary rural Egypt.[107] In effect, Ghosh's nostalgia for these cosmopolitan communities is driven by his disappointment and outrage at the well-known historical events that supplanted them – the European invasion of Asia in the Middle Ages and the onset of Desert Storm in 1991. In this way, Ghosh draws important parallels across the centuries: just as the colonisers were completely antagonistic towards the cosmopolitan norms of bargaining, compromise and understanding that characterised the twelfth-century merchant trading networks, the multilateral forces gathering on the eve of Desert Storm were antagonistic to those transnational groups that disrupted the robust borders and distinct national communities required by the reinstatement of Kuwaiti sovereignty (e.g. Kurdish refugees, migrant workers from Egypt). For Ghosh, both the twelfth-century trading culture and contemporary rural Egypt were 'devoured by that unquenchable, demonic thirst that has raged...for almost five hundred years, over the Indian Ocean, the Arabian Sea and the Persian Gulf'.[108] While Ghosh might express nostalgia for these remarkable communities, he is also interested in showing how this 'unquenchable thirst' of Western power rests upon a teleological, progressive and evolutionary understanding of history that has no room for the personal tales of slaves like Bomma or any of the characters he illustrates with such depth. Ghosh is keen to show how the European invasion of the Middle Ages and the implementation of Desert Storm's 'New World Order' silence those individual stories that contradict the onward march of 'official' history. This is illustrated clearly at the end of the book when they are scanning the television set for traces of their friend Nabeel (a migrant worker in the Gulf) who failed to escape before Desert Storm began. Like the slave Bomma's burial under the sediment of historical documentation, Ghosh concludes that 'Nabeel had vanished into the anonymity of history.'[109]

---

[107] The term 'discrepant cosmopolitanism' is James Clifford's description of the critical anthropology embedded in Ghosh's work: 'His "ancient and settled" fieldsite opens on to complex histories of dwelling and travelling, discrepant cosmopolitanisms' ('The Transit Lounge of Culture', *Times Literary Supplement*, No. 4596, 3 May 1991 p. 8).
[108] Ghosh, *In an Antique Land*, p. 288.
[109] Ghosh, *In an Antique Land*, p. 353.

Does Ghosh's decision to romanticise the heterogeneity of cosmopolitanism rather than the homogeneity of Empire suggest an alternative construction of history? For critics like Viswanathan, Ghosh's 'alternative' nostalgia is problematic because it prevents him from offering concrete political solutions:

Ghosh's syncretism denies the historical reality of religious difference. That is why no matter how moving Ghosh's book might be, and no matter how appealing his humanist call for dissolving barriers between nations, peoples, and communities on the grounds that world civilizations were syncretic long before the divisions introduced by the territorial boundaries of nation-states, the work cannot get beyond nostalgia to offer ways of dealing with what is, after all, an intractable political problem.[110]

While there is certainly a nostalgic tone to the text, I disagree with Viswanathan's argument that it constrains Ghosh's ability to confront the 'intractable political problem' of religious difference. Ghosh is nostalgic for 'discrepant cosmopolitanism' *precisely because* it offers an alternative to the religious, ethnic and cultural conflicts that currently characterise the Middle East. For Ghosh, these 'intractable' political problems must be resisted by the heterogeneous and complex identities that have always existed – and continue to exist – in the region. Ghosh's narrative is not a naïve 'call for dissolving barriers'; rather, it is an illustration of how 'official' history reinforces reified forms of political identity and community at the expense of heterogeneous and contingent ones. To the extent that *In an Antique Land* offers an alternative history that has been dug out of official accounts, it also offers an alternative form of nostalgia – one that hearkens back to a past of difference and heterogeneity rather than certainty and singularity. Very simply, Ghosh's narrative suggests that things have *always been otherwise* than official history tells us. For James Clifford, the careful and critical historical research undertaken by Ghosh suggests that things can be otherwise in the future as well:

Ghosh's account helps us remember/imagine 'world systems', economic and cultural, that preceded the rise of an expansionist Europe. In the late twentieth century it is difficult to form concrete pictures of transregional networks not produced by and/or resisting the hegemony of Western techno-industrial society. These histories of alternate cosmopolitanisms and diasporic networks are redeemable (in a Benjaminian sense) as crucial political visions: worlds 'after' Jews and Arabs, 'after' the West and the 'Rest', and 'after' natives and immigrants.[111]

[110] Guari Viswanathan, 'Beyond Orientalism: Syncretism and the Politics of Knowledge', *Stanford Electronic Humanities Review*, Vol. 5, No. 1, 1996, pp. 9–10.
[111] Clifford, *Routes*, p. 276.

In an Antique Land does not offer easy renditions of 'before' and 'after', which is to say that it does not tell a story of primitive societies coming out of the darkness and into the light. However, it does create the possibility of imagining history differently: by arguing that the past is wholly at odds with stereotypical understandings of the world, Ghosh is also suggesting that the future might also be imagined otherwise.

Alternative histories: the work of remaining present

This chapter has traced the work of nostalgia in contemporary travel writing, and illustrated its ability to govern the previous discourses of genre, subjectivity and space. I am not concerned that travel writers resuscitate the past and project the future, for this imaginary work is central to the fictional ambitions of the genre. But as the analysis of Ritchie, Diski and Ghosh makes clear, contemporary travel writing is at its best when it acknowledges the constraints of traditional history telling, and takes seriously the difficulties of thinking critically about the linear march of time. What makes these three authors significant is their ability to maintain a focus on the anxieties of the present while remaining conscious of how those anxieties shape their accounts of the past and projections of the future. Moreover, by providing alternative accounts of time, these authors automatically disrupt the traditional boundaries of travel writing (can these even be considered travelogues?), the sanctified position of the travel writer (who is being observed here?) and the exotic register of the traveller's destination (isn't this just like home?).

6 Engaging the political: contemporary travel writing and the ethics of difference

> *The Global Soul may see so many sides of every question that he never settles on a firm conviction; he may grow so used to giving back a different self according to his environment that he loses sight of who he is when nobody's around. Even the most basic questions have to be answered by him alone, and when, on the planes where he may make his home, the cabin attendant passes down the aisle with disembarkation forms, it may be difficult for him to fill in any of the boxes: 'Home Address', 'Citizenship', 'Purpose of Visit', even 'Marital Status'. I can answer almost any of these from a variety of perspectives... But though this can be a natural − and useful − enough impulse in response to the question 'Where do you come from?' it becomes more treacherous in answer to the question 'Where do you stand?'*
>
> Pico Iyer[1]

Iyer's own experience of the relationship between authority and hybridity exemplifies one of the main political tensions of this book: on the one hand, there are sovereign structures of power that require loyalty, homogeneity and single-mindedness (e.g. the apparatus of Customs and Immigration), and on the other hand, there are cosmopolitan forms of identity and community that transcend these exclusionary structures (e.g. global souls, travel writers). For me, those opposing formations are best understood as either *colonial visions* that rely on the resuscitated power relations of Empire, or *cosmopolitan visions* that seek to transcend the legacy of Empire through multiculturalism, tolerance and respect for cultural difference. What distinguishes these two positions − and what constitutes the main focus of my argument − are the contrasting strategies by which they engage with difference. Think of it this way: travel writers must go *somewhere else* and meet *strange people* for their work to be considered 'travel writing' in the first place. The point of this book has been to show how contemporary travel writing reveals a particularly challenging formation

---

[1] Iyer, *The Global Soul*, p. 25.

of the struggle between colonial and cosmopolitan visions: all productions of difference in the genre — even the most cosmopolitan — cannot escape the regulating force of Empire. This deference is relatively easy to detect in a travel writer like Theroux who reifies difference according to a cultural hierarchy governed by Western values (i.e. a colonial vision) but is much more difficult to detect in a travel writer like Iyer who shows how 'Global Souls' eschew their cultural differences in favour of a collective commitment to a multicultural future (i.e. a cosmopolitan vision). My point is that while contemporary travel writing claims to have moved away from the authority of Empire — indeed, many authors 'try to act in keeping with the present age of a greater tolerance' — we are, in fact, witnessing the complex rearticulation of Western authority within the most liberal and cosmopolitan gestures.[2]

I have examined how cultural difference is arranged in contemporary travel writing through particular hegemonic formations: a hierarchy of literary forms, a liberal masculine subjectivity, a modern geographical imagination and an evolutionary historical queue. With the help of Foucault, Derrida and others, I have further examined how those arrangements of difference — even the most exclusionary and violent — are never completely totalising. In this way, the deconstructive approach of this book pursues a double function: it identifies and traces the discursive locations of difference in contemporary travel writing but also shows how difference is contradictory, insecure and ambiguous. Moreover, travelogues are not understood as *examples* of difference that symbolise wider trends and events in global politics — this would suggest that travel writing is an innocent bystander in the reproduction of discursive hegemony. Rather, this book argues that travelogues play an *active* role in the reproduction of discursive hegemony and can therefore be held responsible in some measure for the political consequences of those forces. My primary concern is that too many travel writers remain unaware of how their work contributes to and encourages the prevailing discursive hegemonies at work in global politics. For the most part, this means that travel writing is a profoundly *uncritical* literary formation. It is, to use Lyotard's formulation, a genre that exists 'within the limit' — within the boundaries of possibility that common sense allows.[3] While I have been keen to point out the main discursive boundaries that constrain travel writing, I have also revealed

[2] Santiago Henríquez-Jiménez, *Going the Distance: An Analysis of Modern Travel Writing and Criticism* (Barcelona: Kadle Books, 1995) p. 33.
[3] Jean-François Lyotard, *The Postmodern Condition: A Report on Knowledge*, trans. Geoff Bennington and Brian Massumi (Minneapolis: University of Minnesota Press, 1984), p. 80.

significant moments when travelogues push at these boundaries and write 'at' the limit rather than within it. By subjecting the discursive boundaries of travel writing to various contestations, this book has refused the claim that *all* travel writing reproduces difference in violent and unethical ways. Indeed, what makes these texts so politically interesting are those moments when they break out of their discursive limitations and create new possibilities for understanding encounters with difference. It is precisely because travel writing *requires* this encounter with difference that it reveals so much about the shifting authorities that divide us from them, here from there, and the present from the past. With these shifting productions of difference in mind, I want to conclude with the most difficult questions of all: how can we say that one travelogue is *better* or *worse* than another? How do we judge between competing representations of difference in travel writing? And by what criteria can we make these claims? To be sure, many readers, reviewers and critics argue that a particular travelogue is good because it is well written (i.e. it provides an evocative sense of place, rich characterisation, a developed plot and innovative comparisons with home). While the writing itself certainly matters – indeed it is one of the most obvious limitations of Josie Dew's travelogues – this book has consistently argued that the formal aspects of travel writing cannot be divorced from its content. Politically, then, good or bad writing matters *less* than the manner in which a travelogue produces and engages with cultural difference. The first part of Foucault's genealogical method does allow us to fuse form and content and arbitrate between different texts: a travelogue can be judged for whether it critically or uncritically reproduces prevailing formations of power and knowledge. But the deconstructive ethos of this book requires an engagement with *all* of Foucault's method – which means also revealing the discontinuities, contradictions and ruptures in prevailing discursive formations. As Islam remarks, applying the first part of Foucault's method to travel writing only gets us so far: 'At first I thought what bothered me was the narcissism and the racist paranoia so effortlessly strewn across the pages of the books I was reading. Of course, these things bothered me. But I had a suspicion that they were a part of a larger phenomenon.'[4] Indeed, the larger phenomenon in question here is the problem of discrimination: how can we say that one text is better than another without setting up our own criteria, our own moral boundaries and our own guidelines for exclusion? Doesn't the introduction of any criteria – critical or not – contradict the very purpose of a discursive method

[4] Islam, *The Ethics of Travel*, p. vii.

which deconstructs the 'order of things'? How, then, are we supposed to
evaluate and judge travel writing within a post-structural framework?

Ethico-political interpretation: judging encounters with difference

In posing the question of discrimination through a deconstructive
framework, we are forced to address the most common critique of post-
structuralism – that it sanctions ultimate relativity. Critics have argued
that by deconstructing grand narratives, truth claims and transcendental
criteria, post-structuralism maintains that all claims about the world –
no matter how 'true' or 'false' – are equally valid.[5] This suggests that
post-structuralists cannot arbitrate between competing truth claims
because they have done away with the universal standards of truth that
tell us the way the world *really* is. Let me be clear: I think the accusation
that post-structuralism leads to ultimate relativism is erroneous. As
Simon Critchley argues in *The Ethics of Deconstruction*, post-structuralism has *always* been anchored by ethical and political discriminations –
the problem for critics is that post-structural thought collapses the
distinction between the ethical and the political.[6] In effect, there is no
difference between what 'is' and what 'ought' to be the case – our
'empirical' understandings of the political are not divorced from our
'normative' understandings of the ethical. Helpful here is David
Campbell's argument that post-structural analysis employs an 'ethos
of political criticism' in which scholars and practitioners recognise that it
is impossible to stand outside of the world in order to judge it. For
Campbell, we are always invested in the world both politically and
ethically, and those investments are never neutral or objective. Thus,
Campbell is right to critique those methodological approaches in which

[5] These critiques were most vocal in the early 1990s when post-structural ideas were
being disseminated across the social sciences and humanities; see, for example, Moya
Lloyd and Andrew Thacker, eds., *The Impact of Michel Foucault on the Social Sciences
and Humanities* (London: Palgrave Macmillan, 1997), and Tom Cohen, ed., *Jacques
Derrida and the Humanities: A Critical Reader* (Cambridge: Cambridge University
Press, 2002). For an analysis of these critiques in the specific area of International
Relations and global politics, see the essays in the special issue of *International Studies
Quarterly*, Vol. 34, No. 3, 1990, especially Richard Ashley and R. B. J. Walker,
'Reading Dissidence/Writing the Discipline: Crisis and the Question of Sovereignty
in International Relations', pp. 347–416, and also Rob Walker, *Inside/Outside*,
pp. 15–21.

[6] Simon Critchley, *The Ethics of Deconstruction: Derrida and Lévinas* (Oxford: Blackwell,
1992).

scholars and practitioners stand outside of the political world and make judgements according to supposedly universal ethical principles.[7] Indeed, ethics are never 'out there' waiting to be invoked and applied to a particular political situation: '"we" are always already ethically situated, so making judgements about conduct depends less on what sort of rules are invoked as regulations, and more on how the interdependencies of our relations with others are appreciated'.[8] Campbell's point is that one is always already constituted as a political and ethical subject to the extent that one is always already *in relation* with others. Here, Campbell joins Critchley and others in reclaiming deconstruction's responsibility *to* the other by arguing for '*a different figuration of politics, one in which its purpose is the struggle for — on behalf of — alterity, and not a struggle to efface, erase, or eradicate alterity*'.[9]

How then, does this re-imagination of politics and ethics affect wider debates about interpretation, and more specific debates about the interpretation of contemporary travel writing? Instructive here is Roland Barthes' argument that all texts are *polysemic* — that there are always multiple and infinite interpretations of any text.[10] For Barthes, a text does not simply bear the truthful or authentic intentions of the author across to the reader; on the contrary, it has malleable meanings that are produced anew each time a text encounters an audience. As a consequence, there can never be a final interpretation of any text because there is no single incontrovertible truth that is delivered intact from the world to the author, from the author to the text, and from the text to the reader. However, as the correspondence between a real world, a truth, an author and a reader is deconstructed, the charges of relativism ring loud and clear. Recalling White's claims about narrative and history, the inclusion of *any* textual interpretation opens the door for readings that are exclusionary, unethical and possibly violent. Surely there must be *some* interpretations of the world that should be resisted? Critics have argued that White does away with the 'truth'

---

7   Particularly relevant here is Campbell's critique of scholars who discuss the ethics of global politics in terms of an outsider's responsibility, as if 'outsiders' were not always already implicated in political conflicts such as Bosnia: see Campbell, *National Deconstruction*, pp. 11–12.

8   Campbell, *National Deconstruction*, p. 176.

9   Campbell, *National Deconstruction*, p. 191. While Campbell shares Critchley's basic premise about reclaiming post-structuralism as an ethical and political approach, he disagrees with Critchley's assessment of the political. While Critchley thinks it is necessary to supplement Derrida with Lévinasian ethics, Campbell calls for a further step — that Lévinas must be resupplemented with a Derridean notion of the political; see *National Deconstruction*, pp. 181–5.

10   Roland Barthes, *S/Z*, trans. Richard Miller (Oxford: Blackwell, 1990).

as the driving force of history and replaces it with the arbitrary choice of narrative style. In this way, it becomes possible to justify *any* type of history – even one that is wrong, untrue, violent or unethical – as long as it adheres to a conventional narrative form. But as Kansteiner suggests, White's critique leads to a much more profound ontological problem: 'How can we write history successfully, for example, effectively displace unwanted emplotments of the past, without recourse to the concept of historical truth?'[11] Indeed, this question reveals the more general problem of how to judge contemporary travel writing: how can we say that one travelogue is better than another when we have no universal standards to help us arbitrate between competing truth claims? For me, collapsing the ethical and the political and employing an 'ethos of political criticism' allows a genuine engagement with that ontological conundrum that does not capitulate to either ultimate relativism or universal truth. Drawing on both Campbell and Critchley, I want to argue that a travelogue can be judged as 'good' to the extent that it acknowledges, addresses and engages with its ethical and political responsibility to the other.

Political reflexivity and critical thinking: the future of travel writing

As this book has made clear, I am concerned with the absence of both *political reflexivity* and *critical thought* in contemporary travel writing. It seems to me that these texts display a worrying ignorance of how the genre has always been implicated in the political logic of Empire. As a result, contemporary travel writing makes problematic claims about its own literary heritage, the foundations of modern subjectivity, bifurcated global cartography and a teleological historical queue. By ignoring, repressing and displacing the legacy of Empire, travel writers believe it is possible to stand outside of the political and ethical worlds they inhabit. This is why contemporary travelogues are ultimately depoliticising: they cover over the inherited power relations of Empire by telling supposedly neutral and objective stories about encounters with difference. In the hope that future travel writing might become more politically and ethically engaged, I want to make some observations that go some way to foregrounding questions of reflexivity and critical thinking in the

---

[11] Wulf Kansteiner, 'Hayden White's Critique of the Writing of History', *History and Theory*, Vol. 32, No. 2, 1993, p. 274. He goes on to say that White's work has 'struck a widely held, sensitive consensus about the political and social functions of historical writing: the task to render justice and to provide political orientation on the grounds of facticity' (p. 288).

genre. I am aware that the ethos of deconstruction at work in this book does not readily lend itself to constructing 'general criteria' by which we can judge travel writing. With this in mind, the following observations are not intended to construct a final ideal for the genre, or a 'recipe' for judging these texts. Rather, they are suggestions meant to provoke further debate, argumentation and discussion about the ethico-political orientation of travel writing. In this sense, my comments are offered in the spirit of Michael Kowalewski's warning: 'the criticism that seeks to appraise the modern literature of travel must be both judicious and intellectually generous, it must be socially responsible without becoming solemn and prohibitive'.[12]

Generic positions

Travel writer Bettina Selby argues, 'I think if you are writing travel books as such, and that's the genre, you should set out to write the truth. I mean the truth in its essential sense. I think to fictionalise something just for the sake of making a better story, to my mind, lacks responsibility.'[13] To be sure, Selby reproduces a rather narrow conception of travel writing as a genre that privileges non-fiction authority (i.e. truth) over imaginative endeavour (i.e. the art of fictionalising). But it is her point about responsibility that must be challenged, for it implies that to be responsible is to tell the truth. My question, of course, is *which* truth, or more appropriately, *whose* truth. While travel writers are happy to engage simultaneously in fact and fiction, they rarely reflect on the historical conditions under which this conjunction has been established within the genre. While many contemporary travel writers pay homage to their forebears, especially for the 'vivid' or 'dynamic' manner in which writers like Flaubert, Nerval and Burton made a foreign place come alive, this reverence is politically suspect because it does not reveal how the genre itself was − and continues to be − complicit in the reproduction of colonial power relations. To put it another way, how can a liberal and cosmopolitan travel writer like Bill Bryson continue to publish his travelogues *without* commenting on the history of the very genre within which he is working? How can he fail to ask, or even address the basic question: 'What *kind* of book am I writing here?' To be sure, some travel writers have creatively nudged the formal constraints of the genre by altering its narrative

---

[12] Kowalewski, 'Introduction: The Modern Literature of Travel', p. 12.
[13] Travel writer Bettina Selby, interviewed by Santiago Henríquez-Jiménez, in *Going the Distance*, p. 46.

structure – I'm thinking specifically of Chatwin's *The Songlines* here. But formal shifts are not necessarily matched by shifts in content and subject matter – which means that even 'cutting edge' travelogues like *The Songlines* fail to acknowledge how generic, literary and formal constraints have wider political effects. What is missing in contemporary travel writing is a *meta*-conversation about why these texts continue to be so popular in a context of globalisation, media saturation and mass travel, and what they tell us about the ontological condition of mobility. Think of how contemporary novelists like Paul Auster, Jorge Luis Borges and John Fowles deliberately encourage such a meta-conversation with regards to fiction: they call attention to the formal properties of the novel, pass comment on the mechanics of storytelling, make judgements about contemporary political issues and develop innovations in both form and content.[14] The question, of course, is why hasn't the equivalent transformation happened in travel writing?

As all generic boundaries become blurred, we are seeing some texts beginning to resist the generic codes of travel writing and re-imagine its position between fact and fiction. Ghosh's *In an Antique Land*, I think, comes closest to a generic hybrid that actively and self-consciously borrows from anthropology, history, memoir, sociology, geography and autobiography. John Russell argues that the most appropriate label for a travelogue that negotiates between generic and disciplinary authorities is the 'nonfiction novel'.[15] Russell suggests that the multiplicity of generic influences in non-fiction novels turns over the reality principle: when fiction invades the bedrock of fact, neither readers nor writers can be sure which authority to believe. The critical text here is Michael Ondaatje's *Running in the Family* which exemplifies this new literary form by simultaneously blending and disrupting the narrative structure of novels, memoirs and travelogues.[16] Ondaatje is an interesting figure here: not only have his 'unclassifiable' texts foregrounded the theme of travel and the journey metaphor in a variety of literary genres, they have also enjoyed both critical and popular success. A more obvious indication of this 'generic infection' is novels that focus specifically on issues of travel and dislocation. To be sure, migration is a central theme

[14] For a discussion of these meta-conversations in contemporary fiction, see Linda Hutcheon, *The Poetics of Postmodernism* (London and New York: Routledge, 1988).

[15] John Russell, 'Travel Memoir as Nonfiction Novel: Michael Ondaatje's *Running in the Family*', *Ariel*, Vol. 22, No. 2, April 1991, pp. 23–40.

[16] Michael Ondaatje, *Running in the Family* (London: Picador, 1984); for a good analysis of the formal aspects of Ondaatje's disruption, see Linda Hutcheon, 'Running in the Family: The Postmodern Challenge', in Sam Soleki, ed., *Spider Blues: Essays on Michael Ondaatje* (Montreal: Vehicule, 1985).

for post-colonial writers like Salman Rushdie who use hybrid narrators to disrupt prevailing notions of home, self and belonging. However, the most challenging conjunction of fiction, travel and politics is found in Michel Houellebecq's recent novels *Platform* and *Lanzarote* which expose how middle-class tourists – the main readers of contemporary travelogues – perpetuate the same structures of power that lead to child prostitution, environmental destruction and terrorism.[17] It is significant that this 'generic infection' is not limited to the literary landscape – the conventions of travel writing have also been used in academic work to interrogate the theoretical implications of mobility, speed and globalisation. Texts such as Umberto Eco's *Travels in Hyperreality* and Jean Baudrillard's *America* are often called post-modern travelogues because they use the journey metaphor to popularise their critiques of modernity.[18] As the theme of travel becomes central to fictional and academic debates about the global character of modern life, one is drawn to ask whether and how the genre of travel writing is responding. Kowalewski explains this challenge in the following way: 'Word, we might say, needs to get out: not only as a testament to the rich diversity of voices and vantages this writing offers but because an informed sense of the full range of this genre will alter and complicate the kinds of questions we ask of it.'[19] My point is that by embracing the dissolution of sanctified literary boundaries and by encouraging the dissemination of the journey metaphor into other cultural forms, the travelogue can become a more meaningful site for current debates about mobility, location and belonging.

Insecure subjects

By maintaining the anchor of 'non-fiction', travel writers are able to absent themselves from the text and foster the notion that their observations are objective, authentic and truthful. For John Russell, it is precisely these non-fiction strategies that protect travel writers from the kind of upheavals and revolutions that novelists have recently engaged with. As he argues, the characteristics of the 'non-fiction novel' 'are lacking in those travel books whose authors seem manifestly in control of things. The authorian sureness of travelogues like those of

[17] Michel Houellebecq, *Platform*, trans. Frank Wynne (London: William Heinemann, 2002) and *Lanzarote*, trans. Frank Wynne (London: William Heinemann, 2003).

[18] See Holland and Huggan, chapter 4, 'Postmodern Itineraries', in *Tourists with Typewriters*, pp. 157–96 where they discuss 'postmodern travelogues' such as Italo Calvino's *Invisible Cities*, Robert Dessaix's *Night Letters*, Ernest Callenbach's *Ecotopia*, and Melanie McGrath's *Motel Nirvana*.

[19] Kowalewski, 'Introduction: The Modern Literature of Travel', p. 3.

Paul Theroux, Peter Matthiessen, Jan Morris, Tom Wolfe keep them aesthetically out of the running, as far as any claim to the novel form goes.'[20] Unlike travel writing, fiction has a long tradition of unreliable narrators, especially in the Modernist literary tradition. For example, Marlow in Conrad's *Heart of Darkness* and Carraway in Fitzgerald's *The Great Gatsby* disrupt the tradition of 'authorian sureness' and prompt the reader to ask awkward questions about truth and perspective. My point is that the travel writer is unable to release his/her 'authorian sureness' because the genre relies so heavily on the logic of identity/ difference. If the confidence of the travel writer is questioned, it ushers in the difficult problem of subjectivity – of how the self is constructed in the face of difference, and how others are produced as markers of security for the self. Indeed, the reproduction of 'authorian sureness' in travel writing is a deliberate strategy to avoid asking difficult questions about both the role of the travel writer (e.g. Why am I here? What am I doing here?) and the production of others (e.g. What right have I to speak for others?).

Given that travelogues are supposedly based on the theme of mobility, there is a spectacular lack of reflection on the relationship between subjectivity and travel. To be sure, Bill Bryson marvels at the improbability of aeroplanes, Paul Theroux ponders the comforting motion of train travel and Gavin Bell admires the longstanding tradition of canoeing in the Pacific, but none of these authors ask the more difficult question of *why* they are there in the first place. What purpose does a travelogue have? Whose agenda is it serving? What good will it do? What could they, as travel writers, possibly add to a destination that has already been scripted and re-scripted by countless cultural reproductions? Aside from reluctantly admitting that it is a good way to make a living, travel writers fail to engage in a *meta*-conversation about how their own subjectivities are shaped by the competing forces of travel and writing.[21] While Bruce Chatwin got close to asking these difficult questions in his last book *What Am I Doing Here?*, even he fails to interrogate sufficiently how his own subjectivity is constructed in opposition to a whole host of others (e.g. Bedouin, Patagonian, Aboriginal).[22] On the whole, the lack of self-reflexivity in the genre is startling: what exactly *is* Michael Palin doing in the Sahara? What, indeed, is the point of yet *another* journey in which he arbitrarily carves

---

[20] Russell, 'Travel Memoir as Nonfiction Novel', p. 40.
[21] For further explanation on the relationship between travel, subjectivity and writing, see Michael Butor's famous essay 'Travel and Writing', *Mosaic*, Vol. 8, No. 1, Fall 1974, pp. 1–16.
[22] Bruce Chatwin, *What Am I Doing Here?* (London: Vintage, 1998).

up the world? Is there any place left that *hasn't* been subjected to his smug and patronising appreciation of cultural difference?

The unwillingness of travel writers to address the difficulties of representing others reveals the genre's reproduction of power most explicitly. To put it bluntly – and to echo Islam's earlier comments – many travel writers are content to construct a flimsy veneer of civility over the patronising and racist stereotypes that populate their narratives. This smacks of laziness, as travel writers rarely bother to examine the history or reproduction of those stereotypes (e.g. why *are* the Japanese so efficient, and have they always been this way?) or present counter-examples (e.g. like most young adults, Japanese teenagers are inefficient, disgruntled and rebellious). This lack of curiosity is also present in cosmopolitan travel writing: simply celebrating cultural difference in the vein of Bill Bryson (e.g. Japanese efficiency is *wonderful* !) does not avoid the genre's reliance on the identity/difference logic. The point is simple: if this logic continues unchecked and unexamined in the genre, travelogues will continue to reproduce subject positions that are governed by resuscitated colonial power relations. Moreover, travel writers cannot and will not address the ethico-political problems of *encounter* if they are unwilling to question the authority of their own subject positions. Indeed, what *right* do travel writers have to speak for and represent others? Aren't they in the same ethico-political conundrum as contemporary anthropologists, who, as Clifford Geertz rightly argues, can only ever represent others in the language of established power?[23] We know from the 'critical turn' in anthropology that supposedly 'neutral' or 'objective' ethnographies actually do violence to others by shaping and representing them according to prevailing grids of power and knowledge.[24] To the extent that travelogues can be considered popular forms of ethnography, surely the time is right for a 'critical turn' in travel writing?

Perhaps satirical travelogues have begun this shift by unhinging the sacrosanct position of the confident travel writer. For example, the drunken, adolescent and unreconstructed P. J. O'Rourke, or the scared, meek and bored-stiff Mark Lawson do not exhibit the 'authorian sureness' of most travel writers – O'Rourke's confidence is too

---

[23] See especially Clifford Geertz, *Works and Lives: The Anthropologist as Author* (Stanford: Stanford University Press, 1990) and *The Interpretation of Culture* (New York: Basic Books, 1991).

[24] See especially James Clifford, *The Predicament of Culture: Twentieth Century Ethnography, Literature, and Art* (Cambridge, MA: Harvard University Press, 1988) and James Clifford and George Marcus, *Writing Culture: The Poetics and Politics of Ethnography* (Berkeley: University of California Press, 1986).

exaggerated, and Lawson's is too docile. To be sure, satire does not negate the power relations at work in the discourse of liberal subjectivity, but it is one strategy that questions the automatic hierarchy of power between author and other. Travel writers like Younge, Diski and Ghosh exhibit another strategy: because they willingly become vulnerable in the face of otherness, they illustrate how difference resides within the self just as much as it does within the other. The problem, here, is that while satire and vulnerability destabilise the genre's 'authorian sureness', these strategies do not go far enough in questioning the privileged coordinates of liberal subjectivity. Indeed, one is drawn to ask whether the monologic voice of the Western metropolitan author can *ever* engage with cultural difference outside of the legacy of Empire. Certainly, it is not that difficult to see how formal changes could further deconstruct the authorial function – 'heteroglossic' anthologies with both local and foreign writers, multi-vocal narratives or even co-authored texts go some way in this direction. While certainly welcomed, these structural changes do not dismiss the fact that most contemporary travelogues are written by Western metropolitan authors who do not acknowledge the difficulties of representing people and places from other cultures. This convention seems even more anachronistic when we realise that all subjects – including travel writers and those they write about – are constituted *in a context of mobility*. Indeed, Jacques Ranière asks whether our representations of otherness would be *better* if authors took account of the unrelenting mobility of modern life. He argues that it is only by foregrounding the *foreignness* of the author that a mobile 'subject-in-formation' can be articulated:

The foreigner – the naïf, it will be said, he who is not yet informed – persists in the curiosity of his gaze, displaces his angle of vision, reworks the first way of putting together words and images, undoes the certainties of place, and thereby reawakens the power present in each of us to become a foreigner on the map of places and paths generally known as reality. Thus the foreigner loosens what he had bound together.[25]

For Ranière, the condition of being foreign, of being on a voyage, is the 'core political experience of our generation'. My point is that travel writing is the *perfect* genre within which to explore this condition of mobility – not through 'authorian sureness', but rather, through reflexive subjects-in-formation who recognise the foreignness in themselves just as much as they recognise it in others.

[25] Jacques Rancière, *Short Voyages to the Land of the People*, trans. James B. Swenson (Stanford: Stanford University Press, 2003), p. 3.

Spatial contamination

I have argued that contemporary travel writing spatialises the identity/
difference logic in such a way that simple distinctions between here
and there are underscored by more problematic arrangements of West/
Rest, safety/danger, and civilised/uncivilised. Indeed, these distinctions
make it possible for contemporary travel writers to decide *beforehand*
which places count as destinations (and thus extraordinary and exotic)
and which places count as homes (and thus secure and stable). Given
their unreflexive approach to both the genre's history and its identity/
difference logic, it is no surprise that travel writers are equally
unreflexive about its spatial assumptions. It is not just that travel
writers fail to ask '*what* am I doing here?', they also fail to ask 'what
am I doing *here*?' Why did I have to travel halfway around the world to
visit a place *I am already familiar with*? Addressing the genre's spatial
assumptions is a two-step process: firstly, it means identifying the
formations of power that make distinctions between here and there
seem natural and working out who those formations of power actually
serve; and secondly, it means making sense of those asymmetrical
power relations in a context of globalisation. In this sense, the spatial
analysis at work in Said's *Orientalism* was crucial because it revealed
the geographies of Empire − and it is not that difficult to see how the
racist overtones of many contemporary travelogues continue to draw
from an Orientalist logic. But as Foucauldian discourse analysis
suggests, binaries like Orient/Occident are not immutable − they are
articulated in specific contexts, maintained for a period of time and
then disseminated out again only to be rearticulated elsewhere. To be
sure, these continual articulations, disseminations and rearticulations
of power are difficult to track. But travel writing cannot comment on
or shape these circulations until it stops conceiving of the world in
terms of the static geographies of Empire. Post-colonial travel writers
like Pico Iyer have made a start in this direction, and while he might
promote a version of cosmopolitanism saturated with privilege, he does
confront the dynamics of globalisation and mobility that the genre has
so far been ignoring. In this way, Iyer's travelogues must be
distinguished from texts like Kaplan's *The Ends of the Earth* which
claim to confront globalisation (and solve its problems) by resuscitating outdated tropes of Empire and colonialism.

For me, the most compelling re-imagination of the spatial assumptions of travel writing comes from Mary Louise Pratt who argues
that encounters between authors and others take place in the contact
zone − a site where space is both *mediated* and *deterritorialised*. The

contact zone is a contingent and contradictory location in which spatial formations *do not necessarily* take on the binary formations bequeathed by Empire. In other words, space is understood to be discursively constituted rather than ontologically prior. Pratt argues that subjects in the contact zone do not make sense of their spatial location with reference to some transcendental 'reality', but rather, with reference to antecedent representations and prevailing discursive hegemonies. That contemporary travel writers fail to address the mediated nature of their destinations is not surprising – for the most part, travel writers are driven by the idea that it is still possible to access the 'reality' of foreign space. In order for travel writers to accept the discursive construction of their destinations, they would have to engage in another *meta-conversation* – this time about the fundamental spatial categories underscoring the genre of travel writing as a whole. Only then can the automatic placement of authors in the modern West and others in exotic destinations be disrupted, and we can begin to see that the meeting of selves and others in *any* destination is always an encounter between subjects-in-formation. Pratt's argument suggests that the most provocative travelogues are those that ask what happens when sameness and difference crash into one another in heterogeneous sites like the city. In this respect, Stefan Hertmans' *Intercities* combines philosophy, geography, literature and travel writing in order to examine the changing space of 'territoryless' urban landscapes. As he explains:

There are enough descriptions of exotic-looking cities, and anyone wanting to go to Punta Arenas, Dakkar, Baku or Anchorage will, if necessary, see surprising variants of a social culture that has become almost cosmopolitan, with all the attendant advantages and disadvantages. Mexico City, Paris and Singapore are struggling with variants of the same problem.[26]

Hertmans' point is that there are no differences between the world's cities in terms of their spatial characteristics. Because all cities are nodal points for the dissemination of power, they always produce spaces of exclusion (e.g. sequestering people in ghettoes) as well as spaces of freedom (e.g. anonymous public space). Drawing on Derrida's recent work, Hertmans constructs a journey through various 'cities of refuge' that express a 'more open, more democratic morality'. While *Intercities* is not intended as popular travel literature, it does exemplify the kind of text that disrupts our inherited geographies of Empire and reconfigures the space of the journey along more deterritorialised lines.

---

[26] Stefan Hertmans, *Intercities* (London: Reaktion Books, 2001), p. 13.

The time of travel

Not surprisingly, a lack of reflection as to the *what, why, who* and *where* of travel writing is matched by an equal lack of reflection on the *when* of travel writing. By placing themselves at the front of the historical queue, travel writers believe themselves able to provide valuable cultural commentary on the past, and innovative predictions for the future. These pronouncements, of course, can only be made if travel writers assume that history — and the role of travel writing in the formation of that history — is neutral, objective and teleological. In other words, it must seem *natural* that travel writers are more evolved than their chosen destinations (which are stuck in the past) and the others they encounter (who are less civilised). But in positioning themselves as modern subjects at the forefront of the historical queue, travel writers must cover over the very power relations that put them there in the first place. In other words, they must ignore the collusion between travel writing and Empire. Given the possibilities suggested by a re-imagination of genre, subjectivity and space, can travel writers construct narratives in which they do not necessarily occupy the most privileged position in the historical queue? Can they do justice to the genre's complex heritage without reproducing a teleological account of history or resuscitating asymmetrical colonial power relations? When foreign destinations display cultural markers of enlightenment and sophistication, it becomes impossible for travel writers to position them farther back in the historical queue. Indeed, if the end point of the historical queue can no longer be spatially located and protected in the 'evolved' West, there is no *necessary* direction for travel writing to take — which means that despite Fukuyama's claims, the West is not *necessarily* the ideal end point for every culture or society. Post-colonial travel writers are at the forefront of the temporal re-imagination of the genre because their participation in the 'modern' act of travel writing necessarily problematises the historical queue: what are 'they' doing here, in the present tense, joining 'us' in depicting 'them' as historically underdeveloped? Shouldn't 'they' be 'back in time', 'over there' with their own people? My concern is that the Orientalist logic embedded in much contemporary travel writing cannot be resisted unless the genre's much more entrenched teleological understanding of history is exposed and critiqued. This is why I am ambivalent about the cosmopolitan shift in the genre: are post-colonial travel writers *really* accepted as members of a heterogeneous and multicultural genre? Or is it the case — as it is with women authors — that 'even *they* can write travel books!'?

To further illustrate the tentative observations I have set out here, I want to examine how two contrasting travelogues have tried to disrupt both the form and content of the genre. Alain De Botton's *The Art of Travel* (2002) was a bestseller that purported to re-imagine our experiences of travel through insights from philosophy, art and culture. While De Botton's text – and his accompanying television series – offers general comments about travel, I want to argue that *The Art of Travel* is a profoundly apolitical text that actually precludes any critical argumentation. Certainly, De Botton is able to convey the feeling of being overwhelmed by foreignness (e.g. he is lethargic and intimidated in Madrid), but at no point does he question the power relations, structures and forces that allow him to (a) travel freely to a variety of foreign destinations in the first place, (b) peddle 'philosophy-lite' to the middle classes and (c) make authoritative claims about other cultures. For example, his metaphysical blathering during a holiday in Barbados precludes a more engaged political discussion of the tourist industry and his own complicity in those exploitative power relations. Because he is more interested in how the 'universal' experience of travel binds us all together, he fails to see that not everyone – and certainly not the tourist workers in Barbados – can afford to travel for leisure, pleasure and escape. More banal observations abound when De Botton enthuses about Alexander von Humboldt's colonial journey to South America – completely ignoring the less savoury and more damaging elements of that voyage that Mary Louise Pratt has so carefully documented.[27] More generally, De Botton's myopia derives from a narrow-minded understanding of what counts as philosophy: he is only interested in what the Western canon of philosophers, artists and writers – mostly dead, white males – can tell him about travel. It is clear that De Botton is not interested in the political insights of contemporary thinkers like Foucault and Derrida, post-colonial thinkers like Fanon, Said and Spivak, or even radical theorists of travel like Deleuze, Guattari and Van Den Abeele. Indeed, as a commentary on modern travel, De Botton's book is deeply conservative and elitist because it fails to do what Steve Clark suggests *all* critical writing about travel must do: 'acknowledge not only its complicity, but also its power of reconfiguration and aspiration towards a more benign ethics of alterity'.[28]

While travel writers like Younge, Diski and Ghosh begin to address the wider structures of power within which they operate, even their

---

[27] Pratt, *Imperial Eyes*, pp. 111–43.
[28] Clark, 'Introduction', *Travel Writing and Empire*, p. 4.

narratives do not disrupt the seemingly ironclad conjunction of a second-rate literary genre, a 'monarch-of-all-I-survey' authorial position, a home-away-home structure and a teleological historical queue. One text that does manage to push at this conjunction is Julio Cortázar and Carol Dunlop's *The Autonauts of the Global Highway: An Atemporal Journey from Paris to Marseilles* (1983).[29] The most obvious disruptive element of the book is its style: Cortázar and Dunlop are writing in 1982, but they use an eighteenth-century style made popular by early accounts of travel to colonial outposts (e.g. they document the minutiae of the journey as if it were a scientific expedition and address the book directly to a wealthy benefactor). Keen to mimic the rigorous observation of such an expedition, the authors bring out a typewriter at every rest stop along the way. Consequently, the length of the trip – the 'normal' time it takes to get from Paris to Marseilles – is eclipsed by the expanded time it takes to record everything in sight. For Brennan, Cortázar and Dunlop's travelogue is significant because it executes a 'politics of the prank' – it both exposes and sends up 'the literary devices that have eased the task of domination'.[30] For me, *The Autonauts* functions as a comprehensive critique of the discursive structures of contemporary travel writing: its eighteenth-century style foregrounds the impossibility of 'accurate' representations; its dual-authorship unsettles the 'monarch-of-all-I-survey' position of the travel writer; its commonplace journey from Paris to Marseilles refuses the exotic tropes that usually frame travelogue destinations; and its slow pace of recording and documenting punctures the linear timeline. Indeed, it is the lesser-known *Autonauts of the Global Highway*, rather than the bestselling *Art of Travel*, that provides a model for how travel writing might be transformed in a context of globalisation, mobility and deterritorialisation. My point is that if travel writers can draw significance from the genre's precarious positions – between fact and fiction, identity and difference, local and global, and past and present – *without* re-installing hegemonic discourses of difference, it can be resuscitated as a crucial site for political debate and resistance.

Are we there yet? Travel writing as global politics

As a journey in its own right through discourse analysis, literary theory, identity politics, critical geography and historiography, this book must

---

[29] Julio Cortázar and Carol Dunlop, *Los autonautas de la cosmopista: un viaje atemporal Paris–Marsella* (Buenos Aires: Muchnik, 1983); translation from Brennan, *At Home in the World*, p. 191, p. 337, n.52.

[30] Brennan, *At Home in the World*, p. 192.

come full circle and ask what effect these interdisciplinary wanderings might have on the study and practice of global politics. The simplest answer is to say that travel writing is a form of global politics because it reproduces the same discourses of difference that hold our prevailing understandings of the world in place. Moreover, travelogues can help us understand the discursive terrain of global politics because they are an important part of the cultural struggle over how we describe and represent the 'realities' of global life. For example, this book has shown that the hegemonic discourses of difference that arose during colonial rule continue to anchor contemporary narratives about travel – even those that claim a cosmopolitan ethos. But these struggles between colonial and cosmopolitan visions – struggles that touch on difficult issues such as tolerance, equality, justice and multiculturalism – are exactly the same struggles shaping the study and practice of global politics. To be sure, the alignment between travel writing and global politics is expressed most clearly in their shared discourses of difference, but as this book has demonstrated, it is the power relations within that alignment that must be interrogated. My point is that the 'serious' nature of global politics (e.g. conflict, famine, violence) is not derived from unfettered access to a transcendental reality – it is derived from the compelling stories we construct about truth, authenticity and power. By examining the textual character of our claims about global life – their narrative structures, beginnings, middles and ends, grammatical rules, heroes and villains – the strident pronouncements and predictions of global politics are emptied of any final claim to 'the truth'. What results from this inversion is discursive equivalence: travel writing tells us *just as much* about our understandings of the world as the 'serious' claims of global politics. In other words, both 'academic' and 'leisure' texts are engaged in the same negotiations with difference, the same hegemonic articulations and the same normative concerns about the character and direction of global life.

Because this book understands on-going discursive productions of difference as the primary characteristic of the political, it resists any conclusive or transcendental understanding of politics that claims a final triumph over antagonism. To the extent that discourse analysis helps us interrogate our continuing struggles with difference, it continually resists those political understandings that veer towards resolution and narrative closure. With this in mind, the travelogue is an excellent illustration of how discursive power is always characterised by an antagonism between the articulation of hegemony and the inclusion of difference. As this book has demonstrated, that antagonism can be revealed in the relationships between truth claims and falsehoods, selves and others, homes and destinations, and present and past events. But the normative claims of this book go further than that: maintaining the antagonistic character of the political is what prevents excessive violence towards difference and otherness. It seems, then, that travel writing is faced with a profound opportunity: to successfully refute the charge that they are only 'superficial' texts that peddle the acceptable face of a continuing colonial mindset, travelogues must acknowledge, address and engage more explicitly with debates over cultural difference. This is not to say that the creative and aesthetic aspects of the genre should be jettisoned in favour of committed political diatribes. Indeed, one of the things travel writing can teach us is that successful resistance often begins at the level of myth, imagination and storytelling. By politicising the alignment between travel writing and global politics, it is possible to see how the 'real' cultural differences that lead to war, intervention and genocide are constructed from the same discursive terrain as the 'superficial' cultural differences expressed in contemporary travel writing. Moreover, by engaging directly with the difficult issues of cultural difference, travel writing has the opportunity to comment on, shape and intervene in the 'serious' events of global politics.

Bibliography

Adams, Percy G. *Travel Literature and the Evolution of the Novel*. Lexington: University Press of Kentucky, 1983.

Agnew, John. *Geopolitics: Re-visioning World Politics*. London and New York: Routledge, 1998.

Anderegg, Michael, ed. *Inventing Vietnam: The War in Film and Television*. Philadelphia: Temple University Press, 1991.

Anthony, Carolyn. 'Travel Reading for Pleasure', *Publisher's Weekly*, Vol. 237, No. 3, 19 January 1990, pp. 32–4.

Appadurai, Arjun. *Modernity at Large: Cultural Dimensions of Globalization*. Minneapolis: University of Minnesota Press, 1996.

Ashley, Richard and R. B. J. Walker, eds. *International Studies Quarterly* (special edition), Vol. 34, No. 3, 1990.

Bakhtin, Mikhail. *The Dialogic Imagination*, ed. Michael Holquist. Austin: University of Texas Press, 1981.

Banks, Russell, Jan Morris, Robert Stone and William Styron. 'Itchy Feet and Pencils: A Symposium', *New York Times Book Review*, Vol. 96, 18 August 1991, p. 24.

Barber, Lynn. 'Making Waves', *Observer Magazine*, 20 February 2000, pp. 38–41.

Barthes, Roland. *S/Z*, trans. Richard Miller. Oxford: Blackwell, 1990.

Bartkowski, Frances. *Travelers, Immigrants, Inmates: Essays in Estrangement*. Minneapolis: University of Minnesota Press, 1995.

Barton, Geoff, ed. *Travel Writing: Oxford Literary Resources*. Oxford: Oxford University Press, 1993.

Bassnett, Susan. 'Travel Writing and Gender', in Peter Hulme and Tim Youngs, eds., *The Cambridge Companion to Travel Writing*. Cambridge: Cambridge University Press, 2002, pp. 225–41.

Baudrillard, Jean. *The Illusion of the End*, trans. Chris Turner. Cambridge: Polity Press, 1994.

Bauman, Zygmunt. *Globalization: The Human Consequences*. Oxford: Blackwell, 1998.

Behdad, Ali. *Belated Travelers: Orientalism in the Age of Colonial Dissolution*. Durham, NC and London: Duke University Press, 1994.

Bell, Gavin. *In Search of Tusitala: Travels in the Pacific after Robert Louis Stevenson*. London: Picador, 1994.

Bennett, Tony. 'Texts, Readers, Reading Formations', *Literature and History*, Vol. 9, No. 2, 1983, pp. 214–27.

Berndt, Catherine H. 'Review of *The Songlines*', *Parabola*, Vol. 13, No. 1, Spring 1988, pp. 130–32.

Bevis, Richard. *Bibliotheca Cisorientalia: An Annotated Checklist of Early English Travel Books on the Near and Middle East*. Boston: G. K. Hall and Co., 1973.

Beynon, John and David Dunkerley, eds. *Globalization: The Reader*. London: Athlone Press, 2000.

Blacker, Terence. 'Bill's Awfully Big Adventure', *Sunday Times (Culture)*, 11 June 2000, p. 33.

Blanton, Casey. *Travel Writing: The Self & the World*. London and New York: Routledge, 1995.

Blundell, Valda, John Shepherd and Ian Taylor, eds. *Relocating Cultural Studies: Developments in Theory and Research*. London: Routledge, 1993.

Bogel, Frederic V. *The Difference that Satire Makes: Rhetoric and Reading from Jonson to Byron*. Cornell: Cornell University Press, 2001.

Borm, Jan. 'Jonathan Raban's *Coasting* and Literary Strategies in Contemporary British Travel Writing', in Kristi Siegel, ed., *Issues in Travel Writing: Empire, Spectacle, and Displacement*. New York: Peter Lang, 2002, pp. 281–9.

Bracken, Patrick J. and Celia Petty, eds. *Rethinking the Trauma of War*. London: Free Association Books, 1998.

Brennan, Timothy. *At Home in the World: Cosmopolitanism Now*. Cambridge and London: Harvard University Press, 1997.

Brooke-Rose, Christine. 'Historical Genres/Theoretical Genres: A Discussion of Todorov on the Fantastic', *New Literary History: A Journal of Theory and Interpretation*, Vol. 8, No. 1, Autumn 1976, pp. 146–58.

Brockes, Emma. 'Travel Is Nasty', *Guardian (G2)*, 9 June 2003, p. 4.

Bryson, Bill. *African Diary*. London: Doubleday, 2002.

    Down Under. London: Black Swan, 2001.

    A Walk in the Woods. London: Black Swan, 1998.

    Neither Here Nor There: Travels in Europe. London: Black Swan, 1998.

    The Lost Continent: Travels in Small Town America. London: Abacus, 1990.

Butor, Michael. 'Travel and Writing', *Mosaic*, Vol. 8, No. 1, 1974, pp. 1–16.

Buzard, James. *European Tourism, Literature and the Ways to Culture, 1800–1918*. Oxford: Clarendon Press, 1993.

Caesar, Terry. *Forgiving the Boundaries: Home as Abroad in American Travel Writing*. Athens, GA: University of Georgia Press, 1995.

Cahill, Tim. *Road Fever: A High-Speed Travelogue*. London: Fourth Estate, 1992.

Campbell, David. 'Salgado and the Sahel: Documentary Photography and the Imaging of Famine', in Cindy Weber and François Debrix, eds., *Mediating Internationals*. Minneapolis: University of Minnesota Press, 2003, pp. 69–96.

    'Contra Wight: The Errors of Premature Writing', *Review of International Studies*, Vol. 25, No. 2, April 1999, pp. 317–21.

    National Deconstruction: Violence, Identity, and Justice in Bosnia. Minneapolis: University of Minnesota Press, 1998.

    'MetaBosnia: Narratives of the Bosnian War', *Review of International Studies*, Vol. 24, No. 2, April 1998, pp. 261–81.

'Violent Performances: Identity, Sovereignty, Responsibility', in Yosef Lapid and Friedrich Kratochwil, eds., *The Return of Culture and Identity in IR Theory.* Boulder: Lynne Rienner Publishers, 1997, pp. 163–81.

'Political Prosaics, Transversal Politics, and the Anarchical World', in Michael J. Shapiro and Hayward R. Alker, eds., *Challenging Boundaries: Global Flows, Territorial Identities.* Minneapolis: University of Minnesota Press, 1996, pp. 7–32.

Writing Security: United States Foreign Policy and the Politics of Identity. Manchester: Manchester University Press, 1992.

Campbell, Ffyona. *The Whole Story: A Walk around the World.* London: Orion, 1996.

On Foot through Africa. London: Orion, 1994.

Campbell, Mary B. *The Witness and the Other World: Exotic European Travel Writing, 400–1600.* Ithaca: Cornell University Press, 1988.

Camilleri, Joseph A., Anthony P. Jarvis and Albert J. Paolini, eds. *The State in Transition: Reimagining Political Space.* Boulder: Lynne Rienner Publishers, 1995.

Chatwin, Bruce. *What Am I Doing Here?* London: Vintage, 1998.

Anatomy of Restlessness: Uncollected Writings, ed. Jan Borm and Matthew Graves. London: Picador, 1997.

The Songlines. London: Penguin, 1987.

In Patagonia. London: Picador, 1979.

Chatwin, Bruce and Paul Theroux. *Patagonia Revisited.* London: Jonathan Cape, 1985.

Cheah, Pheng and Bruce Robbins, eds. *Cosmopolis: Thinking and Feeling Beyond the Nation.* Minneapolis: University of Minnesota Press, 1998.

Clapp, Susannah. *With Chatwin: Portrait of a Writer.* London: Jonathan Cape, 1997.

Clark, Steve. 'Introduction', in Steve Clark, ed., *Travel Writing and Empire: Postcolonial Theory in Transit.* London and New York: Zed Books, 1999, pp. 1–28.

ed. *Travel Writing and Empire: Postcolonial Theory in Transit.* London and New York: Zed Books, 1999.

Clifford, James. *Routes: Travel and Translation in the Late Twentieth Century.* Cambridge and London: Harvard University Press, 1997.

'No Innocent Eyes: Western Travellers as Missionaries of Capitalism', *Times Literary Supplement*, 11 September 1992, p. 4.

'The Transit Lounge of Culture', *Times Literary Supplement*, No. 4596, 3 May 1991, p. 8.

The Predicament of Culture: Twentieth Century Ethnography, Literature, and Art. Cambridge, MA: Harvard University Press, 1988.

Clifford, James and George Marcus, eds. *Writing Culture: The Poetics and Politics of Ethnography.* Berkeley: University of California Press, 1986.

Cohen, Tom, ed. *Jacques Derrida and the Humanities: A Critical Reader.* Cambridge: Cambridge University Press, 2002.

Connolly, William E. *Identity/Difference: Democratic Negotiation of Political Paradox.* Ithaca: Cornell University Press, 1991.

'Identity and Difference in World Politics', in James Der Derian and Michael J. Shapiro, eds., *International/Intertextual Relations: Postmodern Readings of World Politics*. Lexington: Lexington Books, 1989, pp. 323–42.

Cortázar, Julio and Carol Dunlop. *Los autonautas de la cosmopista: un viaje atemporal Paris-Marsella*. Buenos Airies: Muchnik, 1983.

Critchley, Simon. *On Humour*. London and New York: Routledge, 2002.

The Ethics of Deconstruction: Derrida and Lévinas. Oxford: Blackwell, 1992.

Dalby, Simon. 'The Environment as Geopolitical Threat: Reading Robert Kaplan's Coming Anarchy', *Ecumene*, Vol. 3, No. 4, 1996, pp. 472–96.

'Critical Geopolitics: Discourse, Difference and Dissent', *Environment and Planning D: Society and Space*, Vol. 9, No. 3, 1991, pp. 261–83.

Dalby, Simon and Gearóid Ó Tuathail, eds. *Rethinking Geopolitics*. London and New York: Routledge, 1998.

D'Amore, Louis. 'Tourism – The World's Peace Industry', *Journal of Travel Research*, Vol. 27, 1988, pp. 35–40.

Davidson, Robyn. 'The Trip Trap', edited extract of her introduction to *The Picador Book of Journeys*, *Guardian* (Saturday Review), 4 August 2001, pp. 1–2.

Tracks. London: Picador, 1980.

De Botton, Alain. *The Art of Travel*. London: Hamish Hamilton, 2002.

de Certeau, Michel. *The Practice of Everyday Life*, trans. Steven Rendall. Berkeley and Los Angeles: University of California Press, 1984.

Defert, Daniel. 'The Collection of the World: Accounts of Voyages from the Sixteenth to the Eighteenth Centuries', *Dialectical Anthropology*, Vol. 7, 1982, pp. 11–20.

Deleuze, Gilles and Felix Guattari. *A Thousand Plateaus: Capitalism and Schizophrenia*, trans. Brian Massumi. Minneapolis: University of Minnesota Press, 1987.

Der Derian, James. *Virtuous War: Mapping the Military-Industrial-Media-Entertainment Network*. Boulder: Westview Press, 2001.

Der Derian, James and Michael J. Shapiro. *International/Intertextual Relations: Postmodern Readings of World Politics*. Lexington: Lexington Books, 1989.

Derrida, Jacques. *On Cosmopolitanism and Forgiveness*, trans. Mark Dooley and Michael Hughes. London and New York: Routledge, 2001.

'Conjuring Marxism', in *Spectres of Marx: The State of the Debt, the Work of Mourning, and the New International*, trans. Peggy Kamuf. London: Routledge, 1994.

'Force of Law: The "Mystical Foundation of Authority"', in David Gray Carlson, Drucilla Cornell and Michael Rosenfeld, eds., *Deconstruction and the Possibility of Justice*. London and New York: Routledge, 1992, pp. 3–67.

'Racism's Last Word', in Henry Louis Gates, Jr., ed., *'Race', Writing, and Difference*. Chicago and London: University of Chicago Press, 1986, pp. 329–38.

'The Law of Genre', trans. Avital Ronell, *Critical Inquiry*, Vol. 7, No. 1, 1980, pp. 55–81.

Of Grammatology, trans. Gayatri Chakravorty Spivak. Baltimore: Johns Hopkins University Press, 1976.

Dew, Josie. *The Wind in My Wheels: Travel Tales from the Saddle.* London: Little Brown and Co. Ltd., 1992.

Diski, Jenny. *Stranger on a Train: Daydreaming and Smoking around America with Interruptions.* London: Virago, 2002.

Dittmar, Linda and Gene Michaud, eds. *From Hanoi to Hollywood: The Vietnam War in American Film.* New York: Rutgers University Press, 1990.

Dodd, Philip, ed. *The Art of Travel: Essays on Travel Writing.* London: Frank Cass, 1982.

Dodds, Klaus-John. 'Geopolitics and Foreign Policy: Recent Developments in Anglo-American Political Geography and International Relations', *Progress in Human Geography*, Vol. 18, No. 2, 1994, pp. 186–208.

Dodds, Klaus-John, and David Atkinson, eds. *Geopolitical Traditions: A Century of Geopolitical Thought.* London and New York: Routledge, 2000.

Doel, Marcus A. *Poststructural Geographies: The Diabolical Art of Spatial Sciences.* Edinburgh: Edinburgh University Press, 1999.

Du Gay, Paul. *Production of Culture/Cultures of Production.* London: Sage and Open University Press, 1997.

Duncan, James S. and Derek Gregory, eds. *Writes of Passage: Reading Travel Writing.* London and New York: Routledge, 1999.

Duncan, James S. and David Ley, eds. *Place/Culture/Representation.* London and New York: Routledge, 1993.

During, Simon. 'Popular Culture on a Global Scale: A Problem for Cultural Studies?' *Critical Inquiry*, Vol. 23, No. 4, 1997, pp. 808–34.

Edkins, Jenny. *Trauma and the Memory of Politics.* Cambridge: Cambridge University Press, 2003.

Edmund, Rod. 'The Pacific/Tahiti: Queen of the South Sea Isles', in Peter Hulme and Tim Youngs, eds., *The Cambridge Companion to Travel Writing.* Cambridge: Cambridge University Press, 2002, pp. 139–55.

Epsey, David. 'Comments for Writing the Journey Conference, 1999', http://www.english.upenn/edu/Travel99/Fussell.html.

Fabian, Johannes. *Time and the Other: How Anthropology Makes Its Object.* New York: Columbia University Press, 1983.

Farah, Nuruddin. 'Highway to Hell: The Travel-Writing of the Disaster', *Transition*, Issue 70, Vol. 6, No. 2, Summer 1996, pp. 60–70.

Featherstone, Mike. *Undoing Culture: Globalization, Postmodernism and Identity.* London: Sage, 1995.

Ferguson, Niall. *Empire: How Britain Made the Modern World.* London: Allen Lane, 2003.

Fetherling, Douglas. 'George Woodcock: A Graceful Voyager on a Road Well-Travelled', *Globe and Mail*, 1 May 1993, p. C9.

Foucault, Michel. 'The Ethic of Care for the Self as a Practice of Freedom', in J. Bernauer and David Rasmussen, eds., *The Final Foucault.* Cambridge, MA: MIT Press, 1988.

'Of Other Spaces', *Diacritics*, Vol. 16, Spring 1986, pp. 22–7.

'The Order of Discourse', in Michael, Shapiro, ed., *Language and Politics.* Oxford: Basil Blackwell, 1984, pp. 108–37.

The Foucault Reader, ed. Paul Rabinow. New York: Pantheon Books, 1984.

'The Subject of Power', in H. L. Dreyfus and Paul Rabinow, eds., *Michel Foucault: Beyond Structuralism and Hermeneutics*. Brighton: Harvester Press, 1982.

Power/Knowledge: Selected Interviews and Other Writings 1972–1977. New York: Pantheon Books, 1980.

A History of Sexuality, Vol. I: *An Introduction*, trans. Robert Hurley. New York: Vintage Books, 1980.

Discipline and Punish: The Birth of the Prison, trans. Alan Sheridan. New York: Pantheon Books, 1977.

The Order of Things: An Archaeology of the Human Sciences. New York: Vintage Books, 1973.

Madness and Civilization: A History of Insanity in the Age of Reason, trans. Richard Howard. New York: Random House, 1973.

The Archaeology of Knowledge and the Discourse on Human Language. New York: Pantheon Books, 1972.

Fredrickson, Robert. 'Review of *Tourists with Typewriters*', *Ariel*, Vol. 30, July 1999, pp. 196–8.

Freedman, Aviva and Peter Medway, eds. *Genre and the New Rhetoric*. London: Taylor and Francis, 1994.

Frow, John. 'Tourism and the Semiotics of Nostalgia', *October*, Vol. 57, 1991, pp. 123–51.

Fukuyama, Francis. *The End of History and the Last Man*. London: Penguin Books, 1993.

'The End of History?' *National Interest*, No. 16, Summer 1989, pp. 1–18.

Furlong, Monica. *Flight of the Kingfisher: A Fourney among the Kukatja Aborigines*. London: HarperCollins Publishers, 1996.

Fussell, Paul, ed. *The Norton Book of Travel*. New York: W. W. Norton and Co., 1987.

Abroad: British Literary Travelling between the Wars. Oxford: Oxford University Press, 1980.

Gates, Henry Louis, Jr. 'Writing "Race" and the Difference It Makes', in Gates, Jr., ed., *'Race', Writing, and Difference*, pp. 1–20.

ed. *'Race', Writing, and Difference*. Chicago and London: University of Chicago Press, 1986.

Geertz, Clifford. *The Interpretation of Culture*. New York: Basic Books, 1991.

Works and Lives: The Anthropologist as Author. Stanford: Stanford University Press, 1990.

George, Jim. *Discourses of Global Politics: A Critical (Re)introduction to International Relations*. Boulder: Lynne Rienner Publishers, 1994.

Ghosh, Amitav. *In an Antique Land*. London: Granta Books, 1992.

Gibbons, Fiachra. 'Bryson to Turn Over the Maple Leaf', 2 June 2003, *Guardian (National News)*, p. 11.

Glaser, Elton. 'The Self-Reflexive Traveller: Paul Theroux on the Art of Travel and Travel Writing', *Centennial Review*, Vol. 3, No. 3, Summer 1989, pp. 193–206.

Govier, Katherine, ed. *Without a Guide: Contemporary Women's Travel Adventures*. Toronto: Macfarlane, Walter and Ross, 1994.

Greene, Graham. *The Quiet American*. London: Vintage, 2002.

The Lawless Roads. London: Penguin, 1982.

Journey without Maps. London: Heinemann, 1978.

Gregory, Derek. 'Scripting Egypt: Orientalism and the Cultures of Travel', in James Duncan and Derek Gregory, eds., *Writes of Passage: Reading Travel Writing*. London and New York: Routledge, 1999, pp. 114–50.

Geographical Imaginations. Oxford: Basil Blackwell, 1994.

Griffin, Dustin. *Satire: A Critical Reintroduction*. Lexington: University of Kentucky Press, 1994.

Griffin, Farah J. and Cheryl J. Fish, eds. *Stranger in the Village: Two Centuries of African-American Travel Writing*. Boston: Beacon Press, 1999.

Hall, Stuart. 'The Question of Cultural Identity', in Stuart Hall, David Held and Anthony McGrew, eds., *Modernity and Its Futures*. Cambridge: Polity Press in association with the Open University, 1992, pp. 274–316.

Harstock, Nancy. 'Foucault on Power: A Theory for Women?', in Linda J. Nicholson, ed., *Feminism/Poststructuralism*. London and New York: Routledge, 1990, pp. 157–75.

Hartley, Jenny and Sarah Turvey. *Reading Groups*. Oxford: Oxford University Press, 2001.

Harvey, David. 'Cosmopolitanism and the Banality of Geographical Evils', *Public Culture*, Vol. 12, No. 2, 2000, pp. 529–64.

The Condition of Postmodernity: An Enquiry into the Origins of Social Change. Oxford: Blackwell, 1989.

Hatcher, John. 'Lonely Planet, Crowded World: Alex Garland's The Beach', *Studies in Travel Writing*, Vol. 3, 1999, pp. 131–47.

Hawks, Tony. *Playing the Moldovans at Tennis*. London: Ebury Press, 2001.

Round Ireland with a Fridge. London: Ebury Press, 1999.

Held, David. 'Cosmopolitan Democracy and the New International Order', in David Held, ed., *Democracy and the Global Order: From the Modern State to Cosmopolitan Governance*. Cambridge: Polity Press, 1995, pp. 267–86.

ed. *A Globalizing World? Culture, Economics, Politics*. London and New York: Routledge and Open University Press, 2000.

Held, David and Anthony McGrew, eds. *The Global Transformations Reader: An Introduction to the Globalization Debate*. Cambridge: Polity, 2000.

Henderson, Heather. 'The Travel Writer and the Text: "My Giant Goes with Me Wherever I Go"', in Michael Kowalewski, ed., *Temperamental Journeys: Essays on the Modern Literature of Travel*. Athens, GA and London: University of Georgia Press, 1992, pp. 230–48.

Henríquez-Jiménez, Santiago. *Going the Distance: An Analysis of Modern Travel Writing and Criticism*. Barcelona: Kadle Books, 1995.

Herod, Andrew, Gearóid Ó Tuathail and Susan M. Roberts, eds., *An Unruly World: Globalization, Governance and Geography*. London and New York: Routledge, 1998.

Hertmans, Stefan. *Intercities*. London: Reaktion Books, 2001.

Hetherington, Kevin. *The Badlands of Modernity: Heterotopia and Social Ordering*. London: Routledge, 1997.

Hevda, Beth. *Journey from Betrayal to Trust: A Universal Rite of Passage*. Long Island, NY: Celestial Arts, 1992.

Hirst, Paul and Grahame Thompson. *Globalization in Question: The International Economy and the Possibilities of Governance*. Cambridge: Polity Press, 1996.

Holland, Patrick and Graham Huggan. *Tourists with Typewriters: Critical Reflections on Contemporary Travel Writing*. Ann Arbor: University of Michigan Press, 1998.

Hollis, Martin and Edward Nell. *Rational Economic Man: A Philosophical Critique of Neo-Classical Economics*. Cambridge: Cambridge University Press, 1975.

Houellebecq, Michel. *Lanzarote*, trans. Frank Wynne. London: William Heinemann, 2003.

Platform, trans. Frank Wynne. London: William Heinemann, 2002.

Howarth, David, Aletta J. Norval and Yannis Stavrakakis, eds. *Discourse Theory and Political Analysis: Identities, Hegemonies and Social Change*. Manchester: Manchester University Press, 2000.

Huggan, Graham. 'Maps, Dreams, and the Presentation of Ethnographic Narrative: Hugh Brody's "Maps and Dreams" and Bruce Chatwin's "The Songlines"', *Ariel: A Review of International English Literature*, Vol. 22, No. 1, January 1991, pp. 57–69.

Hughes, Lyn. 'The Reluctant Role Model: An Interview with Robyn Davidson', *Wanderlust*, No. 17, Aug./Sept. 1996, pp. 6–7.

Hulme, Peter. 'Travelling to Write (1940–2000)', in Hulme and Youngs, eds., *The Cambridge Companion to Travel Writing*, pp. 87–101.

Hulme, Peter and Tim Youngs, eds. *The Cambridge Companion to Travel Writing*. Cambridge: Cambridge University Press, 2002.

Hunt, Christopher. *Sparring with Charlie: Motorbiking down the Ho Chi Minh Trail*. London: Bantam Editions, 1997.

Hutcheon, Linda. *A Theory of Parody: The Teachings of Twentieth Century Art Forms*. Champaign, IL: University of Illinois Press, 2000.

The Poetics of Postmodernism. London and New York: Routledge, 1988.

'Running in the Family: The Postmodern Challenge', in Sam Soleki, ed., *Spider Blues: Essays on Michael Ondaatje*. Montreal: Vehicule, 1985.

Islam, Sayed Manzuril. *The Ethics of Travel: From Marco Polo to Kafka*. Manchester: Manchester University Press, 1996.

Iyer, Pico. *The Global Soul: Jet-Lag, Shopping Malls and the Search for Home*. London: Bloomsbury, 2000.

Falling Off the Map: Some Lonely Places of the World. London: Vintage Departures, 1994.

Video Night in Kathmandu and Other Reports from the Not-So-Far East. New York: Vintage Departures, 1988.

Jameson, Frederic. *The Geopolitical Aesthetic: Cinema and Space in the World System*. London: BFI Publishing, 1992.

'Nostalgia for the Present', *South Atlantic Quarterly*, Vol. 88, No. 2, 1989, pp. 517–37.

Janz, Natania and Miranda Davies, eds., *More Women Travel: A Rough Guide Special*. London: Rough Guides, 1995.

Jones, Lisa. *Bulletproof Diva: Tales of Race, Sex and Hair*. London: Penguin, 1995.

Jordan, Rosa. *Dangerous Places: Travels on the Edge*. Lawrencetown, Nova Scotia: Pottersfield Press, 1997.

Kansteiner, Wulf. 'Hayden White's Critique of the Writing of History', *History and Theory*, Vol. 32, No. 3, 1993, pp. 273–95.

Kaplan, Caren. *Questions of Travel: Postmodern Discourses of Displacement.* Durham and London: Duke University Press, 1996.

Kaplan, Robert. *The Ends of the Earth: A Journey at the Dawn of the Twenty-First Century.* London: Macmillan Papermac, 1997.

'The Coming Anarchy', *Atlantic Monthly*, No. 273, 2 February 1994, pp. 44–76.

Balkan Ghosts: A Journey through History. New York: St Martin's Press, 1993.

Keneally, Thomas. *The Place Where Souls Are Born: A Journey into the American Southwest.* London: Sceptre, 1992.

Knight, Charles A. *The Literature of Satire.* Cambridge: Cambridge University Press, 2004.

Kofman, Eleonore and Gillian Youngs, eds. *Globalization: Theory and Practice.* London: Pinter, 2001.

Koshar, Rudi. *German Travel Cultures.* London: Berg Publishers, 2000.

Kowalewski, Michael. 'Introduction: The Modern Literature of Travel', in Kowalewski, ed., *Temperamental Journeys*, pp. 1–16.

ed. *Temperamental Journeys: Essays on the Modern Literature of Travel.* Athens, GA and London: University of Georgia Press, 1992.

Kpomassie, Tété-Michel. *An African in Greenland*, trans. James Kirkup. New York: Harcourt Brace Jovanovich, 1983.

Krist, Gary. 'Ironic Journeys: Travel Writing in the Age of Tourism', *Hudson Review*, Vol. 45, No. 4, Winter 1993, pp. 593–601.

Lacey, Mark J. 'War, Cinema, and International Relations', *Alternatives*, Vol. 28, No. 5, Nov.–Dec. 2003, pp. 611–36.

Laclau, Ernesto and Chantal Mouffe. 'Post-Marxism without Apologies', *New Left Review*, No. 166, Nov./Dec. 1987, pp. 79–106.

Hegemony and Socialist Strategy: Towards a Radical Democratic Politics. London: Verso, 1985.

Lapid, Yosef and Friedrich Kratochwil, eds. *The Return of Culture and Identity in IR Theory.* Boulder: Lynne Rienner Publishers, 1997.

Lasch, Christopher. 'The Politics of Nostalgia', *Harper's Magazine*, Vol. 269, No. 1614, November 1984, pp. 65–70.

Lawrence, Karen R. *Penelope Voyages: Women and Travel in the British Literary Tradition.* Ithaca: Cornell University Press, 1994.

Lawson, Mark. 'A Farewell to Charm', *Guardian (The Guide – Monday)*, 11 October 1999, p. 17.

The Battle for Room Service: Journeys to All the Safe Places. London: Picador, 1993.

Lefebvre, Henri. *The Production of Space.* Oxford: Basil Blackwell, 1991.

Lewis, Reina. *Gendering Orientalism: Race, Femininity and Representation.* London: Routledge, 1996.

Lippard, Lucy. *Different War: Vietnam and Art.* Seattle: Real Comet Press, 1994.

Lisle, Debbie. 'Globalization', in Iain McKenzie, ed., *Political Concepts: A Reader and a Guide.* Edinburgh: Edinburgh University Press, 2005.

'Consuming Danger: Re-Imagining the War-Tourism Divide', *Alternatives*, Vol. 25, No. 1, Jan.–Mar. 2000, pp. 91–116.

'Gender at a Distance: Identity, Performance and Contemporary Travel Writing', *International Feminist Journal of Politics*, Vol. 1, No. 1, June 1999, pp. 66–88.

Lloyd, Moya and Andrew Thacker, eds. *The Impact of Michel Foucault on the Social Sciences and Humanities*. London: Palgrave Macmillan, 1997.

Lowenthal, David. *The Past Is a Foreign Country*. Cambridge: Cambridge University Press, 1985.

Lyotard, Jean-François. *The Postmodern Condition: A Report on Knowledge*, trans. Geoff Bennington and Brian Massumi. Minneapolis: University of Minnesota Press, 1984.

MacCannell, Dean. *Empty Meeting Grounds: The Tourist Papers*. London and New York: Routledge, 1992.

The Tourist: A New Theory of the Leisure Class. New York: Schocken, 1976.

Marriot, Edward. 'Writers from the Boot Camp', *High Life* (British Airways in-flight magazine), April 2003, pp. 70–3.

Massey, Doreen. 'Imagining Globalization: Power-Geometries of Time-Space', in Avtar Brah, Mary Hickman and Mairtin Ghail, eds., *Global Futures: Migration, Environment and Globalization*. Basingstoke: Macmillan, 1999, pp. 27–44.

'Spaces of Politics', in Doreen Massey, John Allen and Phil Sarre, eds., *Human Geography Today*. Cambridge: Polity Press, 1999, pp. 279–94.

'Space-Time, "Science" and the Relationship between Physical Geography and Human Geography', *Transactions of the Institute of British Geographers*, Vol. 24, No. 3, 1999, pp. 261–76.

'Imagining the World', in John Allen and Doreen Massey, eds., *Geographical Worlds*. Oxford: Oxford University Press in association with Open University, 1995, pp. 6–42.

Space, Place, Gender. Cambridge: Polity Press, 1994.

McCamish, Thornton. *Supercargo: A Journey among Ports*. Footscray: Lonely Planet Publications, 2002.

McClintock, Anne and Rob Nixon. 'No Names Apart: The Separation of Word and History in Derrida's "Le Dernier Mot du Racisme"', in Henry Louis Gates, Jr., ed., *'Race', Writing, and Difference*. Chicago and London: University of Chicago Press, 1986, pp. 339–53.

McEwan, Cheryl. *Gender, Geography and Empire: Victorian Women Travellers in West Africa*. Aldershot: Ashgate, 2000.

McGann, Jerome J. *The Textual Condition*. Princeton: Princeton University Press, 1991.

McKenzie, D. F. *Bibliography and the Sociology of Texts*. Cambridge: Cambridge University Press, 1999.

McNally, Tony. *Cloudpuncher*. Liverpool: Pharaoh Press, no date.

Miller, Carolyn R. 'Rhetorical Community: The Cultural Basis of Genre', in Aviva Freedman and Peter Medway, eds., *Genre and the New Rhetoric*. London: Taylor and Francis, 1994, pp. 67–78.

'Genre as Social Action', *Quarterly Journal of Speech*, Vol. 70, 1984, pp. 151–67.

Miller, Jim. 'Literature's New Nomads', *Publisher's Weekly*, Vol. 114, No. 7, 14 August 1989, pp. 50–1.

Milliken, Jennifer. 'The Study of Discourse in International Relations: A Critique of Research Methods', *European Journal of International Relations*, Vol. 5, No. 2, 1998, pp. 225–54.

Mills, Sara. *Discourses of Difference: An Analysis of Women's Travel Writing and Colonialism*. London and New York: Routledge, 1991.

Mills, Sara and Shirley Foster, eds. *An Anthology of Women's Travel Writing*. Manchester: Manchester University Press, 2002.

Molloy, Patricia. 'Theatrical Release: Catharsis and Spectacle in *Welcome to Sarajevo*', *Alternatives*, Vol. 25, No. 1, Jan.–Mar. 2000, pp. 75–90.

Moore, Tim. *French Revolutions: Cycling the Tour de France*. London: Vintage Books, 2002.

Continental Drifter. London: Abacus, 2002.

Frost on My Moustache: The Arctic Exploits of a Lord and a Loafer. London: Abacus, 2000.

Moss, Stephen. '*Down Under* by Bill Bryson', *Guardian*, 5 July 2000, online only at http://www.books.guardian.co.uk/critics/reviews/0,5817,340067,00. html.

Mulberg, Jon. *Social Limits to Economic Theory*. London: Routledge, 1995.

Murtagh, William, and Delta Lightner. 'Robert Louis Stevenson in the Pacific', *Cultural Resource Management*, 19 August 1998, p. 44; http://www.crm.cr.nps.gov/archive/19-8/19-8-15.pdf.

Musgrove, Brian. 'Travel and Unsettlement: Freud on Vacation', in Steve Clark, ed., *Travel Writing and Empire: Postcolonial Theory in Transit*. London: Zed Books, 1999, pp. 31–44.

Naipaul, V. S. *India: A Million Mutinies Now*. New York: Viking, 1990.

India: A Wounded Civilization. New York: Knopf, 1977.

An Area of Darkness. London: André Deutsch, 1964.

The Middle Passage: Impressions of Five Societies, British, French and Dutch, in the West Indies. London: André Deutsch, 1962.

Neilson, Jim. *Warring Fictions: Cultural Politics and the Vietnam War Narrative*. Mississippi: University of Mississippi Press, 1998.

Nixon, Rob. *London Calling: V. S. Naipaul, Postcolonial Mandarin*. Oxford: Oxford University Press, 1992.

O'Hanlon, Redmond. *Congo Journey*. London: Hamish Hamilton, 1996.

In Trouble Again: A Journey Between the Orinoco and the Amazon. London: Penguin Books, 1989.

Ondaatje, Michael. *Running in the Family*. London: Picador, 1984.

Orlikowski, Wanda and JoAnne Yates. *Genre Systems: Structuring Interaction through Communicative Norms*. Cambridge: MIT Press, 1998.

'Genres of Organizational Communication: A Structurational Approach to Studying Communication and Media', *Academy of Management Science Review*, Vol. 17, No. 2, 1992, pp. 299–326.

O'Rourke, P. J. *Age and Guile: Beat Youth, Innocence and a Bad Haircut*. New York: Atlantic Monthly Press, 1996.

Holidays in Hell. London: Picador, 1988.

Ó Tuathail, Gearóid. 'New World Order Geopolitics: Introduction', in Gearóid Ó Tuathail, Simon Dalby and Paul Routledge, eds., *The Geopolitics Reader*. London and New York: Routledge, 1998, pp. 103–13.

'At the End of Geopolitics? Reflections on a Plural Problematic at the Century's End', *Alternatives*, Vol. 22, No. 1, Jan.–Mar. 1997, pp. 33–56.

Critical Geopolitics: The Politics of Writing Global Space. Minneapolis: University of Minnesota Press, 1996.

Ó Tuathail, Gearóid and Simon Dalby, eds. *Critical Geopolitics: A Reader*. London: Routledge, 1998.

Palin, Michael. *Himalaya*. London: Weidenfeld & Nicholson Illustrated, 2004.

Sahara. London: Weidenfeld & Nicholson Illustrated, 2002.

Full Circle. London: BBC Books, 1997.

Pole to Pole. London: BBC Books, 1992.

Around the World in 80 Days. London: BBC Books, 1989.

Parker, Ian. 'I'm Sorry, I Haven't a Crew', *Observer*, 7 September 1997, p. 7.

Pelton, Robert Young, Coskun Anal and Wink Dulles. *Fielding's The World's Most Dangerous Places* (3rd edition). Redondo Beach, CA: Fielding Worldwide Inc., 1998.

Philip, Jim. 'Reading Travel Writing', in Jonathan White, ed., *Recasting the World: Writing After Colonialism*. Baltimore and London: Johns Hopkins University Press, 1993, pp. 241–55.

Phillips, Caryl. *A New World Order: Selected Essays*. London: Vintage, 2001.

A European Tribe. London: Faber, 1987.

Phillips, Richard. 'Decolonizing Geographies of Travel: Reading James/Jan Morris', *Social and Cultural Geography*, Vol. 2, No. 1, 2001, pp. 5–24.

Polanyi, Karl. *The Great Transformation: The Political and Economic Origins of Our Time*. Boston: Beacon Press, 1947.

Pratt, Mary Louise. *Imperial Eyes: Travel Writing and Transculturation*. London and New York: Routledge, 1992.

The Quiet American. Dir. Phillip Noyce, Miramax Films, 2002.

Raban, Jonathan. *Hunting Mr. Heartbreak*. London: Picador, 1991.

Rancière, Jacques. *Short Voyages to the Land of the People*, trans. James B. Swenson. Stanford: Stanford University Press, 2003.

Rennie, Neil. *Far-Fetched Facts: The Literature of Travel and the Idea of the South Seas*. Oxford: Clarendon Press, 1995.

Ritchie, Harry. *The Last Pink Bits: Travels through the Remnants of the British Empire*. London: Sceptre, 1997.

Robertson, Roland. 'After Nostalgia? Wilful Nostalgia and the Phases of Globalization', in Bryan S. Turner, ed., *Theories of Modernity and Postmodernity*. London: Sage, 1990, pp. 45–61.

Robertson, Susan L. 'Defining Travel: An Introduction', in Robertson, *Defining Travel: Diverse Visions*, pp. xi–xxvi.

Defining Travel: Diverse Visions. Jackson: University Press of Mississippi, 2001.

Rose, Gillan. *Visual Methodologies: An Introduction to the Interpretation of Visual Materials*. London: Sage, 2001.

Rosler, Martha. 'In the Place of the Public: Observations of a Traveller', in Ole Bouman and Roemer Van Toorn, eds., *The Invisible Architecture*. London: Academy Editions, 1994, pp. 428–37.

Rushdie, Salman. *Imaginary Homelands: Essays and Criticism 1981–1991*. London: Picador, 1991.

The Jaguar Smile: A Nicaraguan Journey. London: Picador, 1987.

Russell, John. 'Travel Memoir as Nonfiction Novel: Michael Ondaatje's *Running in the Family*', *Ariel*, Vol. 22, No. 2, April 1991, pp. 23–40.

Said, Edward. *Orientalism*. New York: Vintage, 1978.

Saumarez Smith, Charles. 'Upside-Down View of Down Under: Two Outsiders Get Funny Peculiar Ideas about Australia', *Observer*, 2 July 2000, p. 14.

Schechter, Harold and Jonna Gormely Semeiks, eds. *Discoveries: Fifty Stories of the Quest* (2nd edition). Oxford: Oxford University Press, 1992.

Scholte, Jan Aarte. *Globalization: A Critical Introduction*. London: Palgrave, 2000.

Schryer, Catherine F. 'The Lab vs. the Clinic: Sites of Competing Genres', in Aviva Freedman and Peter Medway, eds., *Genre and the New Rhetoric*. London: Taylor and Francis, 1994, pp. 105–24.

Selden, Raman, Peter Widdowson and Peter Brooker, eds. *A Reader's Guide to Contemporary Literary Theory* (4th edition). Hemel Hempstead: Prentice Hall/Harvester Wheatsheaf, 1997.

Shapiro, Michael J. *Reading the Postmodern Polity: Political Theory as Textual Practice*. Minneapolis: Minnesota University Press, 1992.

The Politics of Representation: Writing Practices in Biography, Photography and Policy Analysis. Madison: University of Wisconsin Press, 1988.

Shakespeare, Nicholas. *Bruce Chatwin*. London: Harvill Press, 1999.

Sharp, Joanne P. 'Writing over the Map of Provence: The Touristic Therapy of *A Year in Provence*', in James Duncan and Derek Gregory, eds., *Writes of Passage: Reading Travel Writing*. London and New York: Routledge, 1999, pp. 200–18.

Shaw, Christopher and Malcolm Cross, eds., *The Imagined Past: History and Nostalgia*. Manchester: Manchester University Press, 1989.

Sibley, David. *Geographies of Exclusion*. London: Routledge, 1995.

Siegel, Kristi. 'Introduction: Travel Writing and Travel Theory', in Kristi Siegel, ed., *Issues in Travel Writing*.

ed. *Issues in Travel Writing: Empire, Spectacle and Displacement*. New York: Peter Lang Publishers, 2002.

Smith, Frederik, ed. *The Genres of Gulliver's Travels*. Newark: University of Delaware Press, 1990.

Smith, Steve and John Baylis, eds. *The Globalization of World Politics: An Introduction to International Relations*. Oxford: Oxford University Press, 1997.

Spurr, David. *The Rhetoric of Empire: Colonial Discourse in Journalism, Travel Writing and Imperial Administration*. Durham and London: Duke University Press, 1993.

Stagl, J. and C. Pinney. 'Introduction: From Travel Writing to Ethnography', *History and Anthropology*, Vol. 9, Nos. 2–3, 1996, pp. 121–4.

Staten, Henry. *Wittgenstein and Derrida*. Lincoln and London: University of Nebraska Press, 1984.

Stauth, Georg and S. Bryan Turner. 'Nostalgia, Postmodernism and the Critique of Mass Culture', *Theory, Culture and Society*, Vol. 5, Nos. 2–3, 1988, pp. 509–26.

Stewart, Susan. *On Longing: Narrative of the Miniature, the Gigantic, the Souvenir, the Collection*. Baltimore: Johns Hopkins University Press, 1984.

Stubseid, Anna Stella Karlsdottir. 'Travelogues as Indices of the Past', *Journal of Popular Culture*, Vol. 26, No. 4, 1993, pp. 89–100.

Suganami, Hidemi. 'Stories of War Origins: A Narrativist Perspective on the Causes of War', *Review of International Studies*, Vol. 23, No. 4, 1997, pp. 401–18.

On the Causes of War. Oxford: Oxford University Press, 1996.

Sutcliffe, William. *Are You Experienced?* London: Penguin, 1998.

Swayles, John. *Genre Analysis*. Cambridge: Cambridge University Press, 1990.

Taylor, David. 'Bruce Chatwin: Connoisseur of Exile, Exile as Connoisseur', in Steve Clark, ed., *Travel Writing and Empire: Postcolonial Theory in Transit*. London and New York: Zed Books, 1999, pp. 195–211.

Theroux, Paul. *Dark Star Safari: Overland from Cairo to Cape Town*. London: Hamish Hamilton, 2002.

Sir Vidia's Shadow: A Friendship across Five Continents. London: Hamish Hamilton, 1998.

My Other Life – A Novel. London: Penguin, 1997.

'Chatwin Revisited', *Granta (The Last Place on Earth)*, Vol. 44, 1 June 1993, pp. 213–21.

'First Train Journey', *Granta (New World)*, Vol. 29, 1 December 1989, pp. 167–72.

Riding the Iron Rooster: By Train through China. London: Hamish Hamilton, 1988.

The Old Patagonian Express: By Train through the Americas. New York: Washington Square Press, 1979.

The Great Railway Bazaar: By Train Through Asia. New York: Ballantine Books, 1976.

V. S. Naipaul: An Introduction to His Work. London: André Deutsch, 1972.

Thomas, Nicholas. *Colonialism's Culture: Anthropology, Travel and Government*. Cambridge: Quality Press, 1994.

Thompson, David. 'Their Man in Saigon', *Guardian*, 2 November 2002, p. 18.

Thorpe, Vanessa. 'Bryson Books a Wry Look at the Arabs', *Observer*, 1 June 2003, online only at http://www.observer.guardian.co.uk/uk_news/story/0,6903,968258,00.html.

Thrift, Nigel. *Spatial Formations*. London: Sage, 1996.

Tisdale, Sally. 'Never Let the Locals See Your Map: Why Most Travel Writers Should Stay at Home', *Harper's Magazine*, Vol. 291, No. 1744, September 1995, pp. 66–74.

Todorov, Tzvetan. 'The Journey and Its Narratives', in *The Morals of History*, trans. Alyson Waters. Minneapolis: University of Minnesota Press, 1995, pp. 60–70.

The Conquest of America: The Question of the Other, trans. Richard Howard. Ithaca: Cornell University Press, 1982.

'The Origin of Genres', *New Literary History: A Journal of Theory and Interpretation*, Vol. 8, No. 1, Autumn 1976, pp. 159–70.

Tomlinson, John. *Cultural Imperialism*. London: Pinter Press, 1991.

Turner, Bryan S. 'A Note on Nostalgia', *Theory, Culture and Society*, Vol. 4, No. 1, 1987, pp. 147–56.

Turner, Graeme. *British Cultural Studies*. London: Routledge, 1996.

Urry, John. *The Tourist Gaze: Leisure and Travel in Contemporary Societies.* London: Sage, 1990.

Van Den Abeele, Georges. *Travel as Metaphor: From Montaigne to Rousseau.* Minneapolis and Oxford: University of Minnesota Press, 1992.

'Sightseers: The Tourist as Theorist', *Diacritics*, Vol. 10, No. 4, 1980, pp. 2–14.

Various. 'Images and Narratives in World Politics', Special Issue, *Millennium: Journal of International Studies*, Vol. 30, No. 3, 2001.

Vertovec, Steven and Robin Cohen, eds., *Conceiving Cosmopolitanism: Theory, Context, Practice.* Oxford: Oxford Universtity Press, 2002.

Viswanathan, Guari. 'Beyond Orientalism: Syncretism and the Politics of Knowledge', *Stanford Electronic Humanities Review*, Vol. 5, No. 1, 1996, pp. 9–10, http://www.stanford.edu/group/SHR/5-1/text/viswanathan.html.

Von Martels, Zweder. *Travel Fact and Travel Fiction: Studies on Fiction, Literary Tradition, Scholarly Discovery and Observation in Travel Writing.* Leiden: E. J. Brill, 1994.

Walker, R. B. J. *Inside/Outside: Political Theory as International Relations.* Cambridge: Cambridge University Press, 1993.

Watt, Ian. *The Rise of the Novel: Studies in Defoe, Richardson and Fielding.* Harmondsworth: Penguin, 1963.

Wauters, Ambika. *Journey of Self-Discovery.* London: Piatkus Books, 1995.

Weber, Cindy. *International Relations Theory: A Critical Introduction.* London and New York: Routledge, 2001.

'IR: The Ressurection OR New Frontiers of Incorporation', *European Journal of International Relations*, Vol. 5, No. 4, 1999, pp. 435–50.

Weber, Cindy and François Debrix, eds., *Rituals of Mediation: International Politics and Social Meaning.* Minneapolis: University of Minnesota Press, 2003.

Weldes, Jutta. *Science Fiction and World Politics.* London: Palgrave Macmillan, 2003.

Wheeler, Edward T. 'What the Imagination Knows: Paul Theroux's Search for the Second Self', *Commonweal*, Vol. 121, 20 May 1994, pp. 18–22.

White, Hayden. *The Content of the Form: Narrative Discourse and Historical Representation.* Baltimore: Johns Hopkins University Press, 1987.

The Tropics of Discourse: Essays in Cultural Criticism. Baltimore: Johns Hopkins University Press, 1978.

Metahistory: The Historical Imagination in Nineteenth-Century Europe. Baltimore: Johns Hopkins University Press, 1973.

Williams, Patrick. 'Kim and Orientalism', in Patrick Williams and Laura Chrisman, eds., *Colonial Discourse and Post-Colonial Theory: A Reader.* New York: Columbia University Press, 1994, pp. 480–97.

Wilson, Jason. 'The Travails of Travel Writing', 'On Media' section, *Philadelphia City Paper*, 17–24 June 1999, http://www.citypaper.net/articles/061799/news.onmedia1.shtml.

Wilson, Reul K. *The Literary Travelogue: A Comparative Study with Special Relevance to Russian Literature from Fonvizin to Pushkin.* The Hague: Martinus Nijhoff, 1973.

Yegenoglu, Mayda. *Colonial Fantasies: Towards a Feminist Reading of Orientalism.* Cambridge: Cambridge University Press, 1998.

Younge, Gary. *No Place Like Home: A Black Briton's Journey through the American South.* London: Picador, 1999.

Youngs, Tim. 'Interview with Gary Younge', *Studies in Travel Writing*, No. 6, 2002, pp. 96–107.

Zizek, Slavoj. 'Camp Comedy', *Sight and Sound*, Vol. 10, No. 4, April 2000, pp. 26–9.

Index

Aboriginal land claims 128
Ashe, Arthur 122
Auster, Paul 267
authenticity 80, 156–7, 204, 214–16, 228,
    230

Bagshaw, Geoff 64
Bakhtin, Mikhail 56
Barthes, Roland 264
Bartkowski, Frances 88, 215
    Travellers, Immigrants, Inmates 111–12
Bassnett, Susan 130
Baudrillard, Jean
    America 268
Behdad, Ali 2
Bell, Gavin 230, 269
    In Search of Tusitala 224–9
Blacker, Terence 171
Blanchot, Maurice 34, 56, 58
Blanton, Casey 36, 46, 64, 69, 107–8
Borges, Jorge Luis 267
Bowden, Tim 168
Brennan, Timothy 118–20, 276
Bryson, Bill 24, 100, 105–8, 132, 133,
    241–2, 266, 269, 270
    African Diary 134–7
    Down Under 168–75
    Neither Here Nor There: Travels in Europe
        7–9, 13, 14, 81–3, 101–2
    Walk in the Woods, A 79

Caesar, Terry 29, 30, 35, 40, 43, 50, 54
Cahill, Tim
    Road Fever: A High Speed Travelogue 95–6
Cambridge Companion to Travel Writing
    186–7
Campbell, David 33, 265
    and 'ethos of political criticism' 263–4
Campbell, Ffyona
    On Foot through Africa 86–7

Chatwin, Bruce 27–8, 107–8, 167, 269
    In Patagonia 167
    Songlines, The 61–7, 86, 267;
        see also Rushdie, Salman
Clark, Steve 275
Clifford, James 66, 258–9
colonial vision 3–4, 7, 66, 260, 277
Connolly, Cyril 62
Connolly, William 72–3
Conrad, Joseph 197
    Heart of Darkness 269
Contact zone 187–8, 192, 200, 272
correspondence understanding of
    representation 11
Cortázar, Julio and Carol Dunlop
    *Autonauts of the Global Hughway: An
        Atemporal Journey from Paris to
        Marseilles* 276
cosmopolitan vision 4–5, 8, 10–11, 66, 77,
    108, 118–20, 134, 201, 207, 260,
    261, 270, 277
Critchley, Simon 105, 108–9, 264, 265
    The Ethics of Deconstruction 263

Dalby, Simon 160, 163
Danger, production of 151–2,
    178–86, 201
Danziger, Nick
    Danziger's Travels 92–3
Davidson, Robyn 3, 97
    Tracks 92, 98–9, 127–9
Davis, Angela 124
De Botton, Alain
    The Art of Travel 275, 276
Deleuze, Gilles 275
Derrida, Jacques 5, 23, 249, 273, 275
    on apartheid and race 111
    critique of Fukuyama in 'Conjuring
        Marxism' 235–9
    critique of linear temporality 238–9
    critique of Todorov 59, 60

Derrida, Jacques (cont.)
  'The Law of Genre' 58–61
  Spectres of Marx 235, 238
Desert Storm 257
Dew, Josie 110, 133, 262
  Wind in My Wheels 78–9, 83, 86, 125–7
Didion, Joan 183
difference, production of 6, 24, 40–3, 71,
      83, 125, 201
  in Bill Bryson 8–9
  in Paul Theroux 7, 83–5
disappointment, *see* lament
discourse 11–3
  continuity of 12–3, 23
  discontinuity of 13–7, 23, 59
  of liberal subjectivity 24, 69–133,
      217–18, 261, 268–71
  of literary genre 23–4, 30–67, 217, 261,
      266–8
  materiality of 15–6
  of modern cartography 24–5, 137–202,
      218, 261, 272–3
  of nostalgia 25, 207–59
discourse analysis, Foucauldian 13–18, 277
  ethics of 26
Diski, Jenny 259, 271, 275
  *Stranger on a Train: Daydreaming and
      Smoking around America with
      Interruptions* 245–50
Dreaming Tracks, Aboriginal 62, 64
Dunlop, Carol, *see* Cortázar, Julio

Eco, Umberto
  Travels in Hyperreality 268
Empire 1, 2, 5, 24, 25, 42, 55, 57, 89, 151,
      204, 205, 207, 208, 222, 257, 260,
      261, 265, 271, 273, 274
  British, *see* Ritchie, Harry
  collapse of 3, 11
  persistence of 5, 10, 26, 240, 261, 265
  reassurances of 3
empty spaces 164–72
Endo, Shushako 53

Fabian, Johan 217
Falklands War 244–5
Fangio, Juan 96
Fanon, Franz 275
Farah, Nuruddin 161–3
feminism 110–1, 127, *see* gender
  feminist approaches to travel writing 69,
      124–30; *see also* Mills, Sara,
      Discourses of Difference
fiction, *see* novel
Fielding's The World's Most Dangerous Places
      182

Fitzgerald, F. Scott
  The Great Gatsby 269
Floyd, Harry 121
Foucault, Michel 12, 71, 110, 275
  and genealogical method 210–12,
      230–1, 262
  and geography 139, 188;
    see also heterotopia
  and identity/difference logic 71–2, 90,
      137, 269, 270, 272
  and subjectification 76
  and subjection 76–7
Fowles, John 267
Frankfurt School 13
Freedom Riders 124
Fukuyama, Francis 274; *see also* Derrida,
      Jacques, critique of Fukuyama in
      'Conjuring Marxism'
  'The End of History' 161, 164, 218,
      232–4
Furlong, Monica
  Flight of the Kingfisher 80
Fussell, Paul 19, 29–31, 37, 38, 91

Geertz, Clifford 270
gender
  and embodiment 129–30
  and masculinity 95–100, 125, 198–9
  negotiations 153–4
  and the new man 99–100
  and sexual encounters 129
  and sexuality 130
general poetics, *see* travelogues, generic
      criteria for
geopolitical boundaries 9–10
Ghosh, Amitav 259, 271, 275
  In An Antique Land 251–9, 267
Giles, Ernest 169
globalization
  and contemporary travel writing 2–3, 22,
      24, 25, 75, 113, 119, 124, 176–7,
      204, 209, 267, 272
  debates over 2
  and nostalgia 212–13, 216
  and popular culture 23
global politics, *see* travelogues, and global
      politics
Govier, Katherine 81
Greene, Graham 68–9
Gregory, Derek 138–9
Guattari, Felix 275
guidebook, travel 30, 39, 53–4
Gulliver's Travels 58

Hall, Stuart 109–10
Harstock, Nancy 110

Held, David 4
Hemingway, Ernest 128
Henderson, Heather 216, 218, 221, 223
Hertmans, Stefan
    Intercities 273
heterotopia 188–92, 195, 196, 199, 201
Hetherington, Kevin 190–1
historical queue 203–5, 207–9, 220,
    229, 230, 240, 241, 256, 261,
    274, 276
Ho Chi Minh Trail, *see* Hunt, Christopher
Holland, Patrick, *see Tourists with Type-
    writers*
Holy Grail, search for 44
Houellebecq, Michael 268
    Lanzarote 268
    Platform 268
Huggan, Graham 63; *see also Tourists with
    Typewriters*
Hulme, Peter 113
humour 70, 100–9; *see also* Satire
Hunt, Christopher
    *Sparring with Charlie: Motorbiking down
    the Ho Chi Minh Trail* 192–7

identity/difference, *see* Foucault, Michel
identity politics 70, 110
imperial gaze 69, 87, 240
International Relations, *see* travelogues and
    International Relations
Islam, Sayed Manzuril 142, 151, 189, 262,
    270
Iyer, Pico 115–20, 123, 133, 204, 207–9,
    260, 261, 272
    *Falling Off the Map: Some Lonely Places of
    the World* 165–8, 171–2, 204
    *The Global Soul: Jet-Lag, Shopping Malls
    and the Search for Home* 117–20,
    168
    *Video Night in Kathmandu and Other
    Reports from the Not-So-Far East*
    115–18, 120, 167, 204–7

Jones, Lisa
    *Bulletproof Diva: Tales of Race, Sex and
    Hair* 131
Jordan, Rosa
    Dangerous Places: Travels on the Edge
    152–6, 171–2
journey 35, 36; *see also* travel

Kamal, Yashar 53
Kansteiner, Wulf 265
Kaplan, Caren 113, 114, 213, 216
Kaplan, Robert 24, 79, 165–6, 201
    Balkan Ghosts 209

*The Ends of the Earth: A Journey at the
    Dawn of the 21st Century* 156–64,
    171–2, 179, 233, 272
'The Last Map' 157
Keneally, Thomas 65, 168
    *The Place Where Souls Are Born: A
    Journey into the American Southwest*
    94–5
Kerouac, Jack 197
Kipling, Rudyard 220–1
Kowalewski, Michael 266, 268
Kpomassie, Tété-Michel 87–90, 110

Laclau, Ernesto and Chantal Mouffe
    14–6
lament 214, 216–17, 222, 227–30
Lawson, Mark, 201, 270
    The Battle for Room Service 173–8,
    185–6, 235
Lette, Kathy 170
literary canon, Anglo-American 51–3
Lyotard, Jean François 261

masculinity, *see* gender
Massey, Doreen 7, 203
McCamish, Thornton
    Supercargo: A Journey among Ports
    196–201
McClintock, Anne 111
McDougal Stuart, John 169
Mercator map 138, 150
Miller, Carolyn 56
Mills, Sara
    Discourses of Difference 74–5, 97
monarch-of-all-I-survey 69, 90, 133,
    276
Moore, Tim 241
Morris, Jan 95–100, 130, 168
    Conundrum 130

Naipaul, V. S. 112–15
national character 149
National Geographic 98
neoclassical economics 38–9
Newby, Eric
    A Short Walk in the Hindu Kush 100
Nixon, Rob 111
Nomadology 63
nostalgia, 19, 200, 202, 205, 206, 209–10,
    223, 233; *see also* discourse, of
    nostalgia; *see* globalization and
    nostalgia
    and discursive regulation 217
    for Empire 212–4
Novel 30
    idealization of 50–1

O'Hanlon, Redmond 241
  Congo Journey 209
Ondaatje, Michael 267
  Running in the Family 267
Orientalism 3, 272, 274
  and colonial travel writing 28–9, 72–3
O'Rourke, P.J. 201, 270
  Holidays in Hell 173–5, 178–86
Ortega, Daniel 47, 48
Ó Tuathail, Gearóid 139–40, 161

Palin, Michael 24, 100, 102–8, 132, 133, 269
  Around the World in 80 Days 102
  Full Circle 102–5
  Himalaya 102
  Monty Python's Flying Circus 102, 103
  Pole to Pole 102
  Sahara 102
Paradise mythology 225
paternalism, *see* travelogues, romanticism in
Pax Americana 179
Pax Britannica 240, 245
postcolonial, *see* travelogues, postcolonial approaches to travel writing 1–2, 69
  debates over race 111
poststructuralism and the problem of relativism 263–5
Pratt, Mary Louise 69, 138, 272, 275
  Imperial Eyes 187–8
  see also contact zone, transculturation

Raban, Jonathan 197
Rampo, Edogawa 53
Rancière, Jacques 271
Rand Corporation 154
Ricardo, David 39
Ritchie, Harry 259
  The Last Pink Bits: Travels through the Remnants of the British Empire 240–5, 250
Robertson, Roland 212
Rosler, Martha 150
Rushdie, Salman 119, 268
  The Jaguar Smile: A Nicaraguan Journey 47–50, 54, 114
  Midnight's Children 49
  The Satanic Verses 49, 66
  on Bruce Chatwin's *The Songlines* 65
Russell, Bertrand 246
Russell, John 267, 268

safety, production of 151–2, 173–8, 201
Said, Edward 275; *see also Orientalism*
Sandanista Revolution 47, 49, 89

Sanderson, Mark 171
Satire 173–86, 270; *see also* humour
Sawenko, Toly 64
Schryer, Catherine 56, 57
Selby, Bettina 266
self-deprecation, *see* humour
Shakespeare, Nicholas 67
Sitwell, Edith 62
Sound of Music, The 249
Sowerby, Gary 95
Spivak, Gayatri Chakravorty 275
Steinem, Gloria 153
Stevenson, Robert Louis 224–9
  The Master of Ballantrae 227
Stone, Robert 80
subcontinentalism 48
subjectivity, *see* discourse of liberal subjectivity
Swayles, John 56

Taylor, David 66, 67
Terra Incognita 167
Terra Nullius 166, 167
Theroux, Paul 27–8, 70, 90, 132, 133, 167, 229, 248, 269
  Dark Star Safari: Overland from Cairo to Cape Town 218
  The Great Railway Bazaar: By Train through Asia 2, 50–4, 91, 93, 142–50, 218–23, 230
  The Old Patagonian Express: By Train through the Americas 6–7, 11, 13, 14, 36–43, 45, 218
  on rail travel 218–23
  Riding the Iron Rooster 218
Thomas Cook Travel Book Awards 92, 97, 224
Tisdale, Sally 41, 78, 80, 101
Todorov, Tzvetan 23, 67, 70, 90
  The Conquest of America: The Question of the Other 57
  'The Journey and Its Narratives' 40–7
  limitations of his Structuralist approach 55–8
  'The Origins of Genre' 34–5
tourist gaze 24; *see also* traveller/tourist binary
Tourists with Typewriters 19–23, 31, 70, 100, 113, 114, 117–18, 120, 130, 141–2, 159, 162, 186–7, 212
transculturation 188
travel 31; *see also* journey
traveller/tourist binary 77–83, 141–2, 195
travelogues
  and American foreign policy 163
  and autonomy of travel writer 90–5

and Cultural Studies 18, 21–2
formal elements of 29–30;
   see also discourse of literary genre
generic criteria for 35–44
and global politics 276–8
and International Relations 1–18, 21,
   25
judgement of 262–78
and literary criticism 18–19
literary history of 44–7
post-colonial 112–25
romanticism in 85–7
self-reflexivity in 46, 68–9, 106,
   173
Turner, Bryan S. 213, 214

utopia, *see* discourse of nostalgia
construction of 214–5, 230
deferred 207
ideas of space in 201
utopian ideal 192, 196, 197, 200, 201, 219,
   221

Van Den Abeele, Georges 275
Vargas Llosa, Mario 65
Vietnam War 147–8; *see also* Hunt,
   Christopher
and cinema 192–4
Village Voice 131
Viswanathan, Guari 258
Von Humboldt, Alexander 275

Waugh, Evelyn 197
White, Hayden 31, 39, 239, 264–5
historiography and narrative 31–3,
   231–2
on Marxism 232
Metahistory 32, 231
Windrush 121
Woodcock, George 85

Younge, Gary 128, 132, 271, 275
*No Place Like Home: A Black Briton's
   Journey through the American South*
   120–5, 131